# STANDARD CATALOG OF

# Farm Tractors

## 1890 to 1960

### by C.H. Wendel

## Special Contributors
Craig Anderson
Keith Crawford

## Pricing Panelists

Kurt Aumann
Tom Bitters
John Davis
Tom Detwiler
Dan Ehlerding
Tom Graverson
Ken Guile
Jack Heald
Don Huber
Jeff Huff

Kenneth Johnson
John Kasminski
Wilbert Kerchner
Dennis Lefebers
Byron Lukes
Rick Mannen
Dave Preuhs
Elwyn Suehring
Larry Swenson
Ken Updike
Wayne Witse

Published by

**krause
publications**

**700 E. State Street • Iola, WI 54990-0001**
**Telephone: 715/445-2214**

**www.krause.com**

Please, call or write us for our free catalog of antiques and collectibles publications.
To place an order or receive our free catalog, call 800-258-0929.
For editorial comment and further information, use our regular business telephone at (715) 445-2214.

Library of Congress Catalog Number: 98-84104
ISBN: 0-87341-513-2

Printed in the United States of America

# *Dedication*

*The only thing certain about life is the uncertainty of life itself. Over the past few years this writer has had the pleasure of working with Jon Brecka. He was my editor for* Encyclopedia of American Farm Implements *and he was at work on this book and plans were made for its release in May 2000.*

*On December 23, 1999, Jon left his office at Krause Publications in Iola, bound for home and Christmas with his family. Tragically, he was involved in an automobile accident and critically injured. On Feb. 13, 2000, our friend Jon Brecka passed away.*

*We dedicate this book to the memory of Jon Brecka. May it stand as a tribute to our amiable friend, and to his abilities as one of the best editors we have known in thirty years of book publishing.*

# Table of Contents

# *Introduction*

For nearly 40 years, I've collected literature about old engines, tractors and farm equipment. I admit that what I thought were big prices for a stack of old tractor catalogs some 30 years ago is a bargain price today. Yet I had no interest then or now in the capital appreciation of what I was buying. Instead, I was interested in preserving some of these materials and using them as resource materials for books I wanted to write.

My approach over the years has been to write books that people wanted to read. I have always held that the whole idea of a good book is one that the reader picks up and can't put down until finished (or until sleep intervenes). For me, page after page of corporate history is probably the best method of inducing sleep known to man, but I've always felt that the pages should come alive to the reader—they should be vibrant and carry the message through printed word and pictorial content.

Another important aspect of historical research is accuracy. In perusing various books written in the past 20 years we have noted glaring errors. Sometimes these occur because of typographical errors. Others were based on erroneous information gathered over the decades. Where possible, I have tried to find the primary data (if it exists). Barring that, I have cross-referenced the data to maintain accuracy. Even with all of the precautions, safeguards, file cards and other working tools, this book is certain to contain errors. Companies will be omitted that should have been included, and so on. I apologize in advance for these shortcomings.

---

To improve subsequent editions of this book or if you have literature, directories, pricing, photos, or other information, write to:

**Standard Catalog of Farm Tractors**
**Krause Publications - Book Division**
**700 E. State Street**
**Iola, WI 54990**

# *Tractor Grading Guide*

Condition is one of the most important factors to the price of a tractor. The following is a general grading guide for vintage tractors:

**Condition 1.** A tractor that is new or restored to new condition, both mechanically and cosmetically. Steel wheels may have rubber lugs or flattened rubber tread so it can travel in parades or at shows. A tractor in this condition need not be restored to better than new precision.

**Condition 2.** A tractor that is well restored or an extremely well maintained tractor that can be featured in a parade or used for belt power. It is complete with all correct parts. Iron wheels may have had lugs removed and replaced with rubber cleats or flat tread.

**Condition 3.** A tractor that is functional or restorable. It runs, but it needs restoration or replacement of parts and cosmetics to a fine operating and eye appealing tractor.

**Condition 4.** A tractor that may or may not be functional. It is weathered, wrecked, incomplete or greatly deteriorated, rusty or stripped to the point of being useful for parts only.

# A

**1911 Abenaque tractor**

## Abenaque Machine Works
*Westminster Station, Vermont*

**1908 Abenaque tractor**

Abenaque gas engines first appeared about 1893, being the inventive work of John A. Ostenburg. The latter secured numerous patents for his engines, with the cooling system being a unique feature of many models. In 1908, the company announced this 15 horsepower "gasoline traction engine." Weighing some 5-1/2 tons, it used the company's own stationary engine mounted on a heavy steel chassis. This single-cylinder tractor used an 8-5/8 x 12-1/2-inch bore and stroke; operating speed was 270 rpm.

In 1915, Abenaque Machine Works filed for bankruptcy. The family of Frederick M. Gilbert, one of the company founders, ultimately ended up with the company. After several difficult years, the company again took bankruptcy in 1921, with the assets finally being sold in 1923. Shown here is the 1911 version of the Abenaque tractor. It was a highly refined version of the 1908 model, although it retained the single-cylinder engine. Like the earlier 1908 model, two sizes were offered—15- and 25-horsepower. A unique feature was a choice of three forward speeds along with a reverse gear.

| 1 | 2 | 3 | 4 |
|---|---|---|---|
| — | — | $30,000-$50,000 | — |

## Acason Farm Tractor Company
*Detroit, Michigan*

**Acason attachment for automobiles**

Acason Motor Truck Company was organized in 1915, continuing in the truck business for a decade. Presumably, the Acason Farm Tractor Company was a division of the parent company. The latter first appears in 1918 as a manufacturer of a tractor attachment for automobiles. Little is known of this device, aside from a very few advertisements. However, this tractor conversion was designed specifically for use with the Model T Ford automobile. Acason closed their doors forever in 1925.

| | 1 | 2 | 3 | 4 |
|---|---|---|---|---|
| Conversion Kit | — | — | $1,000 | — |

## Acme Cultivator Company
*Leetonia, Ohio*

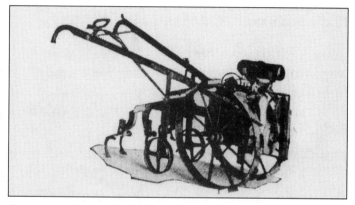

**Acme garden cultivator**

This firm built the Acme and Acme Jr. garden cultivators for some years, beginning in the 1920s. The company appears to have been active as late as 1946. Originally the company appeared at Leetonia, Ohio. Until at least 1948 the firm is shown at Columbiana, Ohio and offering only repair parts for these machines.

| 1 | 2 | 3 | 4 |
|---|---|---|---|
| $950 | $650 | $400 | $250 |

## Acme Harvesting Machine Company
*Peoria, Illinois*

Acme had beginnings at least back into the 1890s, if not earlier. Ostensibly, the company was organized to build grain binders and other harvesting machinery, but by 1918 the firm was offering a unique convertible farm tractor. The tracklayer model shown here was a conversion from their ordinary wheel-type tractor; it was said that the

**Acme tracklayer**

change was relatively easy to make. Probably because of strong competition, and the inability to launch an intensive advertising campaign, the Acme tractor virtually disappears by 1920. A #3 condition Acme tracklayer recently sold for $25,000.

**Acme 12-25 conventional tractor**

Acme's 12-25 conventional tractor, like the twin tracklayer model, was listed in various machinery directories for 1918 and 1919. The model shown here was relatively simple and straightforward in design; it utilized a four-cylinder engine. Aside from a few advertisements and a trade announcement or two, nothing is known of the Acme tractor. In fact, the company itself has its history already shrouded by time. A #3 condition Acme 12-25 recently sold for $20,000.

# Adams-Farnham Company

*Minneapolis, Minnesota*

**Adams-Farnham tractor**

In 1909 this company was incorporated at Minneapolis. The principals were P. W. and G. L. Farnham, along with H. W. Adams. The firm manufactured numerous items, including steam engine governors, gasoline engines, and gasoline tractors. The latter, built only in 1909 and 1910, weighed about 5-1/2 tons. At this time however, there were few statistics for the relatively young tractor industry, so no compilations were as yet available for various makes and models of tractors. Thus, no specifications of the Adams-Farnham have been located. The company quit business in 1911, and in 1915 Harry W. Adams reappears as the general manager of the Common Sense Tractor Company, also of Minneapolis.

# Adams Husker Company

*Marysville, Ohio*

About 1910 Adams began offering their 'Little Traction Gear' to the farmer. It was a complete running gear to which the farmer could mount his own engine, presumably one that was already on the farm. The Adams gear was offered in three sizes, with the No. 0 being for engines up to 9 horsepower. The No. 1 gear could handle engines up to 13 horsepower, and the big No. 2 was capable of handling a 20 horsepower engine. Patent No. 1,118,835 covering this device was issued in 1915. Unfortunately, by this time the

**Adams "Little Traction Gear"**
**#3 condition, No. 0 - $3,500 kit only**

market for convertible outfits was fast diminishing; farmers were instead looking for a small lightweight tractor suitable for any farm task. A #3 condition No. 0 (kit only) is currently valued at $3,500.

# Adams Sidehill Tractor Company

*The Dalles, Oregon*

**Adams Sidehill tractor**

Sometime in the 1920s a special tractor design was developed for use on steep side hills. It was the brainchild of E. G. Adams at The Dalles, Oregon. In 1927 a company was organized to manufacture this unique design, but aside from this illustration in a 1927 issue of *American Thresherman Magazine*, nothing more is known of the company or this unique tractor design.

# Adaptable Tractor Company
*Indianapolis, Indiana*

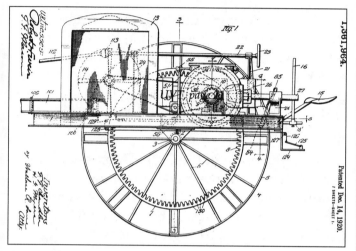

**Adaptable tractor**

The only evidence thus far to make itself known regarding the Adaptable tractor is this 1920 patent drawing. That same year Adaptable was incorporated to manufacture their new design, yet another of the 'universal' designs intended to be adaptable to virtually every farm power use. As with the vast majority of the 'universal' designs, sales were nothing sensational, and this, together with the post-war depression of the time, effectively put an end to the Adaptable Tractor Company, almost before it got started.

# Advance Thresher Company
*Battle Creek, Michigan*

Jack Junkin was a well known tractor and machinery designer. Junkin designed this big Advance 35-70 tractor about 1910, and likewise was a major player in the design of the Twin City tractor of Minneapolis Steel & Machinery Company. A comparison of this tractor with the Twin City 40 illustrates the similarities. When M. Rumely Co. bought out Advance in 1911, Junkin went along with the merger, and was in fact,

**Advance 35-70 tractor**

responsible for polishing out the design of the Rumely Oil Pull tractors. Unfortunately, the Advance 35-70 never got off the ground, and likely never made it past a few prototypes. None of these tractors are known to exist.

# Advance-Rumely Thresher Company
*LaPorte, Indiana*

Much has been written about Advance-Rumely Thresher Company; despite the fact that production of the inimitable Rumely Oil Pull ceased decades ago in 1931, this tractor remains very popular among vintage tractor enthusiasts.

The Author has detailed considerable history of the company in previous titles, including *Encyclopedia of American Farm Tractors (Crestline/Motorbooks: 1979); The Allis-Chalmers Story (Crestline/Motorbooks: 1988); Allis-Chalmers Tractors (Motorbooks: 1992);* and *Unusual Vintage Tractors (Krause: 1996).*

Briefly, the company had roots going back to 1852 when Meinrad Rumely opened a blacksmith and machine shop at Portland, Indiana. By 1856 the company had entered the threshing machine business, and with great demand for the Rumely machine, the business grew rapidly. Until 1882 the company operated as a partnership with Meinrad's brother John under the title of M. & J. Rumely Company. At this point however, Meinrad bought out his brother's interest, forming the M. Rumely Company at LaPorte.

Edward A. Rumely, a grandson of the founder, joined the firm in the early 1900s, and by 1908 was convinced of the need for a 'successful' tractor.

Accordingly, Edward set out to acquire the best minds. These included John A. Secor, the man who probably more than any other, had developed the volume governed engine, and who also was an early proponent of higher compression than had been used formerly.

Edward Rumely was also acquainted with Rudolph Diesel, and was greatly influenced by the latter's ideas regarding high compression engines. Added to the team was William H. Higgins, who was the Rumely factory superintendent.

While certainly there were others involved, Rumely, Secor, and Higgins developed the first prototypes in 1908, with testing being carried out in 1909. The experiments were so successful that the company moved quickly to build a tractor factory, shipping the first tractor on February 21, 1910.

The overwhelming success of the Rumely Oil Pull led the firm to acquire Gaar, Scott & Company, Richmond, Indiana in October 1911, followed by the purchase of Advance Thresher Company, Battle Creek, Michigan. A year later, Rumely bought out the Northwest Thresher Company at Stillwater, Minnesota. The latter had developed a tractor by this time, and it was marketed for a few years as the Rumely GasPull.

In 1912 Rumely acquired the designs for a unique orchard tractor from Joshua Hendy Iron Works, Sunnyvale, California. It was marketed for a time as the Rumely ToeHold tractor, but this model was only in production for a short time, if indeed, it ever went into full production.

During 1913 the company began experiencing financial difficulties, and in 1915 went into receivership. The new firm, Advance-Rumely Thresher Company emerged, but essentially without the Rumely family.

In 1915, probably about the time the firm was reorganized, a new lightweight 8-16 plowing tractor emerged, followed the next year by a larger 12-24 model. Both were out of the market by 1917. Then in 1921 the company announced their new 'line-drive' tractor, a small outfit that was essentially a mechanical horse…the tractor was operated entirely with a pair of leather lines, just like driving a team of horses! A very few of these tractors were built; subsequently the idea was abandoned.

In 1924 Advance-Rumely made the last of their major acquisitions, this time the subject was the Aultman & Taylor Machinery Company at Mansfield, Ohio. The buyout ostensibly put Rumely in a better marketing position, since it eliminated a strong competitor. Unfortunately, the market for big heavyweight tractors was quickly disappearing, so the buyout did little to bolster Rumely's sagging sales.

The Toro Motor Cultivator was acquired in 1927, and it was the basis for the Rumely DoAll tractor, a convertible machine that could be used either as a conventional tractor or as a motor cultivator. Sales were disappointing for the DoAll, and sales for the time-honored Rumely OilPull tractors were weak.

With the onset of the Great Depression in 1929, Advance-Rumely was no longer able to continue on its own, and in 1931 a merger was effected whereby Rumely became a part of Allis-Chalmers Manufacturing Company.

**Rumely 1908 prototype**

In 1908 Rumely began experiments on a new tractor design. Shown here is what would soon become the famous Rumely OilPull. Although this prototype was not equipped with fenders and other niceties, it embodied many of the features that would be characteristic of all OilPull tractors to follow. Especially obvious is the radiator design which would be greatly modified on the production models, but which nevertheless used the engine exhaust to create an induced draft over the radiator tubes.

**Type B, 25-45 OilPull**

The Type B, 25-45 OilPull emerged in 1910, remaining in production during 1911 and 1912. During 1910, the first year of production, a hundred units were built, followed by almost 700 the following year, plus another 150 in 1912. The 25-45 rating meant that the tractor was capable of 25 drawbar and 45 belt horsepower. This rating system was widely used up to about 1930.

| **1** | **2** | **3** | **4** |
|---|---|---|---|
| B 25-45 OilPull | | | |
| $60,000 | $40,000 | $30,000 | $15,000 |

The photograph below, taken at an unknown location, illustrates the 25-45 OilPull coupled to a large plow. In those days, fuel delivery trucks were unknown, with fuel often being delivered in large wooden or steel barrels. The Author has been told that some ingenious engineers chained a full drum to a rear wheel, and drove forward slightly to raise it off the ground. As shown here, fuel is being pumped into the tractor's main fuel tank.

**Type E 30-60 OilPull**

Production of the big 30-60 Rumely tractor began in 1910, and continued until 1923. Nearly 2,500 of these tractors were built during that time. Shown in this photograph with a fourteen-bottom plow, tractors like the 30-60 OilPull were responsible for converting thousands of acres of prairie into tillable and productive farmland. On the belt, the 30-60 was capable of pulling the largest thresher or a large sawmill with relative ease.

**25-45 OilPull**

**Rumely OilPull Type E 30-60 engine**

The power plant of the Rumely OilPull Type E, 30-60 was a huge two-cylinder engine with the cylinders being inclined upward slightly. Above the cylinders is seen the huge carburetor, and to the upper right is seen the magneto and the force-feed lubricating system. Three large clutch shoes are also obvious. They were counterweighted to provide automatic disengagement of the clutch when stopping.

|  | 1 | 2 | 3 | 4 |
|---|---|---|---|---|
| E 30-60 OilPull | $55,000 | $35,000 | $25,000 | $10,000 |

**Type E 30-60 frame**

For the early series of OilPull tractors, also known as the 'heavyweight' style, the chassis design was essentially the same, varying mostly in physical size and dimensions. The foundation was quite simple, but was built to withstand the heaviest loads that might be encountered with a comfortable margin of safety. Note the massive gearing that transmitted power to the drive wheels.

**Rumely Type F 15-30 OilPull**

In the 1911-1914 period Rumely built nearly 2,500 copies of their 15-30 OilPull. This was essentially the same tractor as the larger 30-60 but instead of two cylinders, the 15-30 was a single-cylinder model. None were built in 1915, but the following year the 15-30 re-emerged as the Model F, 18-35 tractor. The slight increase in the horsepower rating came from a small increase in crankshaft speed, as well as capitalizing on the power reserves already built into the tractor. Production ended in 1918.

|  | 1 | 2 | 3 | 4 |
|---|---|---|---|---|
| F 15-30 OilPull | $30,000 | $23,000 | $15,000 | $10,000 |
| F 18-35 OilPull | $33,000 | $26,000 | $18,000 | $10,000 |

With the end of the Model F, 18-35 OilPull in 1918 came the introduction of the new Type G, 20-40 model. This tractor was a two-cylinder design with an 8 x 10 inch bore and stroke, compared to the 10 x 12 cylinder dimensions for the big 30-60. Cold weather operation was always a problem, since in those days there were few suit-

**Type G, 20-40 model**

able anti-freeze solutions available. This was not a problem for the OilPull, since it used oil as a coolant, and thus was never subject to freezing. Production of the 20-40 tractor ended in 1924.

| | 1 | 2 | 3 | 4 |
|---|---|---|---|---|
| G 20-40 OilPull | $17,000 | $15,000 | $12,000 | $6,000 |

**14-28 OilPull tractor**

A 14-28 OilPull tractor first appeared in 1917. Production of this model continued into 1918 when it was slightly modified, and then reappeared as the Type H, 16-30 OilPull. The 16-30

was a very popular tractor, since it was well suited to the average farm. The 30-60 was too large for the average farm, and the 20-40 was well suited to large farms or for pulling a grain separator. However, the 16-30 was ideal for the ordinary grain and livestock farm. Type H, 16-30 tractors used a 7 x 8-1/2 inch bore and stroke, and were rated at 530 rpm. Shown here is a platform view of the 14-28 OilPull.

| | 1 | 2 | 3 | 4 |
|---|---|---|---|---|
| H 16-30 OilPull | $16,000 | $14,000 | $11,000 | $6,000 |

**16-30 OilPull tractor**

When the 16-30 OilPull was tested at Nebraska in 1920 (Test No. 9) it set a record for fuel efficiency. With the high compression engines used in the OilPull tractors, and a comparatively high jacket temperature available with the oil coolant, large quantities of water were necessary to minimize or prevent preignition, especially with low grade fuels. Ordinarily, about a third of the total fuel-water mixture entering the engine consisted of water. In the winter months, when freezing was a problem, high-test gasoline, although more expensive, was often substituted for the kerosene-water mixture of warmer weather.

During the 1918-25 period, Advance-Rumely offered their 12-20 Type K OilPull tractor. Of the same general design as its larger brothers, the 12-20 used a two-cylinder, 6 x 8 inch engine rated at 560 rpm. The tractor was generally underrated for its capacity; for instance, although rated at 20

**12-20 Type K OilPull tractor**

belt horsepower, it was capable of 26 or more horses on the belt. One of the Author's uncles bought a new 12-20 in the early 1920s, using it to operate a corn sheller in the neighborhood for some years, finally trading it off on a truck-mounted corn sheller in the late 1930s.

|  | **1** | **2** | **3** | **4** |
|---|---|---|---|---|
| K 12-20 OilPull | $19,500 | $15,000 | $12,000 | $8,000 |

**Rumely ToeHold tractor**

In 1912 Rumely announced their new ToeHold tractor, a design purchased from Joshua Hendy Iron Works in California. This venture was short-lived, and aside from the initial announcements, very little is known of the ToeHold tractor. Rated at 14 drawbar and 28 belt horsepower, the Toe-Hold was equipped with a two-cycle engine, completely unlike the heavy and substantial engines on which Rumely had built their reputation.

**Advance-Rumely "8-16" tractor**

Advance-Rumely announced their new "8-16" tractor in 1916 for $750 cash, f.o.b. LaPorte, Indiana. It was an approach to the need for light-weight tractors, and like others of its design, met with generally poor farmer acceptance. Rumely also introduced their "12-24" tractor in 1917, with production of both models ending in 1918. The plows could be easily removed so that the tractor could be used for other purposes.

|  | **1** | **2** | **3** | **4** |
|---|---|---|---|---|
| 8-16 | $25,000 | $19,000 | $14,000 | $8,000 |

**GasPull 20-40 tractor - #2 condition $25,000**

GasPull tractors made their first appearance in 1912, subsequent to Rumely's purchase of North-west Thresher Company, Stillwater, Minnesota. Initially the GasPull was rated as a 20-40 tractor, and had been sold under a variety of names prior to the Rumely takeover. However, during 1912 or 1913 the tractor was re-rated downward as a 15-30 model. It remained on the market until 1915, or probably about the time M. Rumely Company was reorganized as Advance-Rumely Thresher Company. A GasPull 20-40 in #2 condition is currently valued at $25,000.

**Advance-Rumely 'line-drive' tractor
#2 condition $15,000**

An aberration from Advance-Rumely was this little 'line-drive' tractor that the company announced in 1921. Fortunately for the company, the design never appears to have gone beyond the prototype stage, although a couple of units were built, with strong indications that both of these still exist in the hands of private collectors (current collector value, #2 condition, is $15,000). So-called line drive tractors were intended to entice farmers unwilling to give up their horses for tractor power, and instead substituting a 'mechanical horse.'

**Light Weight OilPull tractor**

In 1924 Advance-Rumely announced an entirely new line of OilPull tractors. The 'new Light-weight OilPull' was much more compact, and featured a pressed steel frame, replacing the structural steel chassis of earlier models. At the

top of the line stood the 30-60 Type S OilPull, a big tractor with a two-cylinder, 9 x 11 inch engine. Rated speed was 470 rpm. Production of the Type S 30-60 continued into 1928, with only about 500 being built.

|  | 1 | 2 | 3 | 4 |
|---|---|---|---|---|
| S 30-60 OilPull | $30,000 | $25,000 | $17,000 | $8,000 |

**OilPull 25-45 Type R tractor engine**

OilPull 25-45 Type R tractors were part of the 1924-1927 line. All of the Lightweight Series used a completely redesigned engine. Shown here is a cutaway photo illustrating the method of providing forced-feed lubrication to all essential engine parts. This was combined with a splash system in the bottom of the crankcase so that every moving part was always bathed in oil.

|  | 1 | 2 | 3 | 4 |
|---|---|---|---|---|
| R 25-45 OilPull | $17,000 | $13,000 | $10,000 | $6,500 |

The new Lightweight OilPull had all gears enclosed and running in oil. This was a great advantage over the earlier models with their exposed gearing. Another of the first Light-weight series was the 20-35 Type M OilPull. It was very popular, with production totaling nearly 3,700 units during the 1924-1927 production run. The 20-35 was a popular threshing trac-

**20-35 Type M OilPull chassis**

**Type L, 15-25 OilPull**

tor, since it was capable of handling most separators, except for the very largest. It was also quite capable of handling a silo filler, and many other farm power needs.

| | 1 | 2 | 3 | 4 |
|---|---|---|---|---|
| M 20-35 OilPull | $15,000 | $12,000 | $10,000 | $5,000 |

Smallest of the Lightweight OilPull series was the Type L, 15-25 tractor. Over 4,800 of these tractors were built in the 1924-1927 period. It could handle a 24 or 28-inch separator in most cases, especially if the latter was equipped with ball

and roller bearings. A spring-mounted front axle cushioned the tractor, making for easier steering and operation. The Model L was also available as a special Orchard & Vineyard Tractor.

| | 1 | 2 | 3 | 4 |
|---|---|---|---|---|
| L 15-25 OilPull | $17,000 | $13,000 | $11,000 | $5,000 |

For 1928 the Lightweight OilPull Series was slightly modified and re-rated upward on horsepower output. Thus, the earlier 15-25 Type L now became the 20-30 Type W tractor. Initially the Lightweight OilPull tractors used a solid disc

**20-30 Type W OilPull tractor**

flywheel, but its 'sounding board' effect was objectionable since it took normal engine noises and amplified them to unacceptable levels. Thus, many of these tractors were retrofitted with a spoked flywheel instead.

| | 1 | 2 | 3 | 4 |
|---|---|---|---|---|
| W 20-30 OilPull | $12,000 | $10,000 | $8,000 | $5,000 |

**Rumely Oil Pull 25-40 Type X tractor**

Rated to handle four plows or a 32-inch grain separator, the OilPull 25-40 Type X tractor replaced the earlier 20-35 Type M. This model was rated at 700-725 rpm. Both the 20-30 "W" and the 25-40 "X" could be furnished as a special winch tractor for industrial applications. These models were specially equipped with a heavy front-mounted winch. An obvious change between the original Lightweight Series and the second series of 1928 was the relocation of the coolant expansion tank from a position over the engine to just above the radiator. Production of the 25-40 began in 1928 and ended in 1930.

| | 1 | 2 | 3 | 4 |
|---|---|---|---|---|
| X 25-40 OilPull* | $13,000 | $9,000 | $7,000 | $5,000 |
| X 25-40 OilPull** | $11,000 | $8,000 | $6,000 | $4,000 |

* Early style with large flywheel.
** Later style with smaller flywheel.

**Rumely crawler tractor**

Sometime during the 1928-1930 period, Advance-Rumely developed a crawler tractor built over a 20-30 or a 25-40 chassis. Virtually nothing is known of this tractor, except that this original factory photograph exists in the Author's hands, proving that a prototype was actually built. Despite the qualities that may have been embodied in the design, the unfortunate intervention of the Great Depression certainly eliminated the possibility for a sequel.

**Rumely Type Y, 30-50 tractor**

During 1929 Advance-Rumely converted 100 of their earlier Type R 25-45 tractors into the new Type Y, 30-50 model. Another 145 tractors were built and numbered as Model Ys. Design changes were relatively minor, and the increased power output was achieved by raising the high idle speed to 635 rpm. Despite the quality of the 30-50 and other OilPull models, farmers were now beginning to find numerous row-crop tractors on the market. For larger jobs, a great many companies were offering small and compact tractors of the unit frame design on the market. Thus, sales of the inimitable OilPull continued to decline.

| | 1 | 2 | 3 | 4 |
|---|---|---|---|---|
| Y 30-50 OilPull | | | | |
| | $15,000 | $12,000 | $10,000 | $5,000 |

**40-60 Type Z OilPull**

The last of the OilPull tractors was the 40-60 Type Z. Built only in 1929, some of these tractors were converted to Type Z from the earlier Type S, 30-60 model. Sales were so poor that some of these tractors were later fitted backward again to their original 30-60 configuration. After Allis-Chalmers bought out Rumely in 1931, the stocks of remaining OilPull tractors were marketed until depleted. Thus came the end of the venerable Rumely OilPull tractor.

| | 1 | 2 | 3 | 4 |
|---|---|---|---|---|
| Z 40-60 OilPull | | | | |
| | $40,000 | $32,000 | $25,000 | $10,000 |

**Rumely DoAll cultivator**

Advance-Rumely bought out the Toro tractor line in 1927 and began converting it into the Rumely DoAll. This convertible tractor came onto the market in 1928 and remained there until the 1931 buyout by Allis-Chalmers. Unfortunately, the notion of a convertible tractor had already outlived its usefulness. Farmers had already found a taste of the universal farm tractor in the Farmall and others that quickly came onto the market. The hard work of converting a tractor into the cultivator shown here, and then back to a conventional tractor was not a popular idea with most farmers.

**Rumely DoAll tractor**

Rumely DoAll tractors looked just like any small conventional model in their normal mode, but it took lots of work to change it over to cultivating work when necessary to do so. Thus, the DoAll had limited sales in the 1928-1931 period; only about 3,000 units were built. Meanwhile, International Harvester was building its Farmall tractor by the tens of thousands, and this left very little market share for the Advance-Rumely DoAll design.

| | 1 | 2 | 3 | 4 |
|---|---|---|---|---|
| DoAll Tractor | $8,000 | $5,000 | $3,500 | $2,000 |

**Rumely 6A tractor**

In 1930 Advance-Rumely finally moved into conventional tractor designs with their Rumely 6A model. This rather attractive design sold very poorly, since when Allis-Chalmers took over in 1931, there will still some 700 of the 6A tractors on hand. The latter continued selling the 6A until stocks were depleted. Thus, the 6A appears in some tractor directories until 1934. Allis-Chalmers had little interest in promoting the 6A, since they had already developed their own successful tractor line. Thus came the end of Advance-Rumely.

| | 1 | 2 | 3 | 4 |
|---|---|---|---|---|
| 6A | $8,000 | $6,500 | $5,500 | $3,500 |

## Aerco Corporation
*Hollydale, California*

See: Earthmaster Farm Equipment

## Agrimotor Tractor Company
*Wichita, Kansas*

**Mid-West 9-18**

The Mid-West 9-18 appears in the trade directories only for 1921, although it may have been built for a localized market during a longer period. This 3,300 pound tractor was equipped with a Gile two cylinder horizontal engine having a 5 x 6-1/2 inch bore and stroke. It offered only a single forward speed, plus reverse. Very little is known of the company aside from its 1921 listing in the trade directories.

## Ajax Auto Traction Company
*Portland, Oregon*

**Ajax No. 1 tractor**

In 1912 Ajax announced their No. 1 tractor. It used a four-cylinder opposed engine with the crankshaft mounted parallel to the chassis. The cylinders were 6 x 8 inch bore and stroke. The company also offered their No. 2 model, but this four-cylinder opposed engine was built with a 7 x 10 inch bore and stroke. The No. 2 weighed in at some thirteen tons! Little is known of this venture…apparently it ended shortly after it began.

## Ajax-Picrom Company

*San Francisco, California*

Among the many file cards accumulated over the years is this one for Ajax-Picrom Co. The company appears to have built a tractor about 1915, but no additional information has ever been located.

## Alamo Engine & Mfg. Company

*Hillsdale, Michigan*

**Early Alamo tractor**

By 1900 Alamo had already emerged as a major manufacturer of gasoline engines. This early file photo from Alamo illustrates one of the company's earliest attempts at converting an Alamo stationary engine into a usable tractor. The engine is of about 6 horsepower. A simple clutch pulley was used to control the forward movement of the tractor.

A 1905 Alamo catalog illustrates the company's approach to a gasoline traction engine. In this instance a large Alamo engine, probably of 15 or 20 horsepower is mounted on a traction chassis,

**Alamo gasoline traction engine**

but curiously the cooling system is not shown. After a short time in the tractor business, Alamo opted to specialize in the engine business, doing so with great success for many years to follow.

## Albaugh-Dover Company

*Chicago, Illinois*

See: Square Turn Tractor Company

## Albert Lea Tractor & Mfg. Company

*Albert Lea, Minnesota*

**Sexton tractor**

In the August 1917 issue of *Agrimotor Magazine*, George L. Sexton detailed his reasons why small tractors were needed for 'every farm of 60 acres or more.' Seeing this huge need, Sexton organized this Albert Lea company to manufacture the small Sexton tractor. It was equipped with a four-cylinder vertical engine having a 4 x 6 inch bore and stroke, thus giving it about 25 to 30 belt horsepower. The company appears to have its beginnings about 1913, and also appears to have been perpetually short of money; this appears likely because of numerous reorganizations and mergers. Finally in 1917 Albert Lea Grader & Mfg. Company was organized to take over the assets of the tractor company as well as the Albert Lea Grader firm. After this time, little more is to be found concerning the Sexton tractor.

## Alberta Foundry & Machine Company
*Medicine Hat, Alberta*

**14-28 "Canadian" tractor**

In 1919 Alberta Foundry & Machine Company Ltd. came out with their 14-28 "Canadian" tractor. It was the only tractor to be built in the western provinces. The design came from R. B. Hartsough, one of the original partners in the Transit Thresher Company of Minneapolis. A unique feature was a wooden frame that could be shortened or lengthened at the wish of the owner. Another feature was the use of replaceable wooden spokes in the drivewheels. After its initial announcement in 1919, little more was heard of the "Canadian" tractor.

## Allen-Burbank Motor Company
*Los Angeles, California*

The Thorobred 18-30 tractor was marketed by Allen-Burbank Motor Co. in the 1920-1923 period. It was essentially a built-up tractor that used a Beaver four-cylinder motor and a Nuttall

**Thorobred 18-30 tractor**

selective shift transmission. In 1923 the company was merged into Community Mfg. Company, also of Los Angeles, and for further information the reader is directed to that heading

## Algona Mfg. Company
*Algona, Iowa*

Over the past forty years the Author has collected names of engine and tractor manufacturers. For many years we kept these on index cards, and one such card appears for this company. However, we have no record of where we obtained this information, nor have we subsequently found further information on the company.

## Allegheny Gear Works
*Pittsburgh, Pennsylvania*

About 1920 an advertisement appeared for the Allegheny 12-20 3-plow tractor. Priced at $450, it included a 'Buda motor, worm drive, cut steel gears, roller and ball bearings, all moving parts enclosed, complete with governor and fenders.' No illustration of the tractor has been found.

## S. L. Allen & Company
*Philadelphia, Pennsylvania*

S. L. Allen & Co. was actively engaged in manufacturing cultivators by the 1890s; their Planet Jr. line was known around the world. In 1920 the company made a brief entry into the tractor busi-

**Planet Jr.**

ness with their Planet Jr. tractor of 'universal' design. It was designed to handle cultivators, plows, and numerous other implements, and could also be equipped with the sulky shown here for various drawbar work. Production of the Planet Jr. apparently ended in 1921. The company remained active in the cultivator business, eventually building various styles of walk-behind garden tractors. As with many manufacturers, production was suspended on most models during World War Two. Production resumed after the War, but ended again in the early 1950s.

## Allen Tractor Company
*Chicago, Illinois*

Allen Tractor Co. was incorporated at Chicago in 1916. Aside from the corporate announcement, nothing further has been located concerning the company or its products.

## Allen Water Ballast Tractor Company
*location unknown*

Among the many listings gathered over the years comes this one to which reference was made in a magazine article, but without giving the company address. No further information on this company has ever been found.

## Allied Motors Corporation
*Minneapolis, Minnesota*

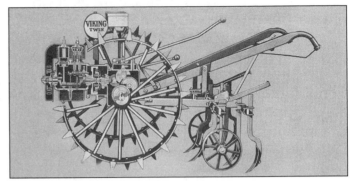

**Allied tractor**

While it is certain that Allied was building and marketing the Viking garden tractors in 1936, along with the Standard Twin, further information regarding the activities of Allied Motors remains elusive. Apparently Allied had bought out the Standard Twin garden tractor about 1930 or 1931, but when they acquired the Viking line is unknown, even though several researchers have attempted to untangle the pertinent events. Perhaps another edition of this book will have enough data to establish the company's activities during the 1930s and subsequently.

## Allied Truck & Tractor Corporation
*Minneapolis, Minnesota*

**Allied 10-20 tractor**

Allied was incorporated in April 1920. Their Allied 10-20 tractor appears in the directories during the 1921-1924 period. Weighing about 4,900 pounds, the 10-20 was a convertible tractor, and is shown here with the sulky truck attached. However, by 1920 the popularity of this design was waning, and just around the corner was the announcement of the Farmall all-purpose row-crop tractor.

## Alligator Tractor Company
*St. Louis, Missouri*

**Alligator Model 66 crawler tractor**

In 1964 Alligator announced their small Model 66 crawler tractor. The 66-G was equipped with a Wisconsin two-cylinder engine, while the diesel model used a Deutz single-cylinder style. Both were of about 53ci displacement, and both models weighed slightly over 2,000 pounds. The Alligator continues to appear during the next two years, but the company's activities after that time are unknown.

| 1 | 2 | 3 | 4 |
|---|---|---|---|
| $2,500 | $2,000 | $1,500 | $500 |

## Allis-Chalmers Mfg. Company
*Milwaukee, Wisconsin*

Allis-Chalmers had its beginnings in 1901 with the merger of Edward P. Allis Company, Fraser & Chalmers, Gates Iron Works, and Dickson Mfg. Company. Until 1914 the company confined its manufacturing efforts to large industrial machinery, everything from gigantic Corliss steam engines to sawmills, flour milling machinery, and a host of other items. However, in 1914 the company took an interest in the tractor business, finally emerging with their 10-18 tractor that year.

Sales of the 10-18 tractor were not at all exciting, but the company moved forward, finally introducing their 15-30, a conventional wheel tractor in 1918. From this point forward Allis-Chalmers tractors made their presence known throughout the industry. Even though the A-C tractor line never was among the top selling tractor brands, it nevertheless earned a position of respect wherever it was used.

In 1929 Allis-Chalmers made history in the tractor business with the introduction of their Model U tractor; it was unique in itself, but more importantly, the Model U was the first American farm tractor to be sold with pneumatic tires. This happened in 1932. Farmers and manufacturers alike scorned the idea at first, but in a short time, farmers were clamoring for rubber tires on their tractors, so the industry followed along, although grudgingly at first.

History was again made in 1933 when Allis-Chalmers introduced its WC row-crop tractor. This lightweight, yet powerful tractor was the first to use a 'square engine' and in this case it was a 4-inch bore and stroke. WC tractors quickly proved themselves as being sturdy, gutsy, and very reliable. By the time production of the WC ended in 1948 the company had built over 178,000 units!

Various other unique features were introduced to the tractor industry during its long career that ended in 1985 by merging into the Deutz interests to form the Deutz-Allis line. Speculation provides many suggestions for the merger. However, viewed in the larger sense, the farm tractor industry of 1985 was no longer able to support the production capacity and facilities of an earlier time.

The Author has compiled several titles relating to Allis-Chalmers. Included is: *Encyclopedia of American Farm Tractors, (Crestline/Motorbooks: 1979); The Allis-Chalmers Story (Crestline/Motor-*

*books: 1988);* and *Allis-Chalmers Tractors (Motorbooks: 1992).* Particularly in *The Allis-Chalmers Story* is the history of Allis-Chalmers delineated. Readers are urged to consult these titles for specific details.

**Allis-Chalmers 10-18 tractor**

Allis-Chalmers introduced their 10-18 tractor in 1914. Its unique design probably did not enhance its sales potential, and as a result, it took until the early 1920s until the company had sold all of the 10-18 tractors it had built. Yet, the company persevered, constantly looking for better designs. Very few 10-18 tractors remain among vintage tractor enthusiasts.

|  | **1** | **2** | **3** | **4** |
|---|---|---|---|---|
| 10-18 | $30,000 | $23,000 | $17,000 | $7,000 |

**Allis-Chalmers 6-12 tractor**

Between 1919 and 1923, Allis-Chalmers offered their 6-12 tractor. It was similar to several of its contemporaries, most notably the Moline Universal. Shown here is a two-row cultivator mounted to the 6-12, but many other implements could be

used just as easily. The cultivator could be easily detached, and for pulling a wagon or other towed implement, a simple sulky attachment was connected to the tractor frame.

|  | **1** | **2** | **3** | **4** |
|---|---|---|---|---|
| 6-12 (with 1-bottom plow) | $15,000 | $11,000 | $6,000 | $4,000 |

**Allis-Chalmers 6-12 and Galion Light Premier road graders**

Rural roads of the 1920s were usually maintained by the farmers within a township. Thus, small road graders were a blessing that permitted the chance to drive into town or in the neighborhood over a relatively smooth road. Shown here is a 6-12 Allis-Chalmers coupled to a Galion Light Premier road grader. With this integral outfit, one man could control the grader and the tractor with relative ease.

**Allis-Chalmers 18-30 tractor**

During 1918 Allis-Chalmers launched their new 18-30 tractor. Its unit frame design was extremely modern for the time; the 18-30 tractor would continue in various forms for several seasons to come. Allis-Chalmers guaranteed the 18-30 to have 3,000 pounds of drawbar pull in low gear; this came from a big four-cylinder engine having a 4-3/4 x 6-1/2 inch bore and stroke. In order to counter competitor's claims, the company noted that "The Allis-Chalmers 18-30 is not an 'assembled' tractor. With the exception of the magneto, carburetor and such special accessories, every part of the tractor is factory-built by the Allis-Chalmers Mfg. Co." The 18-30 shown here is from a 1921 company catalog.

| | 1 | 2 | 3 | 4 |
|---|---|---|---|---|
| 18-30 | $12,000 | $8,000 | $5,500 | $1,850 |

**Allis-Chalmers Model L, 15-25**

2,750 pounds. Rated speed for the four-cylinder engine was 1100 rpm, and featured positive force-feed lubrication. Production of the Model L, 15-25 tractor ended in 1927.

| | 1 | 2 | 3 | 4 |
|---|---|---|---|---|
| Model L, 15-25 | $8,500 | $6,500 | $4,500 | $1,500 |

**Allis-Chalmers 12-20 tractor**

Allis-Chalmers developed their 12-20 tractor during 1920, introducing it early the following year. In September 1921 the 12-20 was tested at Nebraska (Test No. 82) where it performed substantially better than the manufacturer's rating. Shortly afterward Allis-Chalmers re-rated the 12-20 upward to a 15-25 tractor, and even then, it was capable of ample reserve power. Initially at least, the 12-20 was built with a Midwest engine; it was of the four-cylinder style and carried a 4-1/8 x 5-1/4 inch bore and stroke.

| | 1 | 2 | 3 | 4 |
|---|---|---|---|---|
| 12-20 | $12,000 | $8,000 | $5,500 | $1,850 |
| 15-30 | $8,500 | $6,500 | $4,500 | $1,850 |

By the beginning of the 1922 season, Allis-Chalmers had re-rated its 12-20 tractor as the Model L, 15-25. Weighing 4,400 pounds, the 15-25 had a guaranteed drawbar pull in low gear of

**Allis-Chalmers 20-35**

In 1921 or 1922 Allis-Chalmers re-rated the 18-30 tractor upward to a 20-35 rating. This was probably due to the results of Nebraska Test No. 83 of September 1921. The big four-cylinder engine used a 4 x 6-1/2 inch bore and stroke, and was rated at 930 rpm. Removable cylinder sleeves were a standard feature. Production of the 20-35 continued until 1930 when it was replaced with the Model E, 25-40 tractor.

| | 1 | 2 | 3 | 4 |
|---|---|---|---|---|
| 20-35 Short Fender | | | | |
| | $6,800 | $5,500 | $2,500 | $750 |
| 20-35 Long Fender | | | | |
| | $10,500 | $7,500 | $3,200 | $1,850 |

**Allis-Chalmers 15-25 Special Road Maintenance Tractor**

Production of the Allis-Chalmers 15-25 Special Road Maintenance Tractor ran concurrently with the normal production run for the 15-25. However, this modified version used heavier rear wheels, while the fronts were equipped with high ribs for better steering control. The extra weight of the wheels and other special accessories boosted the operating weight of this style to 5,600 pounds.

**Allis-Chalmers Model E, 25-40 tractor**

With the end of the 20-35 in 1930 came its replacement, the Model E, 25-40 tractor. This new model boasted a big four-cylinder engine with a 5 x 6-1/2 inch bore and stroke. Nebraska Test No. 193 of June 1931 revealed 28 drawbar and 47 belt horsepower for this model. Production of the Model E, 25-40 continued until 1936.

| | 1 | 2 | 3 | 4 |
|---|---|---|---|---|
| Model E, 25-40 | | | | |
| | $8,500 | $6,000 | $3,000 | $1,500 |

**Allis-Chalmers Model U, 19-30 tractor**

In 1929 Allis-Chalmers introduced their Model U, 19-30 tractor. This new design was much lighter and more compact than its predecessors, and in fact, production of this highly successful model was continued until 1952. Initially the Model U was equipped with a Continental four-cylinder engine, but in 1932 it was replaced with the company's own engine, having a 4-3/4 x 5 inch bore and stroke. In 1936 this was modified slightly by giving the engine a 4-1/2 inch bore, and of course, slightly more power. The Model U was the first tractor to be equipped with pneumatic tires.

| | 1 | 2 | 3 | 4 |
|---|---|---|---|---|
| Model U, 19-30 | | | | |
| | $5,000 | $3,500 | $1,500 | $500 |

Late in 1930 Allis-Chalmers introduced their Model UC row-crop tractor. It was essentially the same as the Model U standard-tread model, except of course, for the row-crop design. A major feature of the Model UC was the com-

**Allis-Chalmers Model UC row-crop tractor**

pany's development of a "5-minute hitch" system whereby it was possible to simply drive the tractor into the cultivator, using only a pair of pliers to make the necessary connections. Production of the UC tractor continued until 1951.

| | 1 | 2 | 3 | 4 |
|---|---|---|---|---|
| Model UC, 19-30 | | | | |
| Continental Motor | | | | |
| | $8,500 | $3,800 | $2,000 | $1,400 |
| UM Engine | $7,000 | $3,000 | $1,000 | $600 |

**Allis-Chalmers Model WC**

Introduced in 1933, the Model WC was the first tractor in the industry to use a "square engine" meaning that the engine had the same bore and stroke; in this instance, the dimension was 4 inches. From the beginning the WC was a very popular tractor, and by the time production ended in 1948, some 178,000 had been built. Shown here is a 'flat-top' design of 1936. This

meant that the open radiator tank had a "flat" top, as compared with the streamlined series that was initiated in 1938.

| | 1 | 2 | 3 | 4 |
|---|---|---|---|---|
| Model WC Waukesha | | | | |
| | $28,500 | $18,000 | $10,000 | $5,000 |
| WC (unstyled) 1934-38 | | | | |
| | $4,000 | $2,800 | $1,000 | $450 |

**WC row crop on rubber tires**

**WC row crop on steel wheels**

**Model "WC" tractor with wide front axle**

**Model "WC" tractor, single front wheel**

**Cultivating style with dished rear wheels**

**Cultivating style on skeleton steel wheels**

During 1938 the Allis-Chalmers tractor line was streamlined and modernized. Many different configurations were available to suit various crop requirements and farming practices. The standard cultivating style on rubber tires was by far the most popular, although the others were required in certain areas. Production of the WC tractor ended in 1948.

| | 1 | 2 | 3 | 4 |
|---|---|---|---|---|
| Model WC Tractor (styled) | $3,000 | $2,000 | $1,200 | $450 |

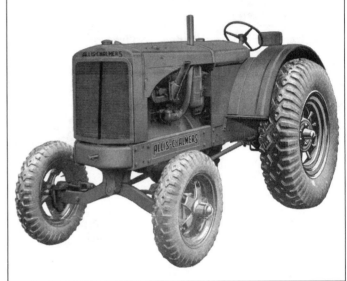

**Allis-Chalmers Model "WF"**

Allis-Chalmers introduced their Model WF tractor in 1937, keeping it in production until 1951. This 23 horsepower tractor was a standard-tread (fixed width) version of the Model WC row-crop tractor. One of the major features was a four-speed transmission with a high gear that permitted road speeds up to 10 mph. Equipped with rubber tires, the WF weighed 3,600 pounds. Pneumatic tires were standard equipment, although steel wheels could also be furnished. When equipped with steel wheels however, fourth gear, or road gear was blocked out and could not be used.

| | 1 | 2 | 3 | 4 |
|---|---|---|---|---|
| Model WF Tractor (unstyled) | $7,000 | $5,000 | $3,200 | $1,200 |
| Model WF Tractor (styled) | $7,000 | $5,000 | $3,200 | $1,200 |

**Model "WD" tractor**

In 1948 the WC tractor was retired, being replaced with a new version known as the WD. A major feature was the 'two-clutch power control system' that was essentially a live pto system. The foot-operated clutch controlled all power operations, while a separate hand clutch could be used to start and stop the tractor, leaving the pto shaft in operation. The WD also offered a full hydraulic system, plus the advantage of power shifting to change the wheel tread width. Eventually these improvements were added to virtually every other tractor on the market. Production of the WD continued into 1954.

| | 1 | 2 | 3 | 4 |
|---|---|---|---|---|
| Model WD Tractor | | | | |
| | $3,500 | $2,000 | $1,000 | $500 |

**Model WD-45**

Introduced in 1953, the WD-45 boasted substantially more horsepower than its predecessor, the

WD. This model had a four-cylinder 226 ci engine with a 4 x 4-1/2 inch bore and stroke. Rated speed was 1400 rpm. The WD-45 was capable of over 45 belt or pto horsepower. Production of the WD-45 ended in 1957. It was available in various chassis configurations, and was also available in diesel or LP-gas models.

| | 1 | 2 | 3 | 4 |
|---|---|---|---|---|
| Model WD-45 Tractor | | | | |
| | $6,000 | $3,500 | $1,200 | $500 |
| Model WD-45 Tractor Buda-Diesel | | | | |
| | $7,000 | $4,000 | $1,200 | $800 |

**Model A standard-tread**

Model A standard-tread tractors were offered in the 1936-1942 period. This style sold rather poorly compared with the WC, but the $1,500 price tag was probably a deterrent. In addition, most farmers saw little need for a standard-tread tractor when their WC row-crop model would do almost everything around the farm. With the onset of World War Two, production ended for the Model A, and did not resume after the war.

| | 1 | 2 | 3 | 4 |
|---|---|---|---|---|
| Model A Tractor | | | | |
| | $14,000 | $8,500 | $5,500 | $2,000 |

Production of the Model B Allis-Chalmers tractor began in 1937, and continued for twenty years. Initially, this small tractor was priced at only $495. Many different attachments were available, including this one-row cultivator. Model B tractors were equipped with a four-cyl-

**Allis-Chalmers Model B tractor**

inder engine having a 3-1/4 x 3-1/2 inch bore and stroke. Rated speed was 1400 rpm. This model used a rear-mounted belt pulley, available as an extra-cost option. Also available was a Model IB tractor, an industrial version of the standard version.

| | 1 | 2 | 3 | 4 |
|---|---|---|---|---|
| Model B Tractor | $2,700 | $1,500 | $750 | $300 |

**Allis-Chalmers Model C tractor**

Between 1940 and 1950 Allis-Chalmers built some 90,000 copies of their Model C tractor. The four-cylinder engine carried a 1/2-inch larger bore at 3-3/8 inches, while the stroke remained the same at 4-1/2 inches. This yielded nearly 22 belt horsepower with an operating speed of 1500 rpm. A host of implements were available

for the Model C, making it an ideal choice for the small farm. In the 1939-1941 period Allis-Chalmers built a few Model RC tractors. The RC was essentially built over the WC chassis but used a smaller engine. Production was suspended during World War Two, and never resumed afterward.

| | 1 | 2 | 3 | 4 |
|---|---|---|---|---|
| Model C Tractor | $2,600 | $1,500 | $750 | $300 |

**Model CA tractor**

Rated at nearly 27 belt horsepower, the Model CA tractor replaced the Model C in 1950. Production of this model continued until 1957. In addition to all the features found on the Model C, the Model CA was equipped with the company's Traction Booster system and their Power Shift rear wheels. The 125 cubic inch engine was also used extensively as a stationary power unit.

| | 1 | 2 | 3 | 4 |
|---|---|---|---|---|
| Model CA Tractor | $2,700 | $1,500 | $750 | $300 |

In a radical departure from conventional design, Allis-Chalmers introduced their Model G tractor in 1948, continuing it until 1955. This small tractor was immensely popular with truck gardeners in particular, although it saw limited use on grain and livestock farms as well. The Model G used a four-cylinder 62ci engine having

**Allis-Chalmers Model G tractor**

a 2-3/8 x 3-1/2 inch bore and stroke. It was rated at 1800 rpm. Many different attachments were available, including a wide variety of cultivators.

|  | 1 | 2 | 3 | 4 |
|---|---|---|---|---|
| Model G Tractor | $3,850 | $2,500 | $1,500 | $700 |

(add $500 for hydraulics)

**Allis-Chalmers D-10 tractor**

Although Allis-Chalmers introduced their D-Series tractors in 1957, the small D-10 did not go into production until 1959; it remained in the line until 1967. Like other D-Series tractors, the D-10 was modified from time to time during the production run. Initially it used a 138.7ci engine having a 3-3/8 x 3-7/8 inch bore and stroke. In late 1961 or early 1962 the engine bore was increased to 3-1/2 inches for a displacement of 149 cubic inches.

|  | 1 | 2 | 3 | 4 |
|---|---|---|---|---|
| D-10 | $7,500 | $5,500 | $4,000 | $1,500 |

**Allis Chalmers D-12 tractor**

In the 1959-1967 period Allis-Chalmers offered their D-12 tractor. Initially, the D-10 and the D-12 used the same 138.7ci engine, but in late 1961 or 1962 this was changed to a larger 149ci motor. The major difference in the D-10 and the D-12 was their operating width. The D-10 stood 58 inches wide, while the D-12 had a width of 69 inches.

|  | 1 | 2 | 3 | 4 |
|---|---|---|---|---|
| Model D12 | $7,500 | $5,500 | $4,000 | $1,500 |

**Allis-Chalmers D-14 tractor**

Built only in the 1957-1960 period, the D-14 tractor was available as a special LP-gas tractor, in addition to the commonly used gasoline engine. Using the four-cylinder, 149ci A-C engine, both models were capable of about 35 pto horse-power. This popular A-C engine featured a 3-1/2 x 3-7/8 inch bore and stroke. Rated speed was 1650 rpm. In 1960 this tractor carried a list price of $2875.

|      | **1** | **2** | **3** | **4** |
|------|------|------|------|------|
| D-14 | $4,000 | $3,000 | $2,500 | $1,800 |

**Allis-Chalmers D-15 tractor**

In the 1960-1967 model years, Allis-Chalmers offered their D-15 tractor in gasoline, diesel, and LP-gas versions. The original series used the same 149ci engine as in the D-14 tractor, but in 1963, the new Series II D-15 was equipped with a larger 160ci engine. This four-cylinder model had a 3-5/8 x 3-7/8 inch bore and stroke. Rated speed was 2000 rpm. In 1967 this model sold for $4430. These tractors were also available in a special High-Clearance version.

Allis-Chalmers D-17 tractors were built in the 1958-1967 period. During this time the D-17 underwent various modifications, finally clos-ing out production with the Series IV. Shown here is the 1958 style, and this one with the sin-gle-front wheel, a style that was popular in cer-tain areas. D-17 tractors were available with gasoline, LP-gas or diesel engines; the gasoline model used a four-cylinder engine with a 4 x 4-1/2 inch bore and stroke for a displacement of

**Allis-Chalmers D-17 tractor**

226ci. The D-17 diesel was equipped with a six-cylinder engine having a 3 9/16 x 4-3/8 inch bore and stroke. All D-17 models were capable of about 53 pto horsepower.

**Allis-Chalmers D-19 tractor**

A short production run, lasting only from 1961 to 1963 is noted for the D-19 Allis-Chalmers trac-tors. Capable of about 70 pto horsepower, the D-19 used a six-cylinder, 262ci engine, and in fact, the D-19 diesel used the same engine as the D-17 diesel. However, the D-17 operated at 1650 rpm, while the D-19 diesel had a governed speed of 2000 rpm.

96

**Allis-Chalmers D-21 tractor**

Allis-Chalmers D-21 tractors were built between 1963 and 1969. This big tractor was available with a gasoline or a diesel engine. The latter was a 426ci, six-cylinder style having a 4 -1/4 x 5 inch bore and stroke. Rated speed was 2200 rpm. Initially the D-21 used a naturally aspirated engine and was capable of about 103 pto horsepower. In 1965 a turbocharger was added and this raised the power level to 128 pto horsepower.

**Model M crawler**

After buying out the Monarch crawler line in 1928 the company continued the Monarch tractors with little change until about 1931 when the Model L crawler appeared. A year later came the Model M, as shown here. It remained in production for a decade, and this was a long time in the rapidly changing tractor business. The standard gauge for the Model M was 40 inches, and the company also offered the Model WM built on a 50-inch track gauge.

**HD-14 crawler**

Production of the HD-Series crawlers began with the HD-14 in 1939, and full production the following year. With 132 drawbar horsepower, the HD-14 weighed in at 29,000 pounds. It was equipped with a GM 6-71 diesel engine, and the latter would characterize the A-C crawler line for some years to come. Numerous models and styles of HD-Series crawlers were built subsequent to 1939 and running until 1965.

| | 1 | 2 | 3 | 4 |
|---|---|---|---|---|
| F 75 Crawler | | | | |
| | $15,000 | $12,000 | $6,000 | $3,000 |
| H 6-Ton Crawler | | | | |
| | $18,000 | $10,000 | $5,000 | $3,000 |
| H 50 Crawler | | | | |
| | $14,000 | $10,000 | $6,000 | $3,000 |
| H-3 & HD-3 Crawler | | | | |
| | $6,000 | $4,500 | $3,000 | $2,00 |
| HD-4 Crawler | | | | |
| | $6,000 | l$4,500 | $3,000 | $2,000 |
| HD-5 Crawler | | | | |
| | $8,000 | $6,000 | $4,000 | $2,000 |
| HD-6 Crawler | | | | |
| | $8,000 | $6,000 | $4,000 | $2,000 |
| HD-7 Crawler | | | | |
| | $9,000 | $7,000 | $3,500 | $1,000 |
| HD-9 Crawler | | | | |
| | $9,000 | $7,000 | $3,500 | $1,000 |
| HD-10 Crawler | | | | |
| | $9,000 | $7,000 | $3,500 | $1,000 |
| HD-10W Crawler | | | | |
| | $9,000 | $7,000 | $3,500 | $1,500 |
| HD-11 Crawler | | | | |
| | $8,000 | $6,000 | $4,500 | $3,000 |
| HD-15 Crawler | | | | |
| | $8,000 | $6,000 | $4,500 | $2,000 |
| HD-16 Crawler | | | | |
| | $8,000 | $6,000 | $4,5000 | $2,000 |

| HD-19 Crawler | | | | |
| --- | --- | --- | --- | --- |
| | $8,000 | $6,000 | $4,500 | $2,000 |
| HD-20 Crawler | | | | |
| | $8,000 | $6,000 | $4,500 | $2,000 |
| HD-21 Crawler | | | | |
| | $10,000 | $8,000 | $4,000 | $2,000 |
| K 35 Crawler | | | | |
| | $8,000 | $6,000 | $4,000 | $1,500 |
| L & LO Crawler | | | | |
| | $9,000 | $7,000 | $4,000 | $1,000 |
| LD Crawler | | | | |
| | $9,000 | $7,000 | $4,000 | $1,500 |
| M Crawler | $6,000 | $4,000 | $2,000 | $500 |
| S & SO Crawler | | | | |
| | $9,000 | $7,000 | $4,000 | $1,000 |

## Alma Mfg. Company
*Alma, Michigan*

A trade note of 1909 indicates that Alma was building the McVicker four-cylinder chain drive tractor. This may have been the same tractor referred to under the heading of *McVicker Engineering Company*, also in this volume.

## Altgelt Tractor Company
*address unknown*

This listing was derived from a magazine article wherein a passing reference was made to the firm, and probably is dated in the 1915-1920 period. No further information has ever been located.

## American-Abell Engine & Thresher Company
*Toronto, Ontario*

American Abell had roots going back to 1847 in the threshing machine business. By 1886 the firm was building *Cock O' The North* steam traction engines. In 1902 the firm was sold jointly to Advance Thresher Co. and Minneapolis Threshing Machine Co. When M. Rumely Co. bought out Advance in 1912, Minneapolis sold their

**American-Abell Universal Farm Tractor**

share for cash to Rumely. In 1911 American-Abell offered 'their' Universal Farm Motor. It was the same tractor being then built by Universal Tractor Co. at Stillwater, Minnesota.

## American Engine & Tractor Company
*Charles City, Iowa*

American announced their 15-30 tractor in 1918. Unfortunately, a photograph of this tractor could not be found. This model was equipped with a Beaver four-cylinder engine having a 4 x 6 inch bore and stroke. It was rather pricey, having a retail tag of $1,895. Production ended shortly after it began, and in 1919 the firm became known as American Tractor & Foundry Company. No trademark or photo shown.

## American Farm Machinery Company
*Minneapolis, Minnesota*

See: Andrews-Kinkade

Among other products, American built the Kinkade garden tractors. The company was incorporated December 24, 1921 and remained in business until 1955. Shown here is one example

**Weber tractor, American Gas Engine Co.**

**Kinkade garden tractor**

of the Kinkade tractor; this one is from the early 1920s. American traced its ancestry to the Andrews Tractor Company, and then the Andrews-Kinkade Tractor Company.

| | 1 | 2 | 3 | 4 |
|---|---|---|---|---|
| Garden tractor | $450 | $200 | $125 | $50 |

## American Fork & Hoe Company
*Montrose, Iowa*

During 1953 this company was listed as the manufacturer for the Gro-Mor garden tractors, as well as for the Held garden tractor. The latter had formerly been built by the Frank Held Tractor Company. Aside from this listing, nothing further has been located.

| 1 | 2 | 3 | 4 |
|---|---|---|---|
| $800 | $600 | $400 | $250 |

## American Gas Engine Company
*Kansas City, Missouri*

The Weber tractor first made its appearance in 1914. American Gas Engine Co. was the resulting reorganization of the Weber Gas Engine Co., also at Kansas City. It is likely that the tractor was at least in development prior to the reorganization of the company. This tractor is identical to that offered concurrently by Phoenix Mfg. Company at Winona, Minnesota. Aside from a few advertisements, little is known of the Weber tractor.

## American Gas Tractor Company

*Minneapolis, Minnesota*

The October 1910 issue of *Gas Review Magazine* discusses the new tractor being developed by American Gas Tractor Company, noting that at the time, they were not yet ready to put it on the market. A table of tractor specifications in the March 1911 issue of *Gas Review* notes that the American used a four-cylinder engine having a 7 x 8 inch bore and stroke for a rating of 60 belt horsepower. Weighing nearly nine tons, the American sold for $3,500. No further information on this tractor has been located.

## American Implement Company

*Cleveland, Ohio*

In 1919 American offered three tractor models. All were equipped with four-cylinder engines. Included was the American Junior, a 10-20 tractor. It used a 3 x 5-1/2 inch bore and stroke. The American was a 15-30 tractor, its engine carried a 3 -3/4 x 5-1/8 inch bore and stroke. Topping the line was the American Combined, a big tractor with a 30-58 horsepower rating. Its four-cylinder engine used a 5-1/2 x 7 inch bore and stroke. Aside from the specifications, no further information has been found, nor have any illustrations been located.

## American Implement Corporation

*Los Angeles, California*

The American garden tractor is listed in the 1948 issue of *Farm Implement News Buyer's Guide*. Their American "General" Model 600 garden tractor weighed 950 pounds and used a Gladden single

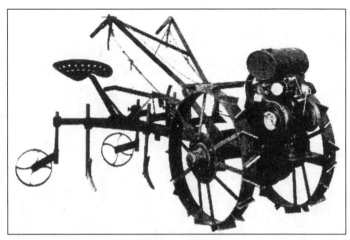

**American "General" Model 600 garden tractor**

cylinder, Model 75 engine; it had a 2-3/4 x 3 inch bore and stroke. Further information on this company has not been found.

| <u>1</u> | <u>2</u> | <u>3</u> | <u>4</u> |
|------|------|------|------|
| $500 | $300 | $200 | $100 |

## American Mfg. Company

*Indianapolis, Indiana*

A trade note of 1913 notes that this company was organized 'to build tractors.' Aside from that, no further information has been located concerning this firm.

## American Merchandise Mart

*Philadelphia, Pennsylvania*

This company offered their Farmwell Jr. garden tractor in the late 1940s. The 1948 *Buyer's Guide* from *Farm Implement News* notes the Farmwell only for this year, and beyond this, no further details have been located.

## American Standard Tractor Company

*Minneapolis, Minnesota*

This firm appears in the 1920 tractor directories, although a suitable illustration of the tractor has not yet been located. The company remained in business until 1922. Rated at 17 drawbar and 23 belt horsepower, this tractor was equipped with the 'American Standard' transmission which was claimed to be very simple and durable. Gilbert Amonsen of Minneapolis secured Patent No. 1,318,471 covering the engine used for the tractor. It was a two-cycle design with a very unusual port design.

## American Steel Tractor Company

*Canton, Ohio*

**American Steel Tractor**

This is a 1947 model built by American Steel Tractor Corporation of Canton, Ohio. It was tested in Nebraska in June 1947. It failed nearly all the tests. The engine overheated under heavy load and the rear end got so hot water had to be poured on it to cool it during the tests. Only five units were ever built and the tractor never made it to the production phase. The results of the Nebraska testing left hard feelings between the engineers and the company, which resulted in the dissolution of the venture.

Of the five tractors built three are known to exist. The tractor in the photo is one sold at the Ed Spiess Auction. It brought $17,000.00.

## American Swiss Magneto Company

*Toledo, Ohio*

Macultivator Company at Sandusky, Ohio apparently went out of business in the late 1920s, probably about 1929 or 1930. At that point the above firm took over the Macultivator line and

continued to offer parts for the Macultivators into the 1950s. Possibly, American Swiss Magneto Co. built the Macultivator for a time after acquiring the company.

| <u>1</u> | <u>2</u> | <u>3</u> | <u>4</u> |
|------|------|------|------|
| $750 | $500 | $200 | $100 |

## American Three-Way-Prism Company

*LaPorte, Indiana*

The September 1914 issue of *Gas Power Magazine* notes that this company was about to begin building a small tractor having 15 drawbar and 24 belt horsepower. It was to be equipped with a four-cylinder vertical engine; total weight of the tractor was about 5,000 pounds. Aside from this mention, no further information has ever been located on the company or its tractor.

## American Tractor & Foundry Company

*Charles City, Iowa*

**Trademark for "Americo" tractors**

This firm was the immediate successor of American Engine & Tractor Company (see page 44). It appears that the company was reorganized or renamed in late 1919 or early 1920. No traces of their tractor(s) have been found. A 1920 issue of the *Patent Office Gazette* illustrates the company trademark for the "Americo" tractors and engines, noting that the company first used this tradename in February 1920. After this time the firm disappears from view.

## American Tractor Company
*Des Moines, Iowa*

This firm is listed in 1916 as the manufacturer of the American Oil Tractor. Rated at 18 drawbar and 35 belt horsepower, the American used a four-cylinder engine with a 5 x 7 inch bore and stroke. The American was of conventional four-wheel design with the engine being placed parallel with the tractor frame and between the rear wheels. It weighed 6,300 pounds and sold for $1,600. Unfortunately, a reproducible photograph could not be located.

## American Tractor Company
*Detroit, Michigan*

No information available.

## American Tractor Company
*Pittsburgh, Pennsylvania*

No information available.

## American Tractor Corporation
*Peoria, Illinois*

**American 15-30**

The American first emerged in 1918, being the work of John W. Kinross. The American 15-30 shown here was replaced with the Yankee 15-25 in 1920. Weighing 4,600 pounds, the American

was priced at $1765. Power was provided by an Erd four-cylinder motor with a 4 x 6 inch bore and stroke. Production of the American and Yankee models ended about 1922.

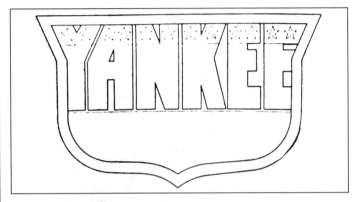

**"Yankee" trademark**

In a trademark application of 1920, American Tractor Corporation claimed that the "Yankee" trademark shown here had first been used April 1, 1918. Chances are that this date closely coincides with the beginning of the company. However, American, like many others of the period, withered under fierce competition and the post-war depression of the early 1920s.

## American Tractor Corporation
*Churubusco, Indiana*

**Terratrac GT-25**

American began building their crawler tractors in late 1949, with full-fledged production coming the following year. In the 1950-53 period American offered the Terratrac GT-25. Weighing less than two tons, the GT-25 had a turning radius of only six feet. Options included a pto shaft, belt pulley, and a hydraulic lift system.

**GT-30 Terratrac**

The GT-30 Terratrac was built from 1951 to 1954. This model was capable of about 25 drawbar horsepower, and like other Terratrac models of the period was available with an optional three-point hitch system. Like other Terratrac crawlers of the period, it used a Continental engine; in this case it was their F-140 model. In the 1951-54 period, American also built the similar GT-34 crawler. Their DT-34, built from 1952 to 1954 was the company's first diesel-powered crawler tractor.

| | **1** | **2** | **3** | **4** |
|---|---|---|---|---|
| GT-30 | $6,000 | $4,000 | $2,500 | $1,000 |

**American "200" crawler**

During 1954 American began a new tractor series with their "200" crawler. This one was similar to the GT-30 model which it replaced. American also introduced their Model 300 crawler in 1954, and it remained in production until 1958. Terra-

trac "400" and Terratrac "500" tractors also made their debut in 1954, with the latter also being equipped with a torque converter; this model was also known as the Terramatic.

**American "600" crawler**

In 1957 American came out with their "600" crawler, the largest that the company had built. Production of this tractor continued until 1962. J. I. Case Company bought out American Tractor Company in 1956, making it the basis for the continuing line of Case crawler tractors. The concept of using a torque converter drive had never been applied to smaller tractors before, although the Allis-Chalmers HD-21 for instance, was equipped with a torque converter. Eventually, Case would use the same concept on their wheel tractors with the Case-O-Matic drive.

## American Tractor & Harvester Company
*Stuttgart, Arkansas*

No information available.

## American Tractor & Implement Company
*Cincinnati, Ohio*

In 1920 the American Ground Hog tractor appeared. Weighing 6200 pounds, it had a 17-1/2 -31 horsepower rating. It featured an Erd four-cylinder engine with a 4 x 6 inch bore and stroke. This tractor listed at $2,800. Aside from a 1920 entry, no further information has been located on this tractor.

## American Well Works

*Aurora, Illinois*

**Aurora traction engine**

American Well Works was established in 1866. With the coming of internal combustion engines, the company developed their own line in the 1890s. As early as 1898 American designed their Aurora traction engine. Production likely continued for only a short time. Aside from a single illustration, few particulars have been found concerning the Aurora tractor from American Well Works.

## Anderson Company

*Minnesota Transfer, Minnesota*

Sometime over the years the Author photocopied a single-page circular describing the Anderson tractor. Aside from the data presented, we have no further information, not even a specific date, although we would estimate this tractor to be of

**Anderson tractor**

about 1915 vintage. Rated at 25 belt horsepower, the Anderson used a four-cylinder engine. With a single drive wheel the complicated differential gearing was eliminated.

## Anderson Foundry & Machine Company

*Anderson, Indiana*

A trade note of about 1915 indicates that Anderson was entering the tractor business, but no further information has been located concerning this venture. Anderson did however, make a substantial mark in the oil and diesel engine business at least into the 1920s.

## Andrews Tractor Company

*Minneapolis, Minnesota*

George C. Andrews organized this company in 1914, ostensibly to build the tractor he had designed. Andrews applied for a patent on the drive mechanism of his tractor. Subsequently, Patent No. 1,311,943 was issued in 1919. A friction-drive transmission provided infinitely variable ground speeds from 1 to 4 mph. Initially at

**Andrews tractor**

least, the Andrews was equipped with a four-cylinder, two-cycle engine that delivered 10 drawbar and 20 belt horsepower. The company was reorganized as Andrews-Kinkade Tractor Company in 1921.

## Andrews-Kinkade Tractor Company
*Minneapolis, Minnesota*

**18-36 Andrews tractor**

In 1921 Andrews Tractor Co. was reorganized as Andrews-Kinkade Tractor Co. Within a very short time, perhaps only a few weeks, the company was again reorganized, this time as American Farm Machinery Company. The latter went on to build the Kinkade garden tractors for some years. During all the corporate changes the company introduced their 18-36 Andrews tractor. This machine used a Climax four-cylinder engine having a 5 x 6-1/2 inch bore and stroke. It was marketed for only a short time.

See American Farm Machinery Company.

## Angola Engine & Foundry Company
*Angola, Indiana*

This firm was in the gasoline engine business by 1904, and was listed as a builder of 'gasoline traction engines' between 1904 and 1909. However, the company built very few engines during its career, ending in 1911. If indeed any number of tractors were built, no images or specifications have been located.

## Ann Arbor Hay Press Company
*Ann Arbor, Michigan*

**Ann Arbor self-propelled hay press**

Ann Arbor had a long career in the hay press business, eventually selling out to Oliver Farm Equipment Company in the 1940s. In 1910 the company offered this self-propelled hay press, one of the earliest self-propelled balers on the market. Although the traction gearing was not heavy enough for heavy drawbar loads, it was at least able to move the machine from place to place without any outside assistance.

## Antigo Tractor Corporation
*Antigo, Wisconsin*

The Antigo Quadpull tractor was listed in various directories between 1921 and 1923. The unique four-wheel-drive design was of interest to some farmers, and with a 15-25 horsepower

**Antigo Quadpull tractor**

rating, the Quadpull was sufficiently large for the average farm. Weighing 4,500 pounds, the Quadpull had all gears enclosed and running in oil.

# Appleton Mfg. Company
*Batavia, Illinois*

**14-28 tractor**

This company was established in 1872 to build various farm machines, including corn shellers, wood saws and feed grinders. By the early 1900s the company had gained considerable status, and in 1917 their 14-28 tractor was announced. By 1919 the tractor was rated downward to a 12-20 model, although it continued to use the same Buda four-cylinder engine. Rated at 1050 rpm, it carried a 4-1/4 x 5-1/2 inch bore and stroke. Production of the 12-20 tractor ended about 1924. The company remained in business until about 1950.

| | 1 | 2 | 3 | 4 |
|---|---|---|---|---|
| 12-20 (1917-24) | | | | |
| | $7,000 | $5,000 | $2,000 | $1,000 |

# Ariens Company
*Brillion, Wisconsin*

**Ariens "C" tiller**

Ariens Company first appears in the trade directories in the 1930s. However, by 1948 the company was the largest of its kind in the country, specializing in garden tillers. Shown here is the Ariens "C" tiller of 1941. It used a 5-1/2 horsepower engine. At the time, Ariens was building similar machines in sizes up to 14 horsepower.

| 1 | 2 | 3 | 4 |
|---|---|---|---|
| $850 | $700 | $400 | $250 |

# A.P. Armington
*Euclid, Ohio*

**Armington 10-20**

During 1921 and 1922 the Armington 10-20 was offered; it carried a list price of $1,100. The Armington featured a friction-drive transmission, thus providing infinitely variable speeds, both forward and reverse. Weighing 3,800 pounds, it used a Waukesha four-cylinder engine with a 3-3/4 x 5-1/4 inch bore and stroke.

# Arnold-Sandberg Machine Company
*Terre Haute, Indiana*

**Arnold-Sandberg tractor**

The April 1911 issue of *Gas Review Magazine* illustrates the Arnold-Sandberg tractor. Weighing 4,300 pounds, it was equipped with a two-cylinder 15 horsepower engine. This tractor certainly has features which would be later embodied in a successful row-crop tractor. Unfortunately, the designers probably never thought of their design as being a row-crop tractor. Aside from their 1911 announcement, it does not appear that the Arnold-Sandberg gained great fame or saw any extensive production. It was developed by D. B. Arnold and others.

# Aro Tractor Company
*Minneapolis, Minnesota*

**Aro small garden tractor**

Aro Tractor Company first appears in the trade directories in 1921. Their small garden tractor was called a 3-6, meaning it had 3 drawbar and 6 belt horsepower. Weighing 1,000 pounds, it was priced at $465. The company apparently remained in business until the late 1920s.

**Aro Trademark**

A trademark application indicates that Aro first used this mark on or about February 1, 1921. Numerous companies attempted to market power cultivators and garden tractors in the 1920s. A few succeeded...most did not.

# Arrow Mfg. Company
*Denver, Colorado*

No illustrations have been found for the Arrow All-Purpose tractor listed in the trade directories for 1948 only. This small tractor was equipped with an Onan two-cylinder engine having a 3 x 2 -3/4 inch bore and stroke. A small, simple little tractor, it used a twin v-belt drive with a tightener as the clutch.

# Arthurdale Farm Equipment Corporation
*Arthurdale, West Virginia*

**Co-Op No. 3**

Duplex Machinery Company at Battle Creek, Michigan sent a Co-op tractor to Nebraska's Tractor Test Laboratory in 1936. (See Test No. 275). A year or so later the name changed to Co-operative Machinery Company, and in 1940 the trade directories listed the above firm as the manufacturer of the Co-op No. 2 and Co-op No. 3 tractors. Shortly afterward, World War Two began, and that all but ended the Co-op tractor line.

## Athey Tractor Company
*Chicago, Illinois*

No information available.

## Atlantic Machine & Mfg. Company
*Cleveland, Ohio*

**Merry Garden Tractor**

In 1920 the Merry Garden Tractor appeared. This walk-behind unit weighed 360 pounds, and was powered by a 2 horsepower engine. By 1924 the Merry was being built by Federal Foundry Supply Co., also of Cleveland. Federal appears only as a parts supplier for the Merry by the early 1930s.

## Atlas Engineering Company
*Clintonville, Wisconsin*

**Atlas tractor**

About 1927 Atlas Engineering Co. was formed as a successor to the Topp-Stewart Tractor Company, also of Clintonville. The latter had its beginnings in 1917, and was organized a year earlier as the Four Wheel Tractor Company. The design was by D. S. Stewart, who was also involved with the Antigo Tractor Company, Antigo, Wisconsin. Stewart's partner was Charles Topp. The model shown here was rated at 30 drawbar and 45 belt horsepower.

|       | 1       | 2 | 3 | 4      |
|-------|---------|---|---|--------|
| Atlas | $15,000 | — | — | $4,500 |

## Aulson Tractor Company
*Waukegan, Illinois*

**Aulson 12-25 tractor**

In 1918 Aulson announced their new 12-25 tractor. Weighing 5,800 pounds, it used a four-cylinder engine having a 5 x 6-1/2 inch bore and stroke. For 1919 the belt horsepower rating was raised to 34 horses, using the same engine as before, but taking advantage of the vastly underrated designation used the previous year. After 1919 the Aulson disappears from the trade directories.

|       | 1 | 2 | 3       | 4 |
|-------|---|---|---------|---|
| 12-25 | — | — | $10,000 | — |

## Aultman & Taylor Machinery Company
*Mansfield, Ohio*

In late 1910 or early 1911 Aultman & Taylor introduced their 30-60 tractor. The early model, as shown here, used an induced draft radiator. Weighing almost 25,000 pounds, the 30-60

**Aultman-Taylor gasoline traction engine**

remained on the market until the company was bought out by Advance-Rumely Thresher Company in January 1924.

**Aultman-Taylor 30-60 tractor**

The square radiator of the earlier models was replaced with a round tubular style in late 1913 or early 1914. Dual fans pulled air through 196 two-inch tubes in the 120 gallon radiator. The four-cylinder engine carried a 7 x 9 inch bore and stroke and was rated at 500 rpm. The 30-60 was capable of pulling over 9,000 pounds on the drawbar. Two clutches were used; one in the flywheel controlled forward ground travel, and one on the belt pulley or bandwheel was used for belt work or for reverse.

| 1 | 2 | 3 | 4 |
|---|---|---|---|
| 30-60 (1911-24) (round rad.) | | | |
| $40,000 | $30,000 | $25,000 | $8,500 |
| Square rad. — | $51,000 | — | — |

**25-50 Aultman-Taylor**

Early in 1915 the 25-50 Aultman-Taylor came on the market. It was virtually a clone of the 30-60 varying primarily in its physical size. The four-cylinder engine used a 6 x 9 inch bore and stroke. The 25-50 remained on the market until 1918.

| 1 | 2 | 3 | 4 |
|---|---|---|---|
| — | $28,000 | — | — |

**Aultman-Taylor 18-36 tractor**

Aultman & Taylor introduced their 18-36 tractor in late 1915. Its four-cylinder engine operated at 600 rpm, and carried a 5 x 8 inch bore and stroke. This model was of the same basic design as the ever-popular 30-60 tractor. However, the smaller sizes found competition very difficult in a market that was being inundated by a host of lightweight tractors. Thus, it appears that the 18-36 was revamped and re-rated as the 22-45 tractor in 1918.

|  | 1 | 2 | 3 | 4 |
|---|---|---|---|---|
| 18-36 and 22-45 (1916-24) | $27,000 | $20,000 | $16,000 | $5,000 |

**Aultman-Taylor 22-45 tractor**

With the 1918 introduction of the 22-45 Aultman-Taylor tractor, the company phased out the 18-36 and 25-50 models. Following the same general design as the 30-60 tractor, the 22-45 used a four-cylinder engine having a 5-1/2 x 8 inch bore and stroke. Weighing almost 13,000 pounds, the 22-45 was the only heavyweight Aultman-Taylor design to use a two-speed transmission. This tractor remained in the Aultman-Taylor line until the 1924 buyout by Advance-Rumely.

**Aultman-Taylor 15-30 tractor**

During 1918 Aultman & Taylor announced their new 15-30 tractor. This was the company's first (and only) entry into lightweight tractor designs,

as compared with the 30-60 and its cousins. The four-cylinder Climax engine used a 5-1/2 x 6 inch bore and stroke. This model was tested at Nebraska under Test No. 31 of July 1920. Production continued until the Advance-Rumely buyout of 1924.

|  | 1 | 2 | 3 | 4 |
|---|---|---|---|---|
| 15-30 | $20,000 | $15,000 | $10,000 | $5,000 |

# F. C. Austin Company
*Chicago, Illinois*

**Austin gasoline road roller**

Austin had a long career in building construction machinery, and offered this gasoline road roller about 1914. It consisted of a huge single-cylinder engine that was built by Austin, along with the heavy framework and ballast which made it an effective road roller.

**Austin 18-35 Multipedal crawler tractor**

About 1916 or 1917 Austin introduced their 18-35 Multipedal crawler tractor. Weighing over five tons, it was equipped with an Automatic four-cylinder engine having a 5-1/2 x 6 inch bore and stroke. Exceptionally long tracks were used; they were carried on six rollers. The final drive was through heavy chain to the bull gears.

**Austin 12-20 crawler tractor**

About 1917 Austin developed their 12-20 crawler tractor. It carried a Buffalo four-cylinder engine having a 4 x 5 inch bore and stroke. The small, compact design of the 12-20 should have gained some popularity in the agricultural trade, but it appears that the company made only a small effort to enter this market. Instead, it appears that most of their efforts were toward the construction industry.

**Austin 20-40 crawler tractor**

In 1919 and 1920 Austin offered their 20-40 crawler tractor. This one was a remodeled and enlarged version of the earlier 18-35 Multipedal design. At this time Austin also announced a big 125 horsepower crawler, rated to pull 12,500 pounds at the drawbar. Their 75-125 model was equipped with a six-cylinder Buffalo engine having a 7-1/2 x 9 inch bore and stroke.

**Austin 12-20 tractor**

Little is known of this 12-20 Austin tractor of 1919. It was apparently a four-wheel-drive design, and is shown here with special road planing equipment. The company was primarily interested in construction machinery, particularly that associated with road building. Thus, the Austin line made little impact on the agricultural market.

**Austin 15-30 tractor**

In 1920 the Austin 15-30 appeared, the only conventional four-wheel design to come from the Austin factories. During 1920 the F. C. Austin Machinery Company was incorporated. It took over the assets of the parent firm, along with a couple of other construction machinery manufacturers. Thus, the Austin 15-30 came to an end, along with the rest of the Austin tractor line; at the time of the merger, the new company apparently ended all efforts in the tractor business.

## Auto Tractor Company
*Chicago, Illinois*

This firm was one of the first to make an attachment whereby an automobile could be converted into a tractor. With this particular attachment the family car could be changed to a tractor with relative ease, and still be ready for church on Sunday or for a family outing. Most farmers, and perhaps their wives as well, held this idea in disdain, so most of the tractor conversion kits never met with great success. This one was available in 1913, and perhaps earlier.

## Auto Tractor Company
*San Francisco, California*

No information available.

## Auto-Track-Tractor Syndicate
*San Francisco, California*

Beginning about 1920 the Auto-Track 30-50 crawler tractor was on the market, remaining there until about 1924. Aside from trade references to this model, little else is known of the company.

**Auto-Track, 30-50**

The 30-50 was equipped with a Buda four-cylinder engine having a 5 x 6-1/2 inch bore and stroke. The spring-mounted track rollers are an unusual feature; extensive use of ball and roller bearings was certainly an asset to the design as well. The 30-50 weighed nearly five tons.

## Automotive Corporation
*Toledo, Ohio*

Probably sometime in 1918 the 12-24 Automotive first appeared. It was a line-drive tractor, using three leather lines to control all operations of the tractor from the towed implement or wagon. Initially the Automotive used a Buda four-cylinder

**Auto-Tractor attachment in use**

**12-24 Automotive**

engine having a 3-3/4 x 5-1/2 inch bore and stroke. Initially the Automotive was built at Fort Wayne, Indiana, but built a new plant and moved to Toledo, Ohio in 1920.

**Automotive 12-24 tractor equipped with a larger Hercules four-cyclinder engine**

Beginning with the 1920 model, Automotive 12-24 tractors were equipped with a larger Hercules four-cylinder engine; the latter used a 4 x 5-1/8 inch bore and stroke. This engine was vastly improved, using a five-bearing crankshaft, along with full force-feed lubrication. Probably due in part to intense competition at the time, the Automotive tractor left the scene about 1922.

## Automotive Motor Plow Company
*Carthage, Missouri*

No information available.

## Autopower Company
*Detroit, Michigan*

# "HELPING HENRY"
# AUTOPOW

In 1916 Autopower Co. began offering special devices that enabled the family car to be used for farm power needs. In some cases this simply consisted of jacking up one hind wheel, attaching a suitable pulley, and connecting a belt to the feed grinder or the wood saw. Among these devices was the "AUTOPOW" and the "HELPING HENRY." The latter was presumably for attachment to the inimitable Ford Model T.

## Avery Company
*Peoria, Illinois*
## Avery Power Machinery Company
*Peoria, Illinois*

**Farm and City Tractor**

Avery Company had its beginnings in 1874, and by 1891 was building steam traction engines. In 1909 the company announced its "Farm and City Tractor." Round wooden plugs in the wheels provided necessary traction, and the final drives were with heavy roller chains. This model was furnished with a four-cylinder engine having a 4 -3/4 x 5 inch bore and stroke. It was capable of 36 horsepower. Production of this model ended in 1914.

| | **1** | **2** | **3** | **4** |
|---|---|---|---|---|
| Farm and City Tractor | | | | |
| | — | $30,000 | $20,000 | $10,000 |

**Avery 25 H.P. tractor**

During 1909 Avery Company built this big single-cylinder tractor. Equipped with a 12 x 18 inch bore and stroke, it should have had about 60 horsepower with a rated speed of 350 rpm. Avery took this tractor to the 1910 Winnipeg Tractor Demonstration, and it performed so poorly that it was withdrawn.

**New Avery tractor**

With Avery's original tractor design of 1910 going down to failure, the company came out with a completely new model in 1911. Rated at 20 drawbar and 35 belt horsepower, this model used a two-cylinder engine having a 7-3/4 x 8

inch bore and stroke. Although this model would undergo further changes and refinements, the design would typify Avery tractors for some years to come.

The New Avery Gas Traction Engine first appeared in 1912, only a few months after the initial prototypes of 1911. The addition of a half-cab and a completely redesigned cooling system were the most obvious changes. Weighing almost six tons, the 20-35 was priced at about $1,800. Production of this model ended in 1915.

| | 1 | 2 | 3 | 4 |
|---|---|---|---|---|
| 20-35 | | — | $28,000 | — |

**Avery "Light Weight" 40-80 Gas and Oil Tractor**

During 1912 Avery Company developed their 40-80 model, announcing it publicly in January 1913. This big $2,650 tractor weighed 22,000 pounds. The four-cylinder engine used a 7 x 8 inch bore and stroke. Rated speed was 600 rpm. The 40-80 designation remained until 1920 when it was tested at Nebraska. Its performance there dictated that the tractor be re-rated as a 45-65, and this occurred in October 1920.

| | 1 | 2 | 3 | 4 |
|---|---|---|---|---|
| 40-80 | $50,000 | $40,000 | $25,000 | $10,000 |

Production of the 12-25 Avery tractor began late in 1912. Weighing 7,500 pounds, the 12-25 was equipped with a two-cylinder engine having a 6-1/2 x 7 inch bore and stroke. Production of

**Avery 12-25 tractor**

this model continued into 1919, and apparently it was discontinued at that time. Sadly, production figures for the Avery tractors have long since vanished.

| | 1 | 2 | 3 | 4 |
|---|---|---|---|---|
| 12-25 | $18,000 | $16,000 | $14,000 | $7,500 |

**Avery 12-25 Nursery Tractor**

About 1916 Avery announced their specially equipped 12-25 Nursery Tractor. This special design featured a high clearance front axle, along with a protective tunnel for tender nursery stock. The half-cab has been removed, and the platform has been modified for this special tractor. Production of this design was probably quite limited.

During 1914 the Avery line grew to include their small 8-16 model. Of essentially the same design as the larger cousins, the 8-16 used a two-

**Avery 8-16 tractor**

cylinder engine with a 5-1/2 x 6 inch bore and stroke. Rated speed was 750 rpm. Although the 8-16 began life with a list price of $900, this was dropped to $700 by 1917. Production of this model continued until about 1922.

| | 1 | 2 | 3 | 4 |
|---|---|---|---|---|
| 8-16 | $18,000 | $16,000 | $14,000 | $7,500 |

**Avery 25-50 tractor**

Avery's 25-50 tractor saw first light in 1914. This model started out with a retail price of $2,300, but eventually this price fell somewhat due to competition. Weighing 12,500 pounds, the 25-50 carried a four-cylinder engine with a 6-1/2 x 7 inch bore and stroke. Production of this model continued into 1922 when it was replaced with an improved model. In 1915 Avery announced electric starting and electric lights as an available option for its tractors. However, it does not appear that this option gained much favor among farmers, since no mention of it has been found in subsequent years.

| | 1 | 2 | 3 | 4 |
|---|---|---|---|---|
| 25-50 | $20,000 | $15,000 | $10,000 | $5,000 |

**Avery 18-36 tractor**

Early in 1916 Avery announced its 18-36 tractor; it came along about the time that the old 20-35 was taken from production. Avery made tractor history in 1916 by being the first tractor manufacturer to use replaceable cylinder sleeves in its tractor engines. This tractor carried a four-cylinder engine using the same 5-1/2 x 6 inch bore and stroke as the little 8-16 tractor, although the latter had but a two cylinder engine. Production of the 18-36 ended about 1921.

|       | 1 | 2 | 3 | 4 |
|-------|---|---|---|---|
| 18-36 | $25,000 | $20,000 | $15,000 | $7,500 |

**Avery 14-28 tractor**

During 1919 Avery added their 14-28 tractor to the line. This broadened the Avery line to eight distinct models, plus several styles of motor cultivators. Due to unrelenting competition at the time, sales of the 14-28 were likely unrewarding, and production ceased by 1922.

|       | 1 | 2 | 3 | 4 |
|-------|---|---|---|---|
| 14-28 | $18,000 | $14,000 | $10,000 | $5,000 |

**Avery 5-10 tractor**

Originally priced at $295 the Avery 5-10 tractor made its debut in January 1916. Of special note, the operator's seat is located ahead of the rear wheels, with a large platform to the rear. This model used a four-cylinder engine rated at 1200 rpm, and carrying a 3 x 4 inch bore and stroke. Production continued at least into 1919.

|      | 1 | 2 | 3 | 4 |
|------|---|---|---|---|
| 5-10 | $7,000 | $5,000 | $3,000 | $1,500 |

**Avery Motor Cultivator**

The Avery Motor Cultivator was first announced in the summer of 1916. The engine and drive train were essentially the same as that of the 5-10 tractor, announced earlier in the year. This design was a one-row cultivator, using the same individual beams and control handles that were then being used on horsedrawn cultivators. This design left the market about 1920, and was then replaced with the Model C, six-cylinder motor cultivator.

**Avery Motor Cultivator Converted into a Motor Corn Planter**

Avery did not limit its motor cultivator to cultivating alone. Other options included a mounted planter, one of the first such units ever built. The motor cultivator with its tricycle chassis design could certainly have been the basis for a row-crop tractor, but that would not come for about a decade after this 1916 Avery Motor Corn Planter was announced.

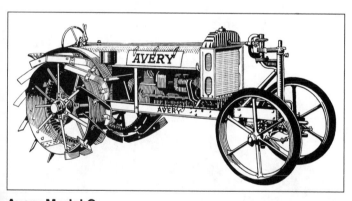

**Avery Model C**

Late in 1919 Avery introduced their Model C, six-cylinder tractor. It replaced the earlier 5-10 model, and permitted the Model C to operate as a two-row cultivator, as well as to handle a corn planter or other implements. Production of this model ended about 1924.

| | 1 | 2 | 3 | 4 |
|---|---|---|---|---|
| Model C | $7,000 | $5,000 | $3,000 | $1,500 |

Along with the standard version of the Model C tractor introduced in 1919 came the special Avery Six-Cylinder Orchard Special Tractor. This model was of course, designed especially for the

**Avery 6-cylinder Orchard Special Tractor**

need of orchardists; the special fenders and smooth hood lines permitted close cultivation near the crop.

**Avery lawn mowing tractor**

About 1920 Avery offered a special lawn mowing tractor built over the 5-10. It consisted of a special extended frame and truck unit to carry the mower gangs. This tractor was built especially for maintaining golf courses and large estates. The odds are that sales of this outfit were indeed limited.

With the introduction of the Model C, six-cylinder tractor in 1919 came the subsequent announcement of a new Avery six-cylinder motor cultivator. This two-row outfit had much more power than the earlier four-cylinder

**Avery six-cylinder motor cultivator**

machine. However, farmers were not especially excited about motor cultivators, so they sold rather poorly. Production of this outfit ended by 1924.

**Avery "Road-Razer"**

Along with the 1919 introduction of the Avery six-cylinder tractor came the Avery "Road-Razer." Built beneath the Model C was a standard road grader blade; it could be completely controlled from the operator's seat. Althought suitable for light grader work, the Model C Road Razer obviously lacked the power for heavy grading.

**Avery TrackRunner mark**

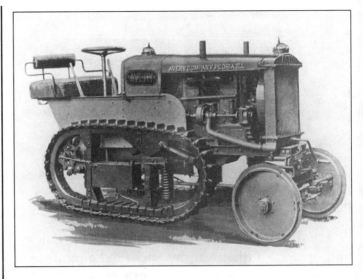

**Avery Track Runner**

The *Patent Office Gazette* provides definite information regarding the Avery Track Runner, noting that this mark was first used on January 8, 1921. The Track Runner was Avery's one and only entry into the crawler tractor business. Unfortunately, the design left things to be desired, so this small tractor never achieved any success. It is unknown whether any of the Track Runner tractors still exist.

**Avery 20-35**

In 1922 Avery revamped its 20-35, giving it a new cellular radiator. Other changes included a full-length hood, wider fenders and a bigger platform. Apparently the canopy or cab remained during the first year, but for 1923, it too was eliminated. With the new models came a change from the dark red finish of earlier years to a simple gray finish with red wheels.

**Avery 25-50 tractor**

During 1922 and 1923 Avery revamped their tractor line, including the intermediate 25-50 model. The tubular readiator of past years was gone, being replaced with a new cellular radiator. This change gave much greater cooling capacity than before. Despite the changes, Avery was, by this time, experiencing serious financial difficulties, and this led to bankruptcy in 1924.

|       | 1        | 2        | 3       | 4       |
|-------|----------|----------|---------|---------|
| 25-50 | $15,000  | $10,000  | $6,000  | $3,000  |

**Avery 45-65 tractor**

The big Avery 45-65 tractor of 1923 was essentially the same as the earlier 40-80 model. The new horsepower rating reflected the results of nebraska Test; No. 44. In this test the 40-80 delivered over 46 drawbar horsepower, but only 69 belt horsepower. Thus, the company re-rated the tractor as the 45-65. Production virtually came to an end with the bankruptcy of 1924, although a few many have been built after the firm reorganized.

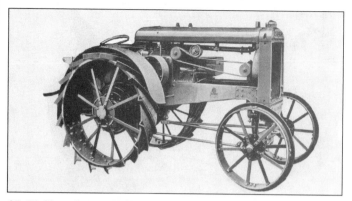

**15-30 New Avery tractor**

About 1921 or 1922 Avery introduced its 15-30 New Avery tractor. This model was of conventional design, using a four-cylinder engine having a 4-1/2 x 6 inch bore and stroke. The crank was carried on a pair of ball bearings. Despite the modern appearance of the 15-30 it appears that sales were far below expectations. Production appears to have ended with the 1924 bankruptcy of the company.

**Avery Ro-Trak**

After the 1924 bankruptcy of Avery Company, the firm reorganized as Avery Farm machinery Company, continuing apace for some years to come. After the reorganization, the company concentrated on its thresher and combines, giving little attention to tractors until the 1938 introduction of the Avery Ro-Trak design. This small tractor featured a Hercules QXB5, six-cylinder engine. Its design included a 3-1/4 x 4-1/8 inch bore and stroke. Production of the ro-Trak was halted in 1941, probably because of the military requirements of World War Two.

|         | 1        | 2       | 3   | 4   |
|---------|----------|---------|-----|-----|
| Ro-Trak | $11,000  | $9,500  | —   | —   |

# B

## B.F. Avery & Sons Company

*Louisville, Kentucky*

**Louisville-Avery Motor Plow**

B.F. Avery & Sons entered the tractor business in 1915 with their Louisville Motor Plow. This 20 horsepower outfit had plows mounted beneath the tractor chassis. They were removable, permitting the tractor to be used for other farm duties. For reasons now unknown, production of the Louisville Motor Plow was very limited, apparently ending altogether by the following year.

**Tru-Draft trademark**

Beginning about 1942, B. F. Avery offered their "A" tractor; it was a dead-ringer for the Cletrac General GG tractor. About 1945 the company again announced their Model V tractor, a small one-plow tractor. Early models used a Hercules IXB-3 four-cylinder engine with a 3-1/4 x 4 inch bore and stroke. Later models carried a Hercules 3 x 4 engine. Production ended with the Model

R, announced in 1950. It used a Hercules four-cylinder, 133 ci engine, and also featured the Avery Tru-Draft hitch system. Minneapolis-Moline Company bought out B. F. Avery in 1951.

|  | 1 | 2 | 3 | 4 |
|---|---|---|---|---|
| Model A | $2,500 | $1,500 | $750 | $400 |
| Model BF | $2,700 | $1,800 | $1,100 | $600 |
| Model BFH | $3,200 | $2,000 | $1,4000 | $800 |
| Model BG | $3,000 | $2,250 | $1,200 | $800 |
| Model V | $2,500 | $1,500 | $750 | $400 |

## Back Auto Plow Company
*Fremont, Nebraska*

No information available.

## Backer Tractor Company
*Royal Oak, Michigan*

No information available.

## Backus Tractor Company
*Alton, Illinois*

**Baby Savidge tractor**

In 1917 the Savidge Tractor Company was organized to build the Baby Savidge tractor. It was the work of William Savidge, and was rated at 8 drawbar and 16 belt horsepower. Subsequent activity was mediocre, and in 1920 the company reappeared as the Backus Tractor Company. The company disappears after that time. This small tractor weighed about 3,500 pounds; retail price for the tractor was $1,395.

# Badley Tractor Company
*Portland, Oregon*

**Angleworm "10" tractor**

Already in 1934 the Angleworm tractor made its appearance. The Angleworm "10" weighed but 2,600 pounds, and was priced at about $950. It was equipped with a Continental four-cylinder motor having a 3-3/8 x 4 inch bore and stroke. The Angleworm remained on the market until the onset of World War Two.

In 1935 the Kultor King garden tractor is listed with Badley Tractor Company. Chances are that the Kultor King made its debut in 1934 or even earlier. Weighing 560 pounds, it was

**Kultor King garden tractor**

equipped with an automotive transmission and axles; power came from a single cylinder engine having a 2-3/4 x 3-1/4 inch bore and stroke.

| | 1 | 2 | 3 | 4 |
|---|---|---|---|---|
| Kultor King | $500 | $350 | $200 | $100 |

**"Angleworm" trademark**

A trademark application filed in 1937 indicates that Joy E. Badley, Portland, Oregon had been using the "Angleworm" trade name in regard to tractors 'since January 1934.' Although a very time consuming task, research of the *Patent Office Gazette* often yields valuable clues about various companies and their activities.

# Bailor Plow Mfg. Company
*Atchison, Kansas*

Bailor was organized in 1912 to build plows, cultivators and numerous other tillage implements. By 1919 the company had developed a two-row motor cultivator that looked remarkably like a

**Two-row motor cultivator**

row crop tractor in its chassis design. However, it does not appear that the company made any efforts toward perfecting its design into a universal farm tractor.

**Single-row motor cultivator**

By 1920 Bailor was also building a small single-row motor cultivator, but like the two-row model, it used a LeRoi four-cylinder engine.

|  | **1** | **2** | **3** | **4** |
|---|---|---|---|---|
| Bailor | $5,000 | $3,000 | $1,500 | $600 |

## Baines Engineering Company
*Canal Dover, Ohio*

A 1921 article on garden tractors includes mention of the Model A and Model B Baines garden tractors. Both were of the same general design, varying primarily in physical size. The various implements available for the Baines garden tractors were Planet Junior designs from S. L. Allen & Company.

## A. D. Baker Company
*Swanton, Ohio*

**Baker 16-30 model**

Baker began building steam traction engines in 1898. By 1920 it was obvious that steam was on the way out, with the tractor coming into dominance. Baker was one of the few companies to attempt a modernized "steam tractor," coming out with their 16-30 model in 1923. (The only one known in existence is in the Ford Museum.) Rated at 16 drawbar and 30 brake horsepower, this model weighed 9,000 pounds. It used an automatic coal stoker; the "radiator" at the front of the tractor is actually the condenser that permitted reusing the condensed steam over and over. A 20-40 model emerged in 1924 (only one is known to exist today), and it was soon re-rated as the 22-45 tractor. Production of the steam tractor apparently ended in 1925.

**22-40 gasoline tractor**

In 1926 Baker introduced the 22-40 gasoline tractor. Initially a Beaver four-cylinder engine was used, but this was changed to a LeRoi four-cylinder; the latter was then used until production essentially ended with the onset of World War Two. The Baker tractors were largely built up of OEM parts, including the transmission, engine, and wheels.

|  | 1 | 2 | 3 | 4 |
|---|---|---|---|---|
| 22-40 | $8,500 | $5,000 | $3,000 | $1,500 |

**Baker 25-50**

The Baker 25-50 first appeared late in 1927, and remained in the trade directories until the late 1940s. However, production after World War Two was probably quite limited. The 25-50 was actually capable of over 43 drawbar and 67 belt

horsepower, and was sometimes known as the 43-67 model. It used a LeRoi four-cylinder engine having a 5-1/2 x 7 inch bore and stroke. Rated speed was 1000 to 1200 rpm.

|  | 1 | 2 | 3 | 4 |
|---|---|---|---|---|
| 25-50 (Wisconsin Motor) | $15,000 | $14,000 | $8,000 | $5,000 |
| 25-50 (Leroi Motor) | $12,000 | $10,000 | $6,500 | $4,000 |

## Baker & Baker
*Royal Oak, Michigan*

In 1913 this tractor manufacturer was bought out by Detroit Tractor Company, also of Royal Oak. The following year the latter moved to Lafayette, Indiana where they continued building the 'Baker' tractor for a time. No images of this tractor have been found.

## Baker Mfg. Company
*Springfield, Illinois*

**Baker heavy crawler tractor**

About 1916 Baker emerged with a heavy crawler tractor, but very little is known of this machine. The company was active until the late 1930s as a manufacturer of road graders, scrapers, and other road machinery. While often listed as a tractor builder, it seems more logical that this reference is to their tractor graders built over a Fordson or an IHC 10-20 tractor.

## Baker Tractor Corporation

*Detroit, Michigan*

The 1919 issue of *Power Wagon Reference Book* lists the Baker tractors, but aside from this reference, we have found no other references to the company.

## Ball Tread Company

*Detroit, Michigan*

Organized in 1912, Ball Tread Company specialized in crawler tractors. The company was bought out by Yuba Construction Company, Marysville, California in 1914. Subsequently the firm was renamed Yuba Mfg. Company; the Ball Tread tractors are referenced under the latter heading.

## Banting Mfg. Company

*Toledo, Ohio*

**"Greyhound" tractor**

About 1927 Banting made a deal with Allis-Chalmers whereby the latter would build the Greyhound tractors, while A-C would sell Banting's Greyhound thresher line. The tractor had a few visible changes, notably, the top radiator tank has 'Greyhound' cast in place instead of 'Allis-Chalmers.' The so-called 'Greyhound' tractors were only marketed for a few years. The Banting brothers operated a repair shop until entering the engine and thresher business about 1918. Only 145 of their steamers were built by the time production ceased in 1922. In 1929 the company was in financial trouble and reorganized as Allis-Chalmers farm equipment dealers. The company remained in existence until 1954.

|  | 1 | 2 | 3 | 4 |
|---|---|---|---|---|
| Greyhound | $6,000 | $4,000 | $2,000 | $1,200 |

## Barnes-Granger Corporation

*Kansas City, Missouri*

Trade references for this company run between 1947 and 1953. The firm built the Pow-R-Queen garden tractor during this time, but no illustrations or specs on this unit have been located.

## Barry Tractor Company

*Muscatine, Iowa*

*No information available.*

## Baskins Tractor Company

*address unknown.*

A trade reference of the early 'teens provides the name of the company as being somewhere in Illinois, but no other information has been found.

## Bates Machine & Tractor Company

*Joliet, Illinois*

This firm was organized in 1919 through the merger of Joliet Oil Tractor Company at Joliet and the Bates Tractor Company of Lansing, Michigan. The latter firm was organized in 1911 by Madison F. Bates and others; he was also the moving force in the Bates & Edmonds Motor Company. They were well known engine builders with their Bulldog engine line.

Joliet Oil Tractor Company was organized in 1913 to build wheel-type and crawler tractors. Bates Machine & Tractor Company continued in the tractor business until 1929. At that time the firm became a division of Foote Bros. Gear & Machine Company. Foote Bros. continued with the Bates line until about 1935, and from then until 1937 the company reappears as Bates Mfg. Company. After 1937, parts only were available from Foot Bros. Gear & Machine Company.

(See Joliet Oil Tractor Company.)

**Model D, 15-22 tractor**

Joliet Oil Tractor Company had begun building their Bates Steel Mule in 1918. A year later Joliet would merge with the Bates Tractor Co. to form Bates Machine & Tractor Co. Various changes were made to the Model D in the following years but the Model D, 15-22 tractor remained on the market until at least 1920.

Introduced in 1921, the Model F apparently replaced the earlier Model D. Both models had the same 18-25 horsepower rating. This model remained in production until the company quit making tractors in 1937. Initially a Midwest

**Model F tractor**

engine was used, but for the 1926-28 period a Beaver engine was substituted, and finally from 1929 to the end of production a LeRoi four-cylinder motor was featured.

**Model G, 25-35 tractor**

The Model G, 25-35 tractor was produced from 1921 to 1928. This model was somewhat larger than the Model F, and used a Beaver four-cylinder engine having a 4-1/2 x 6 inch bore and stroke. Capable of a 4,500 pound drawbar pull, the Model G, like its brothers, made extensive use of ball and roller bearings.

Bates was content to place most of the manufacturing efforts into their unique crawler tractor designs, but in 1921 the company emerged with the Model H, 15-25 wheel tractor. It used the

**Model H, 15-25 wheel tractor**

same engine as the Model F crawler, namely a Midwest four-cylinder style having a 4-1/8 x 5-1/4 inch bore and stroke. Production of the Model H ended in 1924.

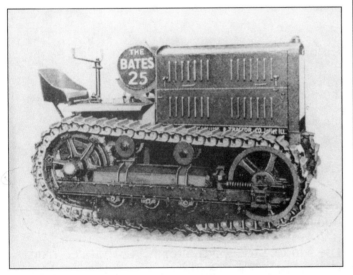

**Industrial 25 model**

The first full-fledged crawler tractor from Bates Machine & Tractor Co. Came in 1924 with their Industrial 25 model. Produced until 1929, it featured a Beaver 4-1/4 x 6 inch engine having four cylinders. Unfortunately, no production figures for the Bates tractors are known to exist.

From 1930 to 1936, Bates offered their Steel Mule Model 35. This model was equipped with a six-cylinder Waukesha engine having a 4-1/2 x 6 inch bore and stroke. The engine used a Ricardo

**Steel Mule Model 35**

head for extra power. The Model 35 featured a completely enclosed drive train with all gears running in oil.

**Model 40 Bates Steel Mule**

Production of the Model 40 Bates Steel Mule ran from 1924 to 1929. A Waukesha four-cylinder engine was used in this model; its four cylinders carried a 5 x 6-1/2 inch bore and stroke. During these years the company was constantly changing and improving its designs.

|  | 1 | 2 | 3 | 4 |
|---|---|---|---|---|
| Model 40 | $10,000 | $7,000 | $4,000 | $1,500 |

**Bates Steel Mule Model 45**

The Bates Steel Mule Model 45 was built in the 1930-33 period. It was essentially an upgrade from the Model 40 crawler, and was actually manufactured by Foote Bros. Gear & Machine Co. In order to maintain the continuum of Bates production, the models built by Foote Bros. are also included under this heading.

**Bates Steel Mule Model 50**

During the 1934-37 period, the Bates Steel Mule Model 50 was on the market. Model 50 crawlers used a six-cylinder Waukesha engine with a Ricardo head. The latter raised the power level

substantially. This engine carried a 4-5/8 x 5-1/8 inch bore and stroke. Rated speed was 1400rpm. Total weight of the Model 50 was 14,000 pounds.

**Model 80 Bates Steel Mule tractor**

Model 80 Bates Steel Mule tractors were marketed between 1929 and 1937. This big tractor weighed over eleven tons, and used a huge Waukesha four-cylinder engine with a 6-1/2 x 7 inch bore and stroke.

**Bates Steel Mule 40 Diesel**

The only Bates Steel Mule diesel design was their "40 Diesel" that was offered in 1937. This $3,100 tractor featured a Waukesha-Hesselman diesel. The four-cylinder design used a 4-1/2 x 5-1/4 inch bore and stroke. The Waukesha-Hesselman was a unique design that used a compression of

150 psi. Fuel was injected as with the full diesel, but a conventional spark plug ignited the fuel. This design saw only limited success, since newer diesel designs were much more simple than the Hesselman. After 1937 the company apparently quit production, but continued to supply repair parts for some years.

## Bates Tractor Company

*Lansing, Michigan*

**Bates Tractor**

Organized in 1911, this firm owed its designs to Madison F. Bates, one of the principals in the Bates & Edmonds Motor Company, also of Lansing. Rated at 30 belt horsepower, the Bates tractor had a working drawbar pull of 2500 pounds, sufficient to pull two or three plows, depending on the circumstances. This tractor weighed 8,000 pounds. The completely hooded engine and the operator's canopy made the design very attractive.

**Bates 10-15 tractor**

Apparently the Bates tractor was built in two sizes of 15 and 30 horsepower. In 1914 the 10-15 model used a single-cylinder horizontal engine; this tractor weighed 5,000 pounds. The 18-30 car-

ried a two-cylinder opposed engine. Also by 1914 the cab had been removed and the tractor had been modified slightly from the original design. Bates continued apace until merging with Joliet Oil Tractor Co. to form the *Bates Machine & Tractor Company* in 1919.

**Bates 15-25 All-Steel tractor**

Near the end of production, Bates came out with their 15-25 All-Steel tractor. Its new features included automotive-type steering, compared to the stiff axle-and-chain steering then in vogue. It also used a Bates-built four-cylinder engine having a 4-3/8 x 5-1/2 inch bore and stroke. It remained on the market for a short time, being replaced with the Bates Model H, 15-25 tractor from Bates Machine & Tractor Company.

## Bauroth Bros.

*Springfield, Ohio*

This company was listed in trade directories as a tractor manufacturer during 1906, 1907, and 1908. Aside from that, no illustrations of their tractor have been found. The company began building gasoline engines in the 1890s.

## Wm. C. Bealmear

*El Monte, California*

In 1945 this firm was listed as the manufacturer of the Western garden tractor, but no other information has been located.

# Bean Spray Pump Company
*San Jose, California*

**Bean Track-pull**

Initially, this firm built its reputation on spray pumps, beginning business in 1884. About 1914 or 1915 the company introduced the Bean Track-pull. This was an unusual design using a single front-mounted track and two carrier wheels at the rear. Initially the company offered their 6-10 Trackpull, but by 1920 the company was also building the Trackpull in an 8-16 model. Both were of the same essential design, differing primarily in the power level produced in each. Production ended in the early 1920s.

# Bear Tractor Company
*New York, New York*

**Bear 25-35 crawler**

Bear began building their 25-35 crawler tractor in 1923. It was powered with a Stearns four-cylinder engine having a 4 x 6-1/2 inch bore and stroke. Weighing 6,000 pounds, it was priced at $4,250. The Bear tractor line was taken over by Mead-Morrison Company at East Boston, Massachusetts in 1925.

|       | **1**   | **2**   | **3**   | **4**   |
|-------|---------|---------|---------|---------|
| 25-35 | $8,000  | $6,000  | $4,000  | $2,000  |

# Beaver Mfg. Company
*Milwaukee, Wisconsin*

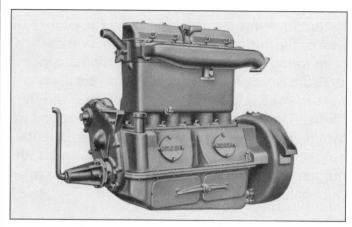

**Beaver engine**

Although Beaver is sometimes listed as a tractor manufacturer, the company instead specialized in building engines for tractors. The Beaver design was frequently specified, with their JA and JB design being shown here. Both utilized four cylinders. The JA carried a 4-1/2 x 6 inch bore and stroke, while the large JB used a 4 -3/4x 6 inch bore and stroke.

# Beaver Tractor Company
*Stratford, Connecticut*

**Beaver garden tractor**

Trade directories list this firm as being the manufacturer of the Beaver garden tractors between 1948 and 1953 but aside from a single illustration, little information on this small tractor has been found.

## Bedford Tractor Company

*Bedford, Indiana*

Except for some correspondence in the possession of the author, very little information has been found concerning this company. Late in 1921 the company developed a 'universal' style tractor, similar to the Hoke, the Indiana, and the Moline Universal. Bedford apparently applied to Moline for a license to build under their patents, but the latter refused to grant a license, and without that, the venture apparently died before production ever began.

## Beeman Tractor Company

*Minneapolis, Minnesota*

**Beeman garden tractor**

Incorporated in 1916, Beeman was one of the early entrants into the garden tractor business. Business continued until the company was reorganized in 1925 as the New Beeman Tractor Company. The firm continues to appear in the trade directories until 1945, where it appears in *Millard's Implement Directory*. The small tractor shown here was rated at 2 drawbar and 4 belt horsepower. Numerous models were built during a long production run.

| 1 | 2 | 3 | 4 |
|---|---|---|---|
| $2,500 | $2,000 | $1,000 | $500 |

## Robert Bell Engine & Thresher Company

*Seaforth, Ontario*

**Model 12-24**

About 1918 this firm got into the tractor business with their 12-24 model. It is likely a Flour City Junior from *Kinnard-Haines Company* of Minneapolis, although this one was sold under the Imperial trade name of Robert Bell Engine & Thresher Company.

**Imperial Super-Drive tractor**

In 1920 Bell offered an Imperial Super-Drive tractor. It had a special spring-cushioned rear wheel drive system. The Imperial 15-30 used a four-cylinder Climax engine having a 5 x 6-1/2 inch bore and stroke.

| | 1 | 2 | 3 | 4 |
|---|---|---|---|---|
| Imperial Super Drive 15-30 | $20,000 | $18,000 | $12,000 | $10,000 |
| Imperial Super Drive 22-40 | $22,000 | $20,000 | $15,000 | $12,000 |

# Belle City Mfg. Company

*Racine, Wisconsin*

**Trackpull crawler**

Belle City manufactured numerous farm machines, and was known particularly as a threshing machine builder. In the late 1920s Belle City began offering their Trackpull crawler tractor attachment. Built specifically for the Fordson tractor, this unit enjoyed lots of popularity for several years.

# Beltrail Tractor Company

*St. Paul, Minnesota*

**Beltrail 12-24 crawler**

Organized in 1917, the Beltrail folks offered a unique crawler design that needed no differential. The steerable front wheels further simplified the design. Their only model was a 12-24 size.

**Beltrail Model B**

**Beltrail trademark**

Beltrail was reorganized in 1918, and about this same time they came out with their Model B; it was nothing more than an improved version of the original 12-20. A Waukesha four-cylinder engine was used; it carried a 3-3/4 x 5-1/2 inch bore and stroke. Production ended during 1920. The Beltrail trademark is also shown. It was first used in April 1918.

# Benjaman Tractor Company

*Dallas, Texas*

In 1918 W. B. Chenoweth filed patent applications on a new tractor design, with Patent No. 1,331,184 and 1,331,185 being issued in 1920. The company proposed three sizes; the Handy Ben as

**Big Ben 20-40**

a 6-12 model, the Little Ben as a 10-20 tractor, and the Big Ben as a 20-40 style. Like several others of the day, it was a hinged frame design. In 1920 the 20-40 had a list price of $1,625.

## Besser Mfg. Company
*Alpena, Michigan*

**Besser tractor**

The February 1918 issue of *Gas Review Magazine* illustrates the Besser tractor. It was rated at 15 drawbar and 30 belt horsepower. Aside from a few 1918 advertisements, nothing more is known of this tractor. Many, if not most, of the early tractor manufacturers were undercapitalized and simply did not have the financing to launch a major advertising and manufacturing effort.

## C. L. Best Gas Traction Company
*San Leandro, California*

Daniel Best became famous for his huge three-wheeled traction engine of 1889. On this first model, Best became a large manufacturer of steam traction engines, but sold out to a competitor, the Holt Mfg. Company in 1908.

A son, C. L. Best, organized the C. L. Best Gas Traction Engine Company in 1910. One of its early crawlers was the Best '75' of 1913, along with numerous other sizes and styles that followed. Finally, Best merged with Holt on April 25, 1925 to form the Caterpillar Tractor Company.

**Best '75'**

The Best '75' came onto the market in 1913. Initially it used a large front tiller wheel for steering, but eventually it was discovered that this was unnecessary, and was removed. The early models of the '75' featured a full-length canopy, and this too was removed by about 1915.

|    | 1 | 2 | 3 | 4 |
|----|---|---|---|---|
| 75 | $75,000 | $60,000 | $30,000 | $10,000 |

In 1918 the Model 75, 40-70 Best crawler had a list price of $5,750. Weighing 28,000 pounds, it carried a huge four-cylinder engine having a 7-3/4 x 9 inch bore and stroke. Although expen-

**Model 75, 40-70 Best crawler**

**Tracklayer 25**

sive, this big crawler had its place, and remained in production until about 1919. The company also built a 45-90 Tracklayer model about 1917.

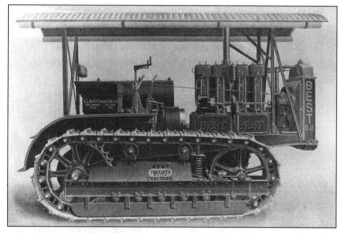

**Best 60 Tracklayer**

Production of the Best 60 Tracklayer apparently began about 1919 and continued up to the 1925 merger with Holt that formed Caterpillar Tractor Company. This popular model featured the company's own four-cylinder engine with a 6-1/2 x 8-1/2 inch bore and stroke. The Best 60 weighed over nine tons.

|        | **1**    | **2**    | **3**   | **4**   |
|--------|----------|----------|---------|---------|
| Best 60 | $20,000 | $15,000 | $8,000 | $5,000 |

The Tracklayer 25 came onto the scene in 1920; this small tractor used a four-cylinder engine with a 4-3/4 x 6-1/2 inch bore and stroke. The cylinders were cast individually, making

repair much simpler, even though this increased the total length of the engine by several inches. The Tracklayer 25 sold for $2,450.

**Tracklayer 30**

During 1920 Best emerged with the Tracklayer 30 model; this tractor apparently used the same engine as the Tracklayer 25. It has been difficult to determine the exact production period for the Tracklayer 25 and the Tracklayer 30 models, but from all appearances, the Tracklayer 30 survived into the Best-Holt merger of 1925.

**Tracklayer 30**

Best likely began producing an early version of the Tracklayer 30 by 1914. A year later the company introduced an orchard version called the

Humpback Thirty. By redesigning the transmission and drive system, the Humpback Thirty had the low profile needed for orchard work.

**Tracklayer 40**

The 1919 version of the Tracklayer 40 illustrates the full canopy and in fact, the same basic designs that the company had been using for several years. The rear-mounted belt pulley came as standard equipment. Sidecurtains were also provided on these machines…they could be rolled down to protect it from the elements.

**Best 60 cruiser model**

Toward the end of Best tractor production their Best 60 cruiser model appeared. This special tractor was designed for higher ground speeds than the standard tractors and used lower grouser bars than those intended for heavy traction. The special buggy top gave some measure of comfort to the operator.

# Bethlehem Motors Corporation
*East Allentown, Pennsylvania*

**Bethlehem 18-36 model**

Beginning in 1918 Bethlehem attempted to enter the tractor business with their 18-36 model. It was powered by a Beaver four-cylinder engine having a 4-3/4 x 6 inch bore and stroke. Weighing 6,200 pounds this model was sold without fenders, probably to help hold down the price. Conversely, having added them might have made the tractor more attractive in its appearance, as well as shielding the operator from a constant dust storm.

# Big Farmer Tractor Company
*Fort Madison, Iowa*

Aside from a trade reference in the 1916 era noting that the company was being organized, no other information has been located.

# Birrell Motor Plow Company
*Auburn, New York*

About 1910 the Birrell Motor Plow appeared, and apparently the manufacturer was looking at the Canadian market with its large expanse of prairie land. It was equipped with a six-bottom Moline plow hung beneath the tractor frame, and used a big four-cylinder engine for power. Little else is known of the Birrell.

# Biwer Mfg. Company

*Cresco, Iowa*

The 1953 *Farm Implement News Buyer's Guide* lists this company as a manufacturer of garden tractors, but no further information has been located.

# Blazer Mfg. Company

*Cleveland, Ohio*

In the 1948-1953 period, and perhaps longer, this firm is listed as the manufacturer of the Gardenette and Soil Blazer garden tractors. No illustrations have thus far been located, nor has any other information come to light.

# Blewett Tractor Company

*Tacoma, Washington*

**Webfoot 53 tractor**

Blewett Tractor Company announced their Webfoot 53 tractor in 1920. It was rated as a 28-53 and was equipped with a Wisconsin four-cylinder Model M engine; the latter had a 5-3/4 x 7 inch bore and stroke. In 1920 this tractor sold for $5,000. Production ended about 1922.

**Webfoot 40 tractor**

Priced at $4,000 the Webfoot 40 tractor was built in 1920 and 1921. It weighed 8900 pounds. Power was provided by a four-cylinder Beaver engine having a 4-3/4 x 6 inch bore and stroke. As evidenced in this illustration, steering was achieved with a single lever.

# John Blue Company

*Huntsville, Alabama*

**G-1000 model**

John Blue Company was established in 1886 as a farm implement manufacturer. At the time the company was in Laurinburg, North Carolina, but moved to Huntsville, Alabama in 1945. Subsequently the firm began building small tractors for market gardeners and nurseries. Shown here is their G-1000 model of the 1970s.

# Blumberg Motor Mfg. Company
*San Antonio, Texas*

**Steady Pull 12-24 model**

In 1915 the Blumberg Steady Pull tractor appeared. Their 12-24 model shown here used a four-cylinder, 4 x 5 engine of their own manufacture. The company continued for a few years, but by 1924 disappears from the scene.

**Steady Pull 9-18 tractor**

The Steady Pull 9-18 tractor first appeared about 1919. This model was of the same basic design as the 12-24 and used a four-cylinder engine having a 3-3/4 inch bore and stroke. At the time a 'square' engine, that is, one having the same bore and stroke, was rather unusual in the tractor industry. For the most part, tractor builders of the time preferred a long-stroke engine; usually the bore was about 70% to 80% of the stroke.

**Blumberg Steady Pull Tractor trademark**

Sometimes the *Patent Office Gazette* yields valuable clues regarding a firm's origins. In this instance, a trademark application of 1921 illustrates that the company had been using the "Blumberg Steady Pull Tractor" mark since April 1915. A simple deduction would be that the company probably started at least a year earlier, since it would have taken at least this long to develop the design and set up a manufacturing operation.

# Boenker Motor Plow Company
*St. Charles, Missouri*

**Boenker's Tractor and Motor Plow**

H. H. Boenker patented this interesting motor plow in 1910; the following year a company was organized to build it. The 1911 Boenker used an Anderson Model E, two-cylinder engine of the opposed horizontal design. The tractor weighed 2,800 pounds and was priced at $1,250. After a few notices in the trade papers the company disappeared from the tractor business.

## Bolens Products Company
*Port Washington, Wisconsin*

See: Gilson Mfg.

**Bolens garden tractor**

Bolens offered their first garden tractor about 1919. Shortly after, numerous attachments were available, including this planter. Numerous designs appeared in the years to follow, although precise production data on the Bolens line has been difficult to document. In the mid-1940s the company became the Bolens Product Division of FMC Corporation.

**Bolens Huski**

The Bolens Huski line was among the first of the so-called compact garden tractors. As with farm tractors, the early garden tractor designs were heavy and cumbersome. Shown here is a Bolens garden tractor of 1948 vintage. The Huski line had its inception in 1946.

**Bolens model 20HD Riding Tractor**

By 1956 the Bolens line included their Model 20HD riding tractor. It incorporated the Bolens Ride-a-matic design and the Versa-Matic drive and reverse. It used both front- and rear-mounted attachments.

## Bollstrom Motors Company
*Marion, Indiana*

A 1918 announcement indicates that this company was being organized with a capitalization of $3 million. After this announcement nothing more is heard of the company or their tractors; presumably neither came to life.

## J.G. Bolte
*Davenport, Iowa*

J.G. Bolte began building his tractors by 1918, and probably for several years before. In 1919 the J. G. Bolte Company was organized to build the 20-40 tractor shown here. Weighing but 5,000 pounds, it

**Bolte 20-40 tractor**

featured a unique steering system which the company called 'The Square Turn' design. After a few trade announcements in 1919, nothing more is heard of this company or its tractors.

## Boring Tractor Corporation
*Rockford, Illinois*

**Boring 12-25**

The Boring tractor was the inventive work of Charles E. Boring who received Patent No. 1,203,304 for his design in 1916. In 1918 the firm was incorporated to build the Boring 12-25. It was equipped with a four-cylinder Waukesha engine having a 4-1/4 x 5-3/4 inch bore and

stroke. For plowing the right-hand drive wheel ran in the furrow, and the left hand driver could be adjusted upward so that the tractor and plow ran level. This tractor had a 1919 price of $1,485. Production ended about 1922.

## Boss Tractor Mfg. Company
*Detroit, Michigan*

In 1915 this company was rechristened as the Chief Tractor Mfg. Company at Detroit. At the time they are said to have been building the "Chief 4" tractors, but no other information has surfaced, nor do we know when Boss Tractor Mfg. Co. was originally organized.

## Boyett-Brannon Tractor Company
*Atlanta, Georgia*

**Boyett tractor**

This was one of Georgia's few tractor builders; they announced this 30 horsepower model in 1913. The completely hooded design was quite unusual for the time, and the operator's cab was a welcome addition. Roller chain drives were used to the drivewheels, and the tractor featured auto-guide steering at a time when most tractors were built with chain steering a stiff front axle.

## David Bradley Mfg. Company

*Bradley, Illinois*

Tractors produced by this company were sold by *Sears, Roebuck & Company*. See this heading for further information.

## Bray Corporation

*Pasadena, California*

This firm is listed in 1948 as a garden tractor manufacturer, but no further information has surfaced.

## Bready Tractor & Implement Company

*Cleveland, Ohio*

**Model A Cultimotor garden**

This company started business already in the early 1920s with their Cultimotor garden tractors. By the late 1940s their Model A, 2-1/2 h.p. model appeared. A variety of front-mounted Bready implements were available. Bready Cultivator Company was the original title of the company but this was changed at some point. Also, the company moved from Cleveland to Solon, Ohio, presumably in the late 1940s or early 1950s. Specific details are lacking on this firm and its products.

## Allen Breed Tractor Company

*Cincinnati, Ohio*

**Allen Breed 30 horsepower tractor**

During 1913 Allen Breed succeeded in perfecting a large 30 horsepower tractor. This unit had several unique features including three forward speeds, something virtually unheard of in those days. The autoguide steering was also a forward step from the stiff axle-and-chain steering that was then in vogue. After mid-1914 no further advertising appears for the Breed tractor, and it is presumed that production ended about that same time.

## Brennan Motor Mfg. Company

*Syracuse, New York*

No information available.

## Brillion Iron Works

*Brillion, Wisconsin*

A line drawing is all that our research has located on the Brillion 24-30 tractor, first advertised in 1916. It featured a two-cylinder engine having a 6 -3/4 x 8 inch bore and stroke; the engine itself

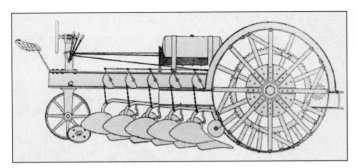

**Brillion 24-30 tractor**

was built by the Brillion people. The tractor sold for $1885. In 1918 the company also offered a 12-24 tractor of the same design. All tractor production appears to have ended in 1918.

## British-Canadian Tractors Ltd.
*Saskatoon, Saskatchewan*

**British-Canadian 15 horsepower tractor**

The *Canadian Thresherman* of 1913 illustrates the British-Canadian 15 horsepower tractor of the period. The company name itself implies that the tractor may have been imported to Canada from Great Britain. Unfortunately, this rear view of the tractor is the only image thus far located.

## Brockway Tractor Company
*Bedford, Ohio*

**Brockway 49G**

Beginning in 1949 Brockway offered two models. Their 49G was a two-plow gasoline tractor that used a Continental F-162 engine. The 49D was a diesel version that was equipped with a Continental GD-157 engine. Production of the Brockway tractor continued at least until 1958 but after that time it disappears from the trade directories.

| | **1** | **2** | **3** | **4** |
|---|---|---|---|---|
| Brockway Tractor | $11,500 | — | — | — |

## Brown Cultivator Company
*Minneapolis, Minnesota*

This firm is listed in the 1921 Minneapolis city directories as being organized by M. F. Hewitt, O. K. Brown, and others. In 1922 the company is no longer listed. It is unknown whether the company survived long enough to produce any of its cultivating tractors.

## Bryan Harvester Company
*Peru, Indiana*

In 1920 Bryan introduced their revolutionary steam tractor design. It employed a small high pressure water tube boiler operating at a pressure of 550 psi. Initially the company offered this 26-70 model. The Bryan was one of the few attempts to market a small high-pressure con-

**Bryan 26-70 model**

densing steam engine to the farm tractor trade. By 1920 the big steam traction engines were on their way out, with the small gasoline tractor taking their place.

**Bryan small 20 horsepower steamtractor**

In the mid-1920s Bryan offered this small 20 horsepower version of their steam tractor. It used a two-cylinder steam engine having a 4 x 5 inch bore and stroke, along with a high pressure water tube boiler operating at 550 psi. The exhaust steam was condensed for reuse, thus cutting down on the need for extra boiler feed water. Ground speed was variable anywhere from 1/8 to 7-1/2 mph. Production ended in the late 1920s.

## W. G. Buck
*Warren, Ohio*

A note in the *American Machinist* for 1915 indicates that this firm was being organized to build tractors. Aside from this notice, no other information has been located.

## Buckeye Mfg. Company
*Anderson, Indiana*

**Buckeye Junior tractor**

Buckeye Junior tractors made their first appearance in 1912. This small crawler design was typical of a time when it was thought that "front wheels" were still necessary for steering. Thus, there were numerous companies building half-track crawlers. The Buckeye Jr. remained on the market until about 1915.

**Buckeye Chain Tread tractor**

The Buckeye Chain Tread tractor appeared in 1917, a year after the company had bought out the Lambert Gas Engine Company, also of Anderson. The Chain Tread had a 16-32 horsepower rating and was powered by a 4-1/2 x 6-3/4 inch four-cylinder engine.

Buckeye introduced this model of their Chain Tread tractor in 1917, shortly before announcing their Trundaar tractor line. Little is known of this particular model, except that it is of an entirely

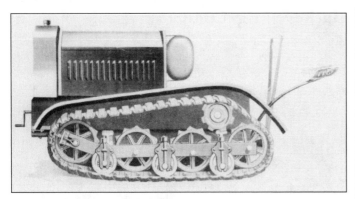

**Buckeye Chain Tread tractor**

different design than its predecessors. A small advertising piece of the day does not denote it as a specific model, simply referring to it as their 'Chain Tread Tractor.'

**Trundaar 20-35 crawler**

In 1917 the company rechristened their Buckeye tractors as the Trundaar line. At the same time, Buckeye announced their 20-35 Trundaar crawler. This was a full-fledged crawler of an entirely new design; it utilized a unique front linkage system that permitted the tracks to oscillate on uneven ground. The 20-35 used a Waukesha four-cylinder engine with a 4-3/4 x 6-3/4 inch bore and stroke.

**Trundaar 25-40 tractor**

Another model of the Trundaar tractor was this 25-40 style. It was rated to pull 4,000 pounds at 2-1/2 mph. This tractor apparently came onto the market in 1920, and seems to have been the replacement for the earlier 20-35 tractor. The 25-40 tractors carried a four-cylinder Waukesha engine with a 5 x 6-1/4 inch bore and stroke.

**Model 10 Trundaar tractor**

Little information has surfaced concerning the Model 10 Trundaar tractor. It was the smallest of the line, and made its debut about 1920. Production of the Model 10, and in fact, for all the Trundaar tractors was probably quite limited, since the firm does not appear in the trade directories after 1923.

**Trundaar**

**Trundaar trademark**

A trademark application of 1918 illustrates the Trundaar trademark and also notes that it was first used on their tractors in September 1917. Thus, the *Patent Office Gazette* provides a valuable historical reference to the company's activities in this regard.

## Buckeye Traction Ditcher Company
*Findlay, Ohio*

From one of the trade papers of the day it is learned that Buckeye was announcing a "new outfit" for 1910. Nothing more was heard of this venture. Finally, in the 1919 *Power Wagon Reference Book* Buckeye is listed as the manufacturer of the Alligator tractor. No specifications or other descriptive information has been found for this company.

## Buffalo-Pitts Company
*Buffalo, New York*

**Buffalo-Pitts tractor**

Buffalo-Pitts had a history going back to 1834 and their early threshers. By the 1880s the com-

pany was building steam traction engines, and in 1910 they came out with their huge 40-70 tractor. It used a three-cylinder engine, and roller chains connected the rear wheels to the bull pinions. Few specs have been found on this tractor, although it remained in the industry listings until at least 1916, and this, despite the fact that the company had gone into receivership in 1914.

**Buffalo-Pitts 40-70 tractor**

The Buffalo-Pitts 40-70 apparently retained the three-cylinder engine until about 1914 when the tractor was revamped and given a four-cylinder vertical engine. Weighing 22,000 pounds, the new style of the 40-70 was listed in the trade directories as late as 1920. Information on the Buffalo-Pitts tractors is exceedingly difficult to find.

## Bulkley-Rider Tractor Corporation
*Los Angeles, California*

No information available.

## Bull Tractor Company
*Minneapolis, Minnesota*

Of all companies to pave the way for the small lightweight farm tractor, Bull was probably the most noticeable. While their design was unique to say the least, it proved that a small and lightweight tractor could be a practical machine as compared to the heavy and cumbersome tractors then on the market. The Little Bull of 1914 sold at only $335 as compared to two or three thousand for one of the 'big' tractors. Historically speaking, it was the Bull that revolutionized the farm tractor industry and brought the small tractor to the farm. In its wake came literally hundreds of companies, all trying to make their mark, and of course, their fortune. Few made it...even the Bull Tractor Company went broke by 1920.

**Little Bull tractor**

In 1914 Bull Tractor Company was incorporated at Minneapolis. Already in 1913 the company displayed the Little Bull at the Minnesota State Fair where it received wide acclaim. The 1914 model had a 5-12 horsepower rating. Weighing but 2,900 pounds, the Little Bull sold for the incredibly low price of $335. Over 3,800 Little Bull tractors were sold between April and December of 1914.

For 1915 the Big Bull emerged. It had a 7-20 horsepower rating, and by 1917 became a 12-24 tractor. The latter used a Toro two-cylinder opposed engine with a 5-1/2 x 7 inch bore and stroke. Through 1917 the Bull tractors were made in the shops of Minneapolis Steel & Machinery Co. However, this contract was cancelled, and eventually a deal was made to build them in the shops of the Toro Motor Company of Minneapolis. Bull merged with Madison Motors Corporation of Anderson, Indiana in 1919 but by 1920 this venture went broke and the remaining parts and inventory was sold to American Motor Parts Company.

# BULL

**Bull tractor trademark**

Various trade notes of the day indicate that the Bull tractor was first demonstrated in September 1913. This is completely substantiated by the *Patent Office Gazette* which illustrates the trademark application for the Bull tractor, noting that it was first used on September 1, 1913.

|  | **1** | **2** | **3** | **4** |
|---|---|---|---|---|
| Little Bull | $30,000 | $25,000 | $15,000 | $8,000 |
| Big Bull | $30,000 | $25,000 | $15,000 | $8,000 |

**Big Bull**

# Bull Dog Tractor Company
*Oshkosh, Wisconsin*

**Bull Dog 30**

For 1920 the Bull Dog 30 was offered. This was a unique four-wheel-drive design powered by a big Waukesha four-cylinder engine having a 5 x 6-1/2 inch bore and stroke. The Bull Dog 30 was listed only in 1920 so apparently it was built only for a short time. It was priced at $4,250.

# Bullock Tractor Company
*Chicago, Illinois*

**Bullock Baby Creeper**

The Creeping Grip tractor was originally built by Western Implement & Motor Co. at Davenport, Iowa. When this company went broke in 1913, H.

E. Bullock, one of the largest stockholders revived the firm as Bullock Tractor Co. Shown here is the Bullock Baby Creeper of 1914. Rated at 20 drawbar and 30 belt horsepower, the Baby Creeper was essentially the same design that had been built at Davenport.

**Bullock Creeping Grip tractor**

Creeping Grip tractors underwent numerous changes after 1914. Four new models were introduced that year; a 12-20, the 20-30, the 30-40, a 45-60, and the big 55-75. The 12-20 remained in production until the company merged with the Franklin Flexible Tractor Company at Greenville, Ohio in 1920 to form the Franklin-Bullock Tractor Co. The 20-30 remained in production for several years, but it does not appear that the other sizes were built for any length of time.

# CREEPING GRIP.

**Creeping Grip trademark**

Bullock Tractor Co. filed a trademark application in 1915 for their Creeping Grip trademark, noting that it had been used since November 9, 1911. This would coincide with the first use of the mark by the predecessor company, Western Implement & Motor Company at Davenport, Iowa.

## Burn Oil Tractor Company

*Peoria, Illinois*

**Burn Oil 15-30**

In 1920 Burn Oil Tractor Co. came out with their 15-30 model. At the time the company was at Peoria, but the 1921 listings indicate that by this time the firm had relocated to Warren, Indiana.

After this the company disappears from the scene. The 15-30 used a two-cylinder horizontal engine having a 6 x 7 inch bore and stroke. Weighing some 5,500 pounds the 15-30 Burn Oil sold for $1,650.

## Burtt Mfg. Company

*Kalamazoo, Michigan*

This company began building gasoline engine by 1902, but a 1914 trade announcement indicates that the firm was anticipating the production of a new three-bottom motor plow. Aside from this note, nothing further has been found concerning the company's activities in the tractor business.

C

## California Tractor Corporation
*San Francisco, California*

During the 1930s and into the 1940s this firm is listed as the manufacturer of the Trojan garden tractors. Despite the listings, no specs or photos of this tractor have been located.

| <u>1</u> | <u>2</u> | <u>3</u> | <u>4</u> |
|---|---|---|---|
| — | — | $3,000 | — |

## W. P. Callahan & Company
*Dayton, Ohio*

Callahan was a well known builder of gasoline engines and is listed as a builder of gasoline traction engines in the 1905-1907 period. No illustrations of their design have been located. The company remained in the gasoline engine business until about 1910.

## Cameron Tractors, Inc.
*New York, New York*

**Cameron tractor**

In the early 1920s Cameron offered their small one-plow tractor. Of rather unique design, it fea-

tured the company's own four-cylinder air-cooled engine; it used a 3-1/4 x 4-1/2 inch bore and stroke. Also included was a belt pulley, mounted in line with the engine and just below the steering wheel. Production of the Cameron continued for only a short time.

## Campco Tractors Inc.
*Stockton, California*

**Campco logo**

A trademark application filed in 1925 is the only evidence found so far on the Campco tractors. According to the application, the Campco mark was first used on December 1, 1919. No illustrations have been located.

## Can-A-Ford Company
*Sparta, Michigan*

This company was organized in 1917 to build a tractor attachment specifically for the Ford Model T automobiles. No other information has been located.

## Canadian Rein Drive Tractors Ltd.
*Toronto, Ontario*

This firm was incorporated for $1 million in 1917. Aside from this information, no further data has been located.

## Canadian-American Gas & Gasoline Engine Company
*Dunville, Ontario*

**Canadian tractor**

A 1911 advertisement illustrates the Canadian tractor, available in 6, 10 and 12 horsepower sizes. This unusual design used a two-cylinder engine that could be governed either with the "hit-and-miss" method or the volume governed method. In addition, the spark could come from a conventional spark plug or from a mechanical igniter. Aside from a few advertisements, no other information has been found for the Canadian tractors.

## Cane Machinery & Engineering Company
*Thibodaux, Louisiana*

**115 Cameco**

In the early 1960s Cameco was organized to build modern field machinery for the sugar cane

industry. By the 1970s the firm was producing the 115 Cameco shown here. Of four-wheel-drive articulated design, the 115 featured a Caterpillar D3304 engine with 100 flywheel horsepower.

**Cameco 235 Powershift tractor**

The Cameco 235 Powershift tractor made its debut about 1975. This big four-wheel-drive tractor was equipped with a Caterpillar 3208 V-8 diesel engine. Capable of 135 flywheel horsepower, the 235 had a working weight of 20,000 pounds. Numerous special features were available especially tailored to the sugar cane harvest.

**405 Cameco tractor**

With a Caterpillar 3208 engine of 210 flywheel horsepower, the big 405 Cameco tractor was available with either a standard direct-drive transmission or a powershift transmission. A Caterpillar planetary axle was also featured, along with an elaborate hydraulic system. Cameco tractors were apparently intended primarily for the sugar cane harvest rather than being built for generalized farming applications.

## Capp Bros.
*Stockton, California*

The Pull-Away garden tractors are listed from Capp Bros. in the 1953 trade directories but no other information has been found.

## J. I. Case Company
## J. I. Case Threshing Machine Company
*Racine, Wisconsin*

Jerome I. Case began in the threshing machine business in 1842. Initially, Case left Oswego County, New York and settled in the small community of Rochester, Wisconsin. Over the next two years Case perfected his design. About that time Case moved to nearby Racine, setting up what would be a huge manufacturing operation. In fact, Case built more threshing machines than anyone else.

The dramatic growth of J. I. Case Threshing Machine Company got another boost with their 1869 introduction of a portable steam engine. It was among the first such engines to be offered to the American farmer and was a hallmark in the beginning of farm power. Subsequently the Case portable led to the development of Case steam traction engines. In this regard, Case quickly rose to the top; this company built more steam traction engines than any other.

In 1876 J. I. Case got into the plow business, forming a separate company that came to be known as J. I. Case Plow Works. This firm had no connection whatever with the J. I. Case Threshing Machine Company aside from the fact that both were founded by J. I. Case himself. The J. I. Case Plow Works made an excellent reputation for itself, eventually building the Wallis tractors. In 1928 the Plow Works was sold out to Massey-Harris. After the sale, Massey-Harris sold out all rights to the Case name to the Threshing Machine Company. Subsequently the latter dropped "Threshing Machine" from the company name, simply calling it J. I. Case Company.

J. I. Case Threshing Machine Company was the first major farm equipment manufacturer to attempt an entry into "gasoline traction engines" as they were originally named. In 1892 the company built a "Paterson" tractor, but despite every effort to perfect the machine, constant problems with carburetion and ignition thwarted its success. The idea was abandoned and nearly two decades would pass before Case would again enter the tractor business.

The first Case tractor appeared in 1911. It was of huge dimensions, but served to help the company launch its first line of tractors in 1912. That year the company launched its 20-40 and 30-60 models, continuing them for several seasons. The tractors that followed are illustrated and described below.

J. I. Case continued in the farm equipment business until 1984 when the company merged with International Harvester Company to form the present-day Case-IH line. Full details of the J. I. Case implement and tractor line may be found in the author's title, *150 Years of J. I. Case* (Crestline/Motorbooks: 1991).

**Paterson tractor**

Also known as the Paterson tractor, the first Case tractor of 1892 was the first to be built by any of the major implement manufacturers of the day. Surprisingly little is known of the 1892 model except that it was plagued with ignition and carburetion problems; the technology of the day simply was not far enough advanced to solve them. It is said that the Paterson tractor resided in a Case warehouse for some years before finally being scrapped.

**Case 30-60 Prototype**

In 1911 J. I. Case came out with a huge 30-60 tractor. This prototype design was somewhat different than the production model of a year later, but no doubt provided its designers with a chance to field test the tractor prior to full production.

**Case 30-60**

Full production of the Case 30-60 tractor began in 1912. Like other tractors of the time, it was built over a heavy structural steel chassis. Due to the great weight of the early tractors the frame was

exceedingly heavy, but in most cases it was over-designed for a comfortable safety factor. Production of the 30-60 continued into 1916.

|  | **1** | **2** | **3** | **4** |
|---|---|---|---|---|
| 30-60 | — | $155,000 | — | — |

**Case 20-40, early style**

The Case 20-40 was a very popular model. Introduced in 1912, the models through 1916 were equipped with a large tubular radiator. The engine exhaust was piped to the top of the radiator, terminating in vertical nozzles that exhausted from the small stack atop the radiator. The action of the exhaust created an induced draft through the radiator tubes, thus cooling the engine automatically.

|  | **1** | **2** | **3** | **4** |
|---|---|---|---|---|
| 20-40 | $28,000 | $25,000 | $18,000 | $10,000 |

**Case 20-40, late style**

Between 1916 and 1919, the last year of production, the Case 20-40 saw a few modifications. The most noticeable was the end of the induced draft radiator and the addition of a fan-cooled cellular radiator. Case 20-40 tractors used a two-cylinder opposed engine with an 8 x 9 inch bore and stroke.

|  | **1** | **2** | **3** | **4** |
|---|---|---|---|---|
| 20-40 late style | | | | |
|  | $25,000 | $20,000 | $15,000 | $7,500 |

**Case 12-25**

Introduced in 1914, the Case 12-25 tractor was the company's first move into the small tractor business. Farmers were clamoring for smaller tractors, since the huge 30-60 tractors were simply of no use to the average farmer. The 12-25 used a two-cylinder opposed engine having a 7-inch bore and stroke. Production ended in 1918.

|  | **1** | **2** | **3** | **4** |
|---|---|---|---|---|
| 12-25 | $28,000 | $25,000 | $18,000 | $10,000 |

**Case 10-20**

An unusual tractor design appeared from Case in 1915. Their 10-20 tractor employed a unique design powered by a four-cylinder engine. Pro-

duction of the 10-20 ended in 1918, but it took another couple of years to sell the remaining inventory. This tractor retailed at $900.

|  | **1** | **2** | **3** | **4** |
|---|---|---|---|---|
| 10-20 | $22,000 | $18,000 | $12,000 | $8,000 |

During 1916 J. I. Case introduced its small 9-18 tractor. This conventional four-wheel design was much more popular than the Case 10-20 with its unique three-wheel configuration. This tractor heralded the beginning of many new features, including the use of an air cleaner as standard equipment. Production ended in 1918.

|  | **1** | **2** | **3** | **4** |
|---|---|---|---|---|
| 9-18 | $16,000 | $10,000 | $7,500 | — |

**Case 10-18**

Production of the 10-18 tractor marked a new era in Case tractor design. This new model was the first Case tractor to use a unit frame. For the 10-18, a single iron casting carried the entire tractor. A four-cylinder Case-built engine was used; it carried a 3-7/8 x 5 inch bore and stroke. Hyatt roller bearings were used throughout the tractor. Production of the 10-18 ended in 1922 when it was replaced with the similar 12-20 model.

|  | **1** | **2** | **3** | **4** |
|---|---|---|---|---|
| 10-18 | $10,000 | $8,000 | $3,000 | — |

**Case 15-27**

Case 15-27 tractors were built between 1919 and 1924. A one-piece cast iron frame was a standard feature and removable cylinder sleeves were part of the design. Another innovative development was the use of a drilled crankshaft and full pressure lubrication of important engine parts. The 15-27 was rerated to the 18-32 model in 1925.

|  | 1 | 2 | 3 | 4 |
|---|---|---|---|---|
| 15-27 | $19,000 | $10,000 | $7,500 | $2,500 |

**Case 22-40**

A heavy structural iron frame supported the big Case 22-40 tractor. Rated to pull 3,700 pounds at the drawbar, this four-cylinder tractor used a 5-1/2 x 6-3/4 inch bore and stroke. Produced between 1919 and 1925, the 22-40 was priced at $3,100. The physical size of the tractor and its hefty price both helped to limit sales of this model.

|  | 1 | 2 | 3 | 4 |
|---|---|---|---|---|
| 22-40 | $13,500 | $10,000 | $7,500 | $2,750 |

**Case 12-20**

In 1921 Case introduced their 12-20 tractor, replacing the earlier 10-18 model. The four-cylinder motor used a 4-1/8 x 5 inch bore and stroke, or a quarter inch larger engine bore than the 10-18. The cylinders were cast en bloc and full force feed lubrication was featured. The 12-20 remained in production until 1928 when it was renamed the Case Model A, but the latter was also dropped by the following year.

|  | 1 | 2 | 3 | 4 |
|---|---|---|---|---|
| 12-20 | $8,000 | $6,000 | $3,500 | $900 |

**Case 40-72**

The huge Case 40-72 first appeared in 1921, with a few more being built in 1922 and 1923. Priced at $4,000 the 40-72 was a huge four-cylinder tractor having a 7 x 8 inch bore and stroke. Capable of over 90 belt horsepower, it was a good choice for large threshing machines, sawmills and for plowing.

|  | 1 | 2 | 3 | 4 |
|---|---|---|---|---|
| 40-72 | $75,000 | $60,000 | $50,000 | — |

**Case 12-20 Industrial tractor**

Case Industrial tractors made their debut in 1925, with this one being built over the little 12-20 model, and in fact, being designated as the 12-20 Industrial Tractor. By 1929 this model was dropped from the line and was replaced with an entirely new tractor design.

| | 1 | 2 | 3 | 4 |
|---|---|---|---|---|
| 12-20 Industrial | $9,000 | $6,500 | $4,000 | $1,500 |

**Case 18-32**

During 1925 Case revamped the 15-27 tractor and re-rated it as the Case 18-32. It used the same four-cylinder 4-1/2 x 6 engine as had been used in the 15-27. Production of the 18-32 ended in 1927 when the Model K tractor appeared; it was essentially the same tractor, but with a different model designator. By 1929 the Model K had also disappeared.

| | 1 | 2 | 3 | 4 |
|---|---|---|---|---|
| 18-32 | $14,000 | $10,000 | $7,500 | $2,500 |

**Case 25-45**

In 1924 Case replaced the 22-40 tractor with their Case 25-45. This model continued until 1927 when it was designated the Model T, although it was essentially the same tractor as before. The 25-45 weighed over 10,000 pounds and used a 5-1/2 x 6-3/4 inch engine. Production ended in 1929.

| | 1 | 2 | 3 | 4 |
|---|---|---|---|---|
| 25-45 | $20,000 | $12,000 | $7,500 | $2,500 |

**Case Model L, 26-40**

J. I. Case introduced an entirely new line of tractors in 1929. The first one was their Model L, also known as the 26-40. It was an entirely new design and carried a Case-built four-cylinder engine with a 4-5/8 x 6 inch bore and stroke. Production of Model L tractors continued into 1940, being then replaced with the Case Model LA.

| | 1 | 2 | 3 | 4 |
|---|---|---|---|---|
| Model L (no updates) | $4,500 | $3,000 | $1,000 | $500 |

| | | | |
|---|---|---|---|
| L Tractor (updates) | | | |
| $3,000 | $2,000 | $1,000 | $500 |
| L Tractor (starter/lights) | | | |
| $4,500 | $3,500 | $1,500 | $750 |
| LA Tractor  $3,000 | $1,900 | $1,100 | $500 |
| LA Tractor (LP) | | | |
| $3,600 | $2,250 | $1,200 | $600 |
| LA Tractor (hydraulic) | | | |
| $3,500 | $2,250 | $1,000 | $500 |

**Case Model L**

Model LI Industrial tractors were available during the same 1929-1940 production run as the Model L farm tractor. This model was essentially the same except for special wheel equipment and a modified transmission.

| | **1** | **2** | **3** | **4** |
|---|---|---|---|---|
| LI Industrial | $5,000 | $3,500 | $1,300 | $1,000 |

Case Model L tractors underwent various modifications during their production run. For instance, in 1934 Case began offering the Model L on full factory rubber instead of the usual steel wheels. The author once owned a 1938 Model L exactly like the one shown here and has always regretted selling it!

**Model LI**

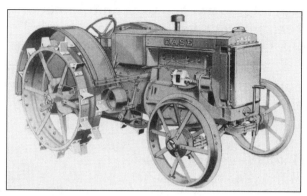

**Case Model C**

Model C Case tractors were a smaller version of the Model L, and except for their physical size and characteristics, looked almost identical. Production of this tractor began in 1929, continuing for a decade after. The company also built a Model CH tractor; it was a special high-clearance model.

|  | **1** | **2** | **3** | **4** |
|---|---|---|---|---|
| C Tractor | $3,500 | $2,500 | $850 | $300 |

**Case Model CI**

Case Model CI tractors were simply an industrial version of the Case Model C farm tractor. This model had a production period approximately the same as the Model C and was intended for factories, warehouses and similar applications where the tractor operated over concrete floors.

|  | **1** | **2** | **3** | **4** |
|---|---|---|---|---|
| CI | $3,750 | $2,500 | $1,000 | $500 |

Although a limited market, the need for orchard tractors brought about the Case Model CO. Built during the same period as the Model C farm tractor, the Model CO was equipped with special fenders and other accessories needed for

**Case Model CO**

this specialized work. All Model C tractors were equipped with a Case-built four-cylinder engine having a 3-7/8 x 5-1/2-inch bore and stroke. Beginning in 1934, Case also built a Model CV Vineyard tractor for a time.

|  | **1** | **2** | **3** | **4** |
|---|---|---|---|---|
| CO | $3,850 | $2,800 | $1,300 | $800 |

**Case Model CC**

Model CC Case tractors were introduced in 1929. This row-crop version was the same as the Model C standard-tread model in many respects. Production of the Model C, the Model CC and other variations continued into 1939 when they were replaced with a new streamlined series.

|  | **1** | **2** | **3** | **4** |
|---|---|---|---|---|
| CC Tractor (1929-1932) | $3,500 | $2,500 | $900 | $300 |
| CC Tractor (1933-1937) | $1,800 | $1,200 | $800 | $300 |
| CC Tractor (1938, starter/lights) | $2,500 | $2,000 | $1,000 | $400 |

**Case Model RC**

The Case Model RC tractors first appeared in 1935. This little tractor had a rating of 11 drawbar and 17 belt horsepower. Like the Model CC tractors, numerous row-crop implements were available, tailored especially to these models. With the introduction of a new tractor line in 1939, Case also began using their "Flambeau Red" finish instead of the time-honored gray enamel.

| | 1 | 2 | 3 | 4 |
|---|---|---|---|---|
| RC Tractor (over top steering) | | | | |
| | $2,500 | $2,000 | $1,000 | $500 |
| RC Tractor (side arm steering) | | | | |
| | $2,750 | $2,000 | $1,000 | $300 |

**Case Model RC**

With the 1939 restyling of the Case tractor line, the Model RC took on a new look that included a

heavy cast iron grille. By this time rubber tires had become very popular. However, with the onset of World War Two and the subsequent shortages, tractor production was very limited and many of those that were built during the war came out of the factory on steel wheels.

| | 1 | 2 | 3 | 4 |
|---|---|---|---|---|
| RC Tractor (sun burst grille) | | | | |
| | $3,000 | $2,500 | $1,500 | $500 |

**Case Model R**

Case Model R tractors came out in 1938. The Model R had the same general appearance as other models of the Case line and was essentially the standard-tread version of the Model RC row-crop tractor. The company also built this model in RO Orchard and RI Industrial models.

| | 1 | 2 | 3 | 4 |
|---|---|---|---|---|
| R Tractor | $3,000 | $2,500 | $1,500 | $500 |
| R Tractor (sun burst grille) | | | | |
| | $3,500 | $3,000 | $1,500 | $500 |

Model LA Case tractors first appeared in 1940, replacing the venerable Model L. Rated at 1100 rpm, the Model LA engine was built by Case and used a 4-5/8 x 6 inch bore and stroke.

**Case Model LA**

This tractor was also available as the Model LAI Industrial tractor and could be furnished with special ricefield equipment when so ordered. Production of the LA continued into about 1952.

As part of a new tractor line, Case introduced their Model D standard-tread tractor in 1939. It was equipped with a Case four-cylinder engine having a 3-7/8 x 5-1/2-inch bore and stroke. Standard-tread tractors are also designated as fixed-width models. In either case the designator portends a design having a wide-front axle with no adjustment for varying tread widths. Row-crop tractors on the other hand, have an adjustable tread width to work in various crops.

|  | 1 | 2 | 3 | 4 |
|---|---|---|---|---|
| D Tractor | $2,500 | $2,000 | $1,200 | $500 |
| D Tractor (hydraulic) | $2,250 | $1,800 | $900 | $300 |

**Case Model D**

| D Tractor (hydraulic, foot clutch) | | | |
|---|---|---|---|
| $3,000 | $2,500 | $1,100 | $300 |
| **D-1 Standard (8,103 built)** | | | |
| $3,000 | $2,000 | $1,000 | $500 |
| **D-1 NT (445 built)** | | | |
| $5,000 | $3,500 | $2,500 | $1,250 |

**Case Model DO with LP gas equipment**

With the introduction of the Model D tractor in 1939, Case also announced their Model DO orchard tractor. In addition, Case began to actively promote the use of LP gas as a tractor fuel in the early 1950s. Shown here is a Case DO tractor of 1952 with LP gas equipment.

|  | 1 | 2 | 3 | 4 |
|---|---|---|---|---|
| DO Tractor (2,879 built) |  |  |  |  |
|  | $5,500 | $4,500 | $2,500 | $1,500 |

Production of the Case Model DC tractors began in 1939 and ended in 1955. This model was very popular and was widely used as a three-plow tractor. Numerous attachments were available for these tractors to further broaden their use. In 1952 Case began to furnish the DC tractors with special LP gas equipment as a factory option.

|  | 1 | 2 | 3 | 4 |
|---|---|---|---|---|
| DC-3 Tractor |  |  |  |  |
|  | $3,000 | $2,500 | $1,600 | $700 |
| DC-4 Tractor |  |  |  |  |
|  | $3,000 | $2,500 | $1,500 | $700 |

**Model DC**

By the time production of the Model DC ended in 1955, this tractor had received numerous modifications. These included a hydraulic system and beginning in 1952, the Case Eagle Hitch system.

|  | 1 | 2 | 3 | 4 |
|---|---|---|---|---|
| DDS Tractor (1,206 built) |  |  |  |  |
|  | $15,000 | $9,000 | $4,500 | $2,000 |
| DE Tractor (16,000 built) |  |  |  |  |
|  | $2,500 | $1,250 | $1,000 | $500 |
| DH Tractor (141 built) |  |  |  |  |
|  | $10,000 | $8,000 | $5,000 | $1,500 |
| DV Tractor (582 built) |  |  |  |  |
|  | $8,000 | $5,500 | $2,500 | $1,500 |
| DI | $3,000 | $2,000 | $1,000 | $500 |

**Model DI Industrial**

Model DI Industrial tractors were a special version for factories and warehouses. Among other things, the DI tractors could be furnished with a special pintle hitch for towing heavy trucks of materials within a factory.

|  | 1 | 2 | 3 | 4 |
|---|---|---|---|---|
| DI Industrial | $3,000 | $2,000 | $1,000 | $500 |

**Model S**

Production of the Model S tractors began in 1940 and ended in 1955. This small tractor used a Case four-cylinder engine having a 3-1/2 x 4 inch bore and stroke. In 1944 the tractor shown here had a list price of $845. However, very few were available due to World War Two.

|  | 1 | 2 | 3 | 4 |
|---|---|---|---|---|
| S Tractor | $2,000 | $1,500 | $700 | $300 |
| S Tractor (hydraulic) | $2,500 | $1,800 | $800 | $300 |

**Case Model SO Orchard tractor**

Case Model S tractors initially used a 3-1/2 x 4 engine, but for 1953 the engine bore was increased to 3-5/8 inches for a 15% increase in the power level. Shown here is a specially built Model SO Orchard tractor.

|  | 1 | 2 | 3 | 4 |
|---|---|---|---|---|
| SO Orchard | $4,000 | $3,200 | $2,000 | $1,000 |

**Model SC row-crop tractor**

Production of the Model SC row-crop tractors closely parallels that of the Model S standard-tread version. Late models of the S and SC tractors could be furnished with live hydraulics. After the power level was raised in 1952 the SC tractors were capable of about 19 drawbar horsepower.

|  | 1 | 2 | 3 | 4 |
|---|---|---|---|---|
| SC Tractor | $1,500 | $1,000 | $600 | $300 |
| SC Tractor (hydraulic) | $3,000 | $2,400 | $1,000 | $350 |
| SC-4 Tractor | $3,500 | $2,500 | $1,500 | $500 |

**Model V tractor**

Model V tractors first appeared in 1939. This small tractor used a Continental four-cylinder engine having a 3 x 4-3/8 inch bore and stroke. The Model V was also available as the Model VI Industrial tractor, complete with electric starter, lights and a pintle hitch. Production of the Model V tractor and its derivatives continued until 1955.

|   | 1 | 2 | 3 | 4 |
|---|---|---|---|---|
| V | $3,000 | $2,500 | $1,200 | $600 |

**Model VA tractor**

Model VA tractors were built in the 1942-1955 period. The Model VA used a Case-built four-cylinder engine having a 3-1/4 x 3-3/4 inch bore and stroke. It was rated at 1425 rpm. By about 1952 electric starter and lights had become standard equipment.

|    | 1 | 2 | 3 | 4 |
|----|---|---|---|---|
| VA | $2,500 | $2,000 | $1,200 | $500 |

**Case Model VC tractor**

During 1939 Case introduced their Model VC tractor, a small one- or two-plow model. This small tractor was built only until 1942 when it was replaced with the Model VAC. At the time, Case was building an extensive line of small tractors, with the largest one being their Model LA of about 45 belt horsepower.

|    | 1 | 2 | 3 | 4 |
|----|---|---|---|---|
| VC | $2,500 | $2,000 | $1,200 | $500 |

**Case Model VAC**

Case Model VAC tractors first appeared in 1942 and with various modifications remained on the market until about 1955. After about 1952 the electric starter and lights came as standard equipment; prior to that time it was a $50 extra-cost option.

|                 | 1 | 2 | 3 | 4 |
|-----------------|---|---|---|---|
| VAC-14 Tractor  | $3,000 | $2,500 | $1,500 | $600 |

**Model VAO (orchard) tractor**

The Case Eagle Hitch lift system was added to the Model VA tractors as an extra-cost option in 1949. It was available on any of the V-Series tractors, including this special Model VAO (orchard) tractor. The VAO tractors went into production in 1943 and continued until 1955.

| | 1 | 2 | 3 | 4 |
|---|---|---|---|---|
| VAO (orchard) | $3,000 | $2,500 | $1,500 | $700 |

**Case Model VAH**

In 1952 Case offered eight different variations of their Model VA tractors. Included was this Model VAH high clearance model. It was designed especially for work in crops where the extra clearance was necessary to avoid damage to the growing plants.

| | 1 | 2 | 3 | 4 |
|---|---|---|---|---|
| VAH | $3,300 | $2,700 | $1,500 | $700 |

**Case 500 Diesel**

Case marketed its first diesel-powered tractor in 1953. Their Case 500 Diesel was a six-cylinder model with 377 cubic inches. This big standard-tread tractor was marketed until 1955. A new feature was optional power steering; this would eventually become standard equipment on all models.

**Case 300 Series**

In 1955 Case introduced an entirely new series of tractors, characterized by the 300 Series. Case offered these tractors in several chassis versions and they could be equipped with a Case-built spark ignition engine or a Continental four-cylinder diesel. The 300 Series tractors were capable of about 23 drawbar and 29 pto horsepower. The 300 Series was built into 1958.

|  | 1 | 2 | 3 | 4 |
|---|---|---|---|---|
| 300 | $3,000 | $2,500 | $1,800 | $500 |
| 300B, 310B & 320B | | | | |
| | $3,000 | $2,500 | $1,800 | $700 |
| 300 & 320 Tractor | | | | |
| | $3,000 | $2,500 | $1,800 | $700 |

**Case 350 LP gas model**

Numerous fuel options were available for Case tractors, including LP gas as shown on this 350 model. Produced in the 1956-58 period, the 350 tractors were a continuation of the earlier 300 Series. The 350 tractors were available only with spark ignition engines using gasoline, distillate, or LP gas

|  | 1 | 2 | 3 | 4 |
|---|---|---|---|---|
| 350 | $3,200 | $2,700 | $1,800 | $800 |

Case 400 Series tractors made their debut in 1955 and replaced the D-Series tractors that had been introduced in 1939. Many different implements were available for the 400 Series tractors.

**Case 400 Series**

This model was available with a gasoline or a diesel engine and was capable of about 50 pto horsepower.

|  | 1 | 2 | 3 | 4 |
|---|---|---|---|---|
| 400 Tractor | $3,500 | $2,500 | $2,000 | $900 |

**400 Cane Tractor**

The 400 Series tractors were available in numerous chassis configurations, including this special high clearance model. It was sold as the 400 Cane Tractor. Due to the limited production of the high clearance models, they carried a substantially higher price than the comparable row-crop tractors.

|  | 1 | 2 | 3 | 4 |
|---|---|---|---|---|
| 400 Cane | $4,500 | $3,200 | $2,700 | $1,200 |

**Case 400**

Case 400 tractors could be furnished in a conventional standard-tread design. The tractor shown here was available as the 400 Diesel Standard, the 400 Super Diesel Standard and the 400 Special Super Diesel Standard. 400 Series Orchard tractors were also available.

**Case 600-B row-crop**

During 1958 Case announced their B-Series tractors; they were in effect, a continuation of the 1955 series, but with changes and improvements. Shown here is a 600-B row-crop model with an adjustable wide-front axle. The Case 600 was also available with a torque converter drive.

**Case 600 Series**

In 1957 the Case 600 Series standard-tread tractor appeared and was apparently on the market for about a year. The six-cylinder Case diesel engine used a 4 x 5 inch bore and stroke; operating speed was 1500 rpm. This tractor had an operating weight of over 7,600 pounds.

|  | 1 | 2 | 3 | 4 |
|---|---|---|---|---|
| 600 Tractor | $4,000 | $2,500 | $1,800 | $800 |

**Case 800**

Case 800 tractors featured the Case-O-Matic drive system. It had the advantages of a torque converter drive, but a lockout lever permitted direct-drive operation as well. The 800 Series tractors were offered in gasoline, diesel and LP gas versions, all having approximately 54 pto horsepower. This model was offered in 1958 and 1959.

|  | 1 | 2 | 3 | 4 |
|---|---|---|---|---|
| 800 | $4,300 | $2,700 | $1,900 | $800 |

**Case 900-B**

The big 900-B Case tractors were built in the 1957-1959 period. This tractor could be furnished in a diesel or gasoline engine; the latter could also be adapted as an LP gas model. Listing at about $5,900 the 900-B used a six-cylinder, 377 ci engine and was capable of about 71 pto horsepower.

| | **1** | **2** | **3** | **4** |
|---|---|---|---|---|
| 900 Tractor | $4,000 | $3,000 | $1,500 | $750 |

**Case 430 tractor**

Case 430 tractors first appeared in 1960, with production ending in 1969. This model used a four-cylinder, 188 ci engine and was available in several chassis styles to suit individual needs.

**Case 530 Series**

The Case-O-Matic drive was a regular feature of the Case 530 Series tractors. Introduced in 1960, the 530 Series models remained in production until 1969. While the Case-O-Matic drive was very popular, it was more expensive and so the company also offered the 530 with a standard sliding gear style. Gasoline, diesel and LP gas versions were available.

**Case 630**

Case 630 tractors came onto the market in 1960, remaining there into 1963. Like others of this period, the 630 could be equipped with a standard transmission or the Case-O-Matic torque converter drive. A four-cylinder engine with 188 ci displacement was used.

| | **1** | **2** | **3** | **4** |
|---|---|---|---|---|
| 630 Tractor | $5,000 | $3,500 | $1,500 | $750 |

**Case 30-Series Case**

Another segment of the 30-Series Case tractors was the 730 model. Built in the 1960-1969 period, this tractor offered an OEM choice of gasoline, diesel, or LP gas engines. The four-cylinder diesel model had a 301 cid, resulting from a 4-3/8 x 5 inch bore and stroke. Detailed performance data on these and other tractors can be found in the author's book, *Nebraska Tractor Tests Since 1920*, (Crestline/Motorbooks: 1985).

**Case row-crop 830**

Topping the Case row-crop tractor line in the 1960-1969 period was the 830 model. This tractor was available in gasoline, diesel and LP gas versions. The four-cylinder, 284 cubic inch spark ignition engine used a 4-1/4 x 5 inch bore and stroke was capable of 65-plus pto horsepower.

**Case 930**

First built in 1960, the big Case 930 tractor was built only in a standard-tread version. The original 930 model remained on the market until 1964 when it was replaced with the new 930 CK model. The suffix refers to the introduction of the new Case Comfort King line. This model was capable of over 85 pto horsepower.

**Case 1200 Traction King**

Case entered the realm of four-wheel-drive tractors in 1964 with their 1200 Traction King model. It was produced until 1969. This big tractor was capable of over 120 pto horsepower. The engine was a Case-built six-cylinder style with a 451 ci displacement. Case 70-Series tractors first appeared in late 1969. Numerous other models appeared subsequently. In 1984 Case and International Harvester merged to form the Case-IH line.

**Case 310 Crawler**

The Terratrac line of crawler tractors was merged into J. I. Case in 1957 when the latter bought out *American Tractor Corporation, Churbusco, Indiana*. The following year Case introduced its 310 crawler tractor, following closely on the lines established by American Tractor. Case marketed this model as an Agricultural Crawler, with a pto shaft, belt pulley and remote hydraulics all available as optional equipment.

**Case 610 crawler**

Case 610 crawlers were built in gasoline and diesel versions and first appeared in 1960. This model was capable of about 60 pto horsepower

and continued the Terramatic transmission and torque converter drive that had been developed by American Tractor Corporation. Power steering was also standard equipment for the 610.

**Case 800 crawler**

The Case 800 crawlers were built in the 1957-1963 period and were then followed by the 810-C crawler. Weighing 7-1/2 tons, the 800 could pull 20,000 pounds and was built in 60 or 54-inch track widths.

Case 1150 crawlers were first built in 1965 and replaced the Case 1000 crawler that had been built under that title since 1957, and in fact, came over to Case from the American Tractor Corporation merger of that year. The 1150 boasted some

**Case 1150 crawler**

100 flywheel horsepower and at the time was the largest machine in the Case crawler tractor line. Subsequently, Case has continued building numerous sizes and styles of crawler tractors.

**Case 450 crawler**

Case 450 crawlers first emerged in 1965 and remained on the market for several years. This tractor weighed nearly five tons and was equipped with a four-speed, dual-range transmission that included a torque converter drive. It was built only with a diesel engine.

## J. I. Case Plow Works
*Racine, Wisconsin*

**Wallis Bear**

Wallis Tractor Company was organized at Cleveland, Ohio in the fall of 1912 by H.M. Wallis and others. Wallis was a son-in-law of J. I. Case and was involved with the J. I. Case Plow Works at Racine. About this same time the Wallis Bear appeared. Rated at about 60 belt horsepower, it was built in small numbers, with the only one known to exist now being owned by W. R. Schmidt & Sons at Upper Sandusky, Ohio.

**Wallis Cub**

By 1913 the Wallis Tractor Co. had moved to Racine and set up shop in the J. I. Case Plow Works. That same year the company announced the Wallis Cub, the first farm tractor with a unit frame design. E. J. Baker Jr., the former editor of *Farm Implement News* once noted that "this was the frameless construction that lifted the myopic lids from the eyes of Henry Ford and led directly to the design of the revolutionary Fordson tractor." The boiler plate frame of the Wallis was protected under Patent No. 1,205,982 with Clarence M. Eason and Robert O. Hendrickson as the patentees. Eason later moved on to the Hyatt Roller Bearing Company.

**Wallis Cub Junior (Model J)**

In 1915 Wallis came out with their Model J, or Cub Junior tractor. This design had a 13-25 horsepower rating and used a four-cylinder engine having a 4-1/2 x 5-3/4 inch bore and stroke. As shown here, the rolled boiler plate frame also served as the oilpan for the engine and terminated at the final drives of the tractor.

**Wallis two-row cultivator**

Wallis offered a motor cultivator in 1919. The unit shown here was of two-row design and used an engine of 12 belt horsepower. Had the company modified the design slightly, they would have anticipated the row-crop design that was soon to come from the Farmall tractor of International Harvester Company.

**Wallis Model K**

Model K Wallis tractors appeared for the first time in 1919. This model had a rating of 15 drawbar and 25 belt horsepower. This tractor used a four-cylinder engine having a 4-1/4 x 5-3/4 inch bore and stroke. It was rated at 900 rpm. Weighing about 3,500 pounds, the 15-25 was capable of at least 2,700 pounds on the drawbar.

**Wallis Model OK 15-27**

Production of the Model K tractor ended in 1922, just as production of the Model OK 15-27 model began. The major difference was that the Model OK used an engine speed of 1,000 rpm, as compared to 900 rpm for the earlier model. Engine dimensions were the same. Few changes were made in the Model OK 15-27 design until it was replaced with the 20-30 Wallis in 1927.

|          | **1** | **2** | **3**   | **4**  |
|----------|-------|-------|---------|--------|
| Model OK | —     | —     | $2,700  | $800   |

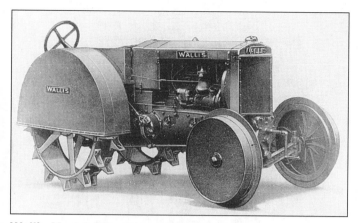

**Wallis Model OK orchard tractor**

Wallis began offering an orchard tractor version of their Model OK tractor in the early 1920s. As with other contemporary models, the orchard design had smooth hoodlines with a re-routed air stack and exhaust pipe. Special fenders were provided and the front wheels had enclosed spokes.

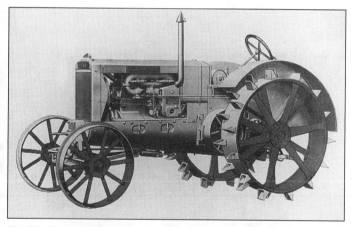

**Wallis Model OK with modifications**

During 1927 Wallis again revamped their proven design. This time the Model OK was modified so that the rated engine speed was raised from 1,000 to 1,050 rpm. Other noticeable changes included a substantial oil bath air cleaner system. Typical of the Wallis designs was the unfortunate placement of the belt pulley inside the left rear wheel. J. I. Case Plow Works sold out to Massey-Harris in 1928. The latter continued building tractors under the Wallis tradename for a few years.

# Caterpillar Tractor Company

*Peoria, Illinois*

Caterpillar Tractor Company resulted from a 1925 merger of Holt Mfg. Co. and C.L. Best Company. Both firms had previously come to a dominant position as manufacturers of crawler tractors. The first year of the merger the new company had sales of nearly $14 million. In 1928, three years after the merger, Caterpillar bought out the Russell Grader Company of Minneapolis, Minnesota. This was the beginning of the Caterpillar grader line.

Caterpillar was the first company to offer a crawler tractor powered by a diesel engine. Work on this project began in 1929, with a completed model ready in October of 1931. Within a short time the company was offering several models of diesel-powered Caterpillar tractors, and was the first tractor manufacturer to opt solely for diesel engines in its fleet, doing so in 1942.

It is difficult to document the exact production dates of the early models up to the late 1930s. Once the company began building the R-Series and the D-Series tractors, establishing the production dates is much easier, but several distinct styles of each model were built during the production runs.

Caterpillar made history with its 320 horsepower D-9 tractor introduced in 1955. At the time, it was the largest tractor ever built.

Although various makes of crawler tractors are oftentimes referred to as "caterpillars" the Caterpillar name and the Cat name are both registered trademarks of Caterpillar Tractor Company. That's why all other crawler tractor manufacturers referred to their machines as crawler tractors, tracklayers and various other names.

Holt and Best merged in 1925 to form Caterpillar Tractor Company. At first the new company selected models from the two different product lines. In 1925, for instance, the new Cat-

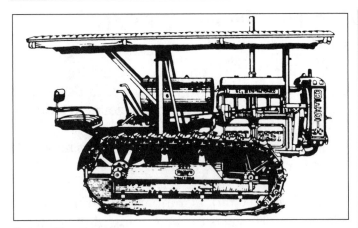

**Caterpillar Best-30**

erpillar line included the old Best 30. This 8,700 pound crawler used a four-cylinder engine with a 4-3/4 x 6-1/2-inch bore and stroke. The Thirty was built until 1931.

**Caterpillar 60**

A close look at the Caterpillar 30 and the Caterpillar 60 for 1925 still reveals the 'Best' trademark in the side of the radiator. By 1927 the 'Holt' and 'Best' tradenames had disappeared. The Caterpillar 60 weighed 19,000 pounds and was powered by the company's own four-cylinder engine having a 6-1/2 x 8-1/2-inch bore and stroke. Production of the Sixty ended in 1931.

| | **1** | **2** | **3** | **4** |
|---|---|---|---|---|
| Caterpillar 60 | | | | |
| | $18,000 | $14,000 | $7,000 | $3,500 |

The Caterpillar 2-Ton of 1925 was essentially the same as the Holt 2-Ton previously introduced. This small tractor weighed only 4,700 pounds, somewhat over two tons. It was

**Caterpillar 2-Ton**

equipped with the company's own four-cylinder engine having a 4 x 5-1/2-inch bore and stroke and used an overhead camshaft. Production continued into 1928.

| | **1** | **2** | **3** | **4** |
|---|---|---|---|---|
| 2 Ton | $10,000 | $7,500 | $4,000 | $2,000 |

**Caterpillar 5-Ton**

Weighing 10,400 pounds the Caterpillar 5-Ton was a carryover from Holt, but remained in the Caterpillar line into 1926. The 5-Ton was a popular intermediate model. It carried a four-cylinder 4-3/4 x 6 inch engine, and like other models, could be equipped with special electric lighting equipment. Production of the 5-Ton ended in 1928.

| | **1** | **2** | **3** | **4** |
|---|---|---|---|---|
| 5-Ton | $18,000 | $14,000 | $7,000 | $3,000 |

**Caterpillar 10-Ton**

The Caterpillar 10-Ton was essentially the same tractor as the Holt 10-Ton built prior to the 1925 Holt-Best merger. Weighing 20,000 pounds, or ten tons, this model was furnished with a big 6-1/2 x 7 inch, four-cylinder engine. Ordinarily this model had a top road speed of 3 mph, but with special gearing it could travel up to 4-3/4 mph. The 10-Ton was built until 1928.

|        | 1        | 2        | 3       | 4       |
|--------|----------|----------|---------|---------|
| 10-Ton | $20,000  | $15,000  | $8,000  | $4,000  |

**Caterpillar Ten**

The Caterpillar Ten first appeared in 1928. This model used a four-cylinder L-head engine with the cylinders and crankcase cast en bloc. Rated at 1500 rpm, this engine used a 3-3/8 x 4 inch bore and stroke. Production of the Ten continued until 1933. The Ten was also available in a special high clearance model.

|     | 1       | 2       | 3       | 4       |
|-----|---------|---------|---------|---------|
| Ten | $4,000  | $3,000  | $2,000  | $1,000  |

**Caterpillar Fifteen**

Caterpillar Fifteen tractors were exactly like the smaller Cat Ten, varying only in physical size. Weighing 5,900 pounds, the Fifteen was capable of 15 drawbar and 20 belt horsepower. It used a four-cylinder L-head engine with a 3-3/8 x 4 inch bore and stroke. Production of the Fifteen continued into 1933.

|            | 1       | 2       | 3       | 4       |
|------------|---------|---------|---------|---------|
| 15, 7C1    | $4,000  | $3,000  | $2,000  | $1,000  |
| 15HC, 1D1  | $4,000  | $3,000  | $2,000  | $1,000  |
| 15, PV1    | $4,000  | $3,000  | $2,000  | $1,000  |

**Caterpillar Twenty**

Priced at $1,900 the Caterpillar Twenty weighed a hefty 7,500 pounds. Introduced in 1928, the Twenty was built as late as 1933. It was capable of over 27 belt horsepower and well over 20 horses on the drawbar. This was equivalent to a maximum drawbar pull of over 4,250 pounds. The Twenty used a four-cylinder engine with a 3-3/4 x 5 inch bore and stroke.

| | 1 | 2 | 3 | 4 |
|---|---|---|---|---|
| 20, IJ, PL1 | $7,000 | $5,5000 | $2,000 | $1,000 |
| 10, 8CI | $8,000 | $5,000 | $3,500 | $1,500 |
| 22, 2FI, IJI | $5,000 | $3,5000 | $2,000 | $750 |

**Caterpillar 25**

The Caterpillar "25", introduced in 1932, was built only into 1933. It used a 4 x 5-1/2-inch engine of four-cylinder design and rated at 1100 rpm. Weighing slightly over 8,000 pounds, the "25" was capable of pulling over 6,000 pounds on the drawbar. Production of the Caterpillar "25" ended in 1933.

| | 1 | 2 | 3 | 4 |
|---|---|---|---|---|
| 25, 3CI | $8,000 | $6,000 | $4,000 | $2,000 |

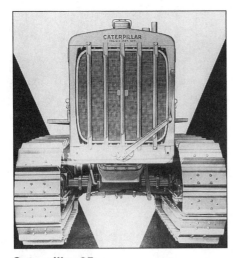

**Caterpillar 35**

Introduced in 1932, the Caterpillar "35" remained in production until 1933. This model

used a four-cylinder engine with a 4-7/8 x 6-1/2-inch bore and stroke. It was rated at 850 rpm. It was capable of nearly 30 drawbar horsepower and almost 40 horsepower was delivered at the belt pulley. Caterpillar gave it a 37-41 horsepower rating.

| | 1 | 2 | 3 | 4 |
|---|---|---|---|---|
| 35, 5CI | $8,000 | $5,000 | $3,000 | $2,000 |

**Caterpillar 50**

The new Caterpillar tractor line of 1932 included the "50", a big 17,000 pound model that retailed for $3,675. The "50" was equipped with a four-cylinder 5-1/2 x 6-1/2-inch engine rated at 850 rpm. In Nebraska Test No. 204 it delivered over 51 belt horsepower and nearly 40 horsepower at the drawbar. Most Caterpillar tractors built into the 1950s were tested at the Nebraska Tractor Test Laboratory. Specific details can be found in the author's book, *Nebraska Tractor Tests Since 1920*; Crestline/Motorbooks: 1985.

| | 1 | 2 | 3 | 4 |
|---|---|---|---|---|
| 50, 5AI | $8,000 | $5,000 | $3,000 | $2,000 |

Production of the Caterpillar "65" began in 1932. Capable of over 78 belt horsepower, this big crawler used a four-cylinder engine having a 7 x 8-1/2-inch bore and stroke. Weighing 12-1/2 tons, the "65" was also capable of delivering a

**Caterpillar 65**

pull of about 6-3/4 tons at the drawbar, or about 68 horsepower. Production of the "65" was apparently quite limited; it appears that production ended by the following year.

**Caterpillar Diesel**

In 1931 Caterpillar became the first company to offer a diesel-powered tractor. Experiments had begun a year earlier and the new design was to become a hallmark of the tractor industry. Caterpillar sent their new "Diesel" to Nebraska's Tractor Test Laboratory in June 1932. On the drawbar, this tractor pulled almost six tons, delivering almost 75 drawbar horsepower. The four-cylinder engine was built by Caterpillar; it used a 6-1/8 x 9-1/4 inch bore and stroke. Production was limited to a few units for this model, but a number of different Caterpillar diesel tractors were on the horizon.

First built in 1932 the Caterpillar "70" was a huge 30,000 pound crawler with a four-cylinder gasoline engine. Rated at 700 rpm, it used a 7 x 8-1/2-inch bore and stroke. It could pull almost

**Caterpillar 70**

18,000 pounds on the drawbar and was capable of almost 78 belt horsepower. The Caterpillar "70" was built as late as 1936.

**Caterpillar 70 Diesel**

Apparently built only in 1932 and 1933, the "70" Diesel was priced at $6,250. Weighing 31,000 pounds, this huge tractor used essentially the same engine as the original "Diesel" although the exterior appearance shows obvious changes. Six forward speeds were available, ranging up to 5 mph.

Topping the Caterpillar tractor line for 1933 was the Diesel "75" crawler. This model weighed over 16 tons and could pull nearly 9-1/2 tons on the drawbar, equivalent to about 80 horsepower.

**Caterpillar Diesel 75**

This huge tractor used a six-cylinder Caterpillar engine with a 5-1/4 x 8 inch bore and stroke. It was rated at 820 rpm. Production of this model continued through 1935.

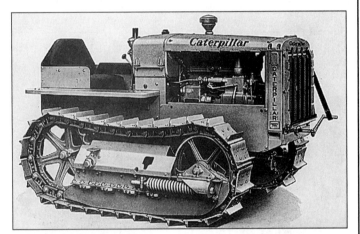

**Caterpillar Twenty-Two**

Production of the Caterpillar Twenty-Two began in 1934, ending in 1939. It used essentially the same four-cylinder, 4 x 5 inch engine as the Caterpillar R-2 model. Weighing 6,200 pounds, the Twenty-Two was priced at $1,450. It had a standard track gauge of 40 inches, but a special 50-inch wide-gauge style was also available.

|  | 1 | 2 | 3 | 4 |
|---|---|---|---|---|
| 22, 2FI, IJI | $5,000 | $3,500 | $2,000 | $1,000 |

A tread width of 42 inches was standard for the Caterpillar Twenty-Eight, introduced in 1933 and continued into the following year. Also available was a special model with a 55-inch

**Caterpillar Twenty-Eight**

track width. The Twenty-Eight was furnished with a four-cylinder engine having a 4-3/16 x 5-1/2-inch bore and stroke. It weighed nearly 7,900 pounds and listed at $1,900.

|  | 1 | 2 | 3 | 4 |
|---|---|---|---|---|
| 28, 4FI | $7,000 | $5,000 | $3,000 | $1,500 |

**Caterpillar Thirty-Five**

Caterpillar introduced the Thirty-Five in 1932; it was tested at Nebraska in June of that year under No. 206. Production of this model continued until 1935. The Thirty-Five used a four-cylinder engine with a 4-7/8 x 6-1/2-inch bore and stroke. It weighed 12,500 pounds and sold for $2,400.

The Caterpillar Thirty-Five Diesel came out in 1933 and was tested at Nebraska in October of that year under No. 217. This tractor used a three-cylinder diesel engine with a 5-1/4 x 8 inch bore and stroke. Rated at 850 rpm, it was capable

**Caterpillar Thirty-Five Diesel**

of about 45 belt horsepower and could exert a maximum drawbar pull of 9,100 pounds. Production of the Thirty-Five Diesel apparently ended in 1935.

**Caterpillar Fifty Diesel**

Production of the Fifty Diesel began in 1933 and ended in 1936. This model used the same 5-1/4 x 8 inch bore and stroke as the Thirty-Five Diesel, but while the latter had but three cylinders, the Fifty Diesel carried four. Initially it was rated at 850 rpm, but by raising the speed to 1,000 rpm, the power level increased substantially, as noted in Nebraska Test Numbers 240 and 241 of 1935.

| | 1 | 2 | 3 | 4 |
|---|---|---|---|---|
| 50 Dsl, 1E1 | $10,000 | $8,000 | $4,500 | $2,500 |

Equipped with its standard 56-inch track width, the Caterpillar Forty sold for $2,575. This figure rose to $2,775 when the tractor was built

**Caterpillar Forty**

with the wide-gauge 74-inch track width. The Forty was a gasoline model with a four-cylinder, 5-1/8 x 6-1/2-inch engine. Production began in 1934 and ended in 1936.

| | 1 | 2 | 3 | 4 |
|---|---|---|---|---|
| 40 5G1 | $10,000 | $8,000 | $4,500 | $2,500 |

**Caterpillar Forty Diesel**

The Caterpillar Forty Diesel was built in the 1934-1936 period. This model weighed in at an impressive 14,700 pounds and was priced at $3,325. The engine was a three-cylinder style having a 5-1/4 x 8 inch bore and stroke. The Forty Diesel was also built with a four-cylinder engine having a 5-1/8 x 6-1/2-inch bore and stroke.

| | 1 | 2 | 3 | 4 |
|---|---|---|---|---|
| 40 Dsl, 3G1 | $8,000 | $6,000 | $3,500 | $1,500 |

**Caterpillar Thirty**

Built only in the 1937 period, the Caterpillar Thirty was in no way related to the earlier Thirty that had been brought in from Best at the time of the 1925 Holt-Best merger. This model weighed about 4-1/2 tons when built with the standard track gauge of 44 inches. Thus built, it was priced at $2,100. The Thirty was designed around a four-cylinder engine having a 4-1/4 x 5-1/2-inch bore and stroke.

|  | 1 | 2 | 3 | 4 |
|---|---|---|---|---|
| 30, S1001, PS1 | | | | |
| | $6,000 | $4,000 | $2,000 | $1,000 |

**Caterpillar R-2 crawler**

Production of the R-2 crawler began in 1934 and continued into 1938, when it was replaced with a new R-2 tractor. This model used a four-cylinder engine with a 4 x 5 inch bore and stroke and operating at 1250 rpm. The R-2 was capable of over 32 belt horsepower.

|  | 1 | 2 | 3 | 4 |
|---|---|---|---|---|
| R-2, IJ Series | | | | |
| | $7,500 | $4,500 | $2,500 | $1,000 |

**Caterpillar R-2 (1938)**

During 1938 Caterpillar revamped the R-2 crawler, giving it an engine with smaller displacement than the original model, but raising the speed to 1,525 rpm from the original 1,250 rpm. With this change, the engine carried a 3-3/4 x 5 inch bore and stroke. Production of this model continued into 1942.

**Caterpillar R-3**

Production of the R-3 Caterpillar tractor began in 1934. Rated at 37 belt horsepower, this tractor was equipped with a four-cylinder engine having a 4-1/2 x 5-1/2-inch bore and stroke. Production of this model was very limited, although there are indications that it was available as late as 1936.

|  | 1 | 2 | 3 | 4 |
|---|---|---|---|---|
| R-3, 5E2501 | $10,000 | $8,000 | $3,500 | $2,000 |

**Caterpillar R-4**

Built in the 1935-44 period, the Caterpillar R-4 was available in a standard track gauge of 44 inches, or a wide-gauge model of 60 inches. This model was also available as a special orchard tractor. A rear pto shaft was available, as was a belt pulley. The R-4 tractor was capable of 35 drawbar and 40 pto horsepower.

|             | 1       | 2       | 3       | 4       |
|-------------|---------|---------|---------|---------|
| R-4, 6G1    | $7,000  | $4,500  | $2,500  | $1,000  |

**Caterpillar R-5**

Production of the R-5 tractor began in 1934 and continued into 1941. After this time the company built diesel-powered tractors exclusively. The R-5 weighed nearly seven tons and was capable of over 54 drawbar horsepower; it could also deliver over 64 horsepower on the belt or the pto shaft. This model was tested at Nebraska in 1934 under No. 224.

|                | 1       | 2       | 3       | 4       |
|----------------|---------|---------|---------|---------|
| R-5, 3R Series | $7,500  | $5,5000 | $3,000  | $1,500  |

**Caterpillar RD-4**

Production of the new RD-4 tractor began in 1936. Initially it was built as the RD-4, but the 'R' was soon dropped from the model designation. The Caterpillar four-cylinder diesel engine was rated at 1,400 rpm and carried a 4-1/4 x 5-1/2-inch bore and stroke.

**Caterpillar D-4**

Caterpillar D-4 tractors were modified at various times during a long production run ending in 1959. About 1947 the engine was modified to include a 4-1/2 x 5-1/2-inch bore and stroke. This increased the power level substantially. About 1954 the D-4 was again modified, including an increase in the rated speed of 200 rpm. By this time the D-4 was capable of over 58 belt horsepower. Eventually though, the D-4 had run its course and was replaced with an entirely new model.

**Caterpillar D-2**

The D-2 tractor first appeared in 1938 and was built in various styles until 1957. Shown here is an early style that is furnished with the special equipment for orchard work. The D-2 used a four-cylinder engine rated at 1,525 rpm and carrying a 3-3/4 x 5 inch bore and stroke. It was capable of about 30 belt horsepower.

**Caterpillar RD-6**

Production of the RD-6, later known as the D-6, began in 1935. Initially, the D-6 used a three-cylinder engine having a 5-3/4 x 8 inch bore and stroke. Weighing about 7-1/2 tons, the D-6 had a list price of about $3,600. The RD-6 was earlier built as the Diesel Forty. Production of this style ended in 1941.

**Caterpillar D-2 (upgraded)**

In 1947 the D-2 was upgraded to a 4 x 5 engine and this increased the power level substantially, with the D-2 now being capable of about 47 belt horsepower. Various other changes were made to the D-2 during its long production run that finally ended in 1957. This tractor weighed about 7,200 pounds.

**Caterpillar D-6**

During 1941 Caterpillar phased out the three-cylinder D-6 tractor and began using a six-cylinder engine in its place. This new model carried a 4-1/4 x 5-1/2-inch bore and stroke with a rated speed of 1,400 rpm. When tested at Nebraska in 1941 under No. 374, the D-6 delivered a maximum pull of almost 17,000 pounds or about 50 drawbar horsepower. Production of various styles of the D-6 continued until 1959.

**Caterpillar RD-7**

With the exception of slightly changed specifications, the RD-7 of 1935 was the same as the Caterpillar Diesel Fifty. The four-cylinder engine used a 5-3/4 x 7 inch bore and stroke and was rated at 61 drawbar and 70 belt horsepower. Weighing over 20,000 pounds, the RD-7 had a maximum drawbar pull of almost 15,000 pounds. Production of this model continued into the late 1950s, albeit with numerous changes along the way.

**Caterpillar RD-8**

Production of the Caterpillar RD-8 began in 1935. This tractor used the same 5-3/4 x 8 inch bore and stroke engine as the D-6 and D-7 tractors, but had six cylinders. This gave the D-8 a capability of over 103 belt horsepower. On the drawbar this tractor was able to pull a load in excess of 20,000 pounds. Total tractor weight was over 33,000 pounds. Various changes and modifications were evident on the D-8 over its long production run that ended in 1955.

**Caterpillar D-9**

The huge Caterpillar D-9 tractor was first built in 1954. Weighing over 33 tons, the D-9 was equipped with a six-cylinder turbocharged engine having a 6-1/4 x 8 inch bore and stroke. At the drawbar, the D-9 demonstrated its capability to pull a load of nearly 57,000 pounds. The D-9 had six forward speeds ranging all the way up to 7 mph.

## C-E Tractor Company
*Toledo, Ohio*
See: Cleveland Engineering Company

**C-E garden tractor**

The C-E garden tractor appeared in the late 1930s. It was powered by a Wisconsin AF-single cylinder engine rated at 5 horsepower. It used a 3-1/4 x 4 inch bore and stroke. Weighing 950 pounds, the C-E also featured a three-speed auto-motive transmission. By the late 1940s parts were still available, but the C-E had apparently gone out of production.

## Centaur Tractor Corporation
*Greenwich, Ohio*

**Centaur tractor**

The Centaur tractor first appeared from Central Tractor Company in 1921. Rated at 10 belt horse-power, the Centaur could be equipped with a wide array of implements built especially for use with this tractor. A 1926 Centaur catalog notes that the Model G, as it was known at the time, weighed 1,220 pounds and was capable of 6 drawbar horsepower. In 1928 the company name was changed to Centaur Tractor Corporation.

|  | 1 | 2 | 3 | 4 |
|---|---|---|---|---|
| Model G | $3,000 | $2,000 | $1,000 | $850 |

**Centaur KV (Klear View)**

Centaur KV (Klear View) tractors first appear in the 1935 directories, indicating that production probably began in 1934. Rated at 22 belt horse-power, the KV was equipped with a LeRoi four-cylinder engine having a 3-1/4 x 4 inch bore and stroke. This unstyled version was built until about 1939.

**Centaur KV**

Production of the Centaur KV tractor began about 1934 and continued with little change until about 1939 when it was given a stylized hood and fenders. Otherwise the tractor was essen-tially the same as before, continuing with the LeRoi D133 four-cylinder engine. A unique fea-ture of the later models was their capability of traveling up to 25 mph on the road. Production of the KV was suspended during World War Two and apparently never resumed after hostili-ties ended.

|  | 1 | 2 | 3 | 4 |
|---|---|---|---|---|
| KV | $3,000 | $2,000 | $1,000 | $500 |

See: Central Tractor Company, Greenwich, Ohio

## Central Machine Works
*Indianapolis, Indiana*

Late in 1911 Central Machine Works announced its new tractor design that featured a friction drive transmission, along with a four-cylinder Clifton engine. Weighing 10,000 pounds, the

**Central Machine Works tractor**

Central is shown here pulling a six-bottom plow. No specifications have been found relative to the size of this tractor, nor in fact, has any other information appeared.

## Central Tractor Company
*Greenwich, Ohio*

**Central Tractor Company Model 6-10**

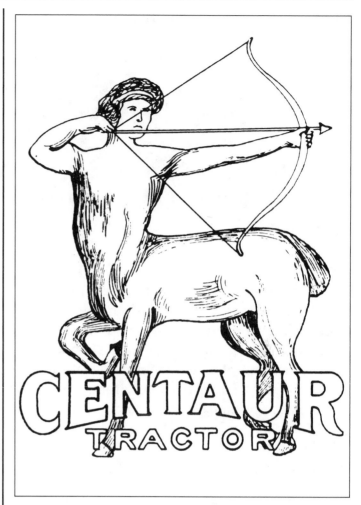

**Centaur trademark**

Two different trademark applications illustrate the Centaur trademarks of 1921. Both appeared in the *Patent Office Gazette*. From these marks it is learned that they were first used on March 3, 1921, and this could very well establish the beginnings of the company at least so far as the Centaur tractor line is concerned.

See: Centaur Tractor Corporation

**CENTAUR**

**Centaur logo**

Organized in 1921 Central Tractor Company specialized in building their Centaur garden tractors. Their 6-10 model was equipped with a LeRoi two-cylinder engine having a 3-1/8 x 4-1/4 inch bore and stroke. In 1928 Central Tractor Co. became the *Centaur Tractor Corporation*.

## Central Tractor Company
*Great Falls, Montana*

This company was incorporated for $25,000 in 1919 to build tractors, but no other information can be found concerning the firm.

# Central Machine Company

*Minneapolis, Minnesota*

**Central Auto Tractor**

In 1912 the Central Auto Tractor appeared at the Minnesota State Fair and gained considerable interest. It used a four-cylinder engine and featured two forward speeds. Rated at 24 belt horsepower, the Central Auto Tractor also featured a relatively unique differential lock for extra traction in slippery spots. Aside from the 1912 mention of this tractor in *Gas Power Magazine*, no further information has been located.

# Challenge Tractor Company

*Minneapolis, Minnesota*

**Challenge Tractor Company tractor**

The December 26, 1916 issue of the Patent Office Gazette contains the trademark application of the Challenge Tractor Company, noting that they first used the mark on October 1, 1916. Aside from this, no other information has been located.

# Champion Tractor Company

*Argo, Illinois*

**Champion Tractor Company 15-30**

Probably beginning in 1918, Champion offered their 15-30 tractor. It retailed for $1,465. The Champion was largely built up of OEM components including the engine and transmission. This tractor used a Buda four-cylinder engine having a 4-1/4 x 5-1/2-inch bore and stroke. Production apparently ended by 1920.

**Champion Tractor Company 17-1/2-32 tractor**

For 1919 and 1920 Champion produced their 17-1/2 - 32 tractor. Like the 15-30 it is shown without fenders, indicating that they were probably an extra-cost option, or that development of the Champion tractors had not yet achieved final completion. Aside from a very few illustrations, little else is known of the Champion tractors.

# Chandler Motor Car Company

*Cleveland, Ohio*

The 1918 issue of the *Farm Implement News Buyer's Guide* lists this well known automobile manufacturer as being a tractor builder. However, no further information has been found in this regard.

# Charter Gas Engine Company
*Sterling, Illinois*

**Charter Gas Engine Company**

About 1887 John Charter built and sold the first successful liquid fuel engine. Although this claim would later be a point of contention, Charter always maintained his claim. In 1889 Charter built the first successful gasoline traction engine, using his own stationary engine over the trucks from a steam traction engine. Although this traction engine operated with considerable success and even greater promise, it appears that this was the beginning and the end of Charter's involvement in the tractor business.

# Chase Motor Truck Company
*Syracuse, New York*

# Chase Tractors Corporation Ltd.
*Toronto, Ontario*

**Chase Motor Truck Company tractor**

Chase Motor Truck Company began building tractors as early as 1908, but their early designs assumed the form of a tractor-roller. The 1908 design shown here was powered by a small air-cooled engine and was intended primarily for use as a roller.

**Chase tractor-roller combination**

By 1913 the Chase tractor-roller combination had been developed to include a three-cylinder, two-cycle engine of 30 belt horsepower. Although more suitable for tractive use than the original machine, its application to heavy traction work was very limited.

**Chase 8-16**

By 1915 Chase had developed a conventional tractor, with this 8-16 using a four-cylinder Waukesha engine. By 1918 the company had upgraded the design to a 9-18 horsepower rating; the new model was built with a Buda four-cylinder engine.

Chase tractors reappear in 1919 at Toronto, Ontario. The 9-18 Buda engine of the 1918 models was replaced with a larger Buda four-cylin-

**Chase 40 horsepower tractor**

**Chase 9-18 with Buda engine**

der design that carried a 4-1/4 x 5-1/2 inch bore and stroke. This gave the Chase a 12-25 horsepower rating.

Little is known of the Chase 40 horsepower tractor of 1915. Weighing some 6,000 pounds, this tractor had a 1916 list price of $1,750. For reasons now unknown the Chase 40 then disappeared from the market. All Chase tractor production ended in 1921.

## Chief Tractor Company
*Detroit, Michigan*

In 1915 this company took over the Boss Tractor Mfg. Company of Detroit. The firm is listed in the *Farm Implement News Buyer's Guide* as late as 1918, but no other information has been found.

## Christensen Engineering Company
*Milwaukee, Wisconsin*

The *Farm Implement News Buyer's Guide* lists this company as a tractor builder from 1909 through 1913. Christensen was a gasoline engine manufacturer and also was well known for its developments in railway air brakes and other railway appliances. No information regarding their entry into the tractor business has been located.

## Cizek Mfg. Company
*Clutier, Iowa*

**Cizek Little John garden tractor**

In the mid-1950s Cizek offered their Little John garden tractor. Shown here with a small trailer, the Little John could be furnished with a variety of different garden tillage implements, lawn sweepers and lawn mowers.

| <u>1</u> | <u>2</u> | <u>3</u> | <u>4</u> |
|---|---|---|---|
| $200 | $150 | $75 | $50 |

## Clarke, Airborne

*Detroit Michigan*

A small 3,000 pound crawler was designed for U.S. Military about 1941. This crawler was positioned into a wooden glider and landed in remote areas to build or repair airfields. A small pull scraper was available from LaPlante-Choate.

Clark used a Waukesha engine and shuttle clutch to four forward and reverse gears. The plant closed after WWII and production was taken over by U.S. Tractor Corp., Warren, Ohio.

## Cleveland Engineering Company

*Cleveland, Ohio*

**Cleveland Engineering Co. C-E garden tractor**

In 1934 Cleveland Engineering Co. announced their new "C-E" garden tractor. Weighing 950 pounds, it was furnished with a single-cylinder air-cooled engine. Numerous attachments were available, including the one-bottom plow shown here. Apparently in the late 1930s the company relocated to Toledo, Ohio, and established the C-E Tractor Company there.

## Cleveland Horseless Machinery Company

*Cleveland, Ohio*

Various trade references indicate that in 1915 and 1916 this firm was building its Baby Johnson tractor, but no illustrations or other information has been located.

## Cleveland Tractor Company

*Cleveland, Ohio*

## Cleveland Motor Plow Company

*Cleveland, Ohio*

**Cleveland Motor Plow Company**

By 1912 Rollin H. and Clarence G. White had developed their own motor plow. Early experiments were successful enough to cause the formation of the Cleveland Motor Plow Company. For reasons unknown however, they chose not to pursue this design, concentrating instead on crawler tractors.

In 1916 Cleveland Motor Plow Company introduced its new Model R crawler. Built only in 1916 and 1917, the Cleveland Motor Plow used either Buda or Waukesha engines, but no specific

**Cleveland Motor Plow company Model R crawler**

data on them has been found. In 1917 the company name was changed to Cleveland Tractor Company.

**Cletrac Model R crawler**

The initial success of the Model R crawler led to the development of the Model H, offered in the 1917-1919 period. This model was equipped with a Weideley engine. Early Cletrac models placed the belt pulley on the front of the tractor, as evident in this photograph.

**Cletrac Company Model W crawlers**

Model W crawlers emerged in 1919 as the replacement for the Model R. The Model W was also known as the 12-20. This tractor used a Weideley four-cylinder engine having a 4 x 5-1/2-inch bore and stroke. The Model W was the first crawler tractor tested at the Nebraska Tractor Test Laboratory. Details may be found in Test No. 45. *(See the Author's title: Nebraska Tractor Tests Since 1920; Crestline/Motorbooks:1985).* Model W crawlers were built until about 1925.

**Cletrac Model F crawler**

Model F Cletrac tractors were built in the 1920-1924 period. This small crawler had a 9-16 horsepower rating and used a four-cylinder engine having a 3-1/4 x 4-1/2-inch bore and stroke. The 'Cletrac' tradename was first used in 1918. Model F used distinctive high drive like many modern crawlers.

**Cletrac Model 20 crawler**

Between 1925 and 1932 Cletrac offered their Model 20 crawler. This model was equipped with the company's own four-cylinder engine having a 4 x 5 inch bore and stroke. While a sizable number of early Cletrac crawlers were used for construction work, the company's chief market was the farmer. Numerous implements were available for use with the Cletrac crawlers.

| | 1 | 2 | 3 | 4 |
|---|---|---|---|---|
| Model 20 | $5,000 | $4,000 | $2,500 | $1,000 |

**Cletrac Model 30A (30-45 tractor)**

The Model 30A tractors were built in the 1926-1928 period. Also known as the 30-45 tractor, this one was followed in 1929 and 1930 with an

improved Model 30B tractor. Model 30 crawlers used a Wisconsin six-cylinder engine having a 4 x 5 inch bore and stroke.

| | 1 | 2 | 3 | 4 |
|---|---|---|---|---|
| Model 30A | $6,000 | $4,000 | $2,500 | $1,000 |

**Cletrac Model 40**

Cletrac Model 40 tractor production began in 1928 and ran until 1931. Subsequently this model was followed by the 55-40; it was essentially the same tractor but with numerous improvements. The Model 40 had a big six-cylinder Beaver engine with a 4-1/2 x 5 inch bore and stroke. Electric starting was a standard feature.

**Cletrac Model 55**

Model 55 Cletrac crawlers were built between 1932 and 1936. This tractor was the immediate successor to the Model 55-40 of 1931 and 1932. By this time the Cletrac crawlers were widely known and used and the company was a major manufacturer of crawler tractors.

**Cletrac Model 100**

In terms of size, the Cletrac Model 100 was one of the largest crawler tractors of its time. Built between 1927 and 1930, the Model 100 used a huge six-cylinder Beaver engine with a 6 x 7 inch bore and stroke. Only about 50 of these huge tractors were built.

**Cletrac Model 15 crawler**

Cletrac introduced their Model 15 crawler in 1931, with production continuing into 1933. At that time the Model 15 was replaced with the Model 20-C, and the latter was available into 1936. Finally, Cletrac replaced the 20-C in 1936

with the Model AG, and production of this model continued into 1942. Model AG crawlers used a Hercules four-cylinder engine having a 4 x 4-1/2-inch bore and stroke.

**Cletrac Model 20-C crawler**

Model 20-C Cletrac crawlers were built between 1933 and 1936. This one carried a four-cylinder Hercules engine having a 4 x 4-1/2-inch bore and stroke. Numerous attachments and accessories were available for special conditions.

|           | **1**    | **2**    | **3**    | **4**    |
|-----------|----------|----------|----------|----------|
| Model 20-C | $5,000  | $3,500   | $2,500   | $1,000   |

**Cletrac 25 tractor**

Cletrac 25 tractors came into being during 1932. Weighing over 3-1/2 tons, the Cletrac 25 was equipped with a Hercules six-cylinder engine having a 3-3/4 x 4-1/4 inch bore and stroke. Model 25 tractors were capable of about 33 belt horsepower.

model used a Hercules six-cylinder engine with a 4-1/4 x 4-1/2 inch bore and stroke. The vast majority of the Cletrac crawlers were rated at the Nebraska Tractor Test Laboratory.

**Cletrac 35 tractor**

The Cletrac 35 tractor was built between 1932 and 1936. Its immediate predecessor was the Cletrac 40-35 and was followed in 1936 with the Cletrac CG crawler; the latter was built until 1942. The three models were so similar that they all used the same parts book.

|  | 1 | 2 | 3 | 4 |
|---|---|---|---|---|
| Cletrac 35 | $5,000 | $4,000 | $2,500 | $1,000 |

**Cletrac Model 40-30**

Model 40-30 Cletrac crawlers were first built in 1930, with production ending the next year. This

**Cletrac Model 40 Diesel**

Model 40 Diesel tractors saw first light in 1935 and a year earlier as the Model 35 Diesel. Sometime in 1935 this became the Model DD Cletrac and production of this model continued into 1936. Power came from a Hercules Model DRXH engine.

**Cletrac Model 80**

The Model 80 Cletrac had its beginnings as the 50-60 Cletrac, built from 1930 to 1932. In the latter year the Model 80 appeared and stayed in the line until 1936. This big crawler had a six-cylinder Her-

**Cletrac Model 80**

cules engine with a 5-3/4 x 6 inch bore and stroke for over 100 belt horsepower. Model 80 Diesel crawlers were offered in the 1933-36 period.

**Cletrac Model E crawler**

Cletrac Model E crawlers first came out in 1934. They were built in several different track widths and were especially designed for farm and field work. In 1938 the Model E was streamlined and this dramatically changed its external appearance. Production of various E-Series crawlers continued until 1940.

**Cletrac OG tractor**

The first Cletrac CG tractor was built in 1936. It was a successor to the Model 35. Capable of nearly 46 drawbar horsepower, the CG weighed almost six tons. This model was built into 1942.

**Cletrac Model D-Series crawler**

Model D-Series Cletrac crawlers first came onto the market in 1937. That year the DG (gasoline) crawler appeared, followed the next season with the DD (diesel) crawler. Production of the DG and its variations continued until 1955, while the DD model remained in production until 1958. Cletrac was bought out by Oliver in 1944.

Beginning in 1936 the F-Series crawlers were built, with the FG gasoline model and the FD diesel tractor. This series replaced the earlier Model

**Cletrac F-Series crawler**

**Cletrac HG (rubber track version)**

80 tractors. The FG was equipped with a huge Hercules HXE six-cylinder engine having a 5-3/4 x 6 inch bore and stroke. At full load this engine burned gasoline at the rate of 12 gallons per hour!

**Cletrac Model HG tractor**

Cletrac Model HG tractors first appeared in 1939 and were built until 1950. The HG was equipped with a Hercules IXA engine capable of about 20 belt horsepower. This small crawler weighed only 3,500 pounds. After Oliver bought out the Cletrac line in 1944 the HG tractor continued in the line for several more years.

An innovative development was the rubber track version of the HG crawler tractors. Cletrac introduced this design in the early 1940s, but

due to problems with the rubber tracks, the company retrofitted virtually all of these tractors with steel tracks.

**Cletrac Model GG General tractor**

In the 1939-1942 period, Cleveland Tractor Company produced their Model GG General tractor. This wheeled version was fairly popular, but because of World War Two, production was suspended. Oliver bought out the Cletrac line in 1944, and after the war was over, production of the General was never resumed. This little tractor used the same engine as the HG crawler and was capable of about 19 belt horsepower.

## Cluff Ammunition Company
*Toronto, Ontario*

This firm is listed as a tractor builder in the 1919 trade directories, but no further information is available.

## C. O. D. Tractor Company
*Minneapolis, Minnesota*

**C.O.D. 1916 model**

Albert O. Espe established a machine shop at Crookston, Minnesota in 1898, and built his first tractor there in 1907. In 1909 the Crookston Mfg. Company was organized to build tractors, but in 1916 the company moved to Minneapolis. The 1916 model shown here had a 13-25 horsepower rating. It was equipped with a two-cylinder engine having a 6-1/2 x 7 inch bore and stroke.

**C.O.D. Model B tractor**

The Model B tractor appeared in 1919. While it had the same 13-25 horsepower rating as the earlier model, several noticeable changes were made, such as the use of a cellular radiator. A. O. Espe was responsible for numerous tractor designs, notably the "Universal" that was built by Union Iron Works and others. Eventually this design was bought out by Rumely and marketed for a time as their GasPull tractor. Production of the C. O. D. tractors ended in 1919.

|   | 1 | 2 | 3 | 4 |
|---|---|---|---|---|
| B | $16,000 | $15,000 | $12,000 | $4,000 |

## Coates Mfg. Company
*Loma Linda, California*

**Coates Little Giant Model A**

For 1948 Coates offered their Little Giant Model A garden tractor. It was equipped with a Lauson RSC single-cylinder engine using a 2 x 1-7/8 inch bore and stroke and capable of 1-1/2 horsepower. The Little Giant made but a brief appearance in the tractor directories but specific production data has not been located.

## Cockshutt Farm Equipment Company Ltd.
*Brantford, Ontario*

**Cockshutt Model 30 tractor**

Cockshutt Model 30 tractors made their first appearance in 1946 with production running until 1956. The Cockshutt 30G gasoline model used a four-cylinder Buda engine with a 3-7/16 x 4-1/8 inch bore and stroke. A Buda four-cylinder, 153 ci engine was used in the 30D diesel model. This tractor was also marketed as the Model E-3 Co-op tractor and as the Farmcrest 30.

| 1 | 2 | 3 | 4 |
|---|---|---|---|
| Model 30 (Gambles-Farmcrest 30) | | | |
| $3,000 | $2,000 | $800 | $325 |

**Cockshutt Model 20**

Model 20 Cockshutt tractors were built between 1952 and 1958. The Model 20 was available with the adjustable-width axle shown here or a conventional tricycle front. Model 20 tractors were built only with a gasoline engine.

| 1 | 2 | 3 | 4 |
|---|---|---|---|
| Model 20 (Black Hawk 20) | | | |
| $4,000 | $3,000 | $1,400 | $450 |

The Cockshutt 40 gasoline tractor was built in the 1949-1957 period. This model used a six-cylinder Buda engine having the same bore and stroke dimensions as the four-cylinder Cockshutt 30. The diesel model carried a Buda six-cylinder

**Cockshutt 40 gasoline tractor**

engine of the same displacement as the gasoline model. Cockshutt 40D diesel tractors were built between 1950 and 1957. The 40D was built primarily for the Canadian market.

| 1 | 2 | 3 | 4 |
|---|---|---|---|
| Model 40 (Black Hawk 40) | | | |
| $3,600 | $2,300 | $1,400 | $425 |

**Cockshutt Golden Eagle tractor**

Cockshutt Golden Eagle tractors were built for the U. S. market, while the identical 40D4 tractor was built for Canada. These tractors were built only in a diesel version and were made in the 1955-57 period.

| 1 | 2 | 3 | 4 |
|---|---|---|---|
| Golden Eagle (Black Hawk) | | | |
| $4,100 | $3,500 | $1,900 | $450 |

**Cockshutt Golden Arrow tractor**

Model 35 tractors were built 1955-57 for sale in Canada, while the Golden Arrow was made only in 1957 for U.S. distribution. While similar, the Golden Arrow is not the same as the Model 35. Both tractors share the same engine, but other parts are different. The Golden Arrow is essentially a "550" with "35" sheet metal. It was also marketed as "Black Hawk." The engine was a GO-198 Hercules.

There is a derivative of the "35" called "35L." Production of the 35L was low. Several have been seen in Canada and the Eastern U.S. They are a Model 35 with 28-inch tires on the back and a low-profile non-arched standard front end. It appears that many were equipped with loaders and back hoe and used for industrial application. Engine was a GO-198 Hercules.

|              | 1       | 2       | 3       | 4     |
|--------------|---------|---------|---------|-------|
| Golden Arrow |         |         |         |       |
|              | $4,750  | $4,000  | $2,000  | $625  |
| Model 35     | $3,700  | $3,000  | $1,400  | $450  |

Gasoline and diesel versions were available for the Cockshutt 50 tractors. This 50 horsepower tractor was made from 1952 to 1957. In addition, the same tractor was sold in the U.S. as the Co-op

**Cockshutt 50**

E-5 tractor. The Cockshutt 50 was tested at Nebraska under No. 487.

|                    | 1       | 2       | 3       | 4     |
|--------------------|---------|---------|---------|-------|
| Model 50 (Black Hawk) |      |         |         |       |
|                    | $4,100  | $3,500  | $2,000  | $550  |

**Cockshutt 540 two-plow model**

The new Cockshutt tractor line for 1958 included the 540 two-plow model shown here. This tractor featured a Continental four-cylinder, 162 ci engine plus a dual-range, six-speed transmission. Production continued until 1961.

|           | 1       | 2       | 3       | 4     |
|-----------|---------|---------|---------|-------|
| Model 540 | $4,400  | $3,000  | $2,000  | $600  |

**Cockshutt 550 model**

For 1958 the Cockshutt tractor line included this 550 model. Available in gasoline and diesel versions, it was equipped with a Hercules engine. Both the gasoline and diesel models were capable of about 35 belt horsepower.

|            | **1**    | **2**    | **3**    | **4**  |
|------------|----------|----------|----------|--------|
| Model 550  | $4,000   | $3,000   | $1,800   | $550   |

**Cockshutt 560 tractor**

A big Perkins four-cylinder diesel engine powered the Cockshutt 560 tractor. For the U. S. market this tractor was offered only in the diesel version, but was otherwise available with a four-cylinder 198 ci gasoline engine. The 560 was rated at about 43 belt horsepower. Production ran from 1958 to 1961.

|            | **1**    | **2**    | **3**    | **4**  |
|------------|----------|----------|----------|--------|
| Model 560* | $4,200   | $2,800   | $1,800   | $500   |

* The early engine was a Perkins L4, similar to Golden Eagle. Later models used a Perkins 4-2700 engine, diesel only.

**Cockshutt 570 tractor**

Cockshutt 570 tractors were built in the 1958-60 period and for 1961 and 1962 were available as the 570 Super Diesel. While sold mainly as a diesel tractor, particularly in the United States, this model was also available with a gasoline engine.

|                  | **1**    | **2**    | **3**    | **4**  |
|------------------|----------|----------|----------|--------|
| Model 570        | $4,600   | $3,000   | $2,200   | $700   |
| Model 570 Super  | $6,500   | $3,100   | $3,000   | $800   |

White Motors Corporation bought out Cockshutt in 1962 and with it, production of the Cockshutt tractors ended. For a time, Oliver (another White acquisition) built tractors with red paint and Cockshutt decals, but they were nevertheless Oliver tractors. One such example is the Cock-

**Cockshutt 1250**

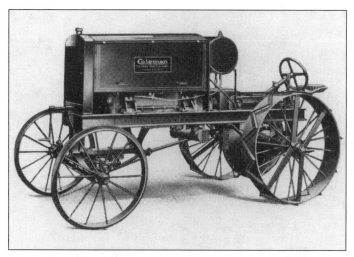

**Coleman tractor, 1917**

shutt 1250 shown here; it is actually an Oliver 1250 model. In addition, White bought Fiat tractors and sold them as the 411R and 411 RG Cockshutt tractors in the 1961-1965 period.

## Coleman Tractor Corporation
*Kansas City, Missouri*

During 1917 Coleman tractors appeared. Rated at 10 drawbar and 20 belt horsepower, the Cole-

man distinguished itself with a worm gear final drive system. A Climax four-cylinder engine was featured.

By 1919 the Coleman tractor had been remodeled and gained a new rating of 16 drawbar and 30 belt horsepower. In this model a Climax four-cylinder engine was used; it had a 5 x 6-1/2-inch bore and stroke. Production of the Coleman ended in 1920 and the company was acquired by Welborn Corporation at Kansas City. In 1921 the Coleman reappeared for a short time from Farmers Mfg. Company, also of Kansas City.

**Coleman tractor, 1919**

## Columbus Machine Company
*Columbus, Ohio*

Columbus Machine Company began building gasoline engines in the late 1890s. In 1905 the company is listed as a manufacturer of "gasoline traction engines" and likely mounted their engines to the Morton Traction Trucks. Nothing further is known of the Columbus tractions, but in 1911 the company began building the Eastman Cable Tractor designed by C. J. Eastman of Washington, D. C. This venture lasted only a short time.

## Columbus Tractor Company
*Columbus, Ohio*

**Columbus Tractor Company Farmer Boy tractor**

This company was organized in 1918 from the ashes of McIntyre Tractor Company, also of Columbus. The latter had been organized to build the Farmer Boy tractor in 1915. It used a Waukesha four-cylinder engine having a 3-3/4 x 5-1/4 inch bore and stroke. Columbus Tractor Co. was apparently out of business by 1920.

## Combination Saw & Tractor Company
*Denton, Texas*

In the late 1940s the Superior Combination Saw & Tractor appeared, remaining on the market at least into the early 1950s. Specific production data has not been located. The Superior was

**Superior Combination Saw & Tractor**

intended to be used as a felling or buck saw, as shown here, and the saw could be removed so that the tractor could be adapted to other uses.

## Comet Automobile Company
*Decatur, Illinois*

**Comet 15-30 tractor**

Comet Automobile Co. began business in 1917 as an automobile manufacturer. In 1919 the company began building the Comet 15-30 tractor. On the automotive side, the company had fairly good sales, but got the fever to expand and by late in 1920 was in serious financial trouble. About this time the Comet 15-30 tractor came to an end and in 1922 the entire factory was sold piece-by-piece at auction.

# Common Sense Tractor Company
*Minneapolis, Minnesota*

**Common Sense Tractor Co. 1915 model**

Common Sense Tractor Co. was incorporated in 1915 to build a unique three-wheel tractor. The original model was rated at 15 drawbar and 25 belt horsepower and this was provided by a four-cylinder engine. The tractor was designed by H. W. Adams who has been identified with several different tractor designs originating in the Minneapolis area.

**Common Sense tractor, V-8 model**

Late in 1916 the Common Sense tractor was modified and fitted with a Herschell-Spillman V-8 engine. This was the first tractor ever equipped

with a V-8. In this instance it had a 3-1/4 x 5 inch bore and stroke for 20 drawbar and 40 belt horsepower. By late 1919 the Common Sense was being offered by Farm Power & Sales Company of Minneapolis; in another year it disappeared from view.

# Commonwealth Tractor Company
*Kansas City, Missouri*

No information available.

# Commonwealth Tractor Company
*Chicago, Illinois*

An advertisement of about 1918 makes reference to the Thorobred tractor, calling it "America's Pedigreed Tractor." The Thorobred people implored interested parties to write for further information. Beyond this, no additional data has been located.

# Community Industries
*Sullivan, Illinois*

In the early 1950s this company appears as the manufacturer of the George garden tractor. No other information has been found.

# Community Mfg. Company
*Los Angeles, California*

**Allen 10-20**

The Allen 10-20 was essentially the same tractor as had been formerly built by *Allen-Burbank Motor Company*. However, the tractor shown here is somewhat different in its exterior appearance, particularly with the addition of a totally enclosed engine compartment and enclosed rear wheels.

**Allen Model A 10-20**

Allen Model A 10-20 tractors were built during 1923 and 1924 by Community Mfg. Company at Los Angeles. They used a Continental four-cylinder engine having a 4-1/8 x 5-1/4 inch bore and stroke. Operating speed was 950 rpm. The Allen 10-20 weighed 3,400 pounds.

## John Compodocina
*Stockton, California*

No information is available on this manufacturer, although it is the author's belief that it was very early, probably prior to 1910.

## Connors Hoe & Tool Company
*Columbus, Ohio*

This company appears at various times in the late 1940s and early 1950s as a garden tractor manufacturer, but no further information has been found.

## Consolidated Gasoline Engine Company
*New York, New York*

Shortly before 1920 this firm came out with their Do-It-All garden tractor. Rated at 6 belt horsepower, it was capable of pulling a one-bottom

**Do-It-All garden tractor**

plow, as shown here. Apparently this machine remained on the market for only a few years; it appears in the trade directories only for 1920.

## Consolidated Implement Mfg. Company
*Ogden, Utah*

No information has been found concerning this company.

## Continental Cultor Co.
*Springfield, Ohio*

**Cultor logo**

Continental began building their 'Cultor' in 1925. The company endured for at least a few years, but vanishes from the trade directories by 1929. If the company endured, it was probably on a limited basis; detailed history of the firm has not been located. The Cultor was designed as an all-around tractor, and to its favor, it was powered by a Ford Model T engine. Since these were in abundance at the time, engine repairs were relatively simple and inexpensive.

# Continental Tractor Company
*Continental, Ohio*

**Continental Tractor Company**

In 1918 this company was organized and incorporated for $100,000. The following year a patent application was filed by O. L. Plettner and W. H. Lowe for the tractor plow shown here. A patent was granted on this application under No. 1,378,196 of May 17, 1921. Meanwhile, Continental attempted to interest other companies in manufacturing the new design, including the then-powerful Moline Plow Company. Very little additional information has surfaced for this design.

# Convertible Tractor Corporation
*St. Paul, Minnesota*

**Megow Convertible Tractor**

Charles F. Megow was an experimental engineer with Ford Motor Company. In 1916 he developed the Megow Convertible Tractor. This was a conversion device that used an automobile engine and chassis, together with suitable traction wheels and gearing. The conversion unit was priced at $325. By 1918 the Me-Go farm tractor was developed, but despite considerable efforts to launch this new tractor, it never reached any sort of production level and disappeared shortly after it was announced.

# A.E. Cook
*Odeboldt, Iowa*

A.E. Cook designed and built a motor plow in 1909, ostensibly with ideas of marketing the new machine. The plans did not materialize and no further information has been located.

# Herman Cook
*Sioux City, Iowa*

**Cook's Auto Thresher**

In 1908 Herman Cook advertised "Cook's Auto Thresher." While not truly a farm tractor in the usual sense of the term, this fully self-contained threshing machine represented a major forward step in threshing machinery. A separate tractor was not required, nor was it necessary to have a long and troublesome drive belt between tractor and thresher. The idea did not catch on and the Cook lasted only a short time.

# Cook & Roberts Machine & Equipment Company
*Oregon City, Oregon*

In 1950 this firm began building their Track-O-Matic garden tractors, with a 1953 model being shown here. Apparently the firm did not endure past 1955, since it disappears from the trade

**Track-O-Matic garden tractor**

directories by that time. The Track-O-Matic was equipped with a 6 hp Wisconsin AEH engine having a 23.0 cid.

# Cooper Engineering Corporation
*Sunland, California*

About 1947 Cooper began building their Moto-Mule garden tractors, with the Model RG-75 of 1948 being shown here. It was a small outfit powered by a Gladden 75 single-cylinder air-cooled engine with a 2.875 x 3.000 inch bore and stroke. The Moto-Mule disappears from trade listings after 1953.

# Co-Operative Mfg. Company
*Battle Creek, Michigan*

**Co-Op No. 1**

With various companies involved, the history of the Co-Op tractor is difficult to untangle. In May 1938 Duplex Printing Press Company at Battle

Creek was dismissed as the manufacturer of the three Co-Op tractor models. In its place came the Co-Operative Mfg. Company, also at Battle Creek. The Co-Op No. 1 shown here weighed only 3,380 pounds. It was powered by a Waukesha four-cylinder engine having a 3-1/4 x 4 inch bore and stroke. Electric starting and lighting came as standard equipment.

|       | 1 | 2      | 3      | 4      |
|-------|---|--------|--------|--------|
| No. 1 | — | $3,500 | $2,300 | $1,000 |

**Co-Op No. 2**

The Co-op tractor line owed its design to Dent Parrett; he had formerly been with the Parrett Tractor Company at Chicago. The original Parrett design went all the way back to 1913. Parrett continued his tractor design work after the company folded about 1922. In 1937 Parrett Tractors appears at Benton Harbor, Michigan, with a Parrett 6 model. The Co-Op No. 2 shown here was a standard-tread design that used a Chrysler Industrial six-cylinder engine; it was built with a 3-1/8 x 4-3/8 inch bore and stroke.

|       | 1 | 2      | 3      | 4    |
|-------|---|--------|--------|------|
| No. 2 | — | $3,000 | $1,800 | $800 |

Co-Op No. 3 tractors for 1938 were built with a six-cylinder Chrysler Industrial engine using a 3-3/8 x 4-1/2-inch bore and stroke. Weighing 5,000 pounds, this tractor featured electric starting and lighting. The Co-Op tractors were also capable of road speeds up to 25 mph. References to the Co-Op tractors will also be found under: Arthurdale Farm Equipment Corporation,

**Co-Op No. 3**

Arthurdale, West Virginia; Farmers Union Central Exchange, St. Paul, Minnesota; and National Farm Machinery Co-operatives, Shelbyville, Indiana.

|       | **1** | **2**   | **3**   | **4** |
|-------|-------|---------|---------|-------|
| No. 3 | —     | $3,000  | $1,800  | $800  |

## Corbitt Company
*Henderson, North Carolina*

**Corbitt tractor**

Richard Corbitt organized the Corbitt Automobile Co. in 1913. Eventually the company began building motor trucks. When Corbitt retired in 1952 the company failed. During the 1956-57 period the company attempted a revival but it also failed. About 1948 the company came out with the Corbitt tractor. Their G-50 model used a gasoline engine,

the K-50 had a kerosene manifold, and the D-50 was a diesel model. All were of about 31 pto horsepower. The Corbitt tractors made a brief reappearance in the 1956-57 revival period.

## Corn Belt Motor Company
*Waterloo, Iowa*

**M&K Farm-Auto**

During 1915 the M & K Farm-Auto was developed and the company attempted raising the capital for full-scale production the following year. The M & K Farm-Auto was fully equipped with Hyatt roller bearings; this was a great advantage over many competitive models of the day with plain babbitt bearings. Rated as a 12-24 model, it used a four-cylinder engine having a 3-3/4 x 5 inch bore and stroke. Unfortunately, the fund-raising efforts failed and little more is known of the M & K Farm-Auto.

## Corn Belt Tractor Company
*Minneapolis, Minnesota*

Corn Belt announced this new tractor in 1914. Rated at 15 belt horsepower, it utilized a front-wheel-drive system. The engine, drivewheel and transmission were all a single unit. This permit-

**Corn Belt tractor**

**Power Horse four-wheel-drive**

ted the tractor to turn in a four-foot radius. Aside from its 1914 announcement, little else is known of the Corn Belt tractor.

## Craig Tractor Company
*Cleveland, Ohio*

**Craig Tractor Company logo**

Incorporated in 1918 for $35,000 the Craig Tractor Company remained in business until about 1922. Their 5,500 pound tractor was powered by a Beaver four-cylinder engine having a 4-3/4 x 6 inch bore and stroke. It sold for $2,385 in 1920. Apparently, Craig built only a single model rated at 15 drawbar and 25 belt horsepower.

## Crockett Bros.
*Stockton, California*

The January 10, 1952 issue of *Farm Implement News* advertises the Power Horse four-wheel-drive tractor from Crockett Brothers. Aside from this advertisement, little else is known of the company and their tractor manufacturing efforts.

See: Harris Mfg. Co.

## Crookston Mfg. Company
*Crookston, Minnesota*

For further information, see under C. O. D. Tractor Company.

## Crosley Motors
*Cincinnati, Ohio*

**Crosley Farm-O-Road combination vehicle**

During 1950 and 1951 Crosley marketed their Farm-O-Road combination vehicle. Ostensibly, it was a tractor, a truck, a mobile power plant and a road vehicle. Numerous farm implements were designed especially for the Farm-O-Road, with a front-mounted mower being shown here.

| | 1 | 2 | 3 | 4 |
|---|---|---|---|---|
| Farm-O-Road | — | $6,250 | — | — |

## Crown Iron Works
*Minneapolis, Minnesota*

This firm is listed as a tractor manufacturer in 1921, but no further information can be found.

## Cultiller Corporation
*New Brunswick, New Jersey*

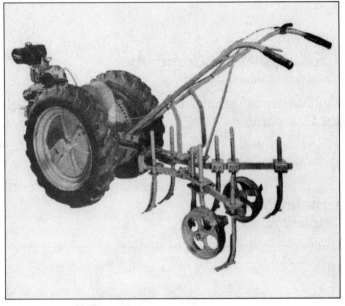

**Cultiller garden tractor**

The Cultiller garden tractor appeared in the late 1940s, probably about 1948. The company is listed in this business as late as 1953. Cultiller garden tractors were equipped with a Clinton single-cylinder engine. Various attachments were available.

## Cultitractor Company
*Minneapolis, Minnesota*

Although this firm was organized in 1918 as a tractor builder, nothing is known of its activities.

## Cultor or Continental Cultor Co.
*Springfield, Ohio*

Articulated motor cultivator using Model "T" engines 1918-1930.

## James Cunningham, Son & Company
*Rochester, New York*

**Cunningham garden tractor**

Organized in 1838, this company rose to be a major carriage builder, and in 1907 began building automobiles, continuing until 1931. Subsequently Cunningham experimented with aircraft and during World War Two was an important defense contractor. In 1947 the company began building a line of garden tractors, apparently continuing until 1955. Most of them used the company's own engines, although one or two models were equipped with Wisconsin air-cooled engines.

## Curtis Form-A-Tractor Company
*Chicago, Illinois*

About 1918 Curtis was offering this tractor attachment, pricing it at $350. This unusual design used leather straps that buckled to the rear wheels so that power could be transmitted to the drive wheels of the attachment. When it

**Curtis tractor attachment**

was desired to use the car on the road, the attachment was uncoupled. By 1920, there were over fifty different companies offering tractor attachments for use with automobiles.

# Curtis Motor Car Company
*Little Rock, Arkansas*

This company was in the automobile manufacturing business during 1920 and 1921. Apparently, the firm also had plans of entering the tractor business and was listed as a tractor manufacturer in 1921. It does not appear that the Curtis tractor manufacturing operation ever became more than a fine idea.

# Cushman Motor Works
*Lincoln, Nebraska*

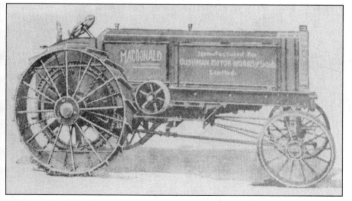

**Cushman 10-22**

About 1917 Cushman entered the farm tractor business in Canada. Initially they offered a 10-22 model, but this was re-rated upward to a 12-24 model in 1918. It was sold as the Macdonald tractor and was built expressly for Cushman. The 12-24 used a Beaver four-cylinder engine having a 4-3/4 x 6 inch bore and stroke. Total weight of the tractor was 5,900 pounds. The venture apparently ended by 1920.

# Custom Mfg. Company
*Shelbyville, Indiana*

**Custom Model C Tractor**

About 1947 the Custom Model C tractor appeared from Custom Mfg. Company. Production continued at Shelbyville into 1949. During the 1950-52 period the Custom was available from Harry A. Lowther Company at Shelbyville. Apparently the company then moved for a short time to Butler, Indiana. By 1953 the Custom Tractor Mfg. Co. appeared at Hustisford, Wisconsin. The Model C Custom tractor shown here was equipped with a Chrysler six-cylinder engine having a 3-1/4 x 4-3/8 inch bore and stroke.

## Custom Tractor Mfg. Company
*Hustisford, Wisconsin*

**Custom tractor**

Beginning in 1953 and continuing for at least a couple of years, the Custom tractor was offered in two sizes, the 96R and the 98R. Both sizes were available in row-crop or standard-tread designs.

The 96R was equipped with a Chrysler six-cylinder engine having a 3-1/4 x 4-5/8 inch bore and stroke, while the 98R used a six-cylinder Chrysler with a 3-7/16 x 4-1/2-inch bore and stroke. Both were equipped with a Gyrol fluid coupling ahead of the transmission.

See also: Custom Mfg. Company and Harry A. Lowther Company.

## Cuyahoga Tractor Sales Company
*Cleveland, Ohio*

This firm was organized and incorporated in 1917 to manufacture farm tractors. No additional information has been found.

# D

## Danielson Mfg. Company
*Independence, Missouri*

The Danielson trade name is listed in the 1919 *Power Wagon Reference Book*. No information has been located concerning this company or its tractors.

## Dart Truck & Tractor Corporation
*Waterloo, Iowa*

Wm. Galloway and C. W. Hellen bought out Dart Mfg. Co. of Anderson, Indiana in 1910 and moved the factory to Waterloo. During 1914 the company was reorganized as the Dart Motor Truck Company and in 1918 the name was changed to Dart Truck & Tractor Company. This continued until 1924 when the company was again reorganized as Hawkeye-Dart Truck Company at Waterloo. In 1925 the company was reorganized as Dart Truck Company and at that time moved to Kansas City, Missouri. Dart tractors were built in the 1918-21 period.

**Dart Blue J Line**

The first Dart tractors appeared in 1918. By 1920 the Dart Blue J line included two models. The 12-25 sold for $1,850 and the larger 15-30 model sold for $2,000. Both tractors used the same chassis and both used Buda four-cylinder engines. The 12-25 carried a 4-1/4 x 5-1/2 inch bore and stroke, while the 15-30 used a 4-1/2 x 6 inch bore and stroke.

## Dauch Mfg. Company
*Sandusky, Ohio*

**15-35 Sandusky tractor**

J. J. Dauch and others formed the Dauch Mfg. Co. in 1914. This was essentially a takeover of the Sandusky Auto Parts & Motor Truck Co. That same year the firm announced their 15-35 Sandusky tractor. It featured a Dauch-built four-cylinder engine with cylinders cast separately. The engine used a 5 x 6-1/2 inch bore and stroke. This model was also sold as the Sandusky Model E tractor.

**10-20 Sandusky tractor**

In January 1917 Dauch Mfg. Co. announced their 10-20 Sandusky tractor. Also sold as the Sandusky Model J, it used a four-cylinder Dauch-built engine having a 4-1/4 x 5 inch bore and stroke. Weighing about 4,900 pounds, this tractor was built into about 1920. By 1921 Dauch Mfg.

Company no longer appears in the tractor directories. The predecessor firm, Sandusky Auto Parts & Motor Truck Co. built various kinds of motor trucks in the 1911-14 period.

## Davis Gasoline Traction Engine Company
*Waterloo, Iowa*

Although this firm was a well established gas engine manufacturer by the mid-1890s, nothing is known of their activities in the 'gasoline traction engine' business. Given the size of the company it seems entirely logical that they may have attempted an entry into the business, but no information has surfaced concerning their activities.

## Dayton-Dick Company
*Quincy, Illinois*

This firm was organized in 1915 by the amalgamation of Leader Engine Co., Detroit, Michigan with the Dayton Foundry & Machine Co., and Hayton Pump Co., both of Quincy. Early in 1919 the company was reorganized as Dayton-Dowd Company. All production ceased by 1924.

**Dayton-Dick Leader tractor**

When Dayton-Dick was organized in 1915 they continued building the Leader tractor that had already been established for some time. The Leader was rated at 12 drawbar and 18 belt horsepower. It used a two-cylinder opposed engine. This tractor weighed about 5,000 pounds and listed at $890.

**Leader 12-18**

By 1917 the Leader 12-18 had been redesigned with a cellular radiator to replace the large cooling tank of the first model. By making this change it was possible to shorten the tractor frame considerably. Adding a partial hood over the engine served to improve the aesthetics. At this time the Leader line also included a 15-25 model, but it was only offered in 1917. Two examples of this model are known to exist; condition #1 value would be $20,000.

**Leader 25-40 tractor with crawler treads**

The 1917 Leader line also included a 25-40 tractor with crawler treads. This model carried a four-cylinder engine having a 6 x 7 inch bore and stroke and could pull about 4,000 pounds. This model remained in production until 1920, but by this time the company was known as Dayton-Dowd.

# Dayton-Dowd Company
*Quincy, Illinois*

**Leader 16-32**

Dayton-Dowd Co. was created in a 1919 reorganization of Dayton-Dick Co. Dayton-Dowd continued building Leader tractors until 1924. Shown here is the Leader 16-32 model that apparantly saw first light about 1920, and continued until all production ended four years later. The 16-32 was equipped with a Climax four-cylinder engine having a 5 x 6-1/2 inch bore and stroke. Weighing 5,000 pounds, the 16-32 sold for $1,725.

**Leader Model C25-40**

Production of the Leader Model C 25-40 tractor began in 1917 under the auspices of Dayton-Dick Company, and continued with Dayton-Dowd until 1920, when production was suspended. Apparently, this model was followed with the Leader GU-Series crawlers in 1920 or 1921.

**Leader GU 16-32**

With the end of the Model C 25-40 tractor in 1920 came the Leader GU 16-32 crawler tractor. By 1921, essentially the same tractor was re-rated upward as an 18-35 model. The GU crawler used the same Climax engine as used in the 16-32 wheel-type tractor previously noted. Weighing 7,500 pounds, this tractor was priced at $2,150. Production of this model apparently ended in 1923.

# Decker Machine & Tractor Company
*Chicago, Illinois*

A trade note in the *American Machinist* indicates that this firm was incorporated at Chicago in 1917. Aside from that, no further information has been found on the company.

# Deere & Company
*Moline, Illinois*

Numerous books have been published relating to the origins of Deere & Company. John Deere came to Grand Detour, Illinois in 1836, and the following year built the first steel plow. Eventually Deere moved to Moline, Illinois where the company's main offices and numerous manufacturing facilities are located.

By about 1910 Deere & Co. was looking at various tractor designs and engaged some of their engineers in development of a lightweight design. Progress was slow and finally in March 1918 the company bought out the Waterloo Gasoline Engine Company for $2.1 million. The venerable Waterloo Boy tractor thus came into the John Deere line and from it came a steady progression of tractors into the present day.

**Melvin tractor**

Deere & Company began serious tractor experiments in 1912 with the Melvin tractor. It was designed by C. H. Melvin, a company engineer. The Melvin closely followed the design of the Hackney tractor. Only a single tractor was built, since the company was not satisfied with the design.

**John Deere Dain tractor**

The John Deere Dain tractor began emerging in 1914. Joseph Dain had founded the Dain Mfg. Company at Ottumwa, Iowa. Deere bought out the company and Joe Dain became a design engineer. After several experimental models, the company built a hundred of the Dain tractors for general distribution in 1919. However, the death of Joe Dain brought the venture to an end.

**B-2 tractor**

During 1915 and 1916 Max Sklovsky designed a new tractor that carried the entire machine in a single frame casting. Mr. Sklovsky is shown here on the seat of a B-2 tractor; it was equipped with a four-cylinder Northway engine. World War One then intervened, experiments on the design were abandoned and were never resumed.

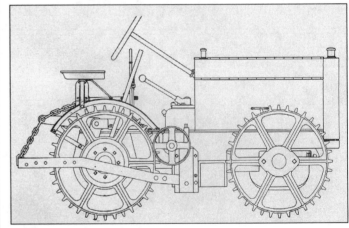

**Silver motor cultivator**

The Silver motor cultivator was an experiment running from 1916 to 1921. During this time Walter Silver came up with several unique designs, but none of them ever attained production status.

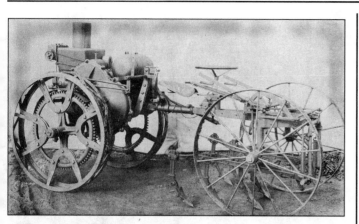

**Walter Silver motor cultivator**

Apparently Deere & Company had some plans of marketing the Walter Silver motor cultivator design, going so far as to apply for a trademark application in July 1917. The new model was to be called the Tractivator and the company claimed first use of the term in June 1917. However, the Tractivator never materialized.

**Model R Waterloo Boy tractor**

Deere & Company finally got into the tractor business with their 1918 buyout of Waterloo Gasoline Engine Company, Waterloo, Iowa. The latter had begun building the Model R Waterloo Boy tractor already in 1914, and it had gained considerable attention in the tractor industry. The Model R was equipped with a two-cylinder engine having a 5-1/2 x 7 inch bore and stroke, but by 1915 the cylinder bore was increased to 6 inches. Deere closed out the Model R in 1918, but by this time the engine bore was raised to 6-1/2 inches. The Waterloo Boy Type R had a single forward speed.

| | **1** | **2** | **3** | **4** |
|---|---|---|---|---|
| Waterloo Boy, R | $35,000 | $28,000 | $20,000 | $10,000 |

**Waterloo Boy Type N tractor**

Waterloo Gasoline Engine Company developed the Waterloo Boy Type N tractor, first building it in 1917. This refined version of the Type R had two forward speeds, but used essentially the same engine. It was of two-cylinder design, using a 6 x 7 inch bore and stroke. When the Nebraska Tractor Tests began in 1920, the Waterloo Boy was the very first tractor to be tested. Production of the Type N continued into 1924.

| | **1** | **2** | **3** | **4** |
|---|---|---|---|---|
| Waterloo Boy, N | $35,000 | $28,000 | $18,000 | $10,000 |
| Waterloo Boy, L & LA | $30,000 | $25,000 | $20,000 | $8,000 |

**Model D**

John Deere Tractor Company released its first version of the venerable Model D in 1923. Initially, this tractor was known as the 15-27. It featured a two-cylinder engine having a 6-1/2 x 7 inch engine rated at 800 rpm. The tractors built up to 1926 used a spoke flywheel but a solid flywheel was used after that time. This model had a two-speed transmission.

**Model D 15-27**

For 1927 John Deere modified and improved the Model D, 15-27 tractor. The power level was raised by increasing the cylinder bore to 6 -3/4 inches but the rated speed remained at 800 rpm. This change alone boosted the maximum belt horsepower by about 7 horses to an output of 36.98. At this time the Model D was also redesigned to use a splined flywheel and crankshaft, compared to the keyed shaft formerly used. Production of this model continued into 1930. During the 1927-1940 period Deere also built a Model DI Industrial tractor.

**Model D 1930-34**

Until 1931 the John Deere D had the steering wheel on the left side, but at that time it was moved to the right side. Also in 1931, the governed speed was raised from 800 to 900 rpm. Various changes along the way brought the net operating weight of the Model D to 4,878 pounds. Electric lights were available as an extra-cost option.

**Model D 1935-38**

A major improvement to the John Deere Model D came in 1935 when it was equipped with a three-speed transmission. Other minor changes took place, but this one stood out above all others. By this time the Model D had a rated brake load of about 37-1/2 horsepower, meaning that it was capable of delivering this load hour-after-hour and day-after-day. At this point the Model D was essentially in its final form from a mechanical viewpoint.

**Model D 1939-53**

In 1939 the John Deere was given a styled hood mainly so that it would conform to the other styled models in the tractor line. By this time rubber tires had become the preferred choice for most farmers, and in addition, electric starting and lighting became optional equipment. When production finally ended in 1953, the John Deere Model D had achieved the longest production run of any tractor in history.

|  | 1 | 2 | 3 | 4 |
|---|---|---|---|---|
| D/15-27 spoked flywheel | | | | |
| 26" | $14,000 | $10,000 | $6,000 | $3,000 |
| 24" | $12,000 | $7,000 | $5,000 | $2,500 |
| D/15-27 solid flywheel | | | | |
| | $5,000 | $3,500 | $1,800 | $800 |

"Nickel Hole" (small flywheel holes) "D" add $1,000

| Model D 1931-34 | | | | |
|---|---|---|---|---|
| | $4,500 | $3,000 | $1,800 | $800 |
| Model D 1935-38 | | | | |
| | $4,500 | $3,500 | $1,800 | $800 |
| Model D 1939-53 | | | | |
| | $4,500 | $3,500 | $1,800 | $500 |

**GP ("General Purpose") tractor**

The GP tractor from 1930 to 1935 used an engine with a 6-inch bore and stroke. It also had a governed speed of 950 rpm. This gave the GP about 25-1/2 belt horsepower. The "GP" stood for "General Purpose" and in fact, the GP could be equipped with numerous implements specially designed for use with this tractor.

**10-20 John Deere (Model GP)**

The 10-20 John Deere, also known as the Model GP, made its debut in 1928. Its immediate predecessor was the Model C tractor which was built in relatively small numbers during 1927. Between 1928 and 1930 the GP was built with a two-cylinder engine having a 5-3/4 x 6 inch bore and stroke. It was rated at 900 rpm. This tractor was capable of almost 25 belt horsepower.

**John Deer GPO**

During the 1931-1935 period, the John Deere GP was also available as a special orchard tractor; this model was designated as the GPO. Its low profile design was further enhanced by the use of special fenders, plus the air intake and exhaust stacks were relocated to permit working under low branches.

**GP Wide-Tread**

The GP Wide-Tread was the first John Deere row-crop tractor. Its engine was the same as the GP Standard-Tread model. During 1932 the Wide-Tread was given a tapered hood for better visibility. Another advantage of this model was the power lift system that quickly became the idea to copy, and various kinds of power lifts soon appeared on almost all row-crop tractors. For model GP specimens with slant plug head add $1,000 to value.

|  | 1 | 2 | 3 | 4 |
|---|---|---|---|---|
| Model GP/Standard-Tread | $5,000 | $3,500 | $2,000 | $1,000 |
| Model GP/Widetread | $10,000 | $7,500 | $5,000 | $2,000 |
| Model GPO | $6,000 | $4,500 | $3,000 | $1,500 |

John Deere Model A tractors made their first appearance in 1934. It was tested at Nebraska's Tractor Test Laboratory in April 1934. In Test No. 222 it revealed a rated belt output of 23-1/2

**John Deer Model A 1934-38**

horsepower. The Model A was among the first to offer an adjustable width wheel tread. Various changes took place in the Model A during its long production run.

**Model A 1938-40**

In 1938 the Model A took on a stylized hood and grille. The Model A tractors built until 1941 used an engine having a 5-1/2 x 6-1/2 inch bore and stroke. It had a governed speed of 975 rpm. An important feature of the Model A was the use of differential brakes geared directly to the bull gears.

**John Deere Model A 1941-47**

In the 1947-1951 period, John Deere Model A tractors were modified to include electric starting, plus a pressed steel frame that was somewhat different from previous models. Already in 1941 the styled John Deere A was given a slight power boost by raising the piston stroke from 6-1/2 to 6-3/4 inches. By the time production

ended in 1951 the John Deere Model A had become the most popular model in the history of the company.

| | 1 | 2 | 3 | 4 |
|---|---|---|---|---|
| Model A | $3,000 | $2,000 | $1,000 | $500 |
| Open fanshaft A | $5,000 | $4,000 | $2,000 | $1,500 |

**John Deere Model AN row-crop**

Following the same production period as the regular row-crop models, the AN and BN tractors differed only in their front wheel design; in this instance a single front wheel was used. This design was especially useful where narrow rows were used. The AN and BN were of the same general appearance; a 1938 example is shown here.

**John Deere BN**

Shown here is a 1951 model of the John Deere BN tractor, with the Model AN being similar. These models used a longer rear axle shaft to provide a wider wheel tread, and also provided greater clearance than the regular row-crop model.

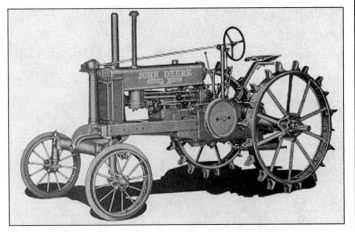

**Model AW**

The AW and BW tractors featured an adjustable front axle width, as well as extra-long rear axles. These tractors were designed especially for bedded crops where it was essential to plant and cultivate without splitting the center. Both models were of the same general appearance and both had production runs approximating that of their row-crop counterparts.

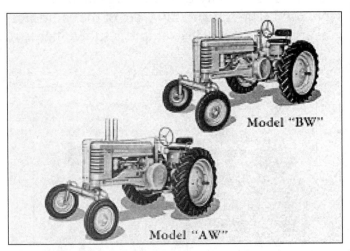

**AW & BW tractor**

A 1951 advertisement of the AW and BW tractors notes, "Except for the front-end assemblies, the 'AW' and 'BW' [tractors] are identical to the single front-wheel type…" Deere also offered a wide variety of integral equipment for both the "N" and "W" models.

**Model AH Hi-Crop model**

During 1951 and 1952 Deere offered the Model AH Hi-Crop model. It was essentially the same tractor as the Model A Row-Crop, but was modified to permit over 32 inches of ground clearance, as well as 48 inches between the axle housings. In the 1951-1953 period Deere offered the Model GH Hi-Crop model. It had the same general appearance but was a modification of the John Deere Model G row-crop tractor.

|  | **1** | **2** | **3** | **4** |
|---|---|---|---|---|
| AH Hi-Crop | $10,000 | — | — | — |

For High Clearance models with 42-inch rear tires add $1,000.

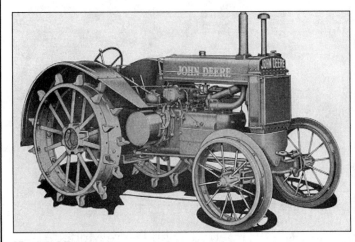

**Model AR tractor**

In the 1935-1940 period Deere offered the unstyled Model AR tractor shown here. This was a standard-tread version of the Model A row-crop tractor. Like the row-crop, it used an engine with a 5-1/2 x 6-1/2 inch bore and stroke until

1941. At that time the Model A tractors were redesigned with a 6-3/4 inch stroke while the bore remained the same.

| | 1 | 2 | 3 | 4 |
|---|---|---|---|---|
| AR unstyled | | | | |
| | $4,500 | $3,000 | $2,000 | $1,000 |

**Model AR styled**

In the 1941-52 period Deere offered the Model AR in a styled version. During this time the AR underwent several changes, although the basic tractor design remained the same. By the time production ended, the AR was equipped with a six-speed transmission and electric starting.

| | 1 | 2 | 3 | 4 |
|---|---|---|---|---|
| AR styled | $4,500 | $3,000 | $2,000 | $1,000 |

with water pump add $500.

**Model AI Industrial tractor**

Model AI Industrial tractors were available in the 1936-1941 period. This style was built with a four-speed transmission and included electric lighting as standard equipment. The AI weighed 4,680 pounds and had a turning radius of 11-1/2 feet.

John Deere Model AO orchard tractors were first built in 1935. The following year the design was streamlined, as shown here. This was essentially an AR standard-tread tractor equipped with special grille, hood and fenders. In addition there were numerous changes to the intake and exhaust stacks, steering wheel and seat location and other modifications.

| | 1 | 2 | 3 | 4 |
|---|---|---|---|---|
| Model AO | $5,000 | $3,100 | $2,000 | $800 |
| Model AO Streamlined | | | | |
| | $10,000 | $7,500 | $4,500 | $1,500 |

**John Deere Model AO orchard tractor AO streamlined**

**1951 Model AO**

In 1940 the Model AR was modified to include the added quarter-inch to the original piston stroke of 6-1/2 inches. Aside from that, its design closely followed that of the concurrent Model A tractor line. This example of 1951 shows the styled hood; this model was equipped with electric starting as standard equipment.

**1938 Model B**

During 1938 the Model B was modified with a longer frame and also during that year was given a stylized hood and grille. It also gained a higher power level with its 4-1/2 x 5-1/2 inch engine. At its rated load, the Model B was thus capable of about 17 horsepower.

**John Deere Model B**

Production of the John Deere Model B began in 1935. The original design with a shorter frame continued until 1937. Model B tractors built into 1938 used a two-cylinder engine having a 4-1/4 x 5-1/4 inch bore and stroke. Like the Model A, it was equipped with a pto shaft and could also be furnished with a hydraulic power lift system for integral equipment.

|  | 1 | 2 | 3 | 4 |
|---|---|---|---|---|
| Model B 1935-37 | $3,500 | $2,500 | $1,500 | $1,000 |
| 4-Bolt front end | $7,000 | — | — | — |

**1941 Model B**

When equipped with rubber tires, the Model B of 1941 was equipped with a road gear of 12 -1/2 mph. This resulted from the new six-speed transmission installed at that time. Engine dimensions remained the same. Model B tractors were extremely popular on small farms as well as an all-around "go-fer" on larger farms.

During 1947 the Model B was once again modified. The most obvious difference was the use of a pressed steel frame. However, the engine was also modified to include a bore of 4-11/16 x 5-1/2 inches. This tweaked the power level slightly, and along with a higher rated speed of

**1947 Model B**

1,250 rpm, the Model B was now rated for a belt load of nearly 25-1/2 belt horsepower. Production of the Model B ended in 1952. The John Deere BN and BW models in the 1935-1940 period are quite similar in appearance to the AN and AW models previously noted.

| | 1 | 2 | 3 | 4 |
|---|---|---|---|---|
| Model B 1938-52 | | | | |
| | $3,500 | $2,300 | $1,100 | $1,000 |

**John Deere model BR**

John Deere Model BR tractors were a standard-tread version of the Model B row-crop models. Design changes, such as the 1938 changeover from a 4-1/4 to a 4-1/2 inch engine, were generally the same as for other models of the B tractor. The four forward speeds ranged from 2 to 6-1/4 mph.

**Model BR**

Model BR tractors gained a larger 4-1/2 inch engine in 1938, as did the rest of the Model B tractor series. Although this model is shown on steel wheels, rubber tires were optionally available. Production of the Model BR tractors ended in 1947.

| | 1 | 2 | 3 | 4 |
|---|---|---|---|---|
| Model BR | $6,500 | $4,500 | $3,800 | $1,500 |

**Model BI**

In the 1936-1941 period, John Deere offered a Model BI Industrial version of the Model B tractor series. It was essentially the same tractor as the Model BR standard-tread, but was suitably modified for use in factories and other industrial applications.

| | 1 | 2 | 3 | 4 |
|---|---|---|---|---|
| Model BI | $8,000 | $6,000 | $3,000 | $1,500 |

**Model BO Orchard tractor**

Production of the Model BO Orchard tractor commenced in 1935 and ended in 1947. This model was essentially the same as the Model BR standard-tread tractor, but was equipped with special fenders and other amenities required for use in orchards and groves.

|  | 1 | 2 | 3 | 4 |
|---|---|---|---|---|
| Model BO | $8,000 | $6,500 | $4,500 | $2,000 |

**John Deere Lindemann crawler**

Between 1939 and 1947 the Lindemann crawler conversion was used with the Model BO tractor chassis. Lindemann Bros. at Yakima, Washington mounted these units on their crawler tracks, with the result being the John Deere-Lindemann crawlers.

|  | 1 | 2 | 3 | 4 |
|---|---|---|---|---|
| Model BO/Lindeman Crawler | $10,000 | $7,500 | $4,000 | $2,000 |

**John Deere Model G**

In November 1937 the John Deere Model G appeared. It was the largest row-crop tractor in the line and was capable of about 34 belt horsepower. The Model G used a two-cylinder engine having a 6-1/8 x 7 inch bore and stroke. Rated speed was 975 rpm. In 1941 the Model G was given a six-speed transmission, with numerous other options being available.

**Model G**

Capable of nearly 40 belt horsepower, the Model G was a full three-plow tractor. By 1947 electric starting was available and this was important for the big two-cylinder engine, especially in cold weather. The Model G was also built in a high clearance design known as the GH Hi-Crop.

|  | 1 | 2 | 3 | 4 |
|---|---|---|---|---|
| Model G (high radiator) | $5,000 | $4,000 | $2,500 | $1,000 |
| (low radiator) | $6,000 | $4,500 | $3,000 | $1,500 |

Introduced in 1939, the Model H tractor was built until 1947. This small two-cylinder model had a maximum output of about 14 belt horsepower. Rated at 1400 rpm, the two-cylinder engine had a 3-9/16 x 5 inch bore and stroke. Operating in road gear, the engine speed could be raised to 1800 rpm for a maximum road speed of 7-1/2 mph.

|  | 1 | 2 | 3 | 4 |
|---|---|---|---|---|
| Model H | $3,500 | $2,500 | $1,800 | $800 |

**Model HN tractor**

Production of the Model HN tractor ran from 1939 to 1947. This small tractor with the single front tire was ideal for crops planted in narrow rows. In addition, Deere built the HWH and HNH special high clearance models in 1941 and 1942.

**Model H tractor**

**Model L**

The first John Deere utility tractor was the Model L, introduced in 1937 and built until 1946. Weighing only 2,200 pounds, the L was equipped with a two-cylinder vertical engine designed by Deere and built by Hercules. It was rated at 1,480 rpm and used a 3-1/4 x 4 inch bore and stroke. This tractor was capable of nearly 10 belt horsepower.

|   | **1** | **2** | **3** | **4** |
|---|---|---|---|---|
| Model L | $5,000 | $4,500 | $2,500 | $1,200 |

(subtract $400 if missing belt pully assembly)

**Model LA tractor**

Deere introduced the Model LA tractor in 1940. This model featured the company's own two-cylinder vertical engine with a 3-1/2 x 4 inch bore and stroke. Operating at a rated speed of 1,850 rpm, this model displayed a maximum of almost

14-1/2 belt horsepower. Production of the Model LA ended in 1946. Deere also built the Model LI Industrial version in the 1938-46 period.

|   | **1** | **2** | **3** | **4** |
|---|---|---|---|---|
| Model LA | $4,000 | $3,000 | $2,000 | $800 |

(subtract $400 if missing belt pully assembly)

**Model M tractor**

In October 1947 Deere & Company sent one of their new Model M tractors to the Tractor Test Laboratory in Lincoln, Nebraska. In Test No. 387 it demonstrated a maximum of nearly 20 belt horsepower. The Model M was equipped with a two-cylinder vertical engine having a 4-inch bore and stroke. It was rated at 1,650 rpm. Production of the Model M ended in 1952.

|   | **1** | **2** | **3** | **4** |
|---|---|---|---|---|
| Model M | $5,000 | $3,500 | $2,000 | $500 |

**Model MT tractor**

Production of the Model MT John Deere tractor ran from 1949 to 1952. It was essentially the same tractor as the Model M, but was of the tricycle chassis design. Despite its small size this tractor could pull over 1,100 pounds at its rated load. The M and MT tractors were built at Deere's Dubuque (Iowa) Works.

|  | 1 | 2 | 3 | 4 |
|---|---|---|---|---|
| Model MT | $4,000 | $3,000 | $2,000 | $500 |

**Model MC crawler**

Using the same engine as the Model M and Model MT tractors, the MC crawler model had a displacement of 101ci. Weighing 4,000 pounds, it could pull over 1,800 pounds on the drawbar. The MC used three track rollers, and offered four forward speeds ranging from 0.8 to 4.7 mph. Model MC crawlers were built from 1949 to 1952.

|  | 1 | 2 | 3 | 4 |
|---|---|---|---|---|
| Model MC Crawler | $9,000 | $7,000 | $4,000 | $2,000 |

**Model R tractor**

In 1949 John Deere introduced their first diesel tractor, the Model R. This big two-cylinder model used a two-cylinder engine having a 5 -3/4 x 8 inch bore and stroke, with a rated speed of 1,000 rpm. The main engine had a displacement of 416 ci and was designed with a 16 to 1 compression ratio. A two-cylinder gasoline engine was used for starting. At maximum load the Model R could develop approximately 48-1/2 belt horse-power. It weighed nearly 7,400 pounds. Production of the Model R ended in 1952.

|  | 1 | 2 | 3 | 4 |
|---|---|---|---|---|
| Model R | $5,500 | $3,000 | $2,000 | $800 |

**John Deere 40 row-crop**

The John Deere 40 was a continuation of the new numbered series that had been introduced with the 50 and 60 tractors in 1952. The 40 row-crop model shown here had a two-cylinder vertical engine with a 4-inch bore and stroke. Although this model had a bare weight of only 3,200 pounds, it was capable of over 17 drawbar horse-power. Production of the 40 row-crop ran from 1953 to 1956.

A three-point hitch was standard equipment for the John Deere Model 40 tractors. Rated at 1,850 rpm, the 40 tractors could pull two plow bottoms in most soils. Extra equipment included a belt pulley, electric lights and pto shaft.

|  | 1 | 2 | 3 | 4 |
|---|---|---|---|---|
| Model 40 Special | $10,000 | $7,500 | $4,500 | $2,000 |
| Model 40 Standard | $5,000 | $3,500 | $2,000 | $1,000 |

**John Deere Model 40**

| Model 40 Utility | | | |
|---|---|---|---|
| $5,000 | $3,500 | $2,000 | $1,000 |

| Model 40 Hi-Crop | | | |
|---|---|---|---|
| $10,000 | $7,500 | $4,500 | $2,000 |

| Model 40 Tricycle | | | |
|---|---|---|---|
| $4,000 | $3,000 | $2,000 | $500 |

| Model 40 Two-Row Utility | | | |
|---|---|---|---|
| $5,000 | $3,500 | $2,000 | $1,000 |

**Model 40-C crawler**

Like other 40-series tractors, the 40-C crawler was built in the 1953-1956 period. It also used the same 101 ci engine that was capable of over 23-1/2 belt

horsepower. Model 40-C crawlers could be furnished with either a four-roller or a five-roller undercarriage, the latter being optional; four rollers were standard.

| | 1 | 2 | 3 | 4 |
|---|---|---|---|---|
| Model 40C Crawler | $9,000 | $7,000 | $3,500 | $1,500 |

**John Deere 50**

In 1952 the end was at hand for the "letter series" tractors, with the new 'number series' models taking their place. The first of these was the John Deere 50. It was available in various styles, although the conventional row-crop design was the most popular. The 50 was designed around a two-cylinder engine having a 4-11/16 x 5-1/2 inch bore and stroke. Rated at 1,250 rpm, it was rated at nearly 21 drawbar horsepower. Production of the John Deere 50 ended in 1956. During 1955 and 1956 this model was also available with an LP gas option.

| | 1 | 2 | 3 | 4 |
|---|---|---|---|---|
| Model 50 | $3,500 | $2,500 | $1,500 | $750 |

The John Deere 60 was built in the 1952-1956 period. Weighing 5,300 pounds, it was powered by a two-cylinder engine having a 5-1/2 x 6-3/4 inch bore and stroke. The engine had a displace-

**John Deere 60 row-crop**

ment of 321 ci and was rated at 975 rpm. This model had a maximum output of approximately 38-1/2 belt horsepower. The 60 was built in numerous axle configurations.

| | 1 | 2 | 3 | 4 |
|---|---|---|---|---|
| Model 60 | $3,000 | $2,000 | $1,000 | $500 |

Two varieties of the 60 Standard were built in the 1952-1956 period. Until 1954 the "low-seat" style was built and during 1955 and 1956 the "high-seat" style was built. Except for this change, the design remained basically unchanged. The standard-tread style was built especially for those whose farming operations required this kind of chassis as compared to the row-crop tractor. Deere also built a 60 Orchard tractor during the same 1952-1956 period.

| | 1 | 2 | 3 | 4 |
|---|---|---|---|---|
| High seat 60 standard | $3,000 | $2,000 | $1,000 | $500 |
| Low seat 60 standard | $4,800 | $3,400 | $2,000 | $1,000 |

Production of the John Deere 70 began in 1953 and continued until 1956. Rated at 975 rpm, the two-cylinder engine had a 5-7/8 x 7 inch bore and stroke. It had a maximum output of about 46

**Model 60 Standard**

**John Deere 70 row-crop**

**Model 70 Standard LP**

belt horsepower. John Deere 70 row-crop tractors were available in various configurations, including a special Hi-Crop model.

|  | **1** | **2** | **3** | **4** |
|---|---|---|---|---|
| Model 70 | $4,000 | $3,000 | $2,000 | $1,000 |

Built during the same 1953-1956 production period as the 70 Row-Crop style, the 70 Standard was likewise available for burning LP gas, as shown here. Model 70 tractors were also built in an All-Fuel version for burning low-grade fuels. In

this instance they were bored out to 6-1/8 inches, while the 7-inch stroke remained the same. This model had a shipping weight of 6,815 pounds.

|  | **1** | **2** | **3** | **4** |
|---|---|---|---|---|
| Model 70 All-Fuel | $5,000 | $4,000 | $3,000 | $1,500 |

Deere's first row-crop diesel came to the market in 1954. The 70 Diesel was built in the standard-tread design shown here, and was also available as a conventional row-crop tractor. This model used a two-cylinder engine with a 6-1/8 x

**John Deere 70 Diesel**

6-3/8 inch bore and stroke, with a rated speed of 1,125 rpm. Starting was by a Deere-built V-4 gasoline starting engine; the latter was equipped with an electric starter. When tested at Nebraska in 1954 (Test No. 528) the 70 Diesel set a new fuel economy record that stood for a number of years. This tractor was capable of over 50 belt horsepower.

| | 1 | 2 | 3 | 4 |
|---|---|---|---|---|
| Model 70 Diesel | $4,000 | $3,000 | $2,000 | $1,000 |

**John Deere 80**

Built only during 1955 and 1956, the John Deere 80 was the largest of the line at the time. Weighing 8,500 pounds, the 80 Diesel had a displacement of 471.5ci from its big two cylinder engine. It used a 6-1/8 x 8 inch bore and stroke. This tractor was capable of over 65 belt horsepower, as well as 46-plus horses at the drawbar.

| | 1 | 2 | 3 | 4 |
|---|---|---|---|---|
| Model 80 | $6,500 | $5,000 | $3,000 | $1,300 |

Introduced in 1956, the Model 320 was equipped with the same two-cylinder vertical, 4 x 4 engine as numerous of its predecessors, such as the Model M. In this instance, the engine was

**Model 320**

rated at 1650 rpm. It was rated at about 21 horsepower. The 320 was built in several chassis configurations.

| | 1 | 2 | 3 | 4 |
|---|---|---|---|---|
| Model 320 | $10,000 | $7,500 | $4,500 | $1,500 |

**Model 420-S standard-tread**

Several styles of the 420 tractor were built beginning in 1956 and continuing into 1958. The 420-S standard-tread model is shown here; it weighed 2,850 pounds. These tractors were equipped with a 4-1/4 x 4 inch two-cylinder vertical engine rated at 1,850 rpm. It was capable of 26 drawbar and 28 belt horsepower.

| | 1 | 2 | 3 | 4 |
|---|---|---|---|---|
| Model 420 | $6,000 | $4,000 | $2,000 | $1,000 |

**Model 520**

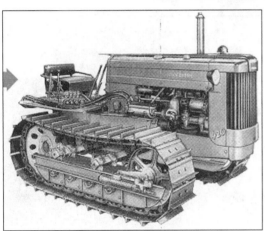

**Model 420-C crawler**

**Model 420-W**

Weighing slightly over 5,000 pounds, the 420-C crawler was offered in the 1956-1958 period. This tractor had the same two-cylinder 4-1/4 x 4 engine as other models in the 420 series. In testing, the 420-C demonstrated a maximum drawbar pull of over 4,800 pounds, although its rated pull was only 2,400 pounds.

|  | 1 | 2 | 3 | 4 |
|---|---|---|---|---|
| Model 420C Crawler | | | | |
|  | $7,000 | $5,000 | $3,000 | $1,500 |

Like others of the 420 series, the 420-W shown here was built at Deere's Dubuque (Iowa) Works. This model had an adjustable width front axle, as well as adjustable rear wheel treads. Production of all 420 models ended in 1958. The 420-W had the same general specifications as others of the 420 series.

Many new features were included on the "20" series tractors. An entirely new combustion chamber was featured on the gasoline and LP-gas models. This Model 520 is shown with the LP-gas option. The two-cylinder engine carried a 4-11/16 x 5-1/2 inch bore and stroke. The propane version used a compression ratio of 8.75 to 1, slightly higher than the gasoline model. This model was capable of about 38 belt horsepower. Production of the 520 tractors ran from 1956 to 1958.

|  | 1 | 2 | 3 | 4 |
|---|---|---|---|---|
| Model 520 | $5,000 | $3,500 | $2,000 | $1,000 |

**Model 720 row-crop**

live pto shaft. The 720 was capable of over 59 belt horsepower and could deliver over 53 horses at the drawbar. Model 720 tractors were available in gasoline, all-fuel and LP-gas models.

|  | 1 | 2 | 3 | 4 |
|---|---|---|---|---|
| Model 720 | $4,500 | $3,000 | $1,500 | $800 |

**John Deere 620 Standard**

John Deere 620 tractors were available in row-crop, standard-tread, orchard and Hi-Crop models. Except for the wheel configuration, all were essentially the same, with the 620 Standard being shown here. The 620 used a 5-1/2 x 6-3/8 inch two-cylinder engine; it was rated at 1,125 rpm. This gave a rated output of nearly 50 belt horsepower. Production of the 620 ran from 1956 to 1958.

|  | 1 | 2 | 3 | 4 |
|---|---|---|---|---|
| Model 620 | $4,500 | $3,000 | $1,500 | $800 |

**Model 720 Diesel**

Built in the same 1956-1958 period as the other "20" series tractors, the 720 was Deere's largest row-crop tractor of the period. Like others of this series, the 720 featured an independent

The 720 Diesel, like the gasoline models, was built in row-crop and standard-tread designs, with the latter being shown here. This tractor carried a two-cylinder engine with a 6-1/8 x 6-3/8 inch bore and stroke. Starting was by a V-type four-cylinder engine having a 2 x 1-1/2 inch bore and stroke. Production began in 1956 and ended in 1958.

**John Deere 820 Diesel**

The big John Deere 820 Diesel had a displacement of over 471ci. This resulted from the two cylinder with a 6-1/8 x 8 inch bore and stroke. Rated speed was 1,125 rpm. Under maximum load, the 820 Diesel could deliver nearly 73 belt horsepower. Like the 720 Diesel, this model also used a V-type four-cylinder starting engine. Production ran from 1956 to 1958.

| | 1 | 2 | 3 | 4 |
|---|---|---|---|---|
| Model 820 (2 cylinder) | | | | |
| | $6,000 | $4,000 | $3,000 | $800 |

**Model 330**

The "30" series tractors were essentially the same as the "20" series tractors except for a modified styling. The little 330 shown here was built either as a Standard or as a Utility tractor. Weighing 2,750 pounds it used a two-cylinder 4 x 4 inch engine with a displacement of 100.5 cubic inches. Production of the 330, like other "30" series tractors ran from 1958 to 1960.

| | 1 | 2 | 3 | 4 |
|---|---|---|---|---|
| Model 330 | $15,000 | $10,000 | $5000 | $15,000 |

**John Deere 430**

The John Deere 430 was built in several different configurations, with the 430 Standard being shown here. The 430 tractors used a two-cylinder, 4-1/4 x 4 inch engine rated at 1,850 rpm. Weighing 3,000 pounds, it was capable of about 27 drawbar horsepower.

| | 1 | 2 | 3 | 4 |
|---|---|---|---|---|
| Model 430 | $8,000 | $6,000 | $4,000 | $1,500 |

**Model 435 Diesel**

Built in the 1958-1960 period, the 435 Diesel was unique in that it used a General Motors two-cylinder diesel engine, vis-à-vis an engine built by Deere & Company. The GM engine was of two-cycle design and used a 3-7/8 x 4-1/2 inch bore and stroke. This engine used a compression ratio of 17 to 1. This tractor had a rated output of nearly 33 pto horsepower.

| | 1 | 2 | 3 | 4 |
|---|---|---|---|---|
| Model 435 | $8,000 | $6,000 | $3,000 | $1,500 |

**John Deere Model 530**

The 530 was a popular John Deere model. Rated at about 39 belt horsepower, it was widely used on smaller farms and also found a place on larger farms. The independent pto shaft was an important feature, and the power-adjustable rear wheels were a popular option. Production of the 530 ran from 1958 to 1960.

| 1 | 2 | 3 | 4 |
|---|---|---|---|
| Model 530 | $7,500 | $5,000 | $3,000 | $1,500 |

**LP-gas 630 Hi-Crop model**

Numerous designs were available in the 630 series, including this LP-gas 630 Hi-Crop model. Although the "30" series tractors included many modern features, they also retained much of the popular design developed in the 1930s, including the hand clutch and the cross-mounted two-cylinder engine. The 630 tractors were capable of nearly 49 belt horsepower.

| 1 | 2 | 3 | 4 |
|---|---|---|---|
| Model 630 | $7,000 | $4,500 | $2,500 | $1,500 |

**John Deere 730 standard-tread tractor**

The John Deere 730 tractors were built in row-crop, Hi-Crop and standard-tread designs. Shown here is a 730 standard-tread tractor equipped for burning LP-gas for fuel. The 730 tractor could also be supplied for burning gasoline or tractor fuel; the latter was known as Deere's All-Fuel engine. Production ran from 1958 to 1960.

| 1 | 2 | 3 | 4 |
|---|---|---|---|
| Model 730 | $7,000 | $4,500 | $2,500 | $1,500 |

**John Deere 730 Diesel Standard model**

While the John Deere 720 Diesel was available only with a gasoline starting engine, the 730 Diesel could optionally be furnished with electric starting. The 730 Diesel Standard model shown here weighed in at 7,800 pounds. It was capable of almost 54 horsepower on the drawbar. Production began in 1958 and ended in 1960.

**John Deere 830 tractor**

John Deere 830 tractors were, like the earlier 820, built only in a standard-tread design. This big tractor used a 24-volt electrical system; this was required to roll over the 471 cubic inch, two-cylinder engine. Production ran from 1958 to 1960. By this time the two-cylinder design had run its course and in 1960 Deere & Company launched a new series of four-cylinder tractors.

|  | **1** | **2** | **3** | **4** |
|---|---|---|---|---|
| Model 830 (2 cylinder) | | | | |
| | $6,500 | $5,000 | $3,000 | $1,500 |
| Model 430C Crawler | | | | |
| | $10,000 | $7,000 | $4,000 | $2,000 |
| Model 8010 | $25,000 | $20,000 | $10,000 | $3,000 |

When evaluating various John Deere models the following features add to the value of tractors on which they are found:

Round-top fenders:   $1,000

Clams:   $300+

Deluxe flat tops with lights and brackets:   $700+

Complete 3-point:   $1,000

Round tube wide front:   $800+

Square tube wide front:   $1,100+

Round-spoke rubber, front and rear:   $2,000

# Wm. Deering & Company
*Chicago, Illinois*

**Wm. Deering & Company prototype**

In 1902 Wm. Deering & Company, McCormick Harvesting Machine Company and others merged to form International Harvester Company. Indications are that Deering had begun gas engine experiments as early as 1891 and by late in the decade the company built an engine-powered mowing machine. Although it gained considerable attention at the time, it never got past a few prototypes and few details of the design have been found.

# Demarest Bros.
*Waldo, Ohio*

Somewhere in the Author's forty years of collecting data on vintage tractors, the name of Demarest Bros. has appeared, but no information on the company or its tractors has been found.

# Denning Motor Implement Company
*Cedar Rapids, Iowa*

Denning Wire & Fence Company was organized at Cedar Rapids, Iowa in 1899. Joseph M. Denning had numerous patents on machinery to weave metal fence.

As early as 1908 the company began experimenting with farm tractors, with a marketable design appearing about 1913. The company name was changed to Denning Tractor Company in 1916, reflecting the firm's new emphasis on tractor production.

Despite the advantages of Denning's lightweight tractor designs, the company went into receivership in 1919 whereupon it was sold to National Tractor Company and shortly after this, to General Ordnance Company of New York City. The latter then sold the 'National' for a short time and then renamed the tractor as the "G-O" model. By 1922 this firm was also in bankruptcy.

**Denning 6-12 tractor**

Denning's little 6-12 tractor was first offered in 1913. Equipped with a two-cylinder, four-cycle engine, it featured a lightweight tubular steel frame. Numerous attachments were available for this tractor, including the one-bottom plow shown here. Late in 1913 the design was changed to include a four-cylinder engine for a major increase in the power level.

**Denning Model B**

Late in 1913 Denning announced the Model B tractor. Of conventional four-wheel design, it used the same tubular steel frame as its predecessor. Rated at 16 drawbar and 24 belt horsepower,

the Model B carried a four-cylinder engine having a 4-3/8 x 5-1/4 inch bore and stroke. Weighing some 3,500 pounds, the Model B sold for $1,200. This model was also known as the Denning Pug Tractor.

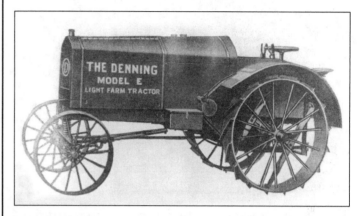

**Denning Model E 10-18 tractor**

During 1916 Denning introduced the Model E, 10-18 tractor. Weighing only 3,600 pounds, it sold for $800. It had many innovative features, including a spring-mounted front axle. Despite its advantages, the Denning saw relatively low production levels, forcing the company into receivership in 1919. Subsequently the company was sold to National Tractor Company, and then again to General Ordnance Company.

## Denver Tractor Company
*Denver, Colorado*

No information can be found concerning this tractor manufacturer.

## Dependable Truck & Tractor Company
*Galesburg, Illinois*

In 1918 this company announced plans for building a factory to make trucks and tractors. Whether the plans materialized, or to what degree, remains unknown.

# Depue Bros. Mfg. Company
*Clinton, Iowa*

**Depue 20-30**

The Depue tractor resulted from the inventive efforts of C. A. Depue. By 1918 the Depue four-wheel-drive tractor had been developed to the point shown here. This resulted from several years of experimental work. It was equipped with a Buda four-cylinder engine having a 4-1/2 x 6 inch bore and stroke. The 20-30 design shown here was built during 1918 and 1919.

**Depue tractor**

Depue redesigned their tractor in 1920, with the most obvious changes being different wheels and a redesigned hood. Production of this tractor continued until about 1924. Although the tractor was in production several years, surprisingly little is known of the design. It does not appear that any Depue tractors remain in existence.

# Homer M. Derr
*Brookings, South Dakota*

**Homer M. Derr tractor**

Early in 1911, Prof. Homer M. Derr offered this tractor design. Since it does not appear that Prof. Derr ever set up a manufacturing operation for this tractor, it is entirely possible that he hoped to induce someone to manufacture the new design. There are no indications that this ever materialized, and it is likely that only this single example was ever built.

# Detroit Engine Works
*Detroit, Michigan*

**Detroit Self-Propelled Portable Outfit**

About 1911 Detroit Engine Works announced their 'Amazing Detroit Self-Propelled Portable Outfit.' As the name implies, this was not so much a tractor as a gas engine that could move itself from one place to another. It featured a Detroit two-cycle vertical engine of 6 horsepower.

**Wadsworth 12 horsepower chain-drive model**

By 1914 the Wadsworth tractors from Detroit Engine Works were available in 6, 8, 12 and 18 horsepower sizes. The engines were of course, built by Detroit. Shown here is a 12 horsepower chain-drive model; it was also available in a heavy duty design using gears rather than chains. The model shown here was priced at $800.

**Wadsworth 18 horsepower two-cylinder model**

The largest of the Wadsworth tractors was this two-cylinder model with 18 belt horsepower. Priced at $990, this model used a 5-1/4 x 5 inch bore and stroke. Like other Wadsworth models, it was rated at 750 rpm. After 1915 the Wadsworth disappeared from the market.

## Detroit Harvester Company
*Detroit, Michigan*

**Farmford logo**

Aside from a trademark application of March 1927, little is known of the Farmford tractor conversion unit from Detroit Harvester Company. No illustrations of this unit have been located.

## Detroit Line Drive Tractor Company
*Detroit, Michigan*
## Detroit Tractor Company
*Detroit, Michigan*
## Detroit Tractor Company
*Lafayette, Indiana*

**Detroit farm tractor**

All of these companies have the same ancestry. Baker & Baker at Royal Oak, Michigan was organized prior to 1913 to build the Baker farm tractors. In March 1913 Detroit Tractor Co. was organized to build the Baker, but the following year the company moved to Lafayette, Indiana, continuing there for a few years. This was a line-drive tractor of the universal frame design and could be attached to any number of farm implements.

## Detroit Tractor Corporation
*Detroit, Michigan*

Aside from a 1949 trade listing, little is known of the history surrounding Detroit Tractor Corporation. Presumably beginning in 1947 or 1948, the

**Detroit 44-16 four-wheel-drive tractor**

company offered its Detroit 44-16 four-wheel-drive tractor. Weighing only 1,660 pounds, it was equipped with a Continental N62, four-cylinder engine. Rated at 1,800 rpm, it had a displacement of 62ci. No other references have been found pertaining to the company after 1949.

## Diamond Iron Works
*Minneapolis, Minnesota*

**American 40-70 model**

Diamond Iron Works had beginnings going back to 1902 as engineers and machinists. In 1911 the company decided to enter the tractor business and entered this American 40-70 model in the 1912 Winnipeg Motor Contest. For reasons now unknown, the company left off building their own tractors by 1914.

Diamond 20-36 tractors were offered in 1913 and 1914. This model used a four-cylinder cross-mounted engine and weighed about 8,000 pounds. Late in 1914 Diamond began building

**Diamond 20-36 tractors**

the Lion tractors on contract, and when this venture failed the company returned to its former specialties of machine work and engineering.

## Diamond Match Company
*Chico, California*

**Diamond Model M crawler**

Beginning in 1914, the Diamond Model M crawler tractor came on the market. Rated at 55 drawbar and 75 belt horsepower, the Diamond M model used a front tiller wheel, as was common practice for large crawlers of the time. Production was apparently of short duration, since the company is listed in various trade directories only for 1914.

## Diamond Tractor Company
*Minneapolis, Minnesota*

The Diamond Tractor Company first appeared about 1915, and as facts later came out, was only a company on paper. It was the brainchild of L. A. La Fond, who billed himself as 'one of the greatest Tractor Engineering Experts in America.' Apparently, Diamond Tractor Company hardly got past being anything more than a sign in an office window. It does not appear that a single tractor was built by this company, although the company seems to have brought in some money from the sale of stock certificates.

## Dice Engine Company
*Anderson, Indiana*

This company often appears as a tractor manufacturer, but the company's main effort was in building engines of all kinds, including those that were used in tractors. This listing is included primarily to emphasize the point.

## Dill Tractor & Mfg. Company
*Little Rock, Arkansas*

**Dill tractor**

Geo. I. Dill organized a company at Harrisburg, Arkansas in 1914 to build a tractor for use in rice fields. Its long frame permitted a grain binder to be mounted directly over the tractor. Owing to the wet conditions typical of rice fields, the Dill tractor was designed with extra wide wheels to provide maximum flotation. The company moved to Little Rock, Arkansas in 1920.

**Dill tractor**

During its career, ending in 1924, Dill produced several tractor models, although they all utilized the same special designs for use in rice fields. This 1920 illustration shows a Dill tractor at work plowing in a typical southern rice field. By the early 1920s many different tractor makers were offering special rice field tractors and this eroded the market to the point that Dill left the tractor business entirely.

## C. H. A. Dissinger & Bros. Company
*Wrightsville, Pennsylvania*

**Dissinger 30 horsepower model**

Dissinger began offering tractors at least by 1904, and perhaps earlier. The company went back to 1892 when they began building gas engines. Shown here is their 30 horsepower model of 1905. Known as the Capital gasoline traction engine, it used the company's own stationary engine as the power source. A unique feature was the two-speed transmission, quite unusual for a 1905 model.

**1905 Dissenger 30 hp "Capital"**

By 1910 the Capital tractors were mounted on springs and pulled on springs. Four different models were available. The 10-20 used an 8 x 12 inch, two-cylinder opposed engine, while the 15-30 carried a two-cylinder engine having a 9 x 14 inch bore and stroke. A 25-45 model was also available; it carried a 6-1/2 x 12 inch bore and stroke. Topping the line was the gigantic 40-80 model; its four cylinders were built with a 10 x 15 inch bore and stroke. Capital traction engines disappeared from the market by 1920.

## Dixieland Motor Truck Company
*Texarkana, Texas*

This firm began building the Dixieland tractors in 1918 and continued until about 1920. Their 12-25 model only weighed 2,800 pounds. Included was a

**Dixieland 12-25 model**

four-cylinder Erd engine having a 4 x 6 inch bore and stroke. Although the Dixieland had a design that could well have become a row-crop tractor, there is no indication that any further effort was made beyond what is shown with this model.

# H. C. Dodge Inc.
*Boston, Massachusetts*

**Spry Wheel**

This company appears in the 1931 issue of *Farm Implement News Buyer's Guide* as the manufacturer of the Spry Wheel garden tractor, and continues to appear as late as 1946. Actually, the Spry Wheel went back to some time before World War One, but the exact origins of the company have not been found. After 1946 the Spry Wheel appears briefly with B. H. Mott & Company, Huntington, West Virginia. The Spry Wheel shown here is a very early version of about 1915.

# Do-It-All Tractor Corporation
*New York, New York*

In 1924 this firm is listed as the manufacturer of the Do-It-All garden tractors, but no other information has been found.

# P. J. Downes Company
*Minneapolis, Minnesota*

Patrick J. Downes first appears as a wholesaler of carriages, wagons and farm implements in 1900. By 1904 the firm of Downes & Morrison appeared, but by 1910 the company was listed as P. J. Downes Company. The Liberty tractor first

**Liberty tractor**

appeared in 1915. Rated as an 18-32 model, it followed conventional lines and gained at least a slight popularity. However, the company is not listed as a tractor manufacturer after 1916.

# Doylestown Machine Company
*Danboro, Pennsylvania*

No information can be found on this company.

# Dubuque Truck & Tractor Company
*Dubuque, Iowa*

**Klumb Model F, 16-32 tractor**

This company offered the Klumb Model F, 16-32 tractor in 1920. The firm was a continuation of the Liberty Tractor Company, organized at Dubuque in June 1919. The latter had its beginnings as Klumb Engine & Machinery Company at Sheboygan, Wisconsin. The Klumb 16-32 used a Climax four-cylinder engine having a 5 x 6-1/2 inch bore and stroke. Nothing is heard of the firm after 1920.

# Duplex Machine Company

*Battle Creek, Michigan*

**Co-Op No. 1**

Duplex Machine Company was the manufacturer of the Co-Op tractors in 1937. Actually, a trademark application indicates that the company first began using the Co-Op trademark on September 10, 1935. Shown here is the Co-Op No. 1. This model was furnished with a four-cylinder Waukesha engine having a 3-1/4 x 4 inch bore and stroke. Weighing 3,400 pounds, the No. 1 had road speeds up to 22-1/2 mph, a full floating rear axle and full electric starting and lighting system.

|  | 1 | 2 | 3 | 4 |
|---|---|---|---|---|
| No. 1 | — | $3,500 | $2,500 | $1,000 |

**Co-Op No. 2**

Weighing 4,050 pounds, the Co-op No. 2 was a standard-tread model. It was designed with a Chrysler Industrial engine of six cylinders, each having a 3-1/8 x 4-3/8 inch bore and stroke. The transmission was a combination sliding gear and constant mesh style and was capable of road speeds up to 28 mph.

|  | 1 | 2 | 3 | 4 |
|---|---|---|---|---|
| No. 2 | — | $3,000 | $1,800 | $800 |

**Co-Op No. 3**

Topping the Co-Op line was the No. 3. This model used a Chrysler Industrial six-cylinder engine with a 3-3/8 x 4-1/2 inch bore and stroke. As with other Co-Op models, electric starting and lighting came as standard equipment. The full-floating rear axle design was an innovative feature that was borrowed from motor trucks and similar applications. Various companies manufactured the Co-Op tractors, but after 1937 the scepter was passed to Co-operative Mfg. Company at Battle Creek, Michigan.

|  | 1 | 2 | 3 | 4 |
|---|---|---|---|---|
| No. 3 | — | $3,000 | $1,200 | $800 |

See also: Arthurdale Farm Equip.; Co-Operative Mfg. Company; Farmers Union Central Exchange; National Farm Machinery Co-Op.

# E

**1911 Eagle 56 horsepower tractor**

In the 1910-1916 period Eagle built a four-cylinder tractor design in three different sizes. The 16-30 used a 6 x 8 inch bore and stroke; the 25-45 was a 7 x 8 inch design and the 40-60 carried an 8-inch bore and stroke. Very little is known of the two smaller sizes, but the larger 40-60 model seems to have been fairly successful. The latter model weighed 19,000 pounds and sold for $2,600.

*Note*: Early 4-cylinder heavyweight models: value would be very high if one could be found.

## E & W Company

*Cedarburg, Wisconsin*

No information has been located for this company.

## Eagle Mfg. Company

*Appleton, Wisconsin*

**1906 Eagle 32 horsepower tractor**

Eagle made their initial entry into the tractor business in 1905 with a two-cylinder tractor having a rating of 32 belt horsepower. This 12,000 pound tractor was built into 1906, after which production was suspended. The company then remained out of the tractor business until 1910. The 32 horsepower model of 1905 used a two-cylinder opposed engine having a 9 -1/4 x 13 inch bore and stroke. Very few were built.

**Eagle Model D Series**

Eagle began building its two-cylinder tractors in 1913, with the Model D Series remaining on the market until 1916. These were built in three sizes; the 8-16 used a 6 x 8 inch bore and stroke, the 12-22 was a 7 x 8 inch model and the 16-30 carried an 8-inch bore and stroke. All sizes had an operating speed of 450 rpm. The Model D typified the Eagle tractor line until 1930.

|         | 1       | 2       | 3       | 4      |
|---------|---------|---------|---------|--------|
| Eagle D | $25,000 | $22,000 | $10,000 | $8,000 |

**Eagle Model F**

Model F Eagle tractors were built in the 1916-1922 period. This series included two models, the 12-22, priced at $1,500 and the 16-30 which sold for $1,825. Both continued with the 8-inch stroke; the 16-30 carried an 8-inch bore, while the 12-22 was an inch smaller in its cylinder diameter.

| | 1 | 2 | 3 | 4 |
|---|---|---|---|---|
| Eagle F | $18,000 | $16,000 | $10,000 | $6,500 |

**Eagle Model H, 13-25 tractor**

The Eagle Model H, 13-25 tractor was essentially a re-rated version of the Model F, 12-22. The Series H tractors were built in the 1922-1930 period. Automotive-type steering was adopted in the Model H tractors, along with other refinements. In 1928 this model listed at $1,100. A substantial number were sold in Canada.

| | 1 | 2 | 3 | 4 |
|---|---|---|---|---|
| Eagle H | $16,000 | $14,000 | $10,000 | $6,500 |

**Model 16-30**

Like other models of the H-Series tractors, the 16-30 was built in the 1922-1930 period. This model was tested at Nebraska in late 1921 under Test No. 80. Although minor problems plagued the test procedures, the 16-30 demonstrated a maximum of 31.8 brake horsepower. At least for purposes of the test and subsequently, for 16-30 Model H tractors sold in Nebraska, the rated engine speed was 500 rpm, compared to the rated speed of 450 rpm that had been used ever since 1913.

**Eagle 20-40 Model H**

Eagle 20-40 Model H tractors were the largest of this series. This two-cylinder model used an 8-inch bore but increased the stroke from 8 to 10 inches. The 20-40 was sold in three different styles, with the 20-40 Regular being shown here; it listed at $1,875. The 20-40 Improved was priced at $2,175.

| | 1 | 2 | 3 | 4 |
|---|---|---|---|---|
| Eagle 20-40 | $16,000 | $14,000 | $10,000 | $6,500 |

**Model 20-40 Special**

The 20-40 Special came along late in the production period, likely in the late 1920s. Ironically, the 20-40 models became very popular, especially in the Canadian market. While this tractor was built in three different styles, Regular, Improved and Special, the difference was primarily in the chassis, wheels and gearing; the engine was essentially the same throughout. Shown here is the Eagle H, 20-40 Special Model.

**Model E, 22-45**

Closing out production of the Eagle two-cylinder tractors was the Model E, 22-45. This was Eagle's largest tractor in the two-cylinder series and used an engine having an 8-1/2 x 10 inch bore and

stroke. Three different chassis and wheel styles were offered. In addition, a number of 20-40 Improved and 20-40 Special models were retrofitted with the larger engine to convert them to 22-45 tractors.

| | 1 | 2 | 3 | 4 |
|---|---|---|---|---|
| Eagle E, 22-45 | $16,000 | $14,000 | $10,000 | $6,500 |

**Model 6A**

In 1930 Eagle phased out its two-cylinder tractors and introduced the new six-cylinder Model 6A. During its first two years of production a Hercules six-cylinder engine was used; it carried a 4 x 4-1/2 inch bore and stroke. In 1932 the company changed to a six-cylinder Waukesha engine having similar specifications as the Hercules. Production of the latter style continued until 1937.

| | 1 | 2 | 3 | 4 |
|---|---|---|---|---|
| Eagle 6A, 22-37 | $7,500 | $6,000 | $4,000 | $1,500 |

Beginning in 1936 the 6B and 6C tractors made their appearance. The 6B used a tricycle design, while the 6C was a standard-tread version. This design carried a six-cylinder Hercules

**Model 6C**

QXB-5 engine with a 3-1/4 x 4-1/8 inch bore and stroke. Production of this model ended in 1938. As late as 1945 the company is listed as Eagle Division, Four Wheel Drive Auto Company.

| 1 | 2 | 3 | 4 |
|---|---|---|---|
| Eagle 6B and 6C, 18-26 | | | |
| $7,500 | $6,000 | $4,000 | $1,500 |

# R. D. Eaglesfield
*Indianapolis, Indiana*

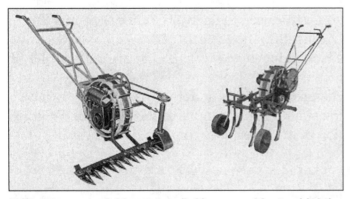

**Unitractor as a sickle mower (left), as a cultivator (right)**

By 1940 the Unitractor garden tractor was on the market. Although it was available at least into the early 1950s, our research has found very little material on these units. Shown here is the Uni-tractor, both as a cultivator and as a sickle mower. By 1948 the company was also building the Eaglesfield NR-6 garden tractor and there may have been other models as well.

| 1 | 2 | 3 | 4 |
|---|---|---|---|
| $500 | $350 | $200 | $75 |

# Earthmaster Farm Equipment
*Hollydale, California*

**Earthmaster "R" garden tractor**

This firm is listed with the Hollydale address, as well as being at Burbank, California. It is also listed at times as being a division of Adel Precision Products Corporation. Our research has found little concerning the corporate history of the company, although it is listed in various tractor directories in 1948 and continues to appear into the early 1950s. Shown here is the Earthmaster "R" garden tractor. It was equipped with a Briggs & Stratton Model N Ultimotor having a 2-inch bore and stroke. Earthmaster also built a Model "S" garden tractor, but we have been unable to find an image suitable for reproduction. Beginning about 1948 the Earthmaster Model C tractor appeared. Weighing only 1,520 pounds, it was equipped with a Continental N62 four-cylinder motor. Three forward speeds were provided and disc brakes were standard equipment. Production of the Earthmaster tractors continued at Burbank, California until about 1955 when the

**Earthmaster Model C tractor**

firm moved to Statesville, North Carolina and operated as the Earthmaster Division of Turner Mfg. Company. The latter kept some Earthmaster models in production until about 1960.,

**Earthmaster Model CN tractor**

Earthmaster Model CN tractors were essentially the same as the Model C tractors except for a slightly different axle width and other variations. In addition, the Model C tractor was also available in a high-crop design known as the Model CH, and the CN model was also available in a high-crop version known as the Model CNH. All models used the Continental four-cylinder N62 engine.

**Model D**

Model D and Model DH Earthmaster tractors were available as early as 1948, with production continuing for several years thereafter. Like the Model C and its variations, the Model D used a Continental N62 engine. Even though the Earthmaster was marketed for well over a decade, very little literature on this tractor has been located during our research, aside from listings in various tractor directories.

| | 1 | 2 | 3 | 4 |
|---|---|---|---|---|
| Model D | $3,500 | — | — | — |

## Eason-Wysong Company
*Topeka, Kansas*

**Autotractor No. 1**

Clarence M. Eason built his Autotractor No. 1 in Meade County, Kansas during 1905. This tractor was built in association with Ansel Wysong. Eason would soon distinguish himself with the Hyatt Roller Bearing Company.

**Eason tractor**

By 1906 Eason had built a somewhat larger tractor than the Autotractor No. 1 of 1905. Within a few years Eason was largely responsible for the first unit frame design as employed on the Wallis Cub tractor. For this design, Eason was granted Patent No. 1,205,982. Eventually, Eason joined the Hyatt Roller Bearing Company. None of the Eason-Wysong tractors ever saw anything resembling full production.

## Eastern Tractor Mfg. Company
*Kingston, New York*

**Gardenaid garden tractor**

Production of the Gardenaid garden tractor apparently began about 1947, continuing into the early 1950s. It was equipped with a 2 horsepower Briggs & Stratton engine. The machine shown here is equipped with a plow, but presumably, there were also other attachments.

| 1 | 2 | 3 | 4 |
|---|---|---|---|
| $500 | $350 | $200 | $75 |

## C. J. Eastman
*Washington, D. C.*

**Eastman Cable Tractor**

The Eastman Cable Tractor appeared in 1911, but nothing has been found to indicate that it ever got past the prototype stage. Apparently this design intended to emulate the European practice of cable plowing. Aside from an illustration and a reference in a 1911 issue of *Gas Power Magazine*, little else is known of the tractor and it is presumed that it never achieved any popularity.

# FARMOBILE

**Farmobile trademark**

A trademark application of January 2, 1908 shows Clyde J. Eastman at Los Angeles, California. This application for the Farmobile claims first use already in January of 1902. It was specifically for an "agricultural cable power wagon." Obviously, Eastman spent a number of years developing his Farmobile, but so far as is known, none of his efforts met with ultimate success.

## Eaton Gas Engine Company
*Eaton, Ohio*

Eaton Gas Engine Company had already been in existence for a few years prior to the 1912 introduction of their Vaughn Gearless tractor. The 'Gearless' reference was not to the traction gearing but to a unique gearless design for the engine

**Vaughn Gearless**

**Ebert tractor**

itself. The two-cylinder engine normally operated under the four-cycle system, but when more power was needed it could be changed over to operate like a two-cycle engine. In 1913 the company had closed its doors, with the assets being taken over by Hoopeston Gas Engine Company, Hoopeston, Illinois.

## Eaton Machine Works
*Jackson, Michigan*

This firm is listed as a tractor manufacturer in 1918, but no other information has been located.

## Eau Claire Implement Company
*Eau Claire, Wisconsin*

This firm was incorporated in 1916 to take over the Opsata Motor Plow Company, also of Eau Claire. No other information has been located.

## Ebert Tractor Company
*Chicago, Illinois*

The Ebert tractor was designed for use with a variety of towed or semi-mounted implements. Much like the Moline Universal and other universal designs, the drive wheels were forward. For ordinary drawbar work, a small caster wheel, barely visible here, was mounted to the back of

the tractor, directly beneath the operators seat. Announced in 1918, the Ebert disappeared shortly after its birth. There are indications that the company may have had its beginnings at Cleveland, Ohio.

## Ebert-Duryea Farm Tractor Company
*Chicago, Illinois*

No information has been found regarding this company.

## Economic Power Company
*Rochester, New York*

Although listed as a tractor manufacturer in a 1900 farm implement directory, no information has been found regarding this company or its tractors.

## Eimco Corporation
*Salt Lake City, Utah*

In the mid-1950s the Eimco crawler tractor appeared in the tractor directories and in fact, the EIMCO 105 was tested at Nebraska in 1957 under No. 628. This model featured a General Motors 4-71 diesel engine and was capable of about 70 maximum drawbar horsepower. Eimco crawlers continued at least into about 1963, but no other information on this design has been located.

**Eimco Power Horse**

About 1939 Eimco began building the Power Horse tractor for a short time. This tractor was developed by Albert Bonham at Clinton, Utah in the 1930s. Eimco built the tractor for a couple of years and then Bonham Company continued until World War Two restricted materials. Allis-Chalmers was quite interested in Bonham's design but never pursued it. In 1949 Harris Mfg. Company took over the design and continued with the Harris Power Horse until about 1964.

## Elderfield Mechanics Company

*Port Washington, Long Island, New York*

**Universal A-20**

For 1920 this firm was offering their Universal A-20 garden tractor. It was rated at one drawbar and four belt horsepower, using a single cylinder engine having a 3-1/2 x 5 inch bore and stroke. Weighing 900 pounds, it is shown here with a one-bottom plow, although other cultivating equipment was also available. No specific production data has been found.

## Electric Tractor Company

*Chicago, Illinois*

This company was organized and incorporated at Chicago in 1916 for $20,000. Aside from the announcement of the firm, no other information has been located.

## Electric Wheel Company

*Quincy, Illinois*

Electric Wheel Company was incorporated in April 1890. As the name implies, the firm was formed to make steel wheels using an innovative electric welding process. Subsequently the firm saw steady growth and in 1941 EWC merged with Peru Wheel Company of Peru, Illinois. The latter dated back to 1851.

Electric Wheel Company became an operating division of Firestone Tire & Rubber Company in 1957.

EWC began experimenting with gasoline tractors as early as 1904 and five years later the company was offering a traction truck. This was a complete tractor chassis to which the farmer could fit his own engine. The company began building its own line of tractors in 1911 and continued in the tractor business until about 1930.

**EWC traction truck**

In 1908 and perhaps earlier, EWC was offering their traction truck. With this outfit a farmer could mount his own engine to the chassis for an instant tractor. In the early years of tractor development, traction trucks gained a slight popularity. Electric Wheel Company offered this device for several years.

**EWC Quincy Model "O"**

During 1911 EWC introduced the Quincy Model "O" tractor. Originally it was rated as a 20-30, but this was soon cut back to a 15-30 horsepower rating. The auto-guide steering, tubular radiator and three-speed transmission were innovative features for a tractor design of 1911. A four-cylinder engine was standard equipment. There are indications that this model was also offered in a 25-45 horsepower size. Production likely ended in 1912 or 1913.

**EWC No. 1**

The No. 1 tractor from EWC emerged late in 1912. Rated at 30 drawbar and 45 belt horsepower, this model weighed nearly five tons. No

information has been located relative to the specifications or production period for this tractor, although it is assumed that the No. 1 remained until about 1917.

**EWC Lightweight Allwork tractor**

In 1915 EWC announced a new lightweight Allwork tractor, but unfortunately, no details of this tractor have been located. Obviously, this model was of two-cylinder design with cylinders opposed and presumably was in the range of 20 belt horsepower.

**1915 Allwork tractor**

A magazine article of 1920 illustrates an Allwork tractor of 1915, noting that it is "still in use on the Gibson Farm, New Brunswick, New Jersey." At the time, getting five years of use from a farm tractor was a meritorious achievement. On the other hand, many of the heavyweight tractors continued in operation for decades with few mechanical problems.

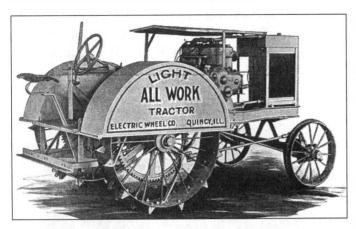

**Light Allwork tractor**

After announcing the Light Allwork tractor in 1915, EWC made numerous changes in the design, although most of them had little or nothing to do with the essential chassis design. An early style, perhaps of about 1916 included dropped fenders. While this was likely done to minimize dust on the operator's platform, it was also a problem in wet and muddy conditions.

**1916 Allwork tractor**

Various EWC advertising indicates that the Allwork design first came out in 1913, undergoing various changes in the following years. For 1916 the Allwork was as shown, with a four-cylinder, 5 x 6 inch engine mounted crosswise and with the belt pulley on the lefthand side of the tractor.

By late 1916 the Allwork tractor had taken what would essentially be it's final form. Initially it was rated as a 12-25 model, but this was raised to a 14-28 rating within a year. Production of this model continued until about 1923.

**Allwork 14-28 tractor**

A platform view of the 14-28 tractor illustrates its design. The company kept the 14-28 very simple, but provided the operator with plenty of room. The hood over the engine was of a unique design and was intended primarily to protect the engine from the weather.

For 1917 and continuing until about 1924, the Allwork kerosene tractor followed essentially the same design as shown here. EWC tractors were among the earliest to use the auto-steer design while many tractors were still using the stiff bolster axle as with steam traction engines. The 14-28 was tested at Nebraska in 1920 (Test No. 53). In 1918 this model retailed for $1,460.

**Allwork II, 12-25 tractor**

Production of the Allwork II, 12-25 tractor began in 1920, but in 1923 it was re-rated as a 14-28 model. This was the first EWC tractor to use an in-line engine, although a unit frame design was not employed. An unusual feature was the front-mounted belt pulley. This model remained in production until 1927.

By 1923 the Allwork II, 12-25 tractor was slightly modified and then became the Allwork Model G tractor. It used a four-cylinder engine with a 4-3/4 x 6 inch bore and stroke. Weighing 4,800 pounds, it sold for $1,500. Production of the Model G ran until 1927.

| | 1 | 2 | 3 | 4 |
|---|---|---|---|---|
| Allwork II/Model G 12-25 | | | | |
| | — | $10,000 | $7,000 | $4,000 |

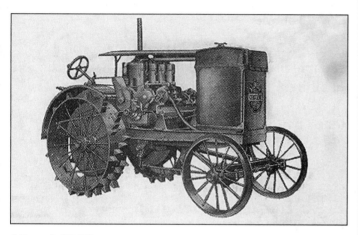

**Allwork 20-38**

Electric Wheel Company offered their 20-38 Allwork tractor in 1922 and 1923. This model used an EWC crossmounted engine having four cylinders with a 5 x 7 inch bore and stroke. Weighing 6,500 pounds, it sold for $1,695.

**Allwork 16-30 tractor**

The four-cylinder engine in the Allwork 16-30 tractor used a 5 x 6 inch bore and stroke. Offered in 1925 and 1926, it sold for $1,395. The price

reduction compared to the 14-28 G, for example, was probably due to the intense competition in the tractor industry.

**Allwork 20-35**

First offered in 1925, the Allwork 20-35 remained in production until the company left the tractor business in 1929. This model used an EWC four-cylinder engine having a 5 x 7 inch bore and stroke. Weighing 6,500 pounds, this model sold for $1,700.

| | 1 | 2 | 3 | 4 |
|---|---|---|---|---|
| 20-35 | $24,000 | $20,000 | $12,000 | $6,000 |

**Allwork 22-40 tractor**

The Allwork 22-40 tractor was first built in 1925. In 1928 it became the Model DA, 22-40 tractor. The 22-40 used an EWC four-cylinder engine having a 5-1/2 x 7 inch bore and stroke. It had a total operating weight of 8,000 pounds. Production ended in 1929.

| | 1 | 2 | 3 | 4 |
|---|---|---|---|---|
| 22-40 | $24,000 | $20,000 | $12,000 | $6,000 |

**Allwork 25-35 crawler**

Electric Wheel Company offered its Allwork 25-35 crawler tractor in 1925 and 1926. This model used the EWC four-cylinder engine with a 5-1/4 x 6 inch bore and stroke. Weighing 9,500 pounds, it could be furnished with electric starter and lights as special equipment. In 1925 EWC also offered a crawler tractor conversion unit for use with the Fordson tractor.

**EWC 5-Ton crawler**

Weighing over 10,000 pounds, the EWC 5-Ton crawler was a 1926 upgrade from the earlier All-work 25-35 model. This tractor carried the same 5-1/4 x 6 inch engine as its predecessor. Production of this model ended in 1928.

Built between 1926 and 1928, the EWC 80 crawler was the largest of all EWC tractors. This one carried a big Waukesha four-cylinder engine having a 6-3/4 x 8 inch bore and stroke. Weigh-

**EWC 80 crawler**

ing 21,000 pounds, the EWC 80 was probably capable of about 80 belt horsepower. Production of all EWC tractors ended in 1929. Perhaps the decision to leave the tractor business was hastened by the onset of the Great Depression.

# Elgin Tractor Corporation
*Elgin, Illinois*

**Elgin tractor**

Waite Tractor Sales Company began marketing the Waite tractor in 1913. The firm got into financial straits by 1916 and was reorganized as Elgin Tractor Corporation at Elgin, Illinois. Within a year the company was again in financial trouble, so the company reorganized and moved to Piqua, Ohio. The Elgin shown here was rated at 9 drawbar and 18 belt horsepower initially, but this was raised to a 10-20 horsepower rating about the time the company moved to Ohio.

# Elgin Tractor Corporation

*Piqua, Ohio*

**Elgin 10-20**

As noted above with the Elgin Tractor Corporation at Elgin, Illinois the company moved to Piqua in 1917. By this time the Elgin 9-18 had been re-rated upward to a 10-20 model. Originally the Elgin used a four-cylinder Buda motor, but when the 10-20 model appeared, power came from a Rutenber motor. When the Elgin was redesigned as a 12-25 model in 1919 an Erd motor was used. After 1920 the Elgin disappears from the scene.

# Ellinwood Industries

*Los Angeles, California*

**Bear Cat trademark**

A trademark application of March 1946 claims first use of the Bear Cat tradename on February 11 of that year. This would effectively note the beginning of production for the Bear Cat and since it was the first of the Ellinwood line, is also the likely beginning of the company.

**Bear Cat tractor**

In July 1946 the Nebraska Tractor Test Laboratory at Lincoln resumed tractor testing following World War Two. The first tractor to be tested was the Bear Cat. Various Ellinwood advertising seems to indicate that several different engines were used, including a Continental AA-7, a Lauson TLC, or a Briggs & Stratton Model A. At the same time the company also developed their own Model 44 engine. Test data may be found in Nebraska Test No. 379.

**Bearcat Jr. garden tractor**

The Bearcat Jr. garden tractor was a smaller version than the Bearcat and was equipped with a Lauson RSC one-cylinder engine having a 2 x 1-7/8 inch bore and stroke. Production appears to have started in 1947.

**Ellinwood Tomcat garden tractor**

Ellinwood Tomcat garden tractors used a single drive wheel and were powered by a Lauson RSC engine, as was used in the Bearcat Jr. garden tractor. Production appears to have ended about 1953, since the Ellinwood line does not appear in the 1954 trade directories.

|  | **1** | **2** | **3** | **4** |
|---|---|---|---|---|
| All Models | $500 | $300 | $150 | $75 |

## G. W. Elliott & Son

*DeSmet, South Dakota*

**Dakota tractor**

This firm began building their Dakota tractor in 1913. That year the company offered two models, one with 25 horsepower and the other with 40 horsepower. The following year saw only the 5-12 model and a 10-20 size. By 1916 the Dakota line included the 7-10 that weighed 2,700 pounds. It sold for $935, although the company attempted to lure prospective dealers with a price of $775 for their copy. Dakota No. 2 tractors weighed 4,300 pounds and listed at $1,500. This model was rated at 14 drawbar and 18 belt horsepower. Nothing more is known of the firm after 1916.

## Ellis Engine Company

*Detroit, Michigan*

Ellis was a well known gasoline engine builder. Their two-cycle models were sold far and wide. At various times the company is listed as a tractor builder, but no images of an Ellis tractor have been located. However, a 1915 catalog for example, illustrates some home-built tractors that used an Ellis engine for power.

## Elwood Tractor Company

*Madison, Wisconsin*

No information has been located for this company.

## Emerson-Brantingham Company

*Rockford, Illinois*

Emerson-Brantingham went all the way back to 1852 when the John H. Manny Company was organized to build a grain reaper. After Manny died in 1856, Ralph Emerson and Waite Talcott took over the firm. Eventually Emerson gained complete ownership and christened the company as Emerson Mfg. Co.

Charles S. Brantingham entered the firm in the 1890s and in 1909 the Emerson-Brantingham Company was formed, with Brantingham as president.

E-B bought out several companies in 1912. Included were: Reeves & Company, Columbus, Indiana; Rockford Engine Works, Rockford, Illinois; Gas Traction Company, Minneapolis, Minnesota; Geiser Mfg. Company, Waynesboro, Pennsylvania and several others.

The E-B tractors were initially the same as the Big Four and the Reeves line, but by 1916 Emerson-Brantingham began building tractors of their own design. Owing perhaps to the lack of funds for new tractor development, the E-B designs languished during the 1920s. In August 1928 the company vanished, being taken over by J. I. Case Company of Racine, Wisconsin.

**Big 4 "30"**

When Emerson-Brantingham bought out the Gas Traction Company in 1913, they acquired the company's full line of tractors. The latter had pioneered the Big 4, the first four-cylinder tractor. Until at least 1916 E-B continued marketing the Big 4 line, including the Big 4 "30" tractor. It had drive wheels over 8 feet high, weighed over ten tons and sold for $2,300. For another $500 this tractor could be purchased as the Model F tractor with three forward speeds.

| | **1** | **2** | **3** | **4** |
|---|---|---|---|---|
| Big 4 "30" (1913) | $50,000 | — | $25,000 | — |

**Big 4 "20" Model D tractor**

The Big 4 "20" Model D tractor made its first appearance in December 1913. Weighing 10,000 pounds, it was powered by a four-cylinder engine having a 5 x 7 inch bore and stroke. It had three forward speeds. Production of the 20-35 Model D continued until about 1920.

**Big 4 "45" tractor**

Emerson-Brantingham introduced the Big 4 "45" tractor in 1913. Weighing 11-1/2 tons, it used a 6-1/2 x 8 inch engine like the Big 4 "30" but instead of four cylinder for the latter, this big tractor used six cylinders. In 1915 this tractor sold for $3,500. It featured extensive use of Hyatt roller bearings and was probably the only one of the so-called 'big tractors' of the day to feature a three-speed transmission.

| | **1** | **2** | **3** | **4** |
|---|---|---|---|---|
| Big 4 "45" (1914-15) | $125,000 | — | — | — |

**Model 40-65 tractor**

Among the 1912 acquisitions of Emerson-Brantingham was the firm of Reeves & Company, Columbus, Indiana. The latter had developed a large 40-65 tractor. E-B made some slight alterations and continued to build it until at least 1920. The four-cylinder 7-1/4 x 9 inch engine was identical to the TC40 engine of Minneapolis Steel & Machinery Company. The latter built the Reeves tractor for E-B.

**Model L, 12-20 tractor**

During 1916 Emerson-Brantingham introduced their Model L, 12-20 tractor. This unique design utilized a drum drive, as shown here. This eliminated the need for a differential gear, since all power was transmitted to a large traction drum. This model used a four-cylinder motor with a 4-1/2 x 5 inch bore and stroke. It weighed about 5,500 pounds. Production continued into 1917.

|  | **1** | **2** | **3** | **4** |
|---|---|---|---|---|
| L 12-20, 3-wheel (1915) | | | | |
| | $18,000 | $13,000 | $8,500 | $4,000 |

**Model Q 12-20 tractor**

E-B presented their Model Q, 12-20 tractor in 1917, probably as a followup to the Model L drum-drive tractor. The design was essentially a scaled-down version of the Big Four "20" tractor. In 1918 the Model Q sold for $1,395. Its four-cylinder engine carried a 4-3/4 x 5 inch bore and stroke.

|  | **1** | **2** | **3** | **4** |
|---|---|---|---|---|
| Q 12-20 | $15,000 | $10,000 | $6,500 | $4,000 |

**Model G, 12-20 tractor**

Through various models, the E-B 12-20 remained in production until the J. I. Case Company takeover of August 1928. Shown here is the Model G, 12-20 tractor of about 1920. Except for minor improvements, it was the same basic tractor as the earlier Model Q.

**E-B 9-18 tractor**

In 1918 the E-B 9-18 tractor appeared. This model had the entire transmission and final drives enclosed to eliminate damage from dust and dirt. All shafts were equipped with Hyatt roller bearings. The four-cylinder engine used a 4-1/8 x 4-1/2-inch bore and stroke. Production of this model appears to have ended about 1920.

The Emerson-Brantingham 12-20 Model AA tractor first appeared in July 1918. The company billed it as a 15-25 for the price of a 12-20. This tractor weighed only 4,700 pounds, almost 2,000

**Model 12-20 AA tractor**

pounds less than the Model Q 12-20 tractor. This model remained in production until the E-B line ended in 1928.

In 1919 Emerson-Brantingham introduced their 20-35 tractor. It was nothing more than an improved version of the Big 4 "20" that had been on the market since 1913. This five-ton tractor used a four-cylinder engine having a 5 x 7 inch bore and stroke. About 1920 the 20-35 disappeared.

**E-B No. 101 Motor Cultivator**

The E-B No. 101 Motor Cultivator first appeared in 1923. It was designed with a friction drive transmission that provided infinitely variable ground speeds. The No. 101 was equipped with a LeRoi four-cylinder motor having a 3-1/8 x 4-1/2-inch bore and stroke. Production of the No. 101 continued until 1928.

**Model 20-35 tractor**

**Emerson-Brantingham 16-32 Model**

Emerson-Brantingham introduced their 16-32 model in 1921 and continued it in production until the company was bought out by J. I. Case Company in 1928. This model used a four-cylinder engine having a 5-1/4 x 7 inch bore and stroke. When J. I. Case bought out E-B, the tractor line ended, but much of the E-B implement line remained intact for several years.

## Empire Tractor Corporation
*Philadelphia, Pennsylvania*

Empire Tractor Corporation was formed after World War Two and built a small tractor using a Willys Jeep engine. There were plenty of these available after the war. Production of the Empire continued only for a few years. Fascination with the rather scarce Empire tractors eventually led to the formation of the Empire Tractor Owners Club with headquarters at Cayuga, New York.

| 1 | 2 | 3 | 4 |
|---|---|---|---|
| — | — | $3,000 | — |

## Engel Aircraft Company
*Niles, Ohio*

No information has been found for this company.

## Engineering Products Company
*Waukesha, Wisconsin*

About 1947 the Economy tractor first appeared. The Economy Standard is shown here and is the model usually illustrated in the trade directories. However, the Economy Deluxe, Economy Spe-

**Economy Standard tractor**

cial, the Jim Dandy and the Power King were also built in the 1947-1954 period. Test No. 483 of 1952 was run at Nebraska's Tractor Test Laboratory where the Economy Special displayed 6.23 belt horsepower.

| | 1 | 2 | 3 | 4 |
|---|---|---|---|---|
| Economy | $600 | $400 | $200 | $100 |
| Deluxe and Special | $3,000 | $2,000 | $1,5000 | $500 |

## Enterprise Machine Company
*Minneapolis, Minnesota*

Enterprise Machine Company was an engine builder at Minneapolis, beginning about 1900. They were designed by Emil Westman who held a number of patents. In the 1910-1917 period Enterprise Machine Co. is listed as a tractor builder in various trade directories, but images of their design have yet to be found. Two sizes of Westman tractors, the 40-45 and the 20-22 (brake horsepower) sizes are listed as late as 1917.

## Erin Motor Plow Company
*Van Etten, New York*

This firm is listed as a tractor manufacturer in 1918, but no further references have been found.

# A.J. Ersted

*San Francisco, California*

A trademark application for the Ersted Auto Cat tractor indicates that this mark was first used on November 14, 1933. Aside from this, no further information has been found.

# Erwin Power Equipment Company

*Omaha, Nebraska*

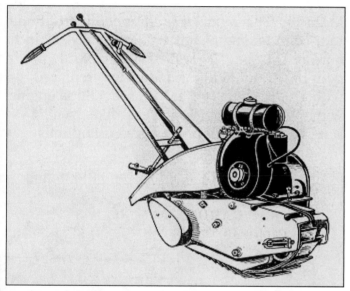

**Erwin Pow-R-Trak "C"**

The Erwin Pow-R-Trak "C" first appears in the trade directories in 1947. Chances are that this design was developed during the previous year. However, there are few other references to this model, leading to the conclusion that is was marketed for only a short time. The Pow-R-Trak Model C weighed only 100 pounds and was equipped with a Clinton 700 engine capable of 1-1/2 horsepower.

# Chester L. Eshelman Company

*Baltimore, Maryland*

By 1954 the Eshelman Riding Tractor was available in 6 and 8 horsepower sizes. The smaller model was equipped with a Wisconsin AKN engine, while the 8 horsepower size used a

**Eshelman Riding Tractor**

Briggs & Stratton Model 23 engine. The smaller model weighed 425 pounds and the 8 hp size weighed 490 pounds.

| 1 | 2 | 3 | 4 |
|---|---|---|---|
| $850 | $500 | $300 | $150 |

# Essex Tractor Company Ltd.

*Essex, Ontario*

**Essex 12-20 tractor**

Nothing is known of this company's beginnings, but by 1919 they were building a two-cylinder Essex tractor with a 10-20 horsepower rating. In 1920 their 12-20 tractor appeared; it listed for $1,000 and was equipped with a Waukesha four-cylinder engine.

In the early 1920s Essex was offering their 15-30 tractor. Of four-cylinder design, it used a Waukesha engine. The price was $1,600. After

**Essex 15-30 tractor**

appearing in the trade directories for a few years the Essex disappears from view and presumably left the tractor business by the mid-1920s.

# Evans & Barnhill
*San Francisco, California*

**Evans & Barnhill logo**

Aside from a trademark application of 1923, nothing is known of this firm as a tractor builder. Apparently the company was building a wide range of farm machinery, including hay presses, plows, cultivators and other equipment, as well as tractors.

# Evans Mfg. Company
*Hudson, Ohio*

**Evans 12-20 Model M tractor**

By 1917 Evans had introduced their 12-20 Model M tractor. This model was equipped with a Buda four-cylinder engine having a 3-3/4 x 5-/12 inch bore and stroke. The 12-20 weighed 3,000 pounds. About 1920 this model was replaced with a 15-30 Evans tractor; it used a Buda engine with a 4-1/2 x 6 inch bore and stroke. Electric starting and lighting were extra-cost options.

**Evans 18-30 tractor**

About 1918 Evans introduced thie 18-30 tractor. For 1919 this model sold at $1,895. During 1920, or probably at the same time that the 12-20 was re-rated to a 15-30, Evans gave the 18-30 a new 20-35 rating. However, by 1921 the Evans tractors disappear from the trade directories.

# F

**Fageol 9-12 tractor**

## Fageol Motors Company
*Oakland, California*

See: Great Western Motor Co.

Fageol was organized in 1912 to build luxury automobiles and orchard tractors. The latter may have taken the form shown here from an undated photograph. This model was called the Fageol Walking Tractor. Production appears to have ended by 1918, about the same time the company quit making cars.

Production of the Fageol 9-12 tractors began in 1918 and continued through 1924. A four-cylinder Lycoming engine was featured; it used a 3-1/2 x 5 inch bore and stroke. In 1922 this tractor was priced at $1,525. The hood vents were much like those used on Fageol buses and trucks of the time. In 1932 the company was reorganized as Fageol Truck & Coach Company, functioning under this title until 1939.

**Fageol Walking Tractor**

# Fairbanks, Morse & Company

*Chicago, Illinois*

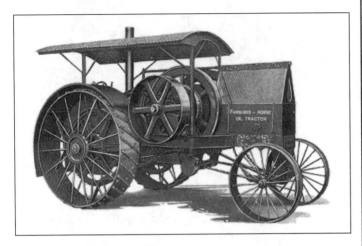

**Fairbanks-Morse 15-25 tractor**

Already in 1909 Fairbanks-Morse began tractor experiments. In 1910 this yielded the 15-25 tractor shown here. The engine was essentially the same as that in the Type N 25 horsepower stationary engine. Rated speed was 250 rpm, and the engine carried a 10-1/2 x 18 inch bore and stroke. Production continued until 1914.

| | **1** | **2** | **3** | **4** |
|---|---|---|---|---|
| 15-25 (1910) — | | — | $25,000 | — |

**Fairbanks-Morse 30-60 tractor**

Concurrently with the 15-25 experiments, Fairbanks-Morse also began developing a larger 30-60 tractor. Initially, it was of a two-cylinder opposed design, but by 1912 it was of the style shown here, using a 10-1/2 x 12 inch bore and stroke. This engine used a crankshaft 5 inches in

diameter! Shipping weight was 28,000 pounds. Production ended in 1914. Only two are known to exist in the U.S.

**10-20 Fair-Mor**

Production of the Fair-Mor tractors began late in 1917. The 10-20 Fair-Mor shown here was really a Reliable built by Reliable Tractor & Engine Company at Portsmouth, Ohio. Fairbanks-Morse marketed this tractor for only a short time; from all appearances, it disappeared from the price lists after 1918.

**12-25 Fair-Mor tractor**

The 12-25 Fair-Mor tractor was in fact built by Townsend Mfg. Company at Janesville, Wisconsin. Roy C. Townsend was earlier associated with Fairbanks-Morse at Beloit, Wisconsin. Roy C. Townsend was largely responsible for the Fairbanks-Morse tractors, and when production ended in 1914, he set up shop at Janesville the following year to build and market his own design. Although the 12-25 Fair-Mor was only marketed for a short time in the United States, it appears that Canadian Fairbanks sold this model until about 1920. However, all tractor production and sales at the Beloit, Wisconsin factories ended in 1918. Only one known specimen remains today.

| | 1 | 2 | 3 | 4 |
|---|---|---|---|---|
| Fair-Mor 10-20 or 12-25 (1917) | $25,000 | — | — | — |

**Fairbanks-Morse garden tractor**

In 1948 Fairbanks-Morse made a brief entry into the garden tractor business with this small outfit. It was equipped with a Lauson RSC or the Lauson TLC engine, and could be furnished with various attachments. Little is known of this unit. It is unlikely that it was actually built by Fairbanks-Morse, but almost certainly was built on contract from another manufacturer. After World War Two, Fairbanks-Morse made a brief but concerted effort to enter various phases of farm and garden equipment lines. The company quickly withdrew from these fields to once again concentrate its efforts on large engines and machinery.

## Fairbury Windmill Company
*Fairbury, Nebraska*

This firm is listed in 1915 as the manufacturers of a 30-60 Auto Tractor. It was designed with a four-cylinder engine and weighed 16,000 pounds. No other information has been found concerning this design.

## Fairmont Gas Engine & Railway Car Company
*Fairmont, Minnesota*

**Fairmont 15-22 tractor**

While this company is much better known for its railway motor cars and engines, the company announced its own tractor in 1914. In 1915 this model was listed as the "Mighty Fairmont" 15-22 and the following year the tractor carried a 16-26 horsepower rating. After 1916 nothing more has been found concerning this tractor.

## Famous Mfg. Company
*Chicago, Illinois*

This company was well known for its hay presses and various other farm machinery. The *Farm Implement News Buyer's Guide* lists this firm as a tractor builder in the 1906-1912 period, but no illustrations of the tractor have ever been located.

## Farm & Home Machinery Company
*Orlando, Florida*

In 1948 Farm & Home Machinery Co. applied for a trademark to cover their line of agricultural implements, including tractors. The company claimed first use of their FARMCO mark in July 1939. No illustrations of the FARMCO tractor have been found.

# Farm Engineering Company
*Sand Springs, Oklahoma*

**Little Chief tractor**

In 1915 the Patch Bros. Tractor Company was organized by A. J. and O. G. Patch, along with J. P. Burke. The latter had formerly been associated with J. I. Case Threshing Machine Company. The partners designed the Little Chief tractor, and in 1916 the firm was reorganized as Farm Engineering Company. The engine itself was unique with a four-cylinder vee design and used a 5-1/2 x 5 inch bore and stroke. This gave it about 45 belt horsepower. For 1916 the Little Chief sold at $1,500 alone, or $1,800 with the plows. Little Chief tractors survived until about 1918.

# Farm Horse Traction Works
*Hartford, South Dakota*

# Farm Horse Traction Works
*Guttenberg, Iowa*

**Farm Horse 15-26**

Organized and incorporated in 1916, Farm Horse Traction Works announced their 15-26 tractor that same year. Weighing 4,800 pounds, it sold for $895. Apparently the Farm Horse remained in production through 1919, but the following year the company moved from South Dakota to Guttenberg, Iowa.

**18-30 Farm Horse tractor**

For 1920 Farm Horse Traction Works announced their new 18-30 Farm Horse tractor. This model used a Climax four-cylinder engine having a 5 x 6-1/2 inch bore and stroke. Weighing 5,000 pounds, the 18-30 sold for $1,685. After the initial announcements at the Iowa factory, nothing more is known of the company.

# Farm Motors Company
*Minneapolis, Minnesota*

In the June 30, 1919 issue of *Farm Implements & Tractors*, the incorporation of Farm Motors Company was announced. Subsequently however, no further information has appeared on this firm.

# Farm Tractor Company
*Indianapolis, Indiana*

In 1913 this firm moved from Indianapolis to Newcastle, Indiana. No information concerning its founding or its subsequent activities in Newcastle have been found.

# Farm Tractor Company
*Fond du Lac, Wisconsin*

This firm was incorporated in 1917 with a capitalization of $20,000. Their claim to fame was a tractor conversion unit whereby an automobile

**Farm Tractor Company tractor**

could be converted for farm tractor purposes. Little is known of the company aside from an occasional advertisement for the conversion unit.

# Farm Power Machinery Company
*Minneapolis, Minnesota*

This company was incorporated in 1912 with a capital of $100,000. Ostensibly, its purpose was to "make gas traction engines in Minneapolis." Beyond this notice, no further information has been found regarding Farm Power Machinery Company.

# Farm-Craft Corporation
*Cleveland, Ohio*

**Farm-Craft R-4**

In 1957 the Farm-Craft R-4 and R-6 garden tractors appeared. These models were the same except for the engines. The R-4 used a Wisconsin ABN engine, while the R-6 was equipped with the Wisconsin AKN engine. Thus, the R-4 was capable of about 4-1/2 horsepower.

**Farm-Craft Model R-8**

With a Wisconsin AEN engine, the Farm-Craft Model R-8 was capable of 8-1/4 horsepower. This model was capable of speeds ranging from 1/2 to 8-1/2 mph. Total weight was 740 pounds. Since the Farm-Craft line only appears briefly, it is assumed that it was built for only a short time.

**R-8-E Farm-Craft tractor**

The R-8-E Farm-Craft tractor used the same Wisconsin AEN engine as the Model R-8. However, this model was equipped with electric starter and generator as standard equipment. In addition the R-8 models could also be furnished with a Vexelmatik automatic gear box as an extra-cost option.

| | 1 | 2 | 3 | 4 |
|---|---|---|---|---|
| All models | $600 | $500 | $300 | $100 |

# Farm-Ette
*Mantua, Ohio*

**Farm-Ette 3-wheel rider**

In the early 1950s the Farm-Ette appeared, remaining until about 1955. The 3-wheel rider shown here was one of several different models, but no specifications of the Farm-Ette line have been located.

| 1 | 2 | 3 | 4 |
|---|---|---|---|
| $200 | $100 | $75 | $25 |

# Farmall Tractor Company
*Cleveland, Ohio*

Farmall Tractor Company was incorporated in 1919 with a capitalization of $100,000. No other information has been found.

# Farmaster Corporation
*Clifton, New Jersey*

**Farmaster FD-33**

The Farmaster FD-33 and FG-33 tractors appear in the trade directories for 1949 and 1950. Since both tractors were tested at Nebraska in August 1949, it is likely that development was under way at least a year before this time. The FD-33 was a diesel model that featured a Buda four-cylinder engine with a 3-7/16 x 4-1/8 inch bore and stroke. Rated at 1650 rpm, it was capable of nearly 24 belt horsepower.

The Farmaster FG-33 gasoline model used a Buda engine of the same bore and stroke dimensions as the FD-33 diesel version. However, the gasoline model was capable of over 28 belt horsepower. The Farmaster FG-33 later became the Mercer 30-CK offered by Mercer-Robinson Company, New York, New York.

| | 1 | 2 | 3 | 4 |
|---|---|---|---|---|
| FD-33 | $12,000 | — | — | — |

# Farmers Mfg. Company
*Kansas City, Missouri*

**Coleman Tractor Company**

Coleman Tractor Company began marketing their tractors in 1918, or perhaps earlier. Production ended in 1920 and the company was taken over by the Welborn Corporation, also of Kansas City. Perhaps Welborn sold manufacturing rights for the Coleman tractor to Farmers Mfg. Company. At any rate, this firm appears in 1921 as building the same essential Coleman 16-30 design. No subsequent listings have been found.

# Farmers Oil Tractor Company
*Mason City, Iowa*

# Farmers Oil Tractor Company
*Watertown, South Dakota*

**Farmers Oil Tractor Co.**

In early 1913 Farmers Oil Tractor Co. announced their new model at Mason City, Iowa. Before the year ended, the company had moved their operation to Watertown, South Dakota. Apparently the latter location was also of short duration, since nothing more can be found concerning the firm. Little is known of the dimensions, but an unusual feature was the location of the cross-mounted engine beneath the tractor chassis.

# Farmers Tractor Company
*Minneapolis, Minnesota*

This firm was incorporated in 1911 as a tractor manufacturer, and appears as late as 1917 as an exhibitor at the Twin City Tractor Show. However, no images of the tractor, or for that matter, any other information, has been found.

# Farmers Tractor Corporation
*Oshkosh, Wisconsin*

**MPM 25-40 tractor**

Since the MPM 25-40 tractor first appears in the 1921 trade directories, it likely saw first light in

1920. This model used a four-cylinder 5-1/2 x 6 inch engine. For reasons unknown, the MPM 25-40 does not appear in the tractor directories after 1921, so production was apparently, quite limited.

# Farmers Tractor Sales Company
*Winnipeg, Manitoba*

**Farmer's Tractor**

The 'Farmer's Tractor' shown here was in reality the same as the tractor offered by Sageng Threshing Machine Company of St. Paul, Minnesota. Farmers Tractor Sales Company offered this model in 1912, the same year that Sageng went into bankruptcy. Thus, it can be assumed that this model was built for only a short time. The Farmer's Tractor was rated at 25 drawbar and 35 belt horsepower.

# Farmers Union Central Exchange
*St. Paul, Minnesota*

As noted under the *Duplex Machinery Co.* heading, the Co-Op tractor line is difficult to follow. After Duplex came *Co-Operative Mfg. Co.* at Battle Creek, and then came Farmers Union Central Exchange. Also involved was Arthurdale Farm Equipment at Arthurdale, West Virginia. Still later came the National Farm Machinery Co-Operative at Shelbyville, Indiana. Despite the

**Co-Op No. 2**

changing company names, the Co-Op No. 2 shown here remained essentially the same as shown under the *Duplex* heading.

**Co-Op No. 3**

The Farmers Union Central Exchange is listed as the manufacturer in 1940, continuing until 1945. First the tractors were built at Battle Creek, then at Arthurdale, then to Shelbyville, and finally to South St. Paul, Minnesota in 1948. Tractor production ended at this plant in 1950. Shown here is the Co-op No. 3 tractor. Both the No. 2 and the No. 3 were tested at Nebraska under No's. 274 and 275.

See also: Co-Operative Mfg. Company; Arthurdale Farm Equipment; Farmers Union Central Exchange; National Farm Machinery Cooperative; Indiana Farm Bureau Co-Op

## Farmobile Mfg. Company
*Columbus, Ohio*

This firm began business in 1909, and there are reports that they demonstrated their tractor at the Winnipeg tractor trials that year. However, no illustrations of the tractor have been found.

## A.B. Farquhar Company
*York, Pennsylvania*

Farquhar had beginnings going back to 1856 and the Pennsylvania Agricultural Works. Eventually the company took the name of A. B. Farquhar Company.

This firm built a wide range of farm implements during its long history. Included were an extensive array of threshing machines, stationary steam engines, steam traction engines and tractors. The company also made a reputation for itself with a line of sawmill machinery. In 1952 the plant was sold to the Oliver Corporation.

**Farquhar 4-40**

By 1913 Farquhar was listed in the trade directories as a tractor builder. By 1915, and perhaps earlier, their 4-40 tractor was available. This big tractor had a four-cylinder engine with 7 x 8 inch cylinders, and apparently was rated at 40 belt horsepower. The rear wheels were 84 inches in diameter with a 24-inch face. Production of this model apparently ended by 1918, with the introduction of the Farquhar 25-50.

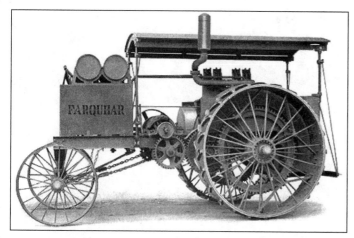

**Farquhar 4-30**

**Farquhar 25-50**

The Farquhar 4-30 appears to have come onto the market about 1913. About 1918 it became the Farquhar 18 or the Farquhar 18-35; the model designator varies from time to time. This model, like the 4-40 tractor, used the company's own engine, but in this instance, the four cylinders carried a 6 x 8 inch bore and stroke. Both tractors used essentially the same chassis, but the diminished size of the 4-30 gave it a total weight of 16,000 pounds, or 3,500 pounds less than the 4-40 tractor.

tractors, and the 25-50 could be furnished with a power steering attachment as an extra-cost option. Production appears to have ended about 1924.

**Farquhar 15-25**

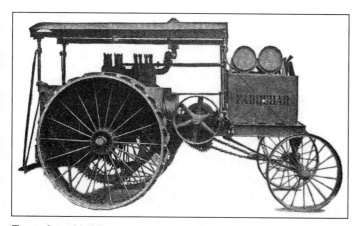

**Farquhar 18-35**

In 1918 the Farquhar 4-30 was named the Farquhar 18 and also the Farquhar 18-35. This model used the same engine as the earlier 4-30, and was apparently of the same essential design. Production of the 18-35 ended about 1924.

In 1918 the Farquhar 4-40 became the 25-50. It was essentially the same tractor as before, but with an increased horsepower rating. A canopy top was standard equipment on the Farquhar

The Farquhar 15-25 tractor made its debut in 1918 so as to be ready for the 1919 market. This model was furnished with a Buda four-cylinder engine having a 4-1/2 x 6 inch bore and stroke. Rated speed was 900 rpm. Total weight of this model was 6,300 pounds. Although regular production of the Farquhar tractor line ended about 1924, it is entirely possible that a few were built to order after that time.

## Farwick Tractor Company
*Chicago, Illinois*

A 1917 trade note indicates that this company was being organized to manufacture tractors, but no further information has been found.

# Fate-Root-Heath Company

*Plymouth, Ohio*

See: Mountain States Engineering

**F-R-H tractor (Plymouth 10-20)**

Introduced in 1933, the F-R-H tractor was also known as the Plymouth 10-20. Standard equipment included a Hercules four-cylinder Model IXA engine with a 3 x 4 inch bore and stroke. The revolutionary lightweight design was also capable of speeds up to 25 mph. By 1935 the Plymouth tractors became known as the Silver King.

**Silver King Model SR38**

The Silver King Model SR38 and the R44 tractors were available during the 1937-1939 period. Both were essentially the same, with the SR38 being set up for 38-inch tread width and the R44 having a 44-inch tread. Through 1935 these tractors used a Hercules IXA 3 x 4 engine, but in 1936 this was changed to a Hercules IXB four-cylinder engine with a 3-1/4 x 4 inch bore and stroke.

**Silver King 3-Wheel**

In April 1936 the Silver King 3-Wheel tractor was sent to Nebraska; the results are shown in Test No. 250. This model used the Hercules IXB, 3-1/4 x 4 engine. Already in 1936 this model had another designation of Model R66, even though it was the identical tractor. The R66 was redesigned with a new hood and grille in 1938.

**R380 tractor**

By 1940 the R38 and R44 models were slightly redesigned and became known as the 380 and 440 tractors. Aside from the new hood and grille, there was little different from the earlier versions. These tractors gained a big reputation with their capability of attaining a 25 mph road speed.

**340 tricycle model**

During 1940 Fate-Root-Heath changed engines in the 340 tricycle model. Instead of the Hercules IXB came a four-cylinder engine designed by F-R-H engineers and built by Continental. It used a 3-7/16 x 4-3/8 inch bore and stroke, and was classified as the F-R-H No. 41 engine. This design was continued until about 1943. The Hercules IXB engine reappeared in the 340 during 1944.

**Model 345 tractor**

During 1945 the Silver King 340 took the new designation of Model 345. Included now was a Continental F-162 engine with a 162cid. Rated at 1,800 rpm, the Model 345 could travel at speeds up to 20 mph. Except for minor changes and new model designators each year, the 345 continued in production until the company closed out the tractor business in 1953. This model was tested at Nebraska in 1949 under No. 424.

**Model 445 Silver King tractor**

Production of the Model 445 Silver King tractor continued essentially the same as the tractor shown here until all production ended in 1953. It used the same Continental F-162 engine as the 3-wheel design. After F-R-H closed out production in 1953, Mountain State Fabricating Company at Clarksburg, West Virginia built the Silver King tractors in the 1955-1957 period.

# Federal Foundry Supply Company
*Cleveland, Ohio*

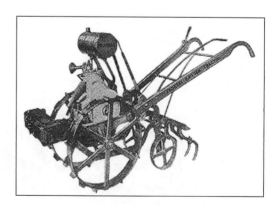

**Merry Garden tractor**

In the early 1920s, Federal Foundry Supply Co. was the successor to Atlantic Machine & Mfg. Company, also of Cleveland. The Merry Garden tractor that had been built by Atlantic became the Federal Model A garden tractor. This model remained on the market, virtually unchanged, at least until the late 1930s.

# Federal Machine & Welder Company
*Warren, Ohio*

**USTRAC crawler**

This company was a successor to the U. S. Tractor Corporation, also of Warren, Ohio. The latter had begun building the USTRAC crawler about 1947, and in 1949 or 1950 Federal appears as the manufacturer. The USTRAC 10A weighed only 3,425 pounds and was powered by a Continental F124 engine. Production continued for only a short time.

| 1 | 2 | 3 | 4 |
|---|---|---|---|
| USTRAC, Crawler (1947) | | | |
| $3,000 | $2,000 | $1,000 | $500 |

# Federal Tractor Company
*Minneapolis, Minnesota*

**Tom Thumb tractor**

In 1917 Federal took over the Tom Thumb Tractor Company, previously established at Minneapolis. The Tom Thumb used an interesting chassis design consisting of a single track at the rear, and steered by two rather large front wheels. It was equipped with a four-cylinder engine capable of 12 drawbar and 20 belt horsepower. The Tom Thumb appears in 1918, but eventually drifts from view, probably leaving the market by 1920.

# Harry Ferguson Inc.
*Detroit, Michigan*

Harry Ferguson began experimenting with plows in 1919. Using a unique linkage system, the Ferguson plow could be connected to a Fordson tractor. In the early 1920s Ferguson contracted with Roderick Lean Company at Mansfield, Ohio to build his plows. The latter went broke in 1924, and the following year, Ferguson-Sherman Inc. was organized at Evansville, Indiana. Ferguson supplied the design and the Sherman brothers furnished the manufacturing facilities and the money. When American production of the Fordson ceased in 1928, so did production of the plows.

Ferguson continued his experiments, and in 1933 he and his associates built the Black tractor (simply because it was painted black). At this juncture the three-point system was essentially developed and included a draft-responsive hydraulic control. Eventually Ferguson persuaded David Brown in England to form David Brown Tractors Ltd., with Harry Ferguson Ltd. as the sales organization. The new tractor was known by various names, including the Ferguson-Brown and the Irish Ferguson.

In a relatively short time Ferguson and Brown were at odds. Ferguson then contacted the Sherman brothers and they in turn were instrumental in introducing Henry Ford to the Ferguson three-point system. Ferguson first demonstrated his design at Ford's home in 1938, and in 1939 came the Ford 9N tractor with the Ferguson system. Ferguson-Sherman Mfg. Corporation was formed on July 1, 1939, to market the new tractor, with Ford actually building the tractor and supplying the capital. In 1942 the sales organization was renamed as Harry Ferguson Inc.

Ford and Ferguson operated on the basis of a verbal agreement made in 1939. Especially after World War Two, Ford executives opined that they should be building and marketing their own tractor. Thus in late 1946 Dearborn Motors was organized as a Ford subsidiary, and began building the 8N Ford tractors.

Now that the Ford-Ferguson agreement was vacated, Ferguson went back to England, and began building Ferguson tractors there. In October 1948 the first Ferguson tractor was completed at Ferguson Park in Detroit. The Ferguson TE-20 was built in England, and the TO-20 was built at Detroit. In August 1951 a larger engine was installed, and the new tractor was known as the TO-30. The TO-35 appeared in 1954. It was of similar design to its predecessors, but had a slightly larger engine bore.

Massey-Harris-Ferguson Limited was announced in August 1953. In 1958 the company changed its name to Massey-Ferguson Ltd.

The Ford 9N, 2N, and others will be found under the *Ford Motor Company* heading.

**TE-20 Ferguson**

As noted above, when the Ford-Ferguson arrangement ended, Harry Ferguson was forced to find a manufacturing facility. Initially, the TE-20 Ferguson, built in England, was shipped to the United States. By October 1948 the TO-20 was being built at Detroit. Nebraska Test No. 392 of May 1948 used the TE-20 with a Continental

four-cylinder engine. The TO-20 of later that year was essentially the same tractor. Production of this model continued into 1951.

**Model TO-30**

Production of the TO-30 began in August 1951 and continued into 1954. The TO-30 used a Continental four-cylinder engine with a 3-1/4 x 3-7/8 inch bore and stroke. This was slightly larger than the 3-3/16 x 3-3/4 inch engine of the TO-20. With this exception there was little difference between the two models. As noted above, the Massey-Harris-Ferguson merger of 1953 effectively ended the Ferguson tractor as a distinct entity.

|       | 1       | 2       | 3       | 4       |
|-------|---------|---------|---------|---------|
| TE-20 | $3,000  | $2,300  | $1,550  | $1,000  |
| TO-20 | $3,500  | $2,400  | $1,500  | $1,000  |
| TO-30 | $3,500  | $2,400  | $1,600  | $1,000  |
| TO-35 | $4,200  | $2,800  | $2,000  | —       |

## Ferguson Mfg. Company
*Belleville, Kansas*

In 1906 the Ferguson Automobile Thresher appeared. This machine was essentially a self-propelled threshing machine. Although it was not designed for drawbar power, it was an early demonstration of the possibilities and the potential for gas power. A caption with this photograph indi-

**Ferguson Automobile Thresher**

cated that the machine was being loaded under its own power onto a Union Pacific rail car for demonstration before an Implement Men's convention in Kansas City. Little else is known of this machine aside from the 1906 photograph.

# Flinchbaugh Mfg. Company
*York, Pennsylvania*

**Flinchbaugh tractor**

Flinchbaugh was an early entrant into tractors and utilized their own engines. The company was building engines by 1900, and commenced tractor experiments shortly after. By 1905 Flinchbaugh was offering this small traction engine with 2 drawbar and 4 belt horsepower. It was equipped with a single cylinder engine having a 4-1/2 x 6 inch bore and stroke. (few known to exist)

| | 1 | 2 | 3 | 4 |
|---|---|---|---|---|
| Flinchbaugh | | $30,000 | | |

**York Little Pet 2 hp**

Production of the York traction engines continued until the company went broke in 1915; the York Little Pet 2 hp model remained throughout the entire production run. Later models of the 2 hp size utilized a much larger water hopper on the engine to provide better cooling, as shown here. This model sold for $340.

**5 hp York tractor**

The 5 and 8 horsepower sizes were capable of 10 and 15 belt horsepower respectively. A 5 hp York tractor is shown here. This model used a two-cylinder engine with a 5 x 7 inch bore and stroke. The 8 hp York carried a 6-1/2 x 9 inch double cylinder engine, weighed 6,000 pounds and sold for $1,425. The smaller 5 hp York was priced at $980. It weighed 4,000 pounds.

**10 hp tractor**

Production of the 10 hp York tractor ended sometime prior to the 1915 dissolution of the company. This model was equipped with a single cylinder engine having a 7-3/4 x 13 inch bore and stroke. It was capable of 14 belt horsepower. The 10 hp size weighed 10,000 pounds and sold for $1,375.

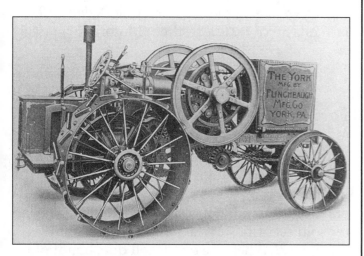

**York 12, 16 and 20 hp tractor**

The 12, 16, and 20 hp York tractors were all of two-cylinder design. Priced at $1,985 the 12 hp model used a 7-1/2 x 12 inch bore and stroke; it was capable of 22 belt horsepower. The 16 hp model could deliver 32 belt horsepower, using an engine with a 7-3/4 x 13 inch bore and stroke; this tractor weighed 16,500 pounds and listed at $2,290. An 8-1/2 x 14 double-cylinder engine was used in the 20 hp model; it could deliver 45 belt horsepower. This size sold for $2,290; it weighed 20,000 pounds.

**Flinchbaugh 40 hp**

About 1913 Flinchbaugh quit building the 25-65 and 40-90 tractors. The 25-65 was designed around a two-cylinder engine having a 10 x 16 inch bore and stroke. This tractor sold for $3,160 and weighed an impressive 24,000 pounds. The big 40-90 style carried a four-cylinder engine with an 8-1/2 x 14 inch bore and stroke. Priced at $4,650, it weighed 32,000 pounds. All sizes of 12 hp and larger could be furnished with power steering as an extra-cost option, and all models featured two forward speeds.

**York 10-Ton Road Roller**

The York 10-Ton Road Roller was essentially built over the 16-32 traction engine. Since the ordinary tractor weighed 8-3/4 tons by itself, the addition of special wheels and auxiliary equipment boosted the total weight to ten tons or more. Production of this model apparently ended about 1913.

**York tractor with locomotive cab**

**Bates Steel Mule "45"**

All York tractors of 8 hp and larger could be specially equipped with a locomotive cab and shielded gearing at extra cost. Another option was the use of oil coolant when the engine was going to be operated in cold climates during freezing weather. The York tractors were built in heavy proportions. For example, the big 40-90 tractor had a 5-inch crankshaft. After the company went broke in 1915 the buildings were sold to Landis Tool Company for $42,500.

## Foos Gas Engine Company
*Springfield, Ohio*

Foos Gas Engine Company developed a successful series of gasoline engines during the 1890s. Subsequently the company began developing their own gasoline traction engine, and in fact, the firm is listed as a traction engine manufacturer as late as 1905. No illustrations of their efforts have been found.

## Foote Bros. Gear & Machine Company
*Joliet, Illinois*

Bates Machine & Tractor Company was taken over by Foote Bros. Gear & Machine Co. in 1929. The latter continued the Bates Steel Mule tractor line until 1935 when Bates Mfg. Company re-emerged. However, the latter left the business in 1937. Two Foote Bros. models were the Bates Steel Mule "35" and the Bates Steel Mule "45"

with the latter being shown here. This model was equipped with a Waukesha six-cylinder engine capable of 45 drawbar horsepower. The Bates "35" is shown in Nebraska Test No. 186, while the Bates "45" is shown in Test No. 187, both of 1931. Further information can be found under the *Bates Machine & Tractor Company* heading, as well as in the Author's title, *Nebraska Tractor Tests Since 1920;* Crestline/Motorbooks, 1985.

## Ford Tractor Company
*Minneapolis, Minnesota*

Ford Tractor Company owed much of its impetus to W. Baer Ewing. The latter organized numerous companies, one of which was the Federal Securities Company at Minneapolis. The latter sold securities in the Power Distribution Company. When the bonds fell due, bondholders had problems getting their money.

The Ford Tractor Company was another of Ewing's enterprises. Allegedly, the concept was to capitalize on the name of Henry Ford. In 1916, virtually anything that had 'Ford' on the nameplate found a ready market. In order to legitimize the plan, one Paul B. Ford was employed and was billed as the designer.

Initially the Ford Tractor Co. was organized as a South Dakota corporation. In November 1916 this company went bankrupt, but while this case was still in litigation, Ewing organized the

Ford Tractor Co. as a Delaware corporation. Sale of $3 million in stock was arranged on a sliding scale so that of the total sale $850,000 went to Ford Tractor Company, and the remaining $2.15 million went to the stock brokers, Robert P. Matches & Company.

A few Ford tractors were built, and a very few still exist. In July 1917 the case of the Ford Tractor Co. came before a United States Grand Jury convened in New York. The company went into receivership in December of that year, and on October 21, 1918 the company was sold at auction. Matches was convicted and sentenced in 1917 on a charge of conspiracy to defraud investors in another case, and Ewing was reported to have organized another tractor company, this time in Canada.

**Ford tractor**

The Ford tractor made its first appearance in 1916, and in December 1917 the company went into receivership. During this relatively short time a few tractors were built. The Ford was of the three-wheel design with two front drivers and a small rear tail wheel. Even if the company had been a previous player in the farm equipment business, the design itself was relatively poor, compared to many other tractors on the 1917 market. Tractors of poor design, little or no aftermarket service, and inadequate performance led to the establishment of the Nebraska Tractor Test law in 1919.

|  | 1 | 2 | 3 | 4 |
|---|---|---|---|---|
| Ford | $22,500 | $15,000 | $10,000 | $5,000 |

## Ford Motor Company

*Detroit, Michigan*

Henry Ford began experimenting with gasoline engines in 1890 and completed his first automobile in 1896. In 1903 the first "Ford" appeared; this led to the introduction of the world-famous Model T in 1908. Over 15 million Model T Ford automobiles were built between 1908 and 1927.

Ford's success with the Model T reinforced his belief that American farmers wanted a small, lightweight, inexpensive tractor. Thus, by 1907 Ford was experimenting with various designs. This led to the 1917 introduction of the Fordson tractor. Over 700,000 Fordsons were built before U. S. production ended in 1928.

Henry Ford was forced to use the Fordson name for his tractors because the rights to the Ford name, as applied to tractors, had already been taken by the Ford Tractor Company at Minneapolis, Minnesota. Further information will be found under the latter heading. However, Ford was not deterred in the least with the Fordson name; the new tractors were built by a subsidiary called Henry Ford & Son.

In 1939 Ford began building the 9N tractor; it embodied the Ferguson three-point hitch system. Henry Ford and Harry Ferguson sealed their deal with a handshake, and this would lead to a host of difficulties for both parties. The result was that the Ford-Ferguson arrangement was terminated in 1946 and Ford began building and marketing their own tractors and implements under the Dearborn Motors Company subsidiary.

**1907 automobile plow**

Henry Ford's early tractor experiments led to the 1907 automobile plow. It used the engine from a 1905 Model B automobile, with the chassis and other parts coming from a Ford Model K. This model was never put into production. Henry Ford himself is seated on this version. Ford would spend money by the hundreds of thousands over the next decade in his quest for the ideal small tractor.

**Experimental Ford tractor**

A 1915 magazine article illustrates two different views of the experimental Ford tractor, noting that Ford intended to market a new tractor by the fall of 1916 and that it would sell in the area of $300. Although Henry came close to a full-fledged production model by late 1916, the price was slightly higher than was originally announced.

**Fordson F**

The tractor manufactured by Henry Ford & Son made its debut in 1917. At first it was known only as a Ford tractor after which the term MOM (Ministry of Munitions) was adopted. The Fordson name was not adopted or used until February of 1918.

At no time has the Fordson been designated as a "22". Instead later references refer to the American-built Fords (1918-1928) as the Fordson "F"; the Irish Fordson (1930-1931) as "N" as was the English Fordson (1932-1945). Ford never made the early Fordson (or MOM) engines. These were farmed out to Hercules as were the wheels, carburetors, manifolds, radiators, etc. All of the first 4,000 or so engines were built by Hercules.

|  | **1** | **2** | **3** | **4** |
|---|---|---|---|---|
| Fordson F 1917-1919 ladder side radiator |  |  |  |  |
|  | $4,200 | $3,200 | $1,500 | $400 |
| Fordson F 1918-1928 (US) |  |  |  |  |
|  | $3,200 | $2,200 | $1,000 | $300 |

1917 MOMs (Henry Ford Tractors) and Fordson hybrids of January-February 1918 are valued highly, especially the first M.O.M. 1,000 with rear oil filters. Add $1,000-$3,000 for MOMs. Add $1,000 or more for half-tracks, and also more for other after-market attachments.

About 1923 the Fordson sprouted fenders, although most advertising we have found does not show the fendered Fordson until 1925. Already in 1918 various editorial writers and agricultural engineers were making negative comments about the Fordson, noting that it had a tendency to tip over backwards under certain conditions. Some engineers noted that the

**Fordson with fenders**

Shortly after the Fordson appeared, various modifications became available. One was an industrial version, and in this case, a front-mounted crane is evident. Several companies built crawler attachments for the Fordson, effectively converting it into a small crawler tractor. Numerous companies built implements and machines especially tailored for use with the Fordson, and Ford Motor Company went so far as to produce a small book called *Fordson Farming* which detailed the products of various manufacturers. U. S. production of the Fordson ended in 1928, and until 1933 a revamped Fordson tractor was built in Cork, Ireland. Production was then shifted to Dagenham, England.

weight of the tractor had not been properly equalized and this was the cause of the problem. However, adding the fenders aided greatly in minimizing the problem.

**Fordson with front-mounted crane**

**Fordson "N" tractor**

The Fordson tested at Nebraska in 1930 was an Irish N. Production of the English N ended in 1945 at which time the E-27-N was introduced. It had the same engine but was now equipped with larger wheels, rear end gears and other emenities. E-27-N means: English-27 hp.-N (same name).

|  | 1 | 2 | 3 | 4 |
|---|---|---|---|---|
| Fordson N 1929-1933 (Ireland) | $3,750 | $2,750 | $1,500 | $500 |
| Fordson N 1934-1938 (England) | $3,500 | $2,500 | $1,300 | $400 |

In 1936 the Fordson Allaround appeared as Ford's first entry with a tricycle style row-crop tractor. This model used the same engine as the standard-tread model. Nebraska Test No.'s 282 and 299 were run on the Fordson Allaround tractor. A noticeable improvement in the Allaround was the addition of a rear pto shaft. Production of the Allaround ended in 1940.

**Fordson Allaround, available on rubber tires or steel wheels**

**Ford 9N**

The first Ford 9N tractor was built in 1939. In Nebraska Test No. 339 it demonstrated 23-1/2 maximum belt horsepower using the company's own four-cylinder engine; the latter carried a 3-3/16 x 3-3/4 inch bore and stroke. The unique feature of the 9N tractor was the fact that it was equipped with Harry Ferguson's unique three-point-hitch system. Although Ford built the tractor, marketing was carried out initially by Ferguson-Sherman Mfg. Corporation of Detroit. Production ended in 1942.

|  | **1** | **2** | **3** | **4** |
|---|---|---|---|---|
| Ford 9-N | $3,000 | $2,250 | $1,750 | $700 |

(For the earliest 1939 models with aluminum hoods and grills, add $1,000-$2,000. For V-8 and 6-cylinder conversions, add $1,000-$2,000.)

**Ford 2N**

Numerous changes had taken place on the Ford 9N subsequent to its introduction in 1939, and many of these changes were embodied in the Ford 2N, introduced in 1942. The onset of World War Two was responsible for the introduction of this new model, due to the restrictions imposed by the war effort. Initially the 2N was offered without an electrical system and without rubber tires. However, the 2N had the electrical system back by the end of 1942, and rubber tires were available, at least occasionally. The 2N was the same as the 9N except for steel wheels and magneto ignition. Production of the 2N ended in 1947.

|  | **1** | **2** | **3** | **4** |
|---|---|---|---|---|
| Ford 2-N | $3,000 | $2,250 | $1,750 | $900 |

**Ford 8N**

Ford 8N tractors made their debut in 1947, with production continuing until 1952. This model used a Ford-built four-cylinder engine with a 3-3/16 x 3-3/4 inch bore and stroke. It was rated at 1,500 rpm on the drawbar, and 2,000 rpm for belt work. The 8N was tested at Nebraska three different times as found in Tests 385, 393 and 443. Test No. 444 used the same 119.7 ci engine but used "tractor fuel" instead of gasoline. In this instance the model was classified as the Ford 8NAN.

|  | **1** | **2** | **3** | **4** |
|---|---|---|---|---|
| Ford 8-N | $3,000 | $,2500 | $2,000 | $800 |

(For 1951 and later with side distributors, add $200.)

For 1953 Ford introduced a new tractor, the Model NAA, also known as the Jubilee model. Ford Motor Company celebrated its fiftieth anniversary in 1953, thus the title. The new NAA used a slightly larger engine than its predecessor, the 8N. In this instance, the four-cylinder motor carried a 3.4375 x 3.60 inch bore and stroke for a displacement of 134 ci. Live hydraulics were standard equipment, and a live pto was available

**Ford Model NAA (Jubilee)**

as an option. Production of the NAA continued into 1954. By this time Dearborn Motors had been merged into the new Tractor & Implement Division of Ford Motor Company. Ford was now ready to enter the tractor and implement business as a major contender.

|  | 1 | 2 | 3 | 4 |
|---|---|---|---|---|
| NAA/Jubilee | $3,750 | $3,000 | $2,200 | $1,000 |

# Four Drive Tractor Company
*Big Rapids, Michigan*

**Four-wheel-drive 20-30 tractor**

John Fitch developed a unique four-wheel-drive tractor by 1913 and organized a company at Ludington, Michigan to manufacture it. The firm was incorporated in 1915, and about that time, moved to Big Rapids, Michigan. Initially the

company built only a 20-30 model. Equipped with a four-cylinder engine, the 20-30 weighed 3,000 pounds.

|  | 1 | 2 | 3 | 4 |
|---|---|---|---|---|
| 20-30 (1918) | $17,000 | $10,000 | $6,500 | $4,000 |

**Fitch Four-Drive 15-30 tractor**

By 1918 the Fitch Four-Drive had undergone obvious changes. Included in the line was the 15-30 tractor. This model was equipped with a Waukesha four-cylinder engine having a 4-1/4 x 5-3/4 inch bore and stroke. Priced at $2,000 the 15-30 weighed 5,100 pounds.

**Fitch Four-Drive 20-35**

The Fitch Four-Drive 20-35 saw little change after about 1918 until production ended in 1930. It featured a Climax four-cylinder engine with a 5 x 6-1/2 inch bore and stroke. The standard tractor weighed 6,000 pounds, but the Model D was also

**Model E, 15-30 Cat tractor**

available with special tamping grousers for packing and rolling. Thus equipped, the 20-35 weighed 10,000 pounds. It could also be furnished with hard rubber tires if so desired.

The Model E, 15-30 Cat tractor first appeared about 1927, and was marketed until the company ceased the tractor business about 1930. This model was tested at Nebraska in 1929 (Test No. 165). The 15-30 Cat used a Waukesha four-cylinder engine having a 4-3/8 x 5-3/4 inch bore and stroke. Weighing 5,800 pounds, it was capable of speeds up to 6 mph. By the late 1920s all Fitch tractors were equipped with ball and roller bearings, as well as Alemite lubrication.

## Four-Wheel Tractor Company

*Clintonville, Wisconsin*

This firm was incorporated in 1916 by D. S. Stewart, Charles Topp, and others. In 1917 the company name was changed to Topp-Stewart Tractor Company. The reader is directed to the latter heading.

## Four Wheel Traction Company

*New York, New York*

**Super 4 Drive trademark**

Aside from a 1930 trademark application, nothing is known of the Four-Wheel Traction Company. The company claimed first use of their "Super 4 Drive" trademark on July 3, 1930.

## Fox River Tractor Company

*Appleton, Wisconsin*

In 1919 the Fox River Tractor Co. was incorporated at Appleton. Ostensibly the first product was to be the 20-40 Fox tractor. This four-cylinder design carried a 5-1/2 x 7-1/2 inch bore and

**20-40 Fox tractor**

stroke. However, the postwar depression and intense competition within the tractor industry caused the company to change its direction from tractor production toward various forage harvesting machines. Less than a dozen Fox tractors were built.

## Franklin Tractor Company
*Greenville, Ohio*

**Franklin 15-30 crawler**

Organized in 1919, Franklin Tractor Co. offered two different crawler models. The Franklin 15-30 shown here was a small 5,500 pound machine equipped with an Erd four-cylinder engine having a 4-1/4 x 6 inch bore and stroke. The larger 18-30 crawler weighed 8,000 pounds and was powered by a Climax four-cylinder, 5 x 6-1/2 inch engine.

**Franklin crawler with front-mounted winch system**

Franklin Tractor Co. offered several variations of its crawler tractors, including this one with a front-mounted winch system. The company applied for a trademark in February 1920 and from all appearances the company only remained in business for a short time, and apparently went into some type of merger with the Bullock Tractor Company of Chicago.

## Franks Tractor Cultivator Company
*Owensboro, Kentucky*

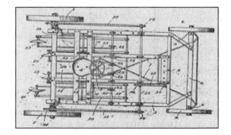

**Franks Tractor Cultivator**

Numerous inventors developed motor cultivators in the 1915-25 period. Few of them were successful, and all of them disappeared with the coming of the row-crop tractors. Franks was organized in 1917 to build this machine, but aside from a few articles announcing the machine, little more is known of either the tractor or the company. Patent No. 1,174,842 was issued for this design.

## Franks Welding Service
*Escondido, California*

This company was listed as a garden tractor manufacturer in 1948, but no other information has been found.

## Frazer Farm Equipment Corporation
*York, Pennsylvania*

**Frazer Farm Equipment tractor**

For 1948 Frazer Farm Equipment was offering this small tractor capable of pulling one 12-inch plow. Power was furnished by a Simar-Swiss single-cylinder engine with a 3 x 3-1/4 inch bore and stroke. It featured six forward speeds ranging up to 4.78 mph in high gear. Production of this model apparently lasted for only a few seasons.

**Frazer Rototiller B1-6**

The Frazer Rototiller B1-6 shown here was very popular among market gardeners. It used the company's own B1-6 engine having a 3 x 3-1/4 inch bore and stroke, and of two-cycle design. By 1953 the Rototiller is listed with Frazer Farm Equipment Company at Auburn, Indiana. No particulars of the company history have been located.

## C.E. Freeman Tractor Company
*Little Rock, Arkansas*

This firm was incorporated for $25,000 in 1919. Beyond this bit of trade information, no other data has been located.

## Frick Company
*Waynesboro, Pennsylvania*

Frick Company was one of the so-called old-line thresher manufacturers. Established in 1853, the company had roots back to 1843 when George Frick built his first grain thresher. Frick began selling steam engines in the 1870s and entered the refrigerating machine business in 1882.

The company announced in early 1913 that they would be selling the tractors produced by Ohio Tractor Company at Columbus, Ohio. This continued for a time, but by 1917 the company had perfected their own tractor design. Production of farm tractors continued until about 1928.

**Frick 12-20**

The Frick 12-20 first emerged in 1918 as the 12-25. It was equipped with an Erd four-cylinder engine having a 4 x 6 inch bore and stroke. In Nebraska Test No. 47 of 1920, the 12-25 wasn't able to muster more than 22.4 belt horsepower, so after the test, it was re-rated as the 12-20 tractor. Weighing 5,800 pounds, the 12-20 was built over 7-inch structural steel channels. Production continued until about 1928.

|  | 1 | 2 | 3 | 4 |
|---|---|---|---|---|
| 12-20 (1918) | $12,000 | $9,000 | $6,500 | $3,500 |

**Frick 15-28 tractor**

Weighing 6,100 pounds, the Frick 15-28 tractor made its first appearance about 1919. This model was powered by a Beaver four-cylinder engine having a 4-3/4 x 6 inch bore and stroke. It was rated at 900 rpm. In Nebraska Test No. 46 of August 1920 the 15-28 demonstrated a maximum of 30 belt horsepower. As with the 12-20, production ended about 1928.

|  | **1** | **2** | **3** | **4** |
|---|---|---|---|---|
| 15-28 (1918) | $12,000 | $9,000 | $6,500 | $3,500 |

## Friday Tractor Company
*Hartford, Michigan*

**Friday O-48 Orchard tractor**

Beginning about 1947 the Friday O-48 Orchard tractor appeared, and remained on the market into the late 1950s. It featured a Chrysler Industrial IND-5 six-cylinder engine with a 3-1/4 x 4-3/8 inch bore and stroke for a displacement of 217.7ci. This tractor featured nine forward speeds ranging from 1.9 to 32.4 mph. The company is listed as building the O-48 tractor as late as 1957, but specific information on the firm has been difficult to locate.

|  | **1** | **2** | **3** | **4** |
|---|---|---|---|---|
| O-48 | $5,000 | $3,000 | $1,000 | $500 |

## Fulton Mfg. Company
*St. Louis, Missouri*

**Do-More garden tractor No. 36CF**

By 1946 Fulton was building their Do-More garden tractor. The line progressed to the point that in 1950 the line included the No. 36CF shown here at the top, with the Fulton No. 50 below. The 36CF was equipped with a Wisconsin ABN single-cylinder engine having a 2-1/2 x 2-3/4 inch bore and stroke, and rated at 3.7 horsepower. The smaller No. 50 was built with a Briggs & Stratton Model N engine. The latter had a 2-inch bore and stroke and was rated at 1.68 continuous horsepower. Production continued at least into the early 1950s.

| 1 | 2 | 3 | 4 |
|---|---|---|---|
| Both models | | | |
| $650 | $500 | $350 | $150 |

**Do-More garden tractor No. 50**

## Fulton Tractor Company

*Anderson, Indiana*

Fulton was incorporated in 1918 with a maximum capitalization of $1 million. It was part of the Madison Motors Corporation, a major player in the engine and tractor business at that time. Aside from a trade note announcing the incorporation of the company, no further data has been found.

## FWD Wagner Inc.

*Portland, Oregon*

Advertising of the early 1960s relates that the FWD Wagner was the "first successful all wheel drive agricultural tractor." Wagner Tractor Company was the original firm, and was later acquired by FWD Corporation of Clintonville, Wisconsin. The latter was eminently successful in four-wheel-drive truck designs going back to World War One, and even before.

**FWD Wagner**

# G

## Gaar, Scott & Company

*Richmond, Indiana*

**Gaar-Scott 40-70**

Gaar-Scott first announced in 1909 that they were planning to enter the tractor business. Early in 1911 their first tractor appeared, the Gaar-Scott 40-70. Weighing 28,000 pounds, this $3,900 tractor featured a four-cylinder engine with a 7-3/4 x 10 inch bore and stroke. Gaar-Scott was an old company that went back to 1849 as a thresher manufacturer. The saga of the Gaar-Scott tractor lasted but a few months after its introduction, for late in 1911 the company was acquired by M. Rumely Company, LaPorte, Indiana. The latter then sold the few remaining tractors as the Gaar-Scott TigerPull. Once the parts inventory was used, production ended. One specimen is known to exist today.

## William Galloway Company

*Waterloo, Iowa*

William Galloway Company was incorporated at Waterloo, Iowa in 1906. From the beginning the Galloway line included gasoline engines as part of an extensive offering of farm equipment. In 1916 the Galloway Farmobile tractor appeared, continuing until 1919. The company took bankruptcy in 1920 and resumed as The Galloway Company Inc. However, the new company was under different management that did not include William Galloway. In 1927 the latter began business again as William Galloway & Sons, and remained in the farm equipment business for some years after. Mr. Galloway died in 1952.

**Farmobile tractor**

The Farmobile tractor was first marketed in 1916. Rated at 12 drawbar and 20 belt horsepower, it used a four-cylinder engine having a 4-1/2 x 5 inch bore and stroke. Galloway made a deal with Great Britain after World War One to sell a substantial number of tractors in the British Isles. History has it that many of the tractors never left the Port of New Orleans where they were to be loaded onto ships for export. Of the remainder, legend has it that Galloway didn't get paid, and as a result, went into bankruptcy. Various factors contributed to Galloway's failure, with the tractor being one of several causes.

|  | **1** | **2** | **3** | **4** |
|---|---|---|---|---|
| Farmobile (1916) | $15,000 | $11,000 | $8,000 | $6,000 |

**Co-Op E-3**

## Gamble-Skogmo, Inc.
*Minneapolis, Minnesota*

In June 1930 the Cockshutt 30 was tested at Nebraska (Test No. 382). Subsequently this tractor was sold in the United States as the Co-Op E-3 tractor or as the Farmcrest sold by the Gamble Stores. Gamble apparently began selling the Farmcrest in 1948, continuing with it into the early 1950s. This model featured a Buda four-cylinder engine with a 3-7/16 x 4-1/8 inch bore and stroke. Capable of about 30 belt horsepower, it also featured a four-speed transmission, 3500 psi hydraulics, and a live pto shaft.

|     | **1** | **2** | **3** | **4** |
|-----|-------|-------|-------|-------|
| E-3 | $2,500 | $1,700 | $800 | $200 |

See: Cockshutt

## The Gamer Company
*Fort Worth, Texas*

In 1913 the Gamer tractor was announced. Designed especially for grubbing and breaking land in one operation, this huge tractor was built

**Gamer tractor**

around a four-cylinder engine having a 10 x 12 inch bore and stroke. The crankshaft was 3-1/2 inches in diameter. The tractor frame consisted of two 12-inch beams weighing 40 pounds per foot. Despite the potential for this tractor, nothing more has been found subsequent to its initial announcement.

# Garden-All Tractor Inc.
*Liberty, Indiana*

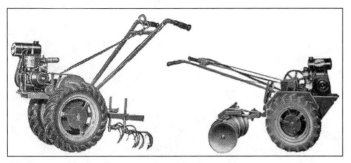

**Cultivette "D" (left), Cultivette "E" (right)**

The Cultivette "D" shown on the left, and the Cultivette "E" shown on the right were essentially the same garden tractor. Both used a Briggs & Stratton NPR-6 engine with a 2-inch bore and stroke. However, the "D" was of smaller physical dimensions and was set up for a 14 to 18 inch wheel tread, while the "E" was capable of an 18 to 28 inch wheel tread.

**Cultivette "S" garden tractor**

Although the Cultivette "S" garden tractor used the same Briggs & Stratton engine as the "D" and "E" models, the "S" used larger tires and was of a somewhat different design. The heavier frame gave it a weight of 277 pounds, compared to 186 pounds for the two smaller models. Production of the Cultivette tractors apparently began about 1947 and continued at least into the mid-1950s.

The Garden-All S2 and S3 tractors were of similar appearance. The S2 model carried a Clinton 1100 engine with a 2-3/8 x 1-7/8 inch bore and stroke for about 3 horsepower. This model weighed 277 pounds. The S3 model used a Wisconsin ABN engine of 4.6 horsepower. Garden-All

**Garden-All S2**

also built an S5 garden tractor. This model used a Wisconsin AKS engine with a 2-7/8 x 2-3/4 inch bore and stroke, for 5 horsepower. The information for the Garden-All line has been derived from trade listings, and for various reasons the entire model line is not always included therein. Likewise, the trade listings offer no historical data on the development and chronology of this or any other company.

**Gard'n Mast'r garden tractor**

Gard'n Mast'r garden tractors featured a Briggs & Stratton Model 23 engine with 8-1/4 horsepower. It used a 3 x 3-1/4 inch bore and stroke. This model was capable of pulling one ten-inch plow, and various other attachments were also available. Total weight of this unit was 810 pounds.

| | 1 | 2 | 3 | 4 |
|---|---|---|---|---|
| All Models | $650 | $500 | $350 | $150 |

## Garden Equipment Company
*Portland, Oregon*

This firm is listed as a manufacturer of garden tractors in 1953, but no further information has been found.

## Garden King Tractor Sales
*Stratford, Connecticut*

**Garden King GRT-3 tractor**

The Garden King GRT-3 tractor appeared in the late 1940s. This unit was powered by a Wisconsin AB-3 single-cylinder, 3 horsepower engine. Aside from a 1948 trade listing, little else has been found on the Garden King line.

| 1 | 2 | 3 | 4 |
|---|---|---|---|
| $650 | $500 | $350 | $150 |

## Garden Tractor & Equipment Company
*Windsor, Ontario*

This firm is first listed in 1946 with their Empire garden tractor. It was built in 3 horsepower and 6 horsepower models, both using a Briggs & Stratton engine. No photographs of this unit have been located.

| | 1 | 2 | 3 | 4 |
|---|---|---|---|---|
| Both Models | | | | |
| | $650 | $500 | $350 | $150 |

## Garden Tractor Sales & Service
*Los Angeles, California*

This company is listed as a garden tractor manufacturer in 1953 but no other information has been found.

## Garvar Tractor Corporation
*New York, New York*

**Garver Model L-20**

The Garvar Model L-20 made its first appearance in the early 1950s, probably about 1952. This 13 horsepower tractor was equipped with a Wisconsin Model TF two-cylinder engine having a 3-1/4 inch bore and stroke. Weighing 1,200 pounds, the L-20 was available with various options, including a rear pto shaft. Aside from a few 1953 trade references, little else is known of this company.

## Gas Traction Company
*Minneapolis, Minnesota*

See: Emerson-Brantingham

The Big Four tractor of Gas Traction Company owed its beginnings to D. M. Hartsough. In 1899 he built a small one-cylinder tractor of 8 horsepower, but soon abandoned this design. The following year he built a 15 horsepower model. Convinced of the possibilities for tractor power, Hartsough built a two-cylinder model in 1901. During 1904 a fourth model was built using a four-cylinder engine with a 4 x 5 inch bore and stroke. This was a dramatic departure in tractor design and was the first successful tractor to be built with a four-cylinder engine.

Hartsough gained the attention of Patrick J. Lyons in 1906, and the Transit Thresher Company was organized to build the tractor. In 1908 the company name was changed to Gas Traction Company.

Emerson-Brantingham Company, Rockford, Illinois bought out Gas Traction Company in 1912.

**Gas Traction Engine**

Transit Thresher Company operated from 1906 to 1908. Shown here is one of the early models of the Gas Traction Engine. The plow guide eased the work of the operator, but this model had only inside wheel guards, and no fenders. Apparently the first production model was built in 1905. The early models were rated at 25 drawbar and 60 belt horsepower. The four-cylinder engine carried a 6 x 8 inch bore and stroke.

**Big 4**

By 1910 Gas Traction Company had billed their tractor as the Big 4. Also, the engine was given a power boost by increasing the bore to 6-1/2

inches from the earlier 6-inch bore. The cylinders were cast singly, and mounted to a massive crankcase. The huge rear wheels were 96 inches in diameter with a 24-inch face.

**Big 4 "30"**

Sometime during 1910 the Big 4 "30" gained a new look with a modified radiator and new fenders. The famous Big 4 trademark, consisting of the number "4" within a circle was first used in December 1910. By this time the company billed itself as the "first and largest builders of four-cylinder farm tractors." James J. Hill, the famous railroad magnate bought a Big 4 in 1910. The company took note of this in its advertising, noting that "on July 23rd (1910) Gas Traction Engine Number 452 was delivered to the James J. Hill Farm at Northcote, Minnesota." In 1912 *Emerson-Brantingham Co.* bought out Gas Traction Company and continued with certain models of the Big 4 line for several years.

|  | **1** | **2** | **3** | **4** |
|---|---|---|---|---|
| Big 4 "30" | $55,000 | $40,000 | $25,000 | — |

## Gasoline Thresher & Plow Company
*Sterling, Kansas*

In 1896 J. A. Hockett and others announced their 'new gasoline traction engine.' The tractor shown here used a two-cylinder tandem engine. According to magazine articles of the day, the machine was built at St. Louis, although the company had its offices in Sterling, Kansas. Few details of the 'Hockett' tractor remain. Apparently it survived for only a short time, and there are no indications

**Hockett tractor**

that anything more than a few prototypes were built. The Hockett is significant in that it was the first "gasoline traction engine" to be advertised for sale in the trade papers of the day.

# Gasport Motor Company
*Gasport, New York*

**Gasport tractor**

By 1911 the Gasport tractor had been developed. Although built especially for orchard work, it was also suitable for other tractor uses. The Gasport used a two-cylinder vertical engine of four-cycle design, and having a 6 x 8 inch bore and stroke. This gave the Gasport about 25 belt horsepower. An interesting feature of the Gasport was the three-speed transmission giving a speed range of 1-1/2 to 3-1/2 mph. It was priced at $1,500. Apparently, the company remained in business for only a short time, since few references can be found after the initial 1911 announcement.

# Gehl Bros. Mfg. Company
*West Bend, Wisconsin*

**Gehl 12-25 tractor**

Gehl introduced their 12-25 tractor in 1916, continuing with it until 1918. This model used a single drive drum for traction. Initially priced at $1,150 it was equipped with a Waukesha four-cylinder engine having a 4-1/2 x 6-3/4 inch bore and stroke. For 1919 the 12-25 was re-rated as a 15-30 model, although it used the same engine as before, and even retained the same rated speed of 900 rpm. After 1919 the Gehl tractor disappears from the trade listings.

# Geiser Mfg. Company
*Waynesboro, Pennsylvania*

**Geiser tractor**

Peter Geiser began building grain threshers in 1850 and organized Geiser Company in 1855. Geiser Mfg. Co. was incorporated in 1869, and the company built its first steam traction engine in 1881. In 1909 the company announced that it was introducing a gasoline tractor; it emerged the following year. This model was a 20 (drawbar) horsepower machine that used a four-cylinder engine having a 7 inch bore and stroke. As with several tractors of the period, induced draft cooling was featured. The engine exhaust was directed upward into the stack, creating an induced draft over the cooling tubes within the radiator.

Emerson-Brantingham Company of Rockford, Illinois bought out Geiser in 1912. E-B continued building the Geiser tractor until the parts inventory was depleted, probably by the end of a year.

| | 1 | 2 | 3 | 4 |
|---|---|---|---|---|
| 20-25 HP (1912) | | | | |
| | $40,000 | $30,000 | $10,000 | $5,000 |

# General Implement Corporation
*Cleveland, Ohio*

**GI garden tractor**

In the 1920s there was a "General" garden tractor built in Cleveland, apparently, by General Implement. This is uncertain as of this writing and should be cleared up in future editions. All values below are for this model only. In 1947 the GI garden tractor took the form shown here. It was equipped with a Wisconsin air-cooled engine of 2-1/2 x 2-3/4 inch bore and stroke, and capable of 3 horsepower. In 1948 the GI 3 horsepower model took on a slightly different appearance but still used the same Wisconsin engine. In addition, it could be furnished with a Gladden engine

of the same size. Curiously, the 1948 line also included the GI 4 H.P. model but it used the same Wisconsin 2-1/2 x 2-3/4 engine as the 3 horsepower size.

| | 1 | 2 | 3 | 4 |
|---|---|---|---|---|
| General | $1,000 | $800 | $600 | $300 |

# General Motors Corporation
*Pontiac, Michigan*

See: Samson

By 1917 Henry Ford had nearly cornered the automobile market with the inimitable Model T. Then in 1918 Ford introduced his Fordson tractor which became an instant success. Bill Durant, chairman of General Motors Corporation was determined to meet this latest Ford challenge with a GMC tractor.

Samson Tractor Works of Stockton, California was purchased and GMC moved this operation to a new plant at Janesville, Wisconsin. Initially GMC continued building the Samson Sieve-Grip tractor, but in December 1918 GMC announced its Samson Model M, priced at only $650. Early in 1919 the Samson Model A was announced, but this larger three-plow tractor never went into production.

During January 1919 GMC announced its Model D Iron Horse. GMC had bought out the rights to the Jim Dandy (later Jerry) motor cultivator, modified its design, and produced the Model D. However, this model was poorly designed and was too limited in its versatility to become popular with farmers. Thus, the Iron Horse did little more than incur huge losses.

Financial losses, an intensely competitive tractor market, and changes in corporate direction were among the reasons that GMC left the tractor market in 1922. The Janesville plant was then converted into a Chevrolet assembly operation.

The GMC Samson Sieve-Grip tractor had originally been developed by Samson Tractor Works, Stockton, California. GMC bought out Samson in early 1918 and set up a tractor factory at Janesville, Wisconsin. The original Samson design was modified to include a GM-built four-

**GMC Samson Sieve-Grip tractor**

cylinder engine with a 4-3/4 x 6 inch bore and stroke. It was capable of 12 drawbar and 25 belt horsepower. The Samson Sieve-Grip was built into 1919.

**Samson Model M tractor**

General Motors announced the Samson Model M tractor in December 1918. This tractor used a 276ci four-cylinder Northway engine with a 4 x 5-1/2 inch bore and stroke. In Nebraska Test No. 27 of 1920 the Model M demonstrated over 19 belt horsepower. Priced at $650, the Model M was complete with fenders, governor, belt pulley, and other items not furnished as regular equipment on the competing Fordson. Production of the Model M continued until 1922 when General Motors left the tractor business completely. The tractor was actually marketed by Samson Tractor Company, Janesville, Wisconsin.

|  | **1** | **2** | **3** | **4** |
|---|---|---|---|---|
| Samson "M" (1918) |  |  |  |  |
|  | $5,000 | $4,000 | $2,000 | $1,000 |

In January 1919 General Motors decided to enter the motor cultivator business, doing so with their Model D Samson Iron Horse. This

**General Motors Model D Samson Iron Horse**

design originated with the Jerry motor cultivator. The hastily contrived Model D was steered somewhat like a crawler tractor, or more accurately, like today's skid-steer loaders. Belts and pulleys were used on each side of the tractor. Weighing 1,900 pounds the Iron Horse was equipped with a Chevrolet four-cylinder 3-11/16 x 4 inch engine. It sold for $450.

## General Ordnance Company
*Cedar Rapids, Iowa*

**G-O tractor**

In May 1919 General Ordnance Co. with offices in New York City, bought out the bankrupt Denning Tractor Company at Cedar Rapids, Iowa. For a few months General Ordnance sold a slightly modified version of the Denning under the National Tractor trademark. By early 1920 the G-O tractor appeared. Two models were offered, the 12-22 and the 14-28. The smaller one used a four-cylinder engine with a 4-1/4 x 5-3/4 inch bore and stroke. This 4,200 pound tractor listed at $1,375. The 14-28 used a four-cylinder 4-1/2 x 5-3/4 inch engine, listed at $1,485, and weighed 4,300 pounds. The G-O was built for only a short time. Advertisements for this tractor disappear by late 1920. Six specimens are known to exist today.

| | 1 | 2 | 3 | 4 |
|---|---|---|---|---|
| G-O (1919) | $17,000 | $12,500 | $8,000 | $3,500 |

## General Tractor Company
*Cleveland, Ohio*

**General 10-12**

The General 10-12 tractor first appeared about 1927. It was of the front-wheel-drive or "universal" design. Power was derived from the company's own two-cylinder engine having a 3-1/2 x 5-1/4 inch bore and stroke. It was also equipped with the company's own planetary transmission that offered speeds from 1 to 3 mph. Weighing 1,600 pounds, the 10-12 sold for $550. About 1927 the 10-12 became known as the 9-12 Model D. After 1932 the 9-12 disappears from the trade listings. For some years after, repairs were available from Cleveland Tractor Company, Cleveland, Ohio.

| | 1 | 2 | 3 | 4 |
|---|---|---|---|---|
| 10-12 (1927) | $4,000 | $3,000 | $2,000 | $900 |

## General Tractor Company
*Detroit, Michigan*

No information has been found regarding this company.

## General Tractor Company
*Seattle, Washington*

**WESTRAK trademark**

Aside from a trademark application, no other information has been found on the WESTRAK design, or for that matter, on General Tractor Co. The mark was first used in April 1948.

## General Tractors Inc.
*Chicago, Illinois*

See: Monarch Tractor Company

**General Tractors 20-12**

Monarch Tractor Company began business at Watertown, Wisconsin in 1913. In 1919 the company reorganized and moved to Chicago, Illinois and operated under the title of General Tractors Inc. The company moved to Springfield, Illinois in 1925 and organized as Monarch Tractor Corporation. During the time in Chicago, General built the Model M, 9-16 crawler, as well as a 20-12 model and the popular Model N, 30-18 crawler. Curiously, when the Model N was tested at Nebraska in 1920 (Test No. 56), the company was listed in the test report at Monarch Tractors Inc., Watertown, Wisconsin. The comings and goings of Monarch in the 1919-1925 period are not well documented, but it is a certainty that the firm moved to Springfield in 1925. Allis-Chalmers bought out Monarch in February 1928.

## Genesee Tractor Company

*Hilton, New York*

Genesee Tractor Company was organized and incorporated in 1915, but no further information has been found.

## Geneva Tractor Company

*Geneva, Ohio*

ADAPTO-TRACTOR

**Adapt-O-Tractor trademark**

Geneva Tractor Co. was organized by Frank E. Jacobs in 1917. By the following year the company had adopted the Adapt-O-Tractor trademark. This covered a conversion unit whereby an automobile could be converted into a tractor. No other information has been found.

## George Tractor Division

*Memphis, Tennessee*

**George Garden Tractor**

In 1948 the George Tractor Division offered their George Garden Tractor. This small 250 pound unit was available with numerous attachments, including the sickle mower shown here. Power was furnished by a single-cylinder, 2-1/2 horsepower Ultimotor engine.

## GFH Corporation

**GFH Corporation "Jerry" trademark**

In 1921 GFH Corporation filed their "Jerry" trademark application for "gas, gasoline, oil, and steam tractors." The company claimed to have first used this mark in May 1920. Aside from this application, no further information has appeared on the company or its tractors.

## Giant Gas Tractor Mfg. Company

*Minneapolis, Minnesota*

H. H. Kryger and others organized the Giant Gas Tractor Mfg. Co. in 1914. Some of their advertising noted that the company was "the mfgr's. of the Kryger gas tractor and Kryger rotary harrow and seeder combined; the best gas tractor on the market; sells on its own merits." The company was listed in the Minneapolis city directories until 1917. Further information has not been found.

## Gibson Mfg. Corporation

*Longmont, Colorado*

In 1949 Gibson filed this trademark application for its tractors and farm implements. The mark plainly includes "tractors." Curiously, the mark claims to have been first used in April 1943.

**Gibson trademark**

However, the Gibson Model D tractor first appears in the trade directories in 1948, with the obvious conclusion that it was on the market sometime in 1947, or perhaps earlier.

**Gibson Model D tractor**

The Gibson Model D tractor first appears in the 1948 tractor directories. This model used a single-cylinder engine, specifically, a Wisconsin Model AEH with a 3 x 3-1/4 inch bore and stroke. It had three forward speeds of 2, 4, and 7 mph. The Model D does not appear in the 1949 directories, leading to the conclusion that this model was taken out of production at that time. It also seems likely that if in fact, Gibson was building tractors already in 1943, it was probably the Model D or one of its ancestors.

| | **1** | **2** | **3** | **4** |
|---|---|---|---|---|
| Gibson D | $2,000 | $1,200 | $500 | $200 |

A Gibson Model H tractor was tested at Nebraska in May 1949. (Test No. 407). Weighing 4,100 pounds, the Model H was equipped with a Hercules IXB-3 four-cylinder engine having a 3-3/4 x 4 inch bore and stroke. This model was

**Gibson Model H tractor**

capable of about 23 belt horsepower. Production of the Model H continued until 1956. In 1957 the Gibson tractors are listed under Western American Industries, also of Longmont, Colorado.

| | **1** | **2** | **3** | **4** |
|---|---|---|---|---|
| Gibson H | $7,500 | $6,200 | $5,000 | $1,500 |

**Gibson Model I tractor**

A Hercules six-cylinder engine was featured in the Gibson Model I tractor. It was rated at 1,800 rpm and used a 3-7/16 x 4-1/8 inch bore and stroke. This model was capable of nearly 40 belt horsepower. Production began about 1948 and continued until about 1956. No serial number lists or specific production data has been located for the Gibson tractor line.

| | **1** | **2** | **3** | **4** |
|---|---|---|---|---|
| Gibson I | $10,000 | $8,500 | $6,500 | $3,000 |

# Gile Tractor & Engine Company
*Ludington, Michigan*

**Gile Model L**

In 1916 the Gile Model L was a simple three-wheel design. Rated at 10 drawbar and 20 belt horsepower, it used a Gile-built two-cylinder engine having a 5-1/2 x 6-1/2 inch bore and stroke. Production of the Gile tractors began in 1913 and continued to about 1919.

|  | **1** | **2** | **3** | **4** |
|---|---|---|---|---|
| Model L (1913) |  |  |  |  |
|  | $18,000 | $14,000 | $10,000 | $6,000 |

**Gile Model XL**

The Gile Model XL tractor was identical to the Model L except that this one had two front wheels, compared to the single front wheel of the Model L. Gile built the Stinson tractor in 1917, and perhaps for a time after that.

The Gile Model K crawler tractor emerged in 1916. This tractor used a slightly larger engine than the Model L, in this case it was two cylin-

**Gile Model K crawler**

ders with a 6 x 6-1/2 inch bore and stroke. This gave the Model K a rating of 12 drawbar and 24 belt horsepower.

**Gile Model Q, 15-35 tractor**

By 1918 the Gile Model Q, 15-35 tractor had emerged. This one used a four-cylinder Gile engine having a 4-3/4 x 6-1/2 inch bore and stroke. Information of the Gile tractors is elusive, but from all appearances, production of the Gile tractors seems to have ended about 1920.

# Gilson Mfg. Company
*Port Washington, Wisconsin*
See: Bolens Products Co.

Gilson Mfg. Company was established at Port Washington in the 1850s. In 1905 the company began building gasoline engines, and shortly

**Gilson tractor**

after they established a factory at Guelph, Ontario. From this factory the Gilson tractors emerged in 1918. Offered in 11-20, 12-25, and 15-30 sizes, the Gilson was built for only a short time. H. W. Bolens, a Gilson stockholder, bought out the company in 1916 and began building the Gilson-Bolens garden tractors. Late model Gilson garden tractors are generally valued at $100 in #2 condition.

## Gladiator Mfg. Company
*Los Angeles, California*

No information has been found on this company.

## Globe Tractor Company
*Stamford, Connecticut*

Globe is listed as a tractor manufacturer in 1919 but no illustrations of their tractors have been found.

## Goodfield Tractor Company
*Goodfield, Illinois*

The 9-18 Goodfield tractor made its debut in 1918. This small tractor had three forward speeds ranging up to 7 mph. Power was derived

**9-18 Goodfield tractor**

from a Gray four-cylinder engine having a 3-3/4 x 5 inch bore and stroke. Apparently the Goodfield remained on the market until 1921 or 1922.

## Goold, Shapley & Muir Company Ltd.
*Brantford, Ontario*

**Goold, Shapley & Muir 45-30 tractor**

Goold, Shapley & Muir had begun building gasoline engines by the early 1900s. In 1909 they entered the tractor business with two models, one of which was the 45-30 shown here. It featured a big two-cylinder opposed engine, also built by Goold, Shapley & Muir.

**Goold, Shapley & Muir 28-20 tractor**

The Goold, Shapley & Muir 28-20 tractor was a smaller version of the big 45-30. It also used a two-cylinder opposed engine of the company's own design and manufacture. These tractors had a special appeal to the Canadian market, but few if any were shipped to the United States.

**Goold, Shapley & Muir Ideal model**

A new tractor design emerged from Goold, Shapley & Muir in 1912. This new Ideal model was much more compact than its predecessors, and even went so far as to use a cellular radiator, much like automotive design. Few details of this model have been available for our research.

**Ideal Kerosene tractor**

The Ideal Kerosene Tractor made its appearance in 1917. This one maintained the use of opposed cylinders, as in previous models. Instead of a cellular radiator, the tractor shown here used hopper cooled cylinders. Advertising of the day noted that "The Ideal Kerosene Tractor drew crowds of interested farmers at the Brandon Plowing Demonstration." This model was rated at 15 drawbar and 30 belt horsepower.

**Goold, Shapley & Muir 12-24 Beaver tractor**

In the 1918-1921 period Goold, Shapley & Muir offered their 12-24 and 15-30 Beaver tractor. It was built with a Waukesha four-cylinder engine having a 4-1/2 x 6-3/4 inch bore and stroke. Operating weight was 5,800 pounds. The Beaver used a friction-drive transmission that offered seven speeds forward or reverse. Goold, Shapley & Muir apparently left the tractor business about 1922.

|        | 1 | 2 | 3 | 4 |
|--------|--------|--------|--------|--------|
| Beaver | $20,000 | $18,000 | $12,000 | $8,500 |

**Graham-Paige 32 hp tractor**

# Graham-Paige Motors Corporation
*Detroit, Michigan*

The Graham-Bradley 32 H. P. tractor was developed in 1937 and was presented to the 1938 market. As the advertising stated, the tractor was 'built by Graham, equipped by Bradley, and proved at Graham Farms.' In fact, the 1940 trade listings show the David Bradley Mfg. Works at Bradley, Illinois as the manufacturer, although it was Graham who actually built the tractor. (Bradley Works was owned and operated by Sears, Roebuck & Company). The 32 H. P. was equipped with the company's own "103" six-cylinder engine. Rated at 1,500 rpm, it used a 3-1/4 x 4-3/8 inch bore and stroke. Additional details of this model can be found in Nebraska Test No. 296.

| | 1 | 2 | 3 | 4 |
|---|---|---|---|---|
| 32 hp | $6,500 | $5,000 | $2,500 | $1,200 |

**Graham-Bradley Model 104**

The Graham-Bradley Model 104 tractor was a standard-tread version of the 32 H. P. unit. Apparently, this model saw first light in 1939. With the onset of World War Two the company apparently ended production of the tractors in favor of military contracts. This likely happened when the company ceased automobile production in November 1941. In 1947 the Graham-

Paige manufacturing entity was sold to Kaiser-Frazer. The Graham-Bradley tractors offered numerous features, including an adjustable drawbar, pto shaft, belt pulley, power lift system, and a wide variety of David Bradley implements.

|  | 1 | 2 | 3 | 4 |
|---|---|---|---|---|
| Model 104 | $8,000 | $6,500 | $4,500 | $2,000 |

# Grain Belt Tractor Company
*Minneapolis, Minnesota*

Grain Belt Tractor Co. 15-35

Grain Belt Tractor Co. began operations at Minneapolis in 1917. Their first model was a 15-35. Weighing about 7,000 pounds, it used a Waukesha four-cylinder engine having a 4-3/4 x 6-3/4 inch bore and stroke. The 15-35 sold for $1,800. Grain Belt initially built its tractors in Minneapolis, but by mid-1917 had moved the factory to St. Cloud, Minnesota. Production of this model continued until about 1919.

By October 1918 the Grain Belt Mfg. Company had been incorporated at Fargo, North Dakota. For reasons now unknown, the company left its Minnesota roots and reorganized at Fargo. The 15-35 continued for a time, but by 1920 the company was building the Grain Belt

Grain Belt 1836

18-36 tractor. It was a redesigned version of the earlier 15-35, and used the same Waukesha engine as before. The company remained in the tractor business at least until 1921.

# Gramont Traction Plow Company
*Springfield, Ohio*

Gramont Traction Plow

In January 1913 the Gramont Traction Plow was announced. Presumably it had been under development for a year or two prior to that time. A. W. Grant and Paul A. Montanus developed this machine and equipped with a 35 horsepower two-cylinder engine. The drive wheels were 2 feet wide and 5-1/2 feet high. Later that same year the company announced a larger traction plow…it carried five bottoms and utilized a 50 horsepower engine. After the initial announcements, nothing more is known of the company or its traction plows.

**Grand Haven BC model**

## Grand Forks Tractor Company
*Fargo, North Dakota*

Grand Forks Tractor Co. was incorporated in 1918 for $250,000. Aside from this, no other information has been found.

## Grand Haven Stamped Products Company
*Grand Haven, Michigan*

Beginning about 1947 Grand Haven offered several different models of garden tractors. The BC model was equipped with a Briggs & Stratton ZZ engine capable of about 6-1/2 belt horsepower, and the CC model was capable of 8 horsepower. These tractors were designed for truck gardeners and could be furnished with numerous attachments, including seeders, cultivators, and sprayers. Production apparently continued for only a short time.

## S. A. Grant
*Thompsonville, Connecticut*

**Squirrel cage garden tractor**

In 1915 S. A. Grant announced his squirrel cage garden tractor. The engine and gearing operated inside the large drive wheel, and a plow can be seen to the rear. Although it does not appear that this particular design made any great headway, various modifications of the squirrel cage design have been offered from time to time.

# Gravely Motor Plow & Cultivator Company
*Dunbar, West Virginia*

**Gravely Garden 2 garden tractor**

About 1927 the Gravely Garden 2 garden tractor appeared. It used a single drive wheel and derived power from the company's own single cylinder engine. The latter used a 2-1/2 x 3 inch bore and stroke. Various attachments were available. Gravely continued to produce this same unit until about 1944.

**Gravely Garden 2 redesigned**

In about 1945 the Gravely Garden 2 was redesigned to include a somewhat larger engine of 3-1/4 x 3-1/2 inch bore and stroke. As with the earlier model, Gravely built their own engine. Although shown here with a sickle mower, the Gravely Garden 2 could be equipped with various attachments. Production of this model continued until 1947.

**Gravely Model D garden tractor**

In 1947 or 1948 Gravely introduced their Model D garden tractor. This one used the same basic engine as the earlier Gravely Garden 2 model, that is, with a 2-1/2 x 3 inch bore and stroke. In fact, the Model D was essentially the same as the early style that began production already in the 1920s.

**Gravely Model L**

The Gravely Model L was essentially the same as the Gravely Garden 2 that had emerged in 1945 or 1946. This style used a 3-1/4 x 3-1/2 inch engine that was capable of over 4 horsepower on a continuous basis. Production of the Model D and Model L tractors continued at least into the late 1950s.

| | **1** | **2** | **3** | **4** |
|---|---|---|---|---|
| All models | $1,000 | $600 | $300 | $100 |

## Gray Company Inc.

*Minneapolis, Minnesota*

In the 1948-53 period, and perhaps for a longer time span, this firm is listed as the manufacturer of the Gardeneer garden tractors. No other information has been found. Specimens would be valued at $800 in any condition.

## Gray Tractor Company

*Minneapolis, Minnesota*

See also: W. Chandler Knapp

**Gray 1908 tractor**

In 1908 W. Chandler Knapp built this small two-cylinder tractor. It used a single rear drive wheel. Knapp was from Rochester, New York but eventually he would become instrumental in the formation of the Gray Tractor Company.

**Knapp Farm Locomotive**

By 1909 the 'Knapp Farm Locomotive' used two drive wheels set close together so as to eliminate the need for a differential. Knapp's early design was one of the first to utilize the drum-drive principle that would later be a salient feature of the Gray tractors.

**Gray tractor 1914**

The tractors up to 1914 used a two-cylinder engine, but in this year the tractor underwent numerous modifications, including the use of a four-cylinder engine. The previous year, 1913, the Wide Drive Drum was first used. Gray Tractor Company was organized at Minneapolis in 1914.

**Gray tractor 1916**

By 1916 the Gray tractor had taken on its essential form that would remain throughout production. A Gray tractor was present at the Power Farming Demonstration held at Fremont, Nebraska in 1914. No doubt the favorable reviews of the Gray were good news to the owners of the company.

The Gray tractor of 1918 would remain virtually unchanged until the company was reorganized in 1925. A couple of different sizes were built, but the Gray 18-36 seems to have been the most popular. This tractor was tested at Nebraska in 1920 (Test No. 22). The 18-36 was equipped with a Waukesha four-cylinder engine having a 4-3/4 x 6-3/4 inch bore and stroke. From its beginnings, all gears were enclosed with the exception of the drive chains to the drum. By 1918 these two were enclosed, and this was an

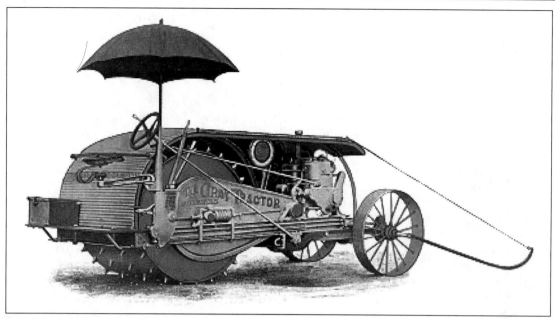

**Gray 18-36 tractor**

important feature compared to other tractors of the day. After the company reorganized in 1925 it appears that their 22-40 Canadian Special was the only model to be built, but this ended too when the company closed its doors in 1933.

|        | **1**    | **2**   | **3**   | **4**   |
|--------|----------|---------|---------|---------|
| 18-36  | $15,000  | $9,500  | $7,200  | $3,000  |

# Great Lakes Tractor Company
*Rock Creek, Ohio*

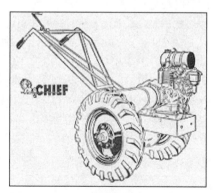

**Chief garden tractor**

By 1947 the Chief garden tractors were available in three sizes of 1, 2, and 2-1/2 horsepower. Apparently, all three models used the same basic chassis, but the engines used were Briggs & Stratton, Continental, and Ultimotor respectively. Numerous attachments were available for these tractors.

**Great Lakes "Jr." garden tractor**

For 1953 Great Lakes offered their "Jr." garden tractor. Priced at $147, it was equipped with a Briggs & Stratton NPR6 or a Kohler K7-2 engine, both rated at 2 horsepower.

The Economy Chief was only slightly larger than the Great Lakes Jr. model; its engine was only rated at 2.2 horsepower. Briggs & Stratton or Kohler engines were used. Priced at $174, the

**Economy Chief**

Economy Chief used two drive wheels, compared to only one on the Jr. model. Both the Jr. and the Economy Chief were built at least into the 1950s.

**Big Chief**

Two different models of the Big Chief were offered in 1953. The "251" used either the Kohler K7-2 engine or the Briggs & Stratton 8R6 engine, both capable of about 7 horsepower. The

Big Chief "303" was the largest of the line, with over 12 horsepower coming from a Kohler K12-2 engine. The "251" sold for $218, while the Big Chief "303" was priced at $268.

|  | 1 | 2 | 3 | 4 |
|---|---|---|---|---|
| All models | $800 | $600 | $200 | $100 |

## Great Western Motor Company
*San Jose, California*

See: Fageol Motors Company

**Great Western 10-15**

After Fageol Motors Company left the tractor business in 1924, Great Western offered this 10-15 Fageol in 1925, and for perhaps a short time afterward. The 10-15 was equipped with a Lycoming four-cylinder engine having a 3-3/4 x 5 inch bore and stroke. Priced at $1,320 this tractor weighed 3,800 pounds. The 10-15 had only a single speed forward and reverse of 2 mph.

## Great Western Tractor Company
*Council Bluffs, Iowa*

About 1919 Great Western was organized at Omaha, Nebraska. Within a few months the company moved to Council Bluffs, Iowa. For about two years this firm built the Great Western

**Great Western Sr. traction 20-30 model**

Sr. tractor, a 20-30 model. The 20-30 was furnished with a Beaver four-cylinder engine having a 4-3/4 x 6 inch bore and stroke. Weighing 4,900 pounds, the 20-30 sold for $1,750.

## Ground Hog Tractor Company

*Detroit, Michigan*

This company was incorporated with a maximum capitalization of $275,000 in 1920. Aside from this no other information has been located.

## Guardian Motors Company

*Norfolk, Virginia*

In 1918 this firm announced a "new truck garden tractor." For reasons unknown, these plans did not materialize, since no other information can be found.

# H

**Hackney Auto Plow**

## Haas Foundry Company
*Racine, Wisconsin*

**Haas tractor**

This company was a major manufacturer of parts for many automotive and tractor companies during World War II, providing parts for Rolls Royce engines and P-51 fighter planes. The president of the company was Edward P. Haas. They built two smaller model tractors, the A and B, and a larger model, the Model D. All were equipped with a three point hitch. Of the smaller models, none are known to exist. The tractor in the photo is thought to be the only remaining Model D.

*Information provided by Dennis Lefebers of Malone, Wisconsin.*

## Hackney Mfg. Company
*St. Paul, Minnesota*

The Hackney Auto Plow was first marketed in 1911. The Hackney was finished in bright red and yellow colors, and included a fully upholstered seat, similar to luxury automobiles of the day. For plowing the drivers were forward, but for road work the tractor was operated with the single steering wheel forward. This was achieved with a unique seat and steering wheel arrangement that permitted the operator to face either direction. Hackney Mfg. Co. continued until 1914 when it was sold to Standard Motor Co., Mason City, Iowa. The latter failed after a short time. Subsequently the Hackney Auto Plow Company was organized in 1917, but a fire wiped out the factory the following year. Within another year or so the Hackney disappeared from the market.

**Hackney Corn-Planter 12-20 tractor**

The Hackney Corn-Planter 12-20 tractor first appeared in 1917. It was not a "corn planter" but was designed for the corn grower. Curiously, the design had great similarities to the true row-crop design that would soon be developed by IHC and their Farmall tractor. At this point, Hackney's chief engineer was John Froehlich, the same man who had developed the Froehlich tractor at Waterloo Gasoline Traction Engine Company in Waterloo, Iowa. Froehlich subsequently left the firm, and eventually the company was bought out by Deere & Company.

**Hagan gasoline traction engine**

**No. 5 Hackney Auto Plow**

The No. 5 Hackney Auto Plow of 1917 was rated at 15 drawbar and 30 belt horsepower. The design was somewhat similar to that of the original Hackney Auto Plow. Although the Hackney did not become a well known, high-production model, the company persevered in the tractor business for a number of years. However, a disastrous fire in January 1918 completely destroyed the Hackney factory and effectively took the company out of the tractor market.

# Hadfield-Penfield Steel Company

*Bucyrus, Ohio*

In the early 1920s this company came out with their 25-40 crawler tractor. It was equipped with a Stearns four-cylinder engine having a 5 x 6-1/2 inch bore and stroke. Weighing 8,500 pounds, the 25-40 offered three forward speeds, enclosed gearing, and a belt pulley. Relatively little is known of the H-P 25-40 crawler; virtually no advertising has been found, and none of these tractors are known to exist. A 1925 trademark application for their "Rigid Rail" tractor indicates that this model name was first used in December 1921. In 1926 the company filed a trademark application for their "crawlerize" tractors, and a few months later applied for the trade name of "Road Hog" as applied to their tractors and road machinery.

# Hagan Gas Engine & Mfg. Company

*Winchester, Kentucky*

This company was organized by Louis T. and Charles Hagan about 1903 to build gasoline engines. In the 1906-1908 period Hagan offered "gasoline traction engines" in sizes from 14 to 50 horsepower. The company's own stationary engines were adapted to this purpose. Few specifics have been found on these traction engines.

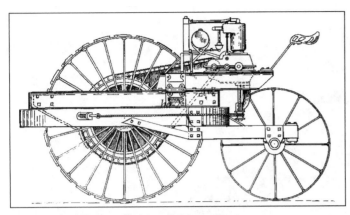

**Drawing of Hagan lightweight tractor**

Hagan continued with engine production until 1918. Somewhere during the 1908-1918 period the company developed a prototype of their new lightweight tractor design, as shown in this drawing. For reasons unknown this design was never produced, and in fact, it is not known of a certainty whether it ever got past the drawing board.

## Paul Hainke Mfg. Company
*Hutchinson, Kansas*

In early 1950 Hainke applied for a trademark protecting their Multivator trade name. No illustrations of the Multivator garden tractor line have been located.

## Hake Tractor Company

No information is available at this time.

## Hamilton Gear & Machine Company
*Toronto, Ontario*

No information has been located regarding this company or its tractors.

## Hamlin Mfg. Company
*Greensboro, North Carolina*

Various references have been found to this company and its garden tractors in the 1947-1953 period, but no photos or specifications have been located.

## Handt Tractor Company
*Waterloo, Iowa*

In 1913 it was announced that this company was being taken over by the National Engine Company, also of Waterloo, Iowa. No other references to either firm have been located.

## Han-D-Trac Company
*Kansas City, Missouri*

**Han-D-Trac**

The Han-D-Trac garden tractor appeared in 1946. Advertising of the time noted that it featured a "monotube chassis, adjustable handles, power take-off and simplified maintenance." Aside from a single reference no other information has been found on this small 5 horsepower unit.

## Haney Corporation
*Philadelphia, Pennsylvania*

**Haney Bull Terrier garden tractor**

In 1947 Haney was offering their Bull Terrier garden tractor. It was equipped with a 12-1/2 horsepower air cooled engine. Little else has been found on the company or its tractors aside from a single reference.

|  | 1 | 2 | 3 | 4 |
|---|---|---|---|---|
| Bull Terrier | $3,500 | $2,300 | $1,500 | $850 |

## Happy Farmer Tractor Company
*Minneapolis, Minnesota*

See: LaCrosse Tractor Co.

**Happy Farmer Tractor Co.**

Organized at Minneapolis in November 1915, the Happy Farmer Tractor Co. began producing tractors by January of the following year. However, LaCrosse Tractor Company was organized at LaCrosse, Wisconsin in late 1916, and it was the direct successor to the short-lived Happy Farmer Tractor Company. Rated at 16 belt horsepower, the Happy Farmer used a two-cylinder opposed cylinder engine with a 5 x 6-1/2 inch bore and stroke.

|  | 1 | 2 | 3 | 4 |
|---|---|---|---|---|
| Happy Farmer | $15,000 | $12,500 | $10,000 | $6,000 |

## A.W. Harpstrite
*Mowequa, Illinois*

In 1907 A. W. Harpstrite designed this motor plow. It was equipped with a Westerfield two-cylinder opposed engine having a 7 inch bore and stroke. By 1908 the machine showed enough

**Harpstrite motor plow**

promise that plans were made for Union Iron Works, Decatur, Illinois to manufacture the new design. For reasons unknown, this venture did not materialize.

## Harris Mfg. Company
*Stockton, California*

**Harris Power Horse 53**

The Harris Power Horse 53 made its appearance in 1952, with one of them being sent to Nebraska's Tractor Test Laboratory in July of that year. Weighing some 5,300 pounds, the Power Horse was equipped with a Chrysler

Industrial six-cylinder engine with a 3-7/16 x 4-1/2 inch bore and stroke. Few details are known about Harris, though apparently the Power Horse was manufactured until 1964.

| 1 | 2 | 3 | 4 |
|---|---|---|---|
| $6,500 | $3,700 | $2,500 | $1,000 |

See: Eimco; Crockett Brothers

## A.T. Harrow Tractor Company
*Detroit, Michigan*

In December 1915 this firm took over the Michigan Tractor Company, also of Detroit; the latter had been organized earlier in the year. Apparently the company had developed an all-wheel drive tractor using a three-wheel design. No other information has been found.

## Hart-Parr Company
*Madison, Wisconsin*

Hart-Parr Company was organized to build gasoline engines in 1896 at Madison, Wisconsin. In 1901 the firm moved to Charles City, Iowa and established the first company to solely build tractors. Their first model appeared in 1902, and in fact, a "Hart-Parr" trademark application notes that their mark was first used on tractors in July of that year.

Although the company moved slowly at first, the new Hart-Parr tractors gained ready acceptance, and by 1906 the firm was well established in the tractor business. Various styles of heavy-weight tractors appeared, ranging all the way up to a gigantic 60-100 model. Although it appears that a few of these were built, little is known about them, and none are known to exist.

Hart-Parr Company underwent an internal upheaval in 1917, with C. W. Hart leaving the company. Subsequently, Hart relocated to Mon-

tana. He developed various enterprises, including the Hart Refineries. Charles H. Parr remained with the firm until his retirement.

The New Hart-Parr tractor of 1918 had been largely the design of C. W. Hart, but had not yet begun production when Hart left the company. Subsequently a whole family of Hart-Parr two- and four-cylinder tractors appeared; they remained on the market until 1930 when they were replaced with new unit frame designs.

Hart-Parr merged with others to form the Oliver Farm Equipment Corporation in 1929. From the legacy of C. W. Hart and C. H. Parr came an entirely new family of Oliver farm tractors. A comprehensive history may be found in the title, *Oliver Hart-Parr*, by C. H. Wendel; Crestline/Motorbooks, 1993.

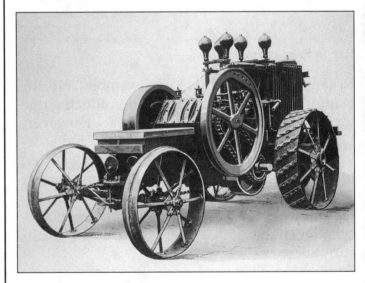

**Hart-Parr No. 1**

The first Hart-Parr tractor, often referred to as Hart-Parr No. 1, was built during 1901 and 1902. Rated at 17 drawbar and 30 belt horsepower, No. 1 used a two-cylinder engine having a 9 x 13 inch bore and stroke. Oil cooling was used. By using an oil coolant the problems of freezing were eliminated, and in addition, a higher cylinder temperature could be maintained. (None known to exist.)

In December 1902 Hart-Parr placed their first advertisement for their tractors. The Hart-Parr 22-45, also known as Hart-Parr No. 2, was avail-

**Hart-Parr 22-45 or Hart-Parr No. 2**

able to farmers. Apparently this model gained considerable attention, and enabled the company to continue with its tractor developments. (None known to exist.)

**Hart-Parr No. 3**

Hart-Parr No. 3 emerged in 1903. It was sold in August of that year to a farmer near Charles City, Iowa. This tractor remained active for over twenty years, and in 1924 the Hart-Parr Company bought the tractor back from the original owner for advertising purposes. No. 3 finally went to the Smithsonian Institution. Certain research indicates that No. 3 may in fact be Hart-Parr No. 4.

|  | **1** | **2** | **3** | **4** |
|---|---|---|---|---|
| No. 3, 18-30 | $125,000 | $100,000 | $80,000 | $35,000 |

**Hart-Parr 17-30**

Weighing almost 7-1/2 tons, the Hart-Parr 17-30 was the first full-fledged production model. Built in the 1903-1906 period, this tractor used a two-cylinder engine having a 9 x 13 inch bore and stroke. Hart-Parr tractors of this era used extra heavy parts throughout and many were used for traction work such as plowing.

**Hart-Parr 17-30 model**

By 1906 Hart-Parr was offering their 17-30 and 22-40 models. Both were of the same general design, but varied substantially in the proportions. The 22-40 weighed 8-1/2 tons and used a big two-cylinder engine having a 10 x 15 inch bore and stroke. These models developed their rated power at 300 rpm.

**Hart-Parr 30-60 "Old Reliable"**

**Hart-Parr 22-40**

Production of the 17-30 and 22-40 tractors ran from 1903 to 1906. Along the way, various changes were made to the design. One such change was a redesigned differential that was included in 1905, along with a revised fuel system. Hart-Parr made heavy use of steel forgings and steel castings in its tractors. This provided greater strength without the added weight required by cast iron components.

|  | 1 | 2 | 3 | 4 |
|---|---|---|---|---|
| 17-30 | $125,000 | $100,000 | $80,000 | $35,000 |
| 22-40 | $90,000 | $80,000 | $60,000 | $25,000 |

Over 4,100 copies of the Hart-Parr 30-60 tractor were built in the 1907-1918 period. This famous tractor took the name of "Old Reliable" and quickly became the most famous of the early Hart-Parr tractors. Rated at 300 rpm, the 30-60 used a 10 x 15 inch bore and stroke. It had a road speed of 2-1/2 mph.

|  | 1 | 2 | 3 | 4 |
|---|---|---|---|---|
| 30-60 | $70,000 | $50,000 | $35,000 | $20,000 |

**Hart-Parr 40-80**

Between 1908 and 1914 Hart-Parr offered their big 40-80 tractor. About 300 of these tractors were built during this time. A unique feature of the 40-80 was the heavy use of steel castings and forgings. The engine cylinders, flywheel, and belt pulley were the only major parts made of cast iron. The big four-cylinder engine was beneath the operators platform with two large exhaust stacks to the rear. The engine used a 9 x 13 inch bore and stroke. (None are known to exist.)

A few copies of the Hart-Parr 60-100 tractor were built in 1911 and 1912. Weighing over 25 tons, this model was powered by a huge four-cylinder engine. Unfortunately, no specifications for this tractor have been located. Apparently, a few of these tractors were shipped, but nothing in the company records indicates whether they were at all successful. The 60-100 remains as one of the largest wheel-type tractors ever built. (None are known to exist.)

**Hart-Parr 15-30**

Hart-Parr began building a 15-30 tractor in 1909. Initially, it used an opposed cylinder engine, but by 1910 the familiar vertical two-cylinder design was selected. The heavy steel canopy was a familiar feature that protected the operator from the elements, as well as providing a measure of protection for the engine in rainy weather. Production of this model ended in 1912.

|       | **1**    | **2**    | **3**    | **4**    |
|-------|----------|----------|----------|----------|
| 15-30 | $70,000  | $50,000  | $35,000  | $20,000  |

**Hart-Parr 20-40 tractor**

In the 1912-1914 period, Hart-Parr offered their 20-40 tractor as a direct successor to the earlier 15-30 model. This tractor had the unique feature of two forward speeds, something rather unusual on a tractor of this size, and built during this time. About 600 of these tractors were built.

|       | **1**    | **2**    | **3**    | **4**    |
|-------|----------|----------|----------|----------|
| 20-40 | $70,000  | $50,000  | $35,000  | $20,000  |

**Hart-Parr 60-100 tractor**

**Hart-Parr 12-27 tractor**

Hart-Parr introduced their 12-27 tractor in 1914. The following year it was superseded by the 18-35

**New Hart-Parr 12-25 tractor**

Oil King; apparently it was little more than a re-rated version of the earlier model. In its 1915-1918 production run, over 2,000 of the 18-35 Oil King tractors were built, making it one of the most popular of the Hart-Parr line up to this time.

|  | **1** | **2** | **3** | **4** |
|---|---|---|---|---|
| 12-27 | $60,000 | $50,000 | $35,000 | $15,000 |
| 18-35 | $66,000 | $50,000 | $35,000 | $15,000 |

**Hart-Parr "Little Red Devil" tractor**

In late 1914 Hart-Parr developed their "Little Red Devil" tractor. It was an entire departure from the previous Hart-Parr tractor line, and was an obvious effort to capture the developing market for small tractors. The Little Devil used a two-cylinder, two-cycle engine. The two-speed transmission had no reverse…instead, to back up the tractor, the engine was reversed, as in marine practice. Only about 700 were built.

|  | **1** | **2** | **3** | **4** |
|---|---|---|---|---|
| Red Devil | $40,000 | $35,000 | $20,000 | $10,000 |

Hart-Parr Company introduced the New Hart-Parr 12-25 tractor in 1918. This model had been developed primarily by C. W. Hart and C. H. Parr during 1917. However, Hart left, or was forced from the company in 1917, and this would be his enduring legacy to the company he had founded with Parr. After a short time this tractor became known as the 15-30 Type A tractor. The 12-25 had an open governor.

|  | **1** | **2** | **3** | **4** |
|---|---|---|---|---|
| 12-25 | $15,000 | $10,000 | $7,000 | $4,000 |

Between 1918 and 1922 over 10,000 of the Hart-Parr 30 tractors were built. Initially, it was the Type A, 15-30 model; the latter was an upgrade of the New Hart-Parr. Originally, the two-cylinder engine used a 6 x 7 inch bore and

**Hart-Parr 30 tractor**

stroke, but this was raised to 6-1/2 inches.
Essentially though, the tractor design remained
the same for a decade.

| | 1 | 2 | 3 | 4 |
|---|---|---|---|---|
| 15-30 Model A | | | | |
| | $7,000 | $5,000 | $3,500 | $1,000 |
| 15-30 Model C | | | | |
| | $5,500 | $4,500 | $3,500 | $1,500 |

**Hart Parr 30**

In Nebraska Test No. 26 of June 1920 the Hart-
Parr 30 demonstrated 20 drawbar horsepower.
An interesting feature was the use of a one-way
oiling system. Lubricant was pumped through a
force-feed lubricator to significant engine parts
and was eventually discharged through overflow
tubes to the ground. The Hart-Parr 30 was
immensely popular with farmers, particularly in
the midwestern states.

In October 1924 Hart-Parr submitted their
new 16-30 tractor for testing at Nebraska, with
the results being tabulated under Test No. 106.
This was the 16-30 Type E tractor; it was built

**Hart-Parr 16-30 tractor**

from 1924 to 1926. Almost 25 drawbar horsepower was demonstrated, and at the belt, the 16-
30 "E" delivered slightly over 37 horsepower.

| | 1 | 2 | 3 | 4 |
|---|---|---|---|---|
| 16-30 Model E & F | | | | |
| | $5,500 | $4,000 | $3,000 | $1,200 |

**Hart-Parr "20" tractor**

Production of the Hart-Parr "20" tractor began in
1921. First it was the 10-20 "B" during 1921 and
1922. In the latter year, this model was modified
slightly and became the 10-20 "C" model. Production of the Type C ran into 1924. The 10-20
"C" used a 5-1/2 x 6-1/2 inch bore and stroke in
its two-cylinder engine. Rated at 800 rpm, it was
capable of about 23 belt horsepower. Only one
Model C is known to exist.

| | 1 | 2 | 3 | 4 |
|---|---|---|---|---|
| 10-20 Model B | | | | |
| | $20,000 | $15,000 | $10,000 | $6,000 |
| 10-20 Model C | | | | |
| | $25,000 | $20,000 | $15,000 | $10,000 |

**Hart-Parr "40"**

As with other Hart-Parr models, the Hart-Parr 22-40 used an engine designed and built within the Hart-Parr factory. In this case, two of the Hart-Parr "20" engines were coupled to yield a four-cylinder engine having a 5-1/2 x 6-1/2 inch bore and stroke. The "40" was built in the 1923-1927 period, and was sent to Nebraska's Tractor Test Laboratory in July 1923. In Test No. 97 it demonstrated over 46 belt horsepower.

|       | 1       | 2       | 3       | 4       |
|-------|---------|---------|---------|---------|
| 22-40 | $8,500  | $7,500  | $6,000  | $2,500  |

**Hart-Parr 12-24 tractor**

Production of the Hart-Parr 12-24 began in 1924. This tractor replaced the earlier Hart-Parr "20". Initially the 12-24 was built with the same 5-1/2 x 6-1/2 engine as was used in the "20." However, this changed in 1926 with the use of a 5-3/4 x 6-

1/2 inch engine. Thus, the power level was raised from about 17 maximum drawbar horsepower to 22 drawbar horsepower. The 12-24 remained in the line until 1928.

|       | 1       | 2       | 3       | 4       |
|-------|---------|---------|---------|---------|
| 12-24 | $6,000  | $5,000  | $4,000  | $2,000  |

**Hart-Parr 18-36 tractor**

Production of the Hart-Parr 18-36 ran from 1926 until 1930. This model replaced the Hart-Parr "30" and was substantially larger than its predecessor. The 18-36 was vastly underrated, delivering over 32 maximum drawbar horsepower in Nebraska Test No. 128 of 1926. This 7,300 pound tractor was also capable of nearly 43 belt horsepower.

|               | 1       | 2       | 3       | 4       |
|---------------|---------|---------|---------|---------|
| 18-36 Model G | $6,000  | $4,500  | $3,000  | $1,500  |
| 18-36 Model H | $6,000  | $4,500  | $3,000  | $1,500  |

Almost 44 drawbar horsepower was manifested for the Hart-Parr 28-50 as shown in Nebraska Test No. 140 of 1927. The 28-50, built in the 1927-1930 period, was a four-cylinder design, using a 5-3/4 x 6-1/2 inch bore and stroke. This big tractor was capable of nearly 65 belt horsepower. On April 1, 1929 the Hart-Parr Company merged with others to form the Oliver Farm

**Hart-Parr 28-50 tractor**

Equipment Corporation. The Hart-Parr name remained for a few years, but with the merger came the end of Hart-Parr as a manufacturing entity. Henceforth, the Oliver name would be a dominant force in the farm tractor industry.

|  | <u>1</u> | <u>2</u> | <u>3</u> | <u>4</u> |
|---|---|---|---|---|
| 28-50 Hart-Parr | $8,500 | $7,000 | $5,000 | $2,000 |
| 18-27 (single wheel Row Crop) | $3,000 | $2,500 | $1,800 | $1,000 |
| 18-27 (dual wheel Row Crop) | $3,000 | $2,500 | $1,800 | $1,000 |
| 18-28 (2-3 plow tractor) | $3,500 | $3,000 | $2,500 | $1,500 |
| 28-44 (3-5 plow tractor) | $3,750 | $3,200 | $2,500 | $1,500 |
| 70 Oliver Hart Parr | $3,000 | $2,400 | $2,000 | $800 |

(Oliver-Hart Parr 70 was built from 1935-1937 when the Hart-Parr name was dropped.)

| 70 Oliver | $2,800 | $2,200 | $1,800 | $800 |
|---|---|---|---|---|

(70 Oliver add $700+ for tiptoe rears and cast fronts.)

## C. W. Hart
*Wauwatosa, Wisconsin*

**Hart tractor**

After C. W. Hart left Hart-Parr Company in 1917 he was in Montana by early the following year. Meanwhile, it appears that he was at Wauwatosa, Wisconsin for a time. Hart continued working on tractor developments with his friend and chief engineer at Charles City, Conrad E. Frudden. The latter went on to be a tractor engineer at Allis-Chalmers for many years. About 1918 the Hart tractor appeared, with one of them being shown here.

**Hart tractor**

The Hart tractor was patented under No. 1,509,293. Hart designed the tractor, apparently with the help of C. E. Frudden. Three of these tractors were built, and Hart eventually shipped them to Montana for use on his wheat ranch. The lure of wheat ranching and the oil refinery business brought an end to Hart's active work in tractor design, with the Hart tractor being the last example.

## Hebb Motors Company
*Lincoln, Nebraska*

In 1918, Hebb Motors Co. filed a trademark application for their "Patriot" tractor, claiming that they had first used this mark on October 1, 1917. Aside from this, no other information on this company has been found.

## Heer Engine Company
*Portsmouth, Ohio*

See: Morton-Heer Company and Reliable Tractor and Engine Company

Chris Heer announced his new four-wheel-drive tractor in 1912. At the time, it was the only FWD tractor on the market. By 1914 it was being built in three sizes; 16-24, 20-28, and 24-32. Apparently they used Heer stationary engines, or modifications thereof for the power plant. Heer had

**Heer FWD tractor**

previously pioneered the development of two-cylinder opposed engines in sizes up to 40 horsepower. The company endured until 1916 when it was reorganized as Reliable Tractor & Engine Company.

## Hefty Tractor Company
*Madison, Wisconsin*

No information has been located for this company.

## Heider Mfg. Company
*Carroll, Iowa*

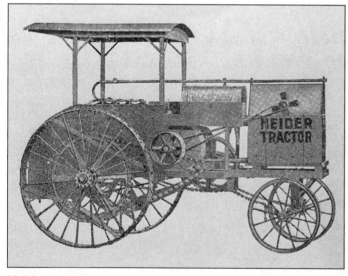

**Heider tractor**

John Heider announced his first tractor in 1911. With it, Heider made the friction drive system famous as a method of power transmission. Weighing only 4,500 pounds, the Heider was equipped with a four-cylinder Waukesha engine having a 4-3/4 x 5 inch bore and stroke. This was one of the first successful tractors of lightweight design.

By 1912 the Heider tractor had been substantially improved. This model caught the attention of Rock Island Plow Company. As a result, the latter began selling the Heider tractors by the

**Heider tractor**

hundreds in 1914. In January 1916, Rock Island bought out the Heider tractor line and continued selling tractors under the Heider name until 1927.

|  | 1 | 2 | 3 | 4 |
|---|---|---|---|---|
| Screen cooled |  |  |  |  |
|  | $32,000 | $25,000 | $12,000 | $7,000 |
| Heider C | $17,000 | $13,000 | $10,000 | $5,000 |
| Heider D | $12,500 | $10,000 | $6,500 | $2,500 |

## Heinss Motor Plow Company
*Fort Wayne, Indiana*

This firm was organized in 1916 but no other information has been found.

## Heinz & Munschauer
*Cleveland, Ohio*

This firm was apparently the antecedent of the Leader Tractor Company of Cleveland; the latter began building tractors in 1948. Heinz & Munschauer appear in a trademark application for the "Leader" trademark dated February 5, 1948. In their application they claim to have first used the "Leader" trademark on January 21, 1945.

## Frank Held Tractor Company
*Columbus, Ohio*

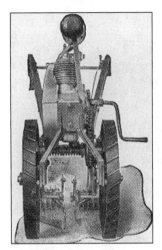

**Gro-Mor Cultivator**

In 1927 the Gro-Mor Cultivator was listed from this firm. It was equipped with a Briggs & Stratton engine having a 2-1/2 inch bore and stroke. Priced at $175, it weighed 200 pounds. Little other information has been found regarding this firm.

| 1 | 2 | 3 | 4 |
|---|---|---|---|
| $2,500 | $2,000 | $1,550 | $500 |

## Joshua Hendy Iron Works
*Sunnyvale, California*

In 1912 M. Rumely Company at LaPorte, Indiana bought out an orchard tractor design from the Hendy people. This became the Rumely Toe-Hold tractor. However, in 1919 the firm is listed as the manufacturer of the Paragon tractor, but no additional information regarding this model has been located.

## Henneuse Tractor Company
*Sacramento, California*

About 1920 Henneuse began offering their Rigid-Rail crawler tractor. It was rated at 25 drawbar and 40 belt horsepower. A Stearns four-cylinder engine with a 5 x 6-1/2 inch engine powered this

**Rigid-Rail crawler**

model. The Rigid-Rail was advertised in 1921, but no other listings or specifications have been located.

## Henry, Millard & Henry Company
*York, Pennsylvania*

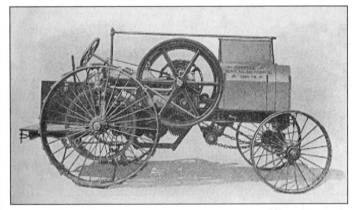

**H.M. & H. tractor**

In 1911 H. M. & H. advertised this single-cylinder tractor. It was apparently available in several different horsepower sizes, and utilized the company's own stationary engines for power. Few specific details regarding this tractor have been found.

By 1914, H. M. & H. was still advertising their single-cylinder tractors. Initially, they were offered under the "Advance" trade name, but by 1914 they were sold as the "HM & H" tractors.

**H.M. & H. tractor**

Shortly after this time the company left the tractor business, concentrating instead on their line of stationary engines.

## Herbert Tractor Company
*Detroit, Michigan*

In 1917 this company was listed as the manufacturer of the 16-32 Herbert tractor. No other information has been found.

## Hercules Tractor Company
*Evansville, Indiana*

This company was incorporated in 1916 for $300,000. Ostensibly, the firm was organized to build farm tractors, but apparently this did not materialize. The company was somehow involved with the Hercules Gas Engine Works and the Hercules Buggy Works, also of Evansville.

## Hero Mfg. Company
*Winnipeg, Manitoba*

In 1911 Hero announced their first tractor. It was designed by Albert O. Espe. The latter had previously designed the Universal tractor, built first by Crookston Mfg. Company, and then by the

**Hero tractor**

Northwest Thresher Company of Stillwater, Minnesota. Hero apparently bought out all of Espe's plans, patents, and foundry patterns as they prepared to put the tractor into production. The plans apparently came to naught, since nothing more can be found regarding the company or its tractors.

## Hession Tractor & Tiller Corporation
*Buffalo, New York*

See: Wheat Tiller & Tractor Company

**Hession tractor**

Hession Tractor & Tiller Corporation was incorporated for $10 million in 1917. Their Hession tractor was available with ordinary steel wheels for farm work, but could also be furnished with hard rubber tires for road work, as shown here. The tractor was sold as the "Hession" into 1919, but during that year the company sold it as the "Wheat" tractor. Rated as a 12-24, it used an Erd four-cylinder engine having a 4 x 6 inch bore and stroke. After 1920 the firm was known as Wheat Tiller & Tractor Corporation.

| | 1 | 2 | 3 | 4 |
|---|---|---|---|---|
| Hession | — | $15,000 | — | — |

## Hicks Tractor Company

*Minneapolis, Minnesota*

**Hicks 12-25 crawler tractor**

This firm was incorporated at Minneapolis in 1916. Late the following year the company relocated to Harvey, Illinois, and by 1918 was situated at Milwaukee, Wisconsin. The company built the Hicks 12-25 crawler tractor, and as shown here, it was a half-track design with front steering wheels. Few specific details of the Hicks 12-25 have been found.

## Highway Tractor Company

*Jackson, Michigan*

This company was incorporated for $2 million in 1917. No other details have been found.

## Hiller Engineering Corporation

*Redwood City, California*

Hiller Yard Hand Model 100 garden tractors appear in trade directories in 1954. The model shown here used a Power Products Model 170 single-cylinder two-cycle motor having a 1-3/4 x

**Hiller Yard Hand Model 100 garden tractor**

1-1/2 inch bore and stroke. Various attachments were available, including a mower, sweeper, cart, roller, and spreader. An interesting attachment was a 10-inch circular saw.

| 1 | 2 | 3 | 4 |
|---|---|---|---|
| $800 | $600 | $200 | $150 |

## J. A. Hockett

*Sterling, Kansas*

J. A. and P. Hockett, R. A. Steward, P. P. Truehart, and W. W. Webb formed the Gasoline Thresher & Plow Company at Sterling in 1893. This company was organized to develop the Sterling gasoline traction engine under development by J. A. Hockett. Given the state of the art in the gas engine business at the time, the venture failed. Further details may be found under the heading, *Gasoline Thresher & Plow Company.*

## Hoke Mfg. Company

*New Carlisle, Indiana*

In 1948 this company was listed as a garden tractor manufacturer, but no other references or photographs have been located.

## Hoke Tractor Company

*South Bend, Indiana*

John I. Hoke announced his first tractor in 1912. At the time, Hoke was located at Washington,

**Hoke tractor**

Indiana. His 'universal' tractor design prompted him to apply for a patent, and indeed, Patent No. 1,073,490 was eventually issued. During 1913 the new company set up a factory at South Bend, Indiana.

**Hoke 12-24 tractor**

The Hoke tractor was built only in one size with a 12-24 horsepower rating. It featured a Waukesha four-cylinder engine having a 4-1/4 x 5-3/4 inch bore and stroke. Despite the quality features of the Hoke tractor, it disappeared from the market after 1917. Whether the company then went into other ventures, or simply closed the doors, is unknown.

|  | **1** | **2** | **3** | **4** |
|---|---|---|---|---|
| Hoke 12-24 | $14,500 | — | $7,500 | — |

# Hollis Tractor Company
*Pittsburgh, Pennsylvania*

**Hollis Type M, 15-25 tractor**

Hollis first appeared with their Type M, 15-25 tractor in 1916 or 1917. This unusual design placed two driving and steering wheels to the front, and support wheels to the rear. A Light four-cylinder engine was used; it had a 3-1/4 x 4-1/2 inch bore and stroke. The Hollis tractor only remained on the market for a short time; apparently it was gone from the scene by 1920.

# J. S. Holmes
*Beloit, Wisconsin*

**Holmes tractor**

Already in 1906, J. S. Holmes began experimenting with a small, lightweight tractor design. By 1908 he had perfected the small tractor shown here. It used a two-cylinder vertical engine, and two forward speeds were provided. Considerable notice was given to the Holmes design, and plans were made to set up a factory for this purpose, but this did not materialize.

## Holmes Mfg. Company
*Port Clinton, Ohio*

**Holmes Little Giant Tractor**

In 1912 Holmes announced their new Holmes Little Giant Tractor. It was rated at 12 brake horsepower and weighed 4,500 pounds. In 1913 the company name was changed to Holmes Tractor Co. Little else is known of the company or its venture into the tractor business, since it disappears from the tractor directories in 1914.

## Holt Mfg. Company
*Stockton, California*

Benjamin Holt demonstrated his first steam-powered tracklayer tractor in 1890. Various steam tracklayers were built in the following years. Holt bought out Daniel Best in 1908 and began building a gasoline-powered tracklayer that year. In 1909 the company bought the Peoria, Illinois factory of Colean Mfg. Company and established a second factory there.

C. L. Best emerged as one of Holt's strongest competitors. In 1925 the two companies merged to form Caterpillar Tractor Company.

**Holt tracklayer tractor**

In the 1890s Benjamin Holt perfected the idea of a tracklayer tractor. For several years to follow, it was steam powered, mainly because gasoline engines were not yet perfected and were very heavy, besides being somewhat unreliable. This large steam powered tracklayer was especially designed to work in soft and mucky soil that was otherwise untouchable with conventional plowing methods.

**Holt gasoline-powered crawler**

In 1908 Holt publicly demonstrated the company's first gasoline-powered crawler tractor. Initially, and for several years to come, a front tiller wheel was used for steering. However, it was eventually discovered that the crawler could be steered on its own tracks and the tiller wheel quickly disappeared.

**Holt-Illinois tractor**

In 1911 the Holt-Illinois tractor appeared for a short time, and was one of the very few entries Holt made into the wheel tractor business. Little is known of this tractor except that it used Holt's 45 horsepower four-cylinder engine, along with the heavy construction that typified all the tractors built by Holt.

**Holt Caterpillar tractor**

By 1912 Holt's Caterpillar tractors had become well known and were very popular in the Canadian provinces. At this time they were offered in 45 and 60 horsepower sizes, both using a four-cylinder engine. With their tremendous tractive force, these machines were virtually unstoppable, especially when compared with the methods then in use.

In 1914 Holt Mfg. Company placed the Caterpillar "18" on the market. It was the smallest of the Caterpillar line, and was designed specifically to work in orchards, vineyards, and small

**Holt Caterpillar "18"**

ranches. The "18" was only 53 inches wide and 53 inches high. Weighing 5,900 pounds, it sold for $1,600.

**Holt Caterpillar 25-45 model**

For 1918 Holt offered their Caterpillar 25-45 model. It weighed 6-3/4 tons, and was equipped with Holt's own four-cylinder engine having a 6 x 7 inch bore and stroke. The canopy and side-curtains were standard equipment intended to protect the engine from the elements. Note the front-mounted belt pulley.

A huge four-cylinder engine with a 7-1/2 x 8 inch bore and stroke was used in the Caterpillar 40-75 tractor. This 1918 model was 104 inches wide, 10 feet high, and 20 feet long; it weighed

**Caterpillar 40-75 tractor**

**Caterpillar Two-Ton tractor**

almost 12 tons. At this point in time the front steering wheel remained for the larger Caterpillar models, but would shortly disappear.

stroke. Three forward speeds were provided, ranging from 2 to 5-1/4 mph. A belt pulley came as standard equipment.

|          | **1**    | **2**   | **3**   | **4**   |
|----------|----------|---------|---------|---------|
| Two-Ton  | $10,000  | $7,500  | $4,000  | $2,000  |

**Caterpillar 70-120 tractor**

**Caterpillar Five-Ton model**

A 1918 offering was the Caterpillar 70-120 tractor. It was one of the largest tractors on the market at the time (if not the largest) and weighed an impressive 24,800 pounds. Power came from a six-cylinder engine having a 7-1/2 x 8 inch bore and stroke. A rear-mounted belt pulley came as standard equipment.

By 1923 the Caterpillar Two-Ton tractor was on the market. This little crawler only weighed 4,000 pounds. It was equipped with a four-cylinder engine having a 4 x 5-1/2 inch bore and

The Caterpillar Five-Ton model was also built as the 25-40 tractor. Weighing 9,400 pounds, it was designed around a four-cylinder engine having a 4-3/4 x 6 inch bore and stroke. This model was still in production at the time of the 1925 Holt-Best merger that formed Caterpillar Tractor Company.

|          | **1**    | **2**    | **3**   | **4**   |
|----------|----------|----------|---------|---------|
| Five-Ton | $18,000  | $14,000  | $7,500  | $3,500  |

Caterpillar Ten-Ton tractors were easily capable of pulling six plows under virtually any conditions. Weighing 19,000 pounds, the Ten-Ton like its contemporaries, was furnished with a

**Caterpillar Ten-Ton tractors**

**Autotiller "12" from Homestead Tractor Corporation**

rear-mounted belt pulley as standard equipment. Power came from a four-cylinder engine having a 6-1/2 x 7 inch bore and stroke.

| | 1 | 2 | 3 | 4 |
|---|---|---|---|---|
| Ten-Ton | $20,000 | $15,000 | $8,5000 | $4,000 |

## Holton Tractor Company
*Indianapolis, Indiana*

This firm announced they were building a new factory in 1915. From it came the Holton 10-16 tractor. This model used a four-cylinder LeRoi engine with a 31/8 x 4-1/2 inch bore and stroke. (The same engine was used in numerous small tractors of the day). Holton advertised this engine into the early 1920s. While this model demonstrates many of the salient features of the row-crop tractor, it was not designed and built as such; the single front wheel was simply a part of the design. Apparently the manufacturer did not consider the potential of using a front-mounted cultivator.

## Homer Laughlin Engine Company
*Los Angeles, California*

No information has been found on this company.

## Homestead Tractor Corporation
*New York, New York*

Sometime during our forty years of collecting data on old tractors we came across the Auto-Tiller "12" from Homestead Tractor Corporation.

Unfortunately, we have no other information on it, nor can we ascertain with certainty what year this tractor was built. We would guess this one to be from the 1920s.

## Hoosier Wheel & Tractor Company
*Franklin, Indiana*

A poor image of the Hoosier 20-35 tractor appears in our book, *Encyclopedia of American Farm Tractors*: Crestline/Motorbooks, 1979. However, we were unable to locate a reproducible picture of this tractor for the present volume. The 20-35 appeared about 1920 and remained on the market for only a short time. It was equipped with a four-cylinder Midwest engine having a 4-1/2 x 6 inch bore and stroke.

## Hoyse Tractor Company
*South Bend, Indiana*

This company was incorporated in 1914 with a capitalization of $90,000. Aside from this, no other information has been found.

## Huber Mfg. Company
*Marion, Ohio*

Edward Huber established a small factory in Marion, Ohio in 1865. By 1880 the company was recognized as a significant builder of steam traction engines and threshing machines. In 1898 the firm built a gasoline tractor, using a VanDuzen gasoline engine. Various problems kept this project from further development, but in 1911 the company returned with the "Farmer's Tractor." The company continued producing tractors until suspended during World War Two. Tractor production never resumed after the Armistice.

**Huber gasoline traction engine**

In 1898 Huber Mfg. Company produced its first tractor. The company bought out Van Duzen Gasoline Engine Company, Cincinnati, Ohio. The latter had been in the engine business for several years. Using a Van Duzen engine, the company proceeded to build a tractor mounted on wheels and gearing from the Huber steam traction engines. The experiment met with poor success and the entire project was abandoned.

**Farmer's Tractor**

During 1910 and 1911 Huber developed their Farmer's Tractor. It used a two-cylinder engine having a 5-3/4 x 6 inch bore and stroke. Tower cooling was used, that is, cooling water was

pumped over inclined screens at the top of the tank for evaporative cooling. This model apparently was marketed for only a couple of years.

**Huber 13-22 Farmer's Tractor**

The 1912 Huber tractor line included a new 13-22 Farmer's Tractor. It may have been no more than an upgrade from the previous Farmer's tractor, but a few magazine advertisements of the day point to it as being a 'new' model. A two-speed transmission was featured, and everything was enclosed but the final drives. Power came from a two-cylinder engine with a 7-inch bore and stroke. Like the original Farmer's Tractor, this one used evaporative cooling with a large tank mounted to the front of the radiator

**Huber 30-60 tractor**

In 1912 the Huber 30-60 tractor appeared. This big tractor had a four-cylinder engine with a 7 x 8 inch bore and stroke. To give some idea of the physical size of this tractor, the rear wheels stood 8 feet tall! The huge tubular radiator carried 95 gallons of water and cooling air was drawn through 175 two-inch tubes. Production of this tractor continued until 1916 when it was super-seded by the big four-cylinder 35-70 model. This model was closed out in 1917.

|  | **1** | **2** | **3** | **4** |
|---|---|---|---|---|
| 30-60 | $55,000 | $40,000 | $32,500 | $20,000 |

**Huber 20-40 tractor**

About 1914 Huber introduced their 20-40 tractor. It was built along the same general lines as the larger 30-60. The 20-40 used a two-cylinder engine. Like the 30-60, production continued until about 1917. Very little data has been found for the 20-40.

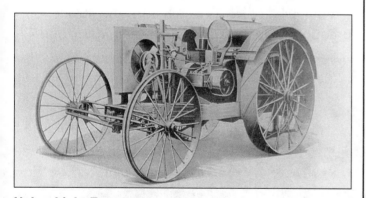

**Huber Light Four tractor**

During 1916 the Huber Light Four tractor appeared. This model weighed 5,200 pounds. Power came from a four-cylinder Waukesha engine having a 4-1/2 x 5-3/4 inch bore and stroke. This model was very popular, even with an initial price tag of $1,085. The Light Four was built until about 1929. Adding to the confusion, the company also built a Super Four 15-30 model in the 1921-25 period.

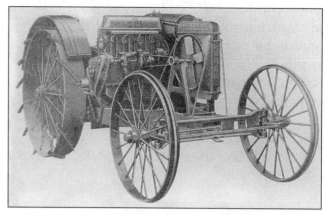

**Huber Super Four 15-30 tractor**

Huber introduced its Super Four 15-30 tractor in 1921. A copy was sent to Nebraska's Tractor Test Laboratory that year where it demonstrated a maximum of almost 45 belt horsepower. This model was equipped with a Midwest four-cylinder engine having a 4-1/2 x 6 inch bore and stroke. By 1923 though, the engine was changed to a four-cylinder Waukesha with a 4-1/2 x 5-3/4 inch bore and stroke. Production of this model continued into 1925. The 1925 *Red Book, page 46,* illustrates and describes the Super 4, 18-36 tractor. It used the same Midwest four-cylinder engine as the earlier Super 4, 15-30 tractor, with a 4-1/2 x 6 inch bore and stroke. There is considerable confusion about some of the Huber models, especially since some of the crossmotor tractors and some of those with in-line engines used the same model designation although they were entirely different tractors

**Huber 25-50 Master Four tractor**

In 1922 Huber introduced the 25-50 Master Four tractor. This model used a Hinkley four-cylinder engine with a 5-1/2 x 6 inch bore and stroke. Rated speed was 1,000 rpm. This model used a drilled crankshaft for full pressure lubrication of the crank journals, and also used drilled connecting rods for perfect lubrication of the wrist pins. Despite the quality features of the 25-50, it was marketed for only a short time.

| 1 | 2 | 3 | 4 |
|---|---|---|---|
| Light Four/Super Four/Master Four | | | |
| $10,000 | $7,000 | $4,000 | $1,500 |

**Huber 18-36 Super Four tractor**

In 1926 Huber began building their new 18-36 Super Four tractor. This unit frame design carried a four-cylinder Stearns engine having a 4-3/4 x 6-1/2 inch bore and stroke. Delivering over 43 belt horsepower in Nebraska Test No. 123, the 18-36 was also capable of 27 drawbar horsepower. By 1929 this model became the Super 4, 21-39 tractor.

In 1926 the Huber Super 4, 20-40 tractor appeared. This model was tested at Nebraska in September of that year. In 1929 the company re-rated it as a 32-45 tractor. Power came from a four-cylinder Stearns engine having a 5-1/8 x 6-1/2 inch bore and stroke.

| | 1 | 2 | 3 | 4 |
|---|---|---|---|---|
| 20-40 | $6,500 | $5,000 | $2,500 | $1,000 |

**Huber's Light Four, 20-36 model**

Advertising for Huber's Light Four, 20-36 model first appeared in 1928. Nebraska Test No. 168 was run on this tractor that year. The 20-36 was equipped with a Waukesha four-cylinder engine having a 4-3/4 x 6-1/4 inch bore and stroke. A unique feature of this engine was the use of a

**Huber Super 4, 20-40 tractor**

**Huber 25-50 Super Four**

Ricardo head. Its unique design added extra power, lowered exhaust temperatures, and reduced spark plug fouling. The 20-36 remained on the market through 1935.

The Huber 25-50 Super Four appeared in 1926. This powerful tractor was capable of nearly 70 belt horsepower, and nearly 50 horsepower on the drawbar. It weighed nearly five tons. Power was derived from a Stearns four-cylinder engine with a 5-1/2 x 6-1/2 inch bore and stroke. By 1929 this tractor was re-rated as the Huber 40-62 tractor.

engine having a 5-1/8 x 6-1/2 inch bore and stroke. In 1929 the *Red Book* shows the same tractor with the same engine as the Huber Super Four 32-43 model. In 1935 the Huber HK tractor was introduced. The 1935 *Red Book* describes this as the "Huber HK 32-45" tractor. However, this was an entirely different tractor than the Huber Super Four 32-45 tractor, also illustrated in the 1935 *Red Book*. About this time the company began offering rubber tires as an extra-cost option. Production continued until being suspended by World War Two. After the war, tractor production was not resumed.

**Huber Super Four 32-45**

The 1928 *Red Book* illustrates the Super Four, 20-40 tractor equipped with a four-cylinder Stearns

**Huber 40-62 tractor**

During 1929 the Huber 25-50 took on a new 40-62 horsepower rating. As noted previously, this tractor was capable of nearly 70 belt horsepower, so the new 62 horsepower rating on the belt was still quite conservative. Production of the 40-62 continued until the onset of World War Two.

| | 1 | 2 | 3 | 4 |
|---|---|---|---|---|
| 40-62 | $10,000 | $8,000 | $6,000 | $2,500 |

**Huber 27-42 tractor**

Production of the Huber HS 27-42 tractor continued until World War Two. This model was a continuation of the Super Four 18-36 that had been introduced in 1925. In 1929 this model was re-rated as the Huber 21-39 and the 1936 *Red Book* designates it as the Huber HS 27-42 tractor. Since manufacturers supplied the information for guides such as *I&T Red Book* and the *Tractor Field Book*, it is presumed that the model designations reflect the wishes of the company sales department.

**Huber Modern Farmer**

The Huber Modern Farmer probably made its first appearance in 1933 or 1934. Weighing less than two tons, it used a Waukesha four-cylinder engine with a 4-1/4 x 5 inch bore and stroke. By 1935 the Model L Modern Farmer appeared.

**Huber Modern Farmer "SC"**

Apparently of short duration was the Huber Modern Farmer "SC" tractor that appeared in 1935. This tractor used a four-cylinder Waukesha engine having a 4-1/8 x 5-1/4 inch bore and stroke. IN 1936 this tractor was apparently replaced with the Modern Farmer "LC" tractor of slightly more horsepower.

**Huber "L" tractor**

By 1936 the Huber "L" tractor appeared. The "L" used a 4-1/2 x 5-1/4 engine for slightly more horsepower, and the most obvious change is the use of solid disk wheels, both front and rear. Production of the Model L continued until suspended by World War Two. The "S" and the larger "L" tractors were both standard-tread design, while the "SC" and "LC" were both tricycle designs.

**Huber Modern Farmer "LC"**

The Modern Farmer "LC" tractor of 1936 was an improved model over the original "SC" tractor of 1935. This one weighed 3,900 pounds and was powered by a Waukesha engine with a 4-1/2 x 5-1/4 inch bore and stroke. Rubber tires were optional equipment, and electric starting and lights could be furnished when ordered, but as an extra-cost option. Production of this model ended with the beginning of World War Two.

**Huber Model B**

The Huber Model B came onto the market in 1936 and was built until 1943. This model included a streamlined hood and rubber tires as standard equipment. Electric starting and lights also came as standard equipment. A four-cylinder Buda engine was used in this model; it carried a 3-13/16 x 4-1/2 inch bore and stroke.

|         | 1       | 2       | 3       | 4     |
|---------|---------|---------|---------|-------|
| Model B | $4,000  | $2,500  | $1,500  | $800  |

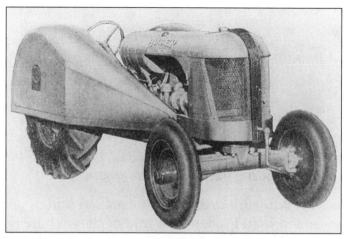

**Huber Model "OB" orchard tractor**

Huber began building their Model "OB" orchard tractor about 1937. It was simply a standard-tread version of the "B" row-crop tractor, plus the addition of the necessary modifications and the special fenders needed for orchard work. It is unlikely that any great number were built, since all tractor production ceased at the beginning of World War Two.

**Huber road grader**

By 1920 Huber Mfg. Company had developed an undermounted road grader that was integrated with a specially modified Light Four tractor. This was the beginning of Huber's entry into the road machinery business. Occasionally this machine is illustrated in Huber's farm machinery catalogs of the day.

After World War Two, Huber once again resumed building road machinery, and indeed continued building a specially modified Model B

**Huber Model B tractor with road grader**

tractor with an extended frame and an under-mounted road grader. The tractor shown here is also equipped with a hydraulically operated front bulldozer blade, and presumably it could also be fitted with a scarifier and other devices.

## Hudkins Tractor Company
*Salina, Kansas*

This company was incorporated for $100,000 in 1918. Aside from this, no other information has been found.

## Huffman Traction Engine Company
*Kenton, Ohio*

**Master Huffman tractor**

The Master Huffman tractor first appeared in 1913. This massive tractor had an 8-foot drive wheel, and was powered by a huge two-cylinder engine of 70 horsepower. It also featured two forward speeds, a feature not often found on large, heavyweight tractors. Aside from the initial announcement, little else is known of the company or its further efforts.

## Humber-Anderson Mfg. Company
*St. Paul, Minnesota*

See: Willmar Tractor Co.

**Little Oak tractor**

The Little Oak tractor first appeared in 1913 with the incorporation of Humber-Anderson. Originally, it was rated at 25 drawbar and 47 belt horsepower. A four-cylinder engine was used; it had a 5-5/8 x 7-1/2 inch bore and stroke. It weighed 9,500 pounds, and could be furnished with a four-bottom mounted plow. For exceptional conditions the rear bottom could be hinged upward if needed. Each plow bottom was furnished with a break pin in case a stone or other object was encountered. In August 1914 the company was reorganized as Willmar Mfg. Company at Willmar, Minnesota. In December 1916 the company was again reorganized, this time as Standard Tractor Company at Stillwater, Minnesota.

|  | **1** | **2** | **3** | **4** |
|---|---|---|---|---|
| Little Oak | — | — | $9,000 | — |

## Hume Mfg. Company
*Hume, Illinois*

Hume was organized in 1913 and eventually received Patent No. 1,068,517 for their design. This tractor was rated at 20 drawbar and 30 belt horsepower, using a four-cylinder engine. Weighing 7,000 pounds, it sold for $1,350. About 1916 a Hume Jr. tractor appeared, but our research has found little information on this

**Hume Jr.**

model. About 1917 the company was bought out by Lyons-Atlas Company of Indianapolis, Indiana who built the same tractor under the "Atlas" name for a short time.

## Hunter Tractor Company
*Los Angeles, California*

**Hunter tractor**

The Hunter was a short-lived tractor that apparently made its first appearance about 1918 or 1919. It was a four-wheel-drive design and featured hard rubber tires. Weighing three tons, it was capable of speeds from 1-1/2 to 12 mph. Power came from a Barker six-cylinder horizontally opposed engine. In 1920, the last year it was listed in the trade directories, the Hunter 15-25 sold for $5,500.

## Huron Engineering Company
*Belleville, Michigan*

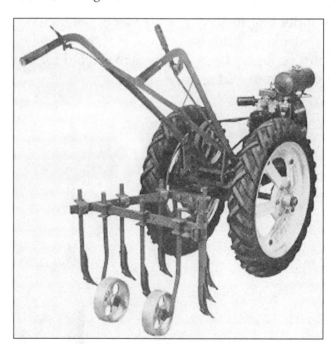

**Huron Model A-2 garden tractor**

The Huron Model A-2 garden tractor appears in the 1948 trade directories. No other references to this model have been found. Powered by a Clinton 1-1/2 horsepower engine, the A-2 rode on 4.00x18 implement tires with the wheel spacing adjustable from 23 to 30 inches. Shipping weight of this model was 270 pounds.

|  | 1 | 2 | 3 | 4 |
|---|---|---|---|---|
| Model A-Z | $500 | $350 | $150 | $45 |

# Huron Tractor Company
*Detroit, Michigan*

**Boyer Four, 12-25 tractor**

The Boyer Four, 12-25 tractor appeared in the 1917 trade directories, the only year in which it is listed. It was equipped with a Waukesha four-cylinder engine having a 4-1/4 x 5-3/4 inch bore and stroke. Little else is known of the Boyer Four, probably because it was marketed for only a short time.

# H. L. Hurst Mfg. Company
*Greenwich, Ohio*

**Hurst 2-4 garden tractor**

In 1920 the Hurst 2-4 garden tractor appeared. Rated at 2 drawbar and 4 belt horsepower, it was equipped with a single-cylinder engine. This outfit weighed 600 pounds and was priced new at $355. It was also known as the Hurst Culti-Plow. The Hurst 2-4 is currently valued at $2,000-$3,000 in any condition.

# I

## Illinois Tractor Company

*Bloomington, Illinois*

**Illinois Motor Cultivator**

The Illinois Motor Cultivator made its appearance in 1916. At the time the company was known as Illinois Silo Company, and by the following year the name was changed to Illinois Silo & Tractor Company. The new motor cultivator was available with a single-cylinder 4 horsepower engine as shown here, or it could be supplied with an 8 horsepower two-cylinder engine if so desired.

The 1917 Illinois Motor Cultivator was vastly improved over the original 1916 model. Power now came from a four-cylinder engine of 16 brake horsepower; it used a 3 x 3-1/4 inch bore and stroke. Through a unique clutch system

**1917 Illinois Motor Cultivator**

built into each drive wheel, the motor cultivator could literally turn in its own tracks. Front caster wheels were used to permit short turns. No Motor Cultivators are known to exist.

**Illinois 12-30 tractor**

Sometime in 1917 the Illinois 12-30 tractor appeared. Weighing 3,700 pounds, it was priced at $1,200. Power came from a Waukesha four-cylinder engine having a 4-1/2 x 5-3/4 inch bore and stroke. A friction drive transmission provided infinitely variable speeds up to 6 mph. This model remained on the market through 1918.

**18-30 Illinois Super-Drive tractor**

By 1918 the company had once again changed its name, this time to Illinois Tractor Company. The following year the 18-30 Illinois Super-Drive tractor appeared. It was powered by a Climax four-cylinder engine having a 5 x 6-1/2 inch bore and stroke. The 18-30 weighed 5,500 pounds and sold for $2,250. This tractor used a unique drive system with springs between the rear wheels and the spokes. It was intended to minimize unwanted strain for both the engine and the load.

| 1 | 2 | 3 | 4 |
|---|---|---|---|
| 18-30 Super Drive (1918) | | | |
| $8,000 | $6,000 | $4,000 | $2,200 |

**Illinois Super-Drive 22-40 tractor**

By 1920 Illinois Tractor Company was offering their Illinois Super-Drive 22-40 tractor. This

model was likely built for only a short time, since the company disappears from the trade directories after 1921. The 22-40 used a four-cylinder Climax engine and weighed 6,200 pounds. Illinois Super-Drive tractors were sold in Canada by Robert Bell Engine & Thresher Company at Seaforth, Ontario under the name of Imperial Super-Drive.

# Imperial Mfg. Company

*Minneapolis, Minnesota*

**Imperial 40-60 tractor**

The Imperial 40-60 tractor first appeared in 1910 from this firm, although they were built already in 1908 by Valentine Bros., also of Minneapolis. The latter merged with the Shock & Hay Loader Co. of Minneapolis to form Imperial in 1910. The 40-60 tractor was actively built as late as 1914, but the company continued to build them on a limited basis as late as 1920. The 40-60 used a four-cylinder horizontally opposed engine with a 7-1/2 x 9 inch bore and stroke. In 1920 this tractor was offered at a price of $4,500. Three specimens are known to exist today.

| 1 | 2 | 3 | 4 |
|---|---|---|---|
| 40-60 (1910) $80,000 | — | — | — |

## Independent Harvester Company
*Plano, Illinois*

Independent was fairly well known as an implement builder, but their efforts in the tractor business remain presently unknown.

## Independent Tractor Company
*Minneapolis, Minnesota*

In 1917 this firm was listed as the manufacturer of The Independent Drive Tractor. No other information has been located.

## Indiana Farm Bureau Co-Op
*Shelbyville, Indiana*

**Co-Op Model C**

In 1945 the Indiana Farm Bureau Co-Op at Shelbyville, Indiana produced a Co-Op Model C tractor. It is believed that only 66 units were built. It used a Continental F124 flathead engine. In 1985 an article appeared in *Gas Engine* magazine that suggested that only three of these exist. At this point it seems that two more have surfaced. It is believed that of those extant only two (or maybe three) are complete and have been restored. The PTO was operated by a roller chain drive. Also, of interest is the fact that an ordinary hex-shaped salt shaker glass was used a sediment bowl. The CO-OP emblem on the front of the front of the tractor is of cast iron. At the 1999 Ed Speiss Classic Tractor Auction a Co-Op C Narrow Front sold for $10,000 and a Wide Front sold for $11,000, both in No. 1 restored condition.

## Indiana Silo & Tractor Company
*Anderson, Indiana*

**Indiana tractor**

The Indiana tractor first appeared in 1918 and remained on the market into the early 1920s. Nebraska Test No. 62 of 1920 demonstrated the 5-10 Indiana as having over 11 belt horsepower, and nearly 6 drawbar horsepower. Weighing 2,200 pounds, it was powered by a LeRoi four-cylinder engine having a 3-1/8 x 4-1/2 inch bore and stroke. Much of the design for the Indiana tractor came from C. A. Schubert of Findlay, Ohio. Eventually the design came to the attention of the Indiana people. It was also sold as the Indiana All 'Round Tractor.

|  | **1** | **2** | **3** | **4** |
|---|---|---|---|---|
| 5-10 (1918) | $8,000 | $5,000 | $3,000 | $1,000 |

## Inexco Tractor Corporation
*New York, New York*

**Inexco Tiger 12 garden tractor, Model IXA-12**

In 1948 Inexco offered their Tiger 12 garden tractor, Model IXA-12. It was powered by a Wisconsin Model TF single-cylinder engine having a 3 x

3-1/4 inch bore and stroke. Various implements were available, and a belt pulley came as standard equipment.

**Inexco Tiger 3 Motor Cultivator**

The 1948 Inexco line also included the Tiger 3 Motor Cultivator. Weighing 440 pounds, this outfit used a sliding motor base to add or release tension on the drive belt as the clutch mechanism. Power came from a choice of a 3-1/2 horsepower Lauson engine, a Wisconsin, or a Clinton. Two forward speeds were provided.

**Tiger tractor PTD6**

For 1950 the Tiger tractor line included the PTD6 shown here. This one is equipped with optional dual rear tires, plus a plow attachment and a sickle mower attachment. Briggs & Stratton or Clinton engines could be specified.

By 1950 the Piedmont Tractor Division of Inexco was building the Tiger tractors at its plant in Fort Lee, New Jersey. The PTD5 shown here

**PTD5**

was quite similar to the concurrent PTD6 model. Numerous attachments were available, as was the choice of a Clinton or a Briggs & Stratton engine. In 1951 the Tiger tractor line was being built by Tiger Tractor Corporation at Keyser, West Virginia.

| | **1** | **2** | **3** | **4** |
|---|---|---|---|---|
| All models | $800 | $600 | $300 | $150 |

## Inland-American Tractor Company
*Eau Claire, Wisconsin*

This firm is listed as a tractor builder in 1921, but no further information has been found.

## Intercontinental Mfg. Company
*Garland, Texas*

**Intercontinental C-26**

The C-26 was apparently developed during 1946 and 1947, since it was already on the market in 1948. This model used a Continental four-cylinder gasoline engine having a 3-7/16 x 4-3/8 inch bore and stroke. This model was tested at Nebraska under Test No. 400 of 1948. It demonstrated a rated output of 20 drawbar horsepower. Production of the Intercontinental tractors continued until about 1960.

|      | **1**    | **2** | **3** | **4** |
|------|----------|-------|-------|-------|
| C-26 | $18,000  | —     | —     | —     |

**Intercontinental D-26 diesel tractor**

Production of the Intercontinental D-26 diesel tractor began in late 1948 or early 1949. This model was quite similar to the gasoline-powered C-26, but used a Buda four-cylinder diesel engine. Rated at 1,800 rpm, it carried a 3-7/16 x 4-1/8 inch bore and stroke. The D-26 was capable of nearly 29 belt horsepower, as shown in Nebraska Test No. 420.

**Cultrac crawler**

In 1950 the Cultrac crawler appeared. This interesting design weighed only 1,750 pounds, and

was equipped with a Waukesha four-cylinder engine with a displacement of 61ci. Designed primarily as a cultivating tractor, it could be used for other jobs as well. Production of this model appears to have continued for only a short time.

**Model DF**

The largest tractor of the Intercontinental line was the Model DF; it first appeared in 1952 or 1953. Nebraska Test No. 498 was run on this tractor in July 1953 and revealed a maximum output of 34 belt horsepower. A four-cylinder Buda diesel engine was used; it carried a 3-3/4 x 4-1/8 inch bore and stroke. This tractor was also designated as the Federal DF. For reasons unknown, Intercontinental is not listed in the trade directories after 1960.

## International Cultivator Company
*Oshkosh, Wisconsin*

During 1921 International Cultivator Co. is listed as a tractor manufacturer. Further details are yet to be found.

## International Gas Engine Company
*Cudahy, Wisconsin*

In late 1914 or early 1915 the Ingeco tractor appeared. Rated at 10 drawbar and 20 belt horsepower, it used a two-cylinder opposed engine. Weight of the tractor was 5,000 pounds, and the

**Ingeco tractor**

retail price was $700. The company remained in the tractor market until a merger created Worthington Pump & Machinery Company. The latter continued to build the tractor for only a short time.

# International Harvester Company
*Chicago, Illinois*

Few companies of any sort, and especially in the farm machinery industry, have the history that has always been associated with International Harvester Company. Cyrus Hall McCormick invented the reaper in 1831, and ever since that time, his name has carried a special mystique shared by few others in the history of agricultural mechanization. In 1981 the Author completed the title, *150 Years of International Harvester,* Crestline/Motorbooks. Its 416 pages and 1,900 photographs show the history of the company through its products.

Deering Harvester Company began operations in 1880, although the company had roots going back to the 1850s. By 1900 the Deering concern was also a huge manufacturer of harvesting machinery.

McCormick, Deering, and several other companies merged in 1902 to form International Harvester Company. Within a couple of years IHC began experimenting with gasoline tractors. This in itself is interesting, since the company never seems to have had much fascination with steam power, even though in 1902 and for another twenty years, steam power reigned supreme on American farms.

To its credit, IHC probably poured more money into research and development of the farm tractor than any of its competitors, at least in the early years. The gamble paid off, because IHC quickly rose to the forefront in the tractor industry. The challenge of the Fordson tractor only served to goad the company into accelerated research work on a truly practical row-crop tractor. Full production of the Farmall row-crop tractor began in 1924. It revolutionized the thinking of not only what a row-crop tractor should look like, but also how it should perform!

By 1930 the IHC tractor line was already the most extensive of any American manufacturer. Farm tractors were available in row-crop and standard-tread designs. The IHC crawler tractor line was developing, and several styles of IHC Industrial tractors were available. Curiously, the company did not enter the garden tractor business, although with the huge dealer network and product loyalty enjoyed by IHC, the odds are that garden tractors would have been very successful.

Despite the quality of the IH tractor and equipment lines, the company veered into financial problems due in part to the depressed agricultural economy of the 1980s. Thus, it eventually merged with J. I. Case to form today's Case-IH product line.

**International Harvester Company Auto-Mower**

International Harvester Company began building tractors in 1906. One of the predecessors, McCormick Harvesting Machine Company, began developing an "Auto-Mower" a decade earlier. Although it was not well accepted, and apparently never got past a very small production, it certainly indicates the mindset of company engineers: Gasoline power would be the coming thing in the mechanization of agriculture.

**Deering Harvester Company mower**

Deering Harvester Company began experimenting with a self-powered mowing machine as early as 1891. One of these machines even went to the Paris Exhibition of 1900. Although it attracted considerable attention, it was impractical for a variety of reasons and never went into full production.

**International Harvester gasoline tractor**

By 1906 International Harvester was producing gasoline tractors. Already in 1889 S. S. Morton's friction drive traction trucks were attracting attention. With this chassis almost any gasoline engine could be mounted as the power unit. International Harvester did so with their newly designed gasoline engines. Various styles of friction-drive tractors were built in the following years.

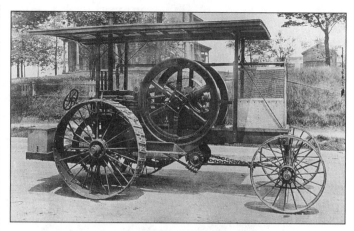

**International Harvester gasoline tractor**

For 1907 the International Harvester gasoline tractor was given an improved appearance over the initial offering. This model shows a 15 horsepower IHC Famous engine mounted on the frame, along with an evaporative cooling tank mounted to the front. In 1908 alone, IHC sold almost 630 of these tractors. The 15 horsepower Type A used a single-cylinder engine with an 8 x 14 inch bore and stroke; a larger 20 horsepower model had a 9 x 15 inch bore and stroke.

|  | **1** | **2** | **3** | **4** |
|---|---|---|---|---|
| 15 hp | — | $70,000 | $50,000 | $20,000 |
| 20 hp | $110,000 | — | — | — |

**International Harvester three-cylinder tractor**

By 1908 International Harvester was looking past the single-cylinder tractors that comprised the line. This three-cylinder experimental tractor emerged. Rated at 40 horsepower, it used a 7 x 9 inch bore and stroke. It was entered in the 1908 Winnipeg tractor trials and performed fairly well, but apparently IHC engineers weren't impressed because nothing more was heard of the tractor after that time.

**IHC Type B**

The IHC Type B tractors were similar to the Type A. The 20 horsepower size was the most popular. Type A tractors went into production in 1907 and ended in 1916. The Type B was built between 1910 and 1917. In addition, a Type B, two-speed model was also built in the 1910-1917 period.

**IHC Type C Mogul tractor**

The 20 horsepower IHC Type C Mogul tractor first appeared in 1909. Beginning about this time, and for some years to come, Mogul engines were sold by McCormick implement dealers, and

Titan tractors were sold by Deering dealers. All this had to do with a long, convoluted anti-trust suit resulting because of the 1902 merger. In 1911 IHC added the 25 horsepower Mogul to the line; both styles went out of production in 1914. The last reported sale of a 20hp Type C, in about 1997, was for $35,000.

**IHC Mogul 45 tractor**

In 1911 IHC introduced the Mogul 45 tractor. This big two-cylinder model was among the first to leave Harvester's new Chicago Tractor Works; the IHC Titan tractors were mostly produced at Milwaukee Works. Initially at least, the Mogul 45 used the cooling system shown here; it would change by 1912.

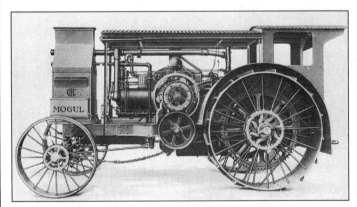

**IHC Mogul 30-60**

By 1912 the IHC Mogul 45 had taken the form shown here. Late that year the company revised the tractor slightly and called it the Mogul 30-60. Over 2,400 IHC Mogul 45 and Mogul 30-60 tractors were built between 1911 and 1917. This model used a big two-cylinder opposed engine with a carburetor for each cylinder. A small 1 horsepower engine was used to turn the big flywheels for starting.

**Mogul Jr.**

With the 1911 introduction of the Mogul 45 came the single-cylinder Mogul Jr. 25 horsepower tractor. It was quite similar in design to the Mogul 45. During late 1912 or early 1913 this tractor was given a 15-30 horsepower rating. Production of the 15-30 continued into 1915. During 1912 and 1913 IHC produced a similar 10-20 model, but little information can be found on this tractor.

**Mogul 12-25**

The Mogul 12-25 actually saw first light in 1911, but was then built as the Mogul 10-20 (no relation to the Mogul 10-20 of a few years later). In

1912 it was christened the Mogul 12-25 and was the first of the IHC production models to actually look at a lightweight design. Production of this model continued into 1918.

|  | **1** | **2** | **3** | **4** |
|---|---|---|---|---|
| 12-25 | $35,000 | $25,000 | $15,000 | — |

**IHC Type D Titan**

Production of the IHC Type D Titan 25 horsepower tractor began in 1910 and ended in 1914. The model was originally sold as a 20 horsepower tractor, but was upgraded about 1912. A single-cylinder engine was used; it had an 8-3/4 x 15 inch bore and stroke.

**Titan**

While McCormick farm machinery dealers were busy selling Mogul tractors, the Deering dealers were geared up to sell the Titan tractor line. For a number of years the various components of IHC were forced by government edict to operate as separate companies, albeit under the IHC corporate umbrella. The Titan 45 first appeared in

**Titan 15-30 tractor**

1911. It was sold under this rating until 1913 when it was revamped and re-rated as the Titan 30-60. The last reported sale of an early Titan 45, in 1999, was for $116,000.

**Titan 30-60 tractor**

About 1913 the Titan 45 became the Titan 30-60 tractor. Its outward appearance changed slightly, but in 1915 the 30-60 took on an entirely new appearance with an enclosed cab and a cellular radiator. A friction-drive starting engine was used to roll over the flywheels of the big engine for starting. Production of the Titan 30-60 ended in 1917. The last reported sale, in 1998, was for $120,000.

The first 12-25 Titan tractor appeared at Milwaukee Works in 1915. This model remained in production until 1916 when it was re-rated as the 15-30 Titan. Production continued through 1917; then, it was slightly altered and became known as the International Titan 15-30. On these tractors, each cylinder had its own mixer and needle valve, so it required some careful adjustment to get each cylinder properly tuned.

**International Titan 15-30 tractor**

Production of the International Titan 15-30 tractor began in 1918 and continued into 1921. This model used a four-cylinder engine having a 5-1/4 x 8 inch bore and stroke. For 1918 this model had a list price of $1,900. Despite this, over 5,500 of these tractors were built in the 1918-1921 period.

| | 1 | 2 | 3 | 4 |
|---|---|---|---|---|
| Titan 15-30 | $26,000 | $22,000 | — | — |

**IHC Titan Type D, 18-35 tractor**

The IHC Titan Type D, 18-35 tractor was produced between 1912 and 1915. This model was essentially built over the Titan 30-60 chassis, but with a smaller engine. Production of this model was very limited; less than 300 left the production line. Two specimens are known to exist.

| | 1 | 2 | 3 | 4 |
|---|---|---|---|---|
| Titan 18-35 D | — | $70,000 | — | — |

**IHC Mogul 8-16 tractor**

IHC got into the tractor business in a big way with their 1914 introduction of the IHC Mogul 8-16 tractor. It used a single-cylinder engine of hopper cooled design for the ultimate in simplic-

ity. The 8-16 engine had an 8 x 12 inch bore and stroke. Production of the 8-16 continued into 1917, and during that time the company built over 14,000 of the 8-16 Mogul tractors. At this point the 8-16 was replaced with the similar, but improved, Mogul 10-20.

| | 1 | 2 | 3 | 4 |
|---|---|---|---|---|
| Model 8-16 | | | | |
| Tin Hopper | $25,000 | $22,000 | $17,000 | $7,000 |
| Cast Hopper | $22,000 | $20,000 | $15,000 | $5,000 |

**Harvester Mogul 10-20**

Harvester began building the Mogul 10-20 in late 1916, with both the 8-16 and the 10-20 being available late that year, and early into 1917. This model had a single-cylinder engine with an 8-1/2 x 12 inch bore and stroke. New features included two forward speeds and the addition of fenders. Over 8,900 of these tractors were built in the 1916-1919 period.

| | 1 | 2 | 3 | 4 |
|---|---|---|---|---|
| Mogul 10-20 | $30,000 | $25,000 | $20,000 | $10,000 |

International Harvester introduced its motor cultivator in 1916 and continued building them into 1918. Contrary to expectations, this machine did not become popular, and it took two years after production ended to sell the last of them. Harvester modified this machine extensively, hoping that it could be adapted to a variety of farm machines, and become the basis for a uni-

**International Harvester motor cultivator**

**International 8-16**

versal tractor. This finally came to pass when the company decided to build 200 of its new Farmall row-crop tractors for 1924. (Only a few are known to exist.)

First built in 1917, the International 8-16 was a four-cylinder lightweight model. It followed the 8-16 Mogul tractor production, and despite numerous changes the International 8-16 remained in production until 1922. Early in the production period, Harvester also adapted this tractor as an Industrial model by replacing the steel wheels with hard rubber tires.

**IHC Titan 10-20 tractor**

**International 8-16**

Between 1916 and 1922 IHC built over 78,000 of the IHC Titan 10-20 tractors. From its introduction, the Titan 10-20 was phenomenally popular, and indeed was the first tractor for many farmers. It was powered by a two-cylinder engine having a 6-1/2 x 8 inch bore and stroke. In Nebraska Test No. 23 the 10-20 Titan delivered nearly 14 drawbar horsepower. In 1919 the 10-20 got full-length rear fenders, and the rated speed was raised from 500 to 575 rpm. About this time an Ensign carburetor replaced the simple mixer used on earlier models.

In 1920 Harvester sent the International 8-16 to Nebraska's Tractor Test Laboratory. In Test No. 25 it demonstrated over 18-1/2 belt horsepower. The 8-16 was equipped with the company's own four-cylinder engine having a 4-1/4 x 5 inch bore and stroke. This little tractor only weighed 3,650 pounds and marked the company's entry into the design and production of lightweight tractors.

|  | 1 | 2 | 3 | 4 |
|---|---|---|---|---|
| 8-16 |  |  |  |  |
| First Year | $11,000 | $9,000 | $7,000 | $3,500 |
| Later | $9,000 | $7,5000 | $3,500 | $2,500 |

|  | 1 | 2 | 3 | 4 |
|---|---|---|---|---|
| 10-20 Titan | $13,000 | $10,000 | $8,000 | $4,000 |

**International 15-30 tractor**

During 1921 IHC began producing their 15-30 tractor. It marked the end for heavyweight designs and was the first IHC tractor to use the unit frame design. All parts were enclosed, and a single casting ran from the radiator to the bull gears. The engine crankshaft was carried by two massive ball bearings. Numerous options were available, including a rear pto shaft. Using the company's own four-cylinder engine, the 15-30 demonstrated nearly 33 belt horsepower in Nebraska Test No. 87 of 1922. The engine carried a 4-1/2 x 6 inch bore and stroke. About 1926 the rated engine speed was raised from 1,000 to 1,050 rpm; this gave the 15-30 nearly 35 belt horsepower.

The McCormick-Deering 15-30 was modified in 1929. A major change was the use of a 4-3/4 inch engine bore, compared to 4-1/2 inches in earlier tractors. In Nebraska Test No. 156 the New 15-30 demonstrated over 40 belt horsepower. This model was known as the 15-30, the New 15-30, and as the 22-36, depending on where it was sold. At one time, the Author was told by a former company official that export tractors were taxed on the basis of horsepower. Obviously, a nameplate bearing 15-30 was taxed less than one reading 22-36. Production of this model ended in 1934. During its 1921-1934 production run, nearly 100,000 were built.

|  | **1** | **2** | **3** | **4** |
|---|---|---|---|---|
| 15-30 HP | $3,500 | $1,900 | $1,200 | $900 |

**McCormick-Deering 15-30**

**McCormick-Deering 10-20 tractor**

Introduced in 1923, the McCormick-Deering 10-20 tractor remained in production until 1939. Over 215,000 were built during this period. Nebraska Test No. 95 was run on this tractor in 1923, with specifications showing the four-cylinder, 4-1/4 x 5 inch engine operating at 1,000 rpm. In 1927 the 10-20 returned, with the only major difference being a rated speed of 1,025 rpm. In Test No. 142 the 10-20 delivered nearly 25 belt horsepower. Numerous variations were available for the 10-20, as was a variety of special equipment. Pneumatic tires became optionally available in the late 1930s.

|  | 1 | 2 | 3 | 4 |
|---|---|---|---|---|
| 10-20 HP | $3,000 | $1,500 | $1,000 | $750 |

Limited production of the Farmall tractor began in 1924, with full production beginning the following year. In September 1925 a McCormick-Deering Farmall was sent to Nebraska and underwent Test No. 117. It demonstrated 12.7 maximum drawbar horsepower. Rated at 1,200 rpm, the Farmall used a four-cylinder engine having a

**Farmall tractor**

3-3/4 x 5 inch bore and stroke. Many attachments were designed for the Farmall (Regular) tractor, and numerous modifications were made during a production run that ended in 1932.

|  | 1 | 2 | 3 | 4 |
|---|---|---|---|---|
| Regular | $2,200 | $1,500 | $1,000 | $500 |

**Farmall F-20**

Production of the Farmall F-20 began in 1932 and ended in 1939, with almost 149,000 units being produced. The F-20 was first tested at Nebraska under No. 221 of 1934. In this test it demonstrated over 23 belt horsepower using kerosene fuel. In Test No. 264 of 1936 the F-20 delivered almost 27 belt horsepower using distillate fuel. Test No. 276 of the same year again showed nearly 27 belt horsepower. For many farmers the F-20 was their first row-crop tractor, and indeed was their only tractor. Numerous axle and chassis designs were available, along with a wide range of implements.

|  | 1 | 2 | 3 | 4 |
|---|---|---|---|---|
| F-20 | $2,300 | $1,700 | $1,000 | $500 |

**International Harvester F-30 tractor**

Late in 1931 International Harvester introduced its F-30 tractor. Production of the F-30 continued until 1939. Test No. 198 was run at Nebraska in October 1931 for the F-30. It demonstrated almost 33 maximum belt horsepower at the rated speed of 1,150 rpm. The four-cylinder engine carried a 4-1/4 x 5 inch bore and stroke. By the mid-1930s the F-30 was also available with rubber tires as an extra-cost option; steel wheels were still the standard equipment at this time.

|      | 1      | 2      | 3      | 4    |
|------|--------|--------|--------|------|
| F-30 | $3,500 | $2,700 | $1,600 | $900 |

**W-30**

The W-30 was a standard-tread version of the F-30 row-crop tractor. Rated at 19 drawbar and 31 belt horsepower, the W-30 was comparable in size to the McCormick-Deering 10-20, yet it had a power level akin to the McCormick-Deering 15-30. Production of this model ran into 1938, and

by 1935 it was available with pneumatic rubber tires as an extra-cost option. The W-30 was also available as a special Orchard Tractor; this option included special fenders and other accessories.

|      | 1      | 2      | 3      | 4    |
|------|--------|--------|--------|------|
| W-30 | $2,500 | $1,700 | $1,100 | $800 |

**Farmall F-12 tractor**

A four-cylinder engine with a 3 x 4 inch bore and stroke was used in the Farmall F-12 tractor. Production of this model began in 1932 and ended in 1938. By 1934 the F-12 was available on pneumatic tires as an extra-cost option, making it one of the first IHC tractors to offer rubber tires. In Nebraska Test No. 212 of 1933 the F-12 demonstrated nearly 12-1/2 drawbar horsepower using gasoline fuel. Test No. 220 was run shortly afterward using distillate fuel, and showed slightly a slightly diminished performance.

|              | 1      | 2      | 3      | 4    |
|--------------|--------|--------|--------|------|
| F-12         | $2,000 | $1,500 | $1,000 | $300 |
| F-12 Waukesha |        |        |        |      |
|              | $3,500 | $2,200 | $1,500 | $800 |

A standard-tread version of the Farmall F-12 was the W-12 tractor. Built in the 1934-1938 period, this model displayed over 12-1/2 drawbar horsepower in Nebraska Test No. 229. This

**W-12**

model was also built as the I-12 Industrial model as well as the Fairway-12, a special tractor built for use on golf courses and large estates.

| | **1** | **2** | **3** | **4** |
|---|---|---|---|---|
| W-12 | $3,500 | $2,200 | $1,500 | $800 |
| I-12 | $4,500 | $3,200 | $2,500 | $1,200 |
| O-12 | $5,000 | $4,000 | $2,800 | $1,800 |

**IHC O-12 Orchard tractor**

Between 1935 and 1938 IHC built almost 2,400 copies of the O-12 Orchard Tractor. This one was especially designed for use in orchards, groves, and vineyards. Retailing at about $800, it was normally equipped with rubber tires. This tractor had a top speed of about 7-1/2 mph, considerably faster than was possible with steel wheels.

Production of the Farmall F-14 tractor began in 1938 and ended the following year. This model evolved from the earlier F-12 model, and was nearly identical. In fact, the major change was raising the rated engine speed from 1,400

**Farmall F-14 tractor**

rpm to 1,650 rpm. The F-14 is shown here with the optional wide-front axle. Various chassis designs were available, as with the former F-12. In addition, this basic design was also available as the W-14 Wide-Tread model, the O-14 Orchard, and the I-14 Industrial.

| | **1** | **2** | **3** | **4** |
|---|---|---|---|---|
| F-14 | $2,250 | $1,750 | $1,200 | $900 |
| W-14 | $4,000 | $3,100 | $2,400 | $1,000 |
| I-14 | $6,200 | $5,100 | $3,000 | $1,500 |
| O-14 | $6,800 | $5,500 | $3,500 | $2,500 |

**International Harvester W-40 tractor**

In the 1934-1940 period International Harvester built their W-40 tractor. This standard-tread design saw total production of about 6,500 units during that time. In Nebraska Test No. 269 the W-40 delivered almost 50 belt horsepower on distillate fuel. This was the first tractor from Harvester to use a six-cylinder engine; in this case it carried a 3-3/4 x 4-1/2 inch bore and stroke. Technically, there was no "straight" W-40. The WA-40 (which is least plentiful) has a gasoline engine. The WK-40 has a pre-heater manifold for burning kerosene.

**McCormick-Deering WD-40**

The first wheel-type tractor in America to use a diesel engine was the McCormick-Deering WD-40, introduced in 1934. Nebraska Test No. 246 saw a maximum output of nearly 49 belt horsepower. The WD-40 used a four-cylinder engine having a 4-3/4 x 6-1/2 inch bore and stroke. It was rated at 1,100 rpm. By the time production ended in 1940, almost 3,400 of these tractors had been built. A unique starting system was used in the WD-40. In basic terms, the engine started as an ordinary gasoline engine, and through an automatic system, changed over to diesel operation after a certain number of engine revolutions.

|  | 1 | 2 | 3 | 4 |
|---|---|---|---|---|
| WK-40 | $5,500 | $3,500 | $2,800 | $1,000 |
| WA-40, WD-40 | $10,000 | $8,000 | $6,000 | $1,500 |

In 1939 International Harvester Company launched an entire new series of streamlined tractors. Included was the Farmall A. This small tractor used a four-cylinder engine of 3 x 4 inch

**International Harvester Company Farmall A**

bore and stroke. In Nebraska Test No. 329 the Farmall A developed over 16 drawbar horsepower. While most of these tractors were sent out with electric starting, it remained a $31 option over the base price of $575. Production of the Farmall A ended in 1947.

|  | 1 | 2 | 3 | 4 |
|---|---|---|---|---|
| A | $2,700 | $2,000 | $1,500 | $700 |

**Farmall B tractor**

Farmall B tractors were built in the 1939-1947 period. This model used the same basic engine as the Farmall A, but was capable of greater tread width adjustment. For the Farmall B, this ranged from 64 to 92 inches, compared to a range of 40 to 68 inches for the Farmall A. In 1940 the Farmall B sold for about $600.

|  | 1 | 2 | 3 | 4 |
|---|---|---|---|---|
| B | $2,500 | $1,700 | $1,200 | $500 |

Farmall Model AV tractors were simply a high-clearance version of the ordinary Farmall A. Except for the special parts needed to raise the

**Farmall Model AV tractor**

tractor profile, the same basic engine and chassis was used. Production also ran during the same 1939-1947 period as the Farmall A.

|        | 1       | 2       | 3       | 4     |
|--------|---------|---------|---------|-------|
| AV     | $3,200  | $2,300  | $1,700  | $900  |

**Farmall Super A tractor**

Between 1948 and 1954 IHC built the Farmall Super A tractor. It continued to use the same four-cylinder, 3 x 4 inch engine as was used in the Farmall A, and was rated at 1,400 rpm. In Nebraska Test No. 329 the Super A yielded over 18 belt horsepower.

|         | 1      | 2      | 3      | 4     |
|---------|--------|--------|--------|-------|
| Super A | $3,200 | $2,500 | $1,700 | $900  |

**Farmall H tractor**

The Farmall H and Farmall M tractors both featured adjustable rear wheel treads. In addition, both tractors had the same wheelbase for better implement interchangeability. The Farmall H used a four-cylinder engine having a 3-3/8 x 4-1/4 inch bore and stroke. Rated at 1,650 rpm, this tractor displayed a maximum of over 26 belt horsepower in Nebraska Test No. 333. Production of the Farmall H ran until 1953 when it was replaced with the Farmall Super H tractor.

**Farmall Super H tractor**

During 1953 and 1954 International Harvester built the Farmall Super H tractor. This model used a four-cylinder IH C-164 engine with a 3-1/2 gx 4-1/4 inch bore and stroke. Rated at 1,650 rpm it delivered slightly over 31 belt horsepower.

|             | 1      | 2      | 3      | 4     |
|-------------|--------|--------|--------|-------|
| H, Super H  | $2,500 | $1,500 | $1,100 | $600  |

**Farmall M**

From the time of its introduction in August 1939 the Farmall M was one of the most popular farm tractors in America. By the time production ended in 1952, over 288,000 of these tractors had been sold. Nebraska Test No. 328 demonstrated over 34 drawbar horsepower, and nearly 40 belt horsepower. These power levels made the Farmall M the ideal size for its time. Rated at 1,650 rpm, the Farmall M carried a four-cylinder engine having a 3-7/8 x 5-1/4 inch bore and stroke. The Farmall M was available in several configurations, including the MV High Clearance model. A host of attachments were built especially for the Farmall M and Farmall H tractors. Both used the same frame and the same wheelbase to provide better interchangeability of mounted implements.

Introduced in 1941, the Farmall MD was one of the first row-crop diesel-powered tractors in America. It used an engine similar to that pioneered by the WD-40, and with the same 3-7/8 x 5-1/4 inch cylinder dimensions as the gasoline-powered Farmall M. In Nebraska Test No. 368

**Farmall MD**

the Farmall MD demonstrated 31-1/2 drawbar horsepower. Production of the Farmall MD continued until 1952 when it was replaced with the Farmall Super MD model.

During 1953 and 1954 International Harvester built their Super M and Super M-TA tractors. This model boasted 43 drawbar horsepower due to an increased engine bore which went from 3-7/8 to 4 inches. Other new features included

**Super M and Super M-TA**

faster field speeds, double-disc brakes and direct-power hydraulic control. The Torque Amplifier system permitted on-the-go shifting in tough conditions for greater operating efficiency.

The Farmall Super MV and the Farmall Super MDV were high-clearance versions of the regular models. With this style there was over 30 inches of clearance under the front axle. High-clearance tractors were used for certain crops where the extra height was needed to prevent damage to growing plants. Aside from the altered specifications required by the high-clearance equipment, there was virtually no difference between the MV models and the Super M tractors.

**Farmall Super MV**

**Farmall Super MD diesel tractor**

Farmall Super MD diesel tractors were built during 1953 and 1954. This model used a 264ci, four-cylinder engine having a 4 x 5-1/4 inch bore and stroke. Rated at 1,450 rpm, it delivered almost 47 belt horsepower in Nebraska Test No. 477. The basic tractor weighed about 6,000 pounds; this photo shows the Super MD at work in Test No. 477.

|         | **1**    | **2**    | **3**    | **4**    |
|---------|----------|----------|----------|----------|
| M       | $3,200   | $2,250   | $1,200   | $800     |
| Super M | $3,500   | $2,500   | $1,600   | $1,000   |
| MD      | $4,200   | $3,000   | $1,900   | $900     |

Between 1948 and 1951 International Harvester offered the Farmall C tractor. During this relatively short production run, almost 80,000 units were sold. In Nebraska Test No. 395 of 1948 the Farmall C demonstrated nearly 19 belt

**Farmall C tractor**

horsepower at its rated load. The four-cylinder IH engine used a 3 x 4 inch bore and stroke. In 1951 this model was replaced with the Farmall Super C.

**Farmall Super C tractor**

The Farmall Super C was marketed in the 1951-1954 period. During that time about 98,000 units were built. This model was essentially the same tractor but had a slightly larger engine. While the earlier one had a four-cylinder, 3 x 4 engine, the Super C had a 3-1/8 x 4 inch bore and stroke. In Nebraska Test No. 458 the Super C delivered almost 23 maximum belt horsepower.

|  | 1 | 2 | 3 | 4 |
|---|---|---|---|---|
| C, Super C | $3,000 | $2,100 | $1,500 | $500 |

The smallest of the IH tractor line was the Farmall Cub. Introduced in 1947, it remained virtually unchanged for a decade. The Cub went to Nebraska in 1947 with the results being cataloged in Test No. 386. The Cub delivered about 9-1/4 maximum belt horsepower, using a four-cylinder engine with a 2-5/8 x 2-3/4 inch bore

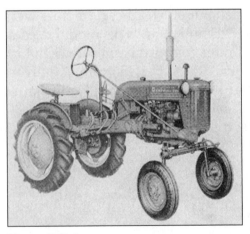

**Farmall Cub**

and stroke. Thousands of these tractors were sold, and a substantial number remain in use today, a half century after they were introduced.

|  | 1 | 2 | 3 | 4 |
|---|---|---|---|---|
| Cub | $3,200 | $2,500 | $1,500 | $750 |

**McCormick-Deering W-4**

The McCormick-Deering W-4 tractor was simply a standard-tread version of the Farmall H row-crop tractor. Introduced in 1940, it remained on the market until 1953. W-4 tractors used the same IH-built C-152 four-cylinder engine as on the Farmall H. Steel wheels or rubber tires were available for this model, although the latter was far more popular. In 1953 and 1954 Harvester built a slightly improved Super W-4 tractor.

|      | **1**   | **2**   | **3**   | **4**  |
|------|---------|---------|---------|--------|
| W-4  | $2,700  | $2,200  | $1,500  | $750   |

**W-6 tractor**

Rated at about 33 drawbar horsepower, the W-6 tractor came onto the market in 1940 and

remained in production until 1952. That year it was replaced with the Super W-6 and the latter continued until 1954.

Nebraska Test No. 355 demonstrates the W-6 with a maximum output of 36 belt horsepower. This tractor used a four-cylinder engine with a 3-7/8 x 5-1/4 inch bore and stroke. This tractor was also available as an O-6 orchard design with special fenders and other accessories.

|      | **1**   | **2**   | **3**   | **4**  |
|------|---------|---------|---------|--------|
| W-6  | $3,200  | $2,500  | $1,700  | $800   |

**WD-6 Diesel tractor**

Production of the WD-6 Diesel tractor ran concurrently with the W-6 and Super W-6 gasoline models, that is, from 1940 until 1954. In Nebraska Test No. 356 the WD-6 delivered nearly 35 belt horsepower. Rated at 1,450 rpm, the four-cylinder engine used a 3-7/8 x 5-1/4 inch bore and stroke. WD-6 tractors used the same gasoline starting system as the WD-40 introduced some years earlier.

|       | **1**   | **2**   | **3**   | **4**  |
|-------|---------|---------|---------|--------|
| WD-6  | $3,400  | $2,700  | $1,700  | $800   |

Topping the IHC tractor line was the W-9 tractor. This standard-tread model was capable of 52 belt horsepower. The IHC-335 four-cylinder engine was used. It was the same engine as was used in the T-9 crawler tractor, namely,

**IHC W-9 tractor**

with a 4.4 x 5.5 inch bore and stroke. This 1940 model is shown with steel wheels, but rubber tires were far more popular. Production continued until 1953.

**IHC WD-9**

Production of the IHC WD-9 paralleled that of the gasoline-powered W-9 tractor. It used a four-cylinder IH engine with a 4.4 x 5.5 inch bore and stroke. At its rated speed of 1,500 rpm this tractor delivered over 46 belt horsepower in Nebraska Test No. 370. In 1953 this model was replaced with the Super WD-9. The latter used a 4.5 x 5.5 inch bore and stroke, but the same rated speed of 1,500 rpm that was used in its predecessor. This model remained in production until 1956.

|      | **1**   | **2**   | **3**   | **4**  |
|------|---------|---------|---------|--------|
| W-9  | $3,500  | $2,700  | $1,800  | $800   |
| WD9  | $3,750  | $3,000  | $2,200  | $800   |

**T-20 TracTracTor**

The T-20 TracTracTor saw first light in 1931. For several years previously the company had experimented with various designs built around the 10-20 and 15-30 tractors. A few of these even saw limited production. This model used the same basic engine as found in the Farmall F-20 tractor. Production of the T-20 continued into 1939.

|       | **1**   | **2**   | **3**   | **4**   |
|-------|---------|---------|---------|---------|
| T-20  | $8,000  | $6,000  | $3,000  | $1,000  |

**International Harvester T-35**

International Harvester introduced their T-35 (gasoline) and TD-35 (diesel) crawlers in 1936. Both remained in production until 1939. The T-35 was built with a six-cylinder IH engine having a 3-5/8 x

4-1/2 inch bore and stroke. TD-35 tractors used a four-cylinder IH diesel having a 4-1/2 x 6-1/2 inch bore and stroke. In Nebraska Test No. 279 the T-35 yielded nearly 36 drawbar horsepower.

|  | **1** | **2** | **3** | **4** |
|---|---|---|---|---|
| T-35, TD-35 | $8,000 | $6,000 | $3,000 | $1,000 |

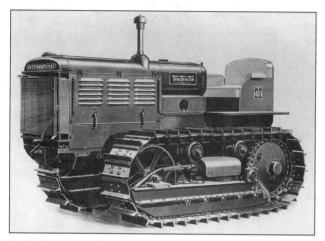

**T-40 TracTracTor**

Production of the T-40 TracTracTor began in 1932 and continued into 1939. This model was capable of over 44 drawbar horsepower. Power came from a six-cylinder IH engine having a 3-3/4 x 4-1/2 inch bore and stroke. The engine was rated at 1,750 rpm. Total weight was nearly 13,000 pounds.

**TD-40 TracTracTor**

The TD-40 TracTracTor used the same engine as the WD-40 wheel tractor. Rated at 1,200 rpm, it was capable of over 48 drawbar horsepower. Like the WD-40, this model had the unique starting system, whereby the engine was started as a gasoline

engine, complete with magneto and carburetor. After 900 revolutions the engine automatically converted over to diesel operation. Production of this model ran from 1933 and ended in 1939.

|  | **1** | **2** | **3** | **4** |
|---|---|---|---|---|
| TD-40 | 48,000 | $6,000 | $3,000 | $1,500 |

**TD-18 crawler**

A new line of IH crawlers emerged in late 1938 with the introduction of the TD-18. This model remained in production until 1949 when it was replaced with the TD-18A; the latter was built until 1955. In Nebraska Test No. 318 the TD-18 delivered over 72 drawbar horsepower. However, the big TD-18A demonstrated almost 84 horsepower on the drawbar. The engine was of six-cylinder design, using a 4-3/4 x 6-1/2 inch bore and stroke.

|  | **1** | **2** | **3** | **4** |
|---|---|---|---|---|
| TD-18 | $7,000 | $5,000 | $3,000 | $1,000 |

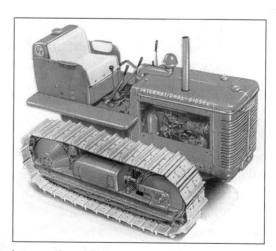

**International T-6**

The International T-6 and TD-6 tractors were introduced in 1939 and remained in production until 1956. Both were virtually identical except that the T-6 used a gasoline engine, and of course the TD-6 was equipped with a diesel. Nebraska Test No. 345 was run on the TD-6 and showed a maximum of 34-1/2 belt horsepower; Test No. 346 on the T-6 elicited about 37 brake horsepower. Both the gasoline and diesel engines were of four-cylinder design and used a 3-7/8 x 5-1/4 inch bore and stroke.

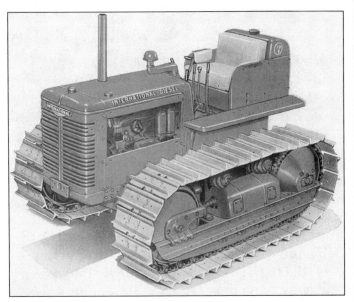

**T-9 crawler**

Built in the 1939-1956 period, the T-9 and TD-9 crawlers were virtually identical except for the style of engine. The IH-built four-cylinder engine of the T-9 was the same four-cylinder engine as used in the W-9 tractor; it had a 4.4 x 5.5 inch bore and stroke. The T-9 appears in Nebraska Test No. 372. Capable of about 44 brake horsepower, the TD-9 used a four-cylinder IH engine having the same 4.4 x 5.5 inch bore and stroke as its gasoline-fired counterpart. Rated speed was 1,400 rpm.

Production of the huge TD-24 crawler began in 1947. Weighing over 20 tons, it was powered by an IH six-cylinder diesel engine with a 5-3/4 x 7 inch bore and stroke for a displacement of 1090ci. Production continued until 1959. This big tractor boasted 148 drawbar horsepower, and for a time, was the largest crawler tractor on the market. For further details of this and other tractors from International Harvester, the reader is referred to

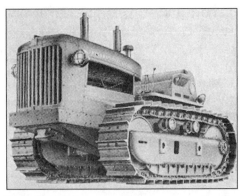

**TD-24 crawler**

the Author's title, *150 Years of International Harvester*, Crestline/Motorbooks: 1981, and our title, *Nebraska Tractor Tests Since 1920*, Crestline/Motorbooks: 1985. The latter illustrates virtually all of the IH tractors marketed through 1985, including those past the time frame of this book.

## Interstate Engine & Tractor Company
*Waterloo, Iowa*

**Plow Boy 10-20 tractor**

In 1915 the Board of Directors for Sandy McManus Inc. of Waterloo opted for a more conservative approach than had been exercised by McManus. The company was then reorganized as Interstate Engine & Tractor Company. One of the new tractor models from this firm was the Plow Boy 10-20 tractor. It was equipped with a Waukesha four-cylinder engine having a 3-1/2 x 5-1/4 inch bore and stroke. The tractor retailed for $675.

**Plow Man "30"**

The Plow Man "30" from Interstate was also rated at 13 drawbar horsepower; about 1916 this model was given a 15-30 horsepower rating. Power came from a Buda four-cylinder engine with a 4-1/4 x 5-1/2 inch bore and stroke. By 1919 the company was in financial trouble and reorganized as the Plow Man Tractor Company, but the latter firm remained in business for only a short time.

## Iron Horse Tractor Company
*Kansas City, Missouri*

See: Sweeney Tractor Company

## Iron Horse Tractor Company
*Minneapolis, Minnesota*

This company was organized in 1916, with one of its principals having been formerly associated with the Lion Tractor Company, also of Minneapolis. No further information has been found, leading to the conclusion that the company never materialized except perhaps for a prototype model.

## Iron Horse Sales Company
*Los Angeles, California*

**Iron Horse**

A small tractor called the Iron Horse emerged from this firm in 1920. Aside from a single advertisement, no other information has emerged. From all appearances, the engine was something less than 10 horsepower.

## Isaacson Iron Works
*Seattle, Washington*

**"Farm Dozer" trademark**

In 1940 this firm applied for protection of its "Farm Dozer" trademark, claiming first use of the mark in November 1939. Aside from this, no other information has emerged on the company or its tractors.

# J

although no illustrations of these models have been found. A 1955 directory illustrates the Farmaster 150 tractor from Jenson; at this time the company was located at Burbank, California. The Farmaster 150 was equipped with a two-cylinder Wisconsin Model TFU engine and had a total displacement of 54ci.

## W. S. Jardine
*Omaha, Nebraska*

**Van Nostrand Rotary Plow**

In 1913 Jardine announced the Van Nostrand Rotary Plow. The large drum was adorned with curved spikes, not unlike a similar machine from Allis-Chalmers. Little is known of this machine; it does not appear that it was ever put into production, except for a few prototypes.

## Jenson Mfg. Company
*Alhambra, California*

**Farmaster 150 tractor**

In 1948 the Jenson and J. M. C. garden tractors were listed in some of the farm directories,

## Jewell Tractor & Truck Company
*Boston, Massachusetts*

This company appears as a tractor builder in a 1918 trade directory, but no other information has been found.

## Jiffy Till
*La Mesa, California*

**Magic Hoe from Jiffy Till**

In 1950 and 1951 the Magic Hoe appears from Jiffy Till. This was a dedicated design and does not appear to have been a multiple-use tractor. The Magic Hoe is shown here; it used a 2-1/2 horsepower Briggs & Stratton engine. The Model 2A was equipped with a 5 horsepower Clinton engine; a larger 3B model was built with an 8-1/4 horsepower motor. Little other information has surfaced on the company or its products.

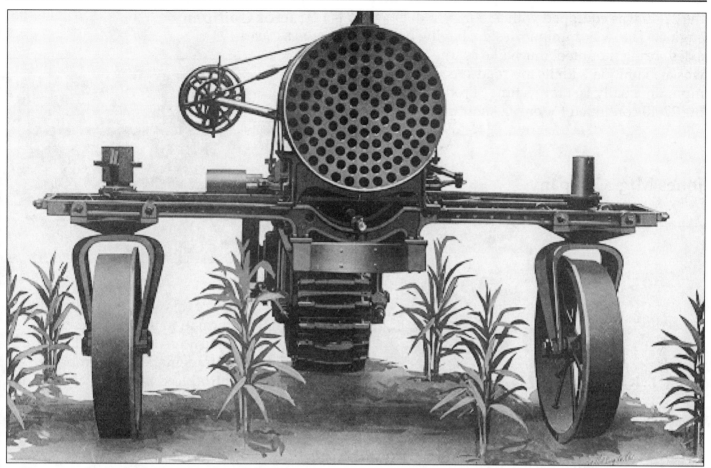

**Bates "Steel Mule" tractor**

## Johnson Farm Equipment Company
*Streator, Illinois*

This firm is listed as the manufacturer of the Johnson garden tractors in the 1948-1953 period, but no other information has been located.

## Joliet Oil Tractor Company
*Joliet, Illinois*

See: Bates Machine & Tractor Company

Joliet introduced their first tractor late in 1913. By June of the following year they had adopted the "Steel Mule" trademark. Rated at 13 drawbar and 30 belt horsepower, the Steel Mule carried a four-cylinder engine having a 4 x 6 inch bore and stroke. It weighed 5,800 pounds and had two forward speeds. The single rear crawler track was 15 inches wide. Production of the Steel

Mule continued into the 1919 merger of Joliet with the Bates Tractor Company. The result was *Bates Machine & Tractor Company*, noted previously in this book.

**Joliet 22-40 wheel tractor**

In 1914 Joliet introduced their 22-40 wheel tractor. Although no specifications have been found, the 22-40 was equipped with a four-cylinder engine. This was a unique design, having both axles spring mounted, much like a large truck. It was also unique with its top road speed of 10 mph, unusually fast for its time. Production of the 22-40 continued for only a short time.

## Jones Mfg. Company
*Colby, Kansas*

**Colby Plow Boy tractor**

Jones Mfg. Company was organized in 1909 and built the first Colby Plow Boy tractor that year. Several were built and sold during 1910, and the design gained the attention of the farm press that year. For reasons unknown, nothing more is heard from the company after that time. Little is known of the tractor specifications except that it carried a big four-cylinder engine capable of 30 drawbar horsepower. Designed specifically for drawbar work, the Colby Plow Boy was double-geared.

## Joy-McVicker Company
*Minneapolis, Minnesota*
See: McVicker Engineering Company

## J-T Tractor Company
*Cleveland, Ohio*

**J-T 16-30 crawler**

Tracing the history of this company is difficult, since the only information that has been found consists of magazine advertisements. The firm first used its "J-T" trademark in December 1917 and apparently introduced the 16-30 crawler at that time. Weighing 7,000 pounds, the 16-30 used a four-cylinder Chief engine.

**J-T crawler 16-32**

By the early 1920s the J-T crawler tractor had been upgraded slightly to a 16-32. It also shows evidence of a redesigned hood and radiator, along with a front-mounted belt pulley. Three large carrier rollers were used on each side, and apparently, no top roller was needed.

**J-T tractor, 1925 model**

In 1925 the J-T tractor was again modified. A fully hooded engine was now used, along with protection for the bottom track rollers. The engine itself was now a Model KU Climax with four cylinders having a 5 x 6-1/2 inch bore and stroke. The J-T tractors disappear from the directories after 1930.

## Jumbo Steel Products
*Azusa, California*

**Jumbo Steel Products tractor**

By late 1947 this tractor was available from Jumbo Steel Products. It used a 217ci Chrysler six-cylinder engine, and five forward speeds were available, ranging from 5 to 20 mph. Very little information has been found on this tractor, and presumably, it was built for only a short time.

# K

## Kansas City Hay Press Company
*Kansas City, Missouri*

**K-C Gasoline Traction Engine**

The K-C Traction Gasoline Engine made its first appearance in 1908. It used the K-C Lightning gasoline engine, already in production. This unique engine was of the opposed piston design. While one piston was connected to the crankshaft in the usual manner, the other was connected by extended rods to a pair of outer cranks. Production of this model lasted for only a short time.

**K.C. Prairie Dog**

The K.C. Prairie Dog made its appearance about 1914 or 1915. This tractor used a single rear drive wheel. Power came from a Waukesha four-cylinder engine having a 4-1/4 x 5 inch bore and stroke. This gave the tractor a rating of 12 drawbar and 25 belt horsepower. This model remained in production until about 1917.

**Prairie Dog Model L, 9-18 tractor**

Production of the Prairie Dog Model L, 9-18 tractor began in 1917 and continued until about 1920. In 1919 the company name was changed to Kansas City Hay Press & Tractor Company, reflecting a desire to gain quantity production and sales of this unit. The 9-18 used a four-cylinder Waukesha engine having a 3-3/4 x 5-1/4 inch bore and stroke. In 1920 it was re-rated as a 10-18 model.

**15-30 Model D Prairie Dog tractor**

In 1920 Kansas City Hay Press announced their new 15-30 Model D Prairie Dog tractor. This one was built with a Waukesha four-cylinder engine having a 4-1/2 x 6-1/4 inch bore and stroke. This model was built for only a year or so, since Kansas City Hay Press Company disappears from the tractor trade directories by 1922. No Kansas City Hay Press Tractors are known to exist today.

## Kansas Mfg. Company
*Wichita, Kansas*

This company was incorporated in 1913, ostensibly to build tractors, but no other information has been found.

## Kardell Truck & Tractor Company
*St. Louis, Missouri*

**Four-in-One tractor**

In 1917 Kardell announced their Four-in-One tractor. Shown here as a motor plow, it could also be used for other farming operations. In addition, a separate chassis was available whereby it could be converted to a truck if so desired. This tractor used a four-cylinder Waukesha engine having a 4-1/2 x 5-3/4 inch bore and stroke. Weighing some 5,100 pounds the 20-32 retailed at $1,600. Production continued into 1918 or perhaps slightly later.

About 1918 the Kardell Utility tractor with an 8-16 horsepower rating appeared. By the following year it was re-rated as a 10-20 tractor. A Wisconsin four-cylinder engine was used; it had a 4 x

**Kardell Utility tractor**

5 inch bore and stroke. About 1921 the company was bought out by Oldsmar Tractor Company of Oldsmar, Florida.

## Kaws Tractor Company
*Indianapolis, Indiana*

This firm was incorporated in 1919 to build tractors, but no other information has been found.

## Kaywood Corporation
*Benton Harbor, Michigan*

**Kaywood Model D tractors**

Kaywood Model D tractors first appear in the 1936 tractor directories. The company continues to appear until 1946. This model weighed in at 3,000 pounds and was equipped with a four-cyl-

**12-24 Keck-Gonnerman**

inder Hercules IXB engine; it had a 3-1/4 x 4 inch bore and stroke. Aside from listings in the tractor directories for a short time, little other information has been found on the Kaywood tractors.

|  | 1 | 2 | 3 | 4 |
|---|---|---|---|---|
| Model D | — | — | $9,750 | — |

## KC 4-Drive Sales Company
*Kansas City, Missouri*

No information has been located on this firm or its tractors.

## Horace Keane Aeroplanes Inc.
*New York, New York*

**"Ace" trademark**

In November 1920 the above company filed the "Ace" trademark shown here, claiming first use of the mark a year earlier, as applied to tractors. No further information has been found.

## Keck-Gonnerman Company
*Mt. Vernon, Indiana*

Keck-Gonnerman Company began business in 1873 as a steam engine and thresher manufacturer. In 1917 the company entered the tractor business with their 12-24 model. It used a two-cylinder engine having a 6-1/2 x 8 inch bore and stroke. This model was modified in 1920 with the use of a larger 7-1/4 x 8 inch engine and a new 15-30 power rating. Production of this model continued into the late 1920s.

**18-35 Kay-Gee tractor**

In 1928 Keck-Gonnerman introduced their 18-35 Kay-Gee tractor. This model used a Buda four-cylinder engine with a 4-1/2 x 6 inch bore and stroke. This tractor has a remarkable resemblance to the Rock Island 18-35 introduced about the same time, and used the same Buda four-cylinder engine. Curiously, Keck-Gonnerman increased the engine bore to 4-3/4 inches by 1931, keeping this size until 1935.

**Kay-Gee 25-50 tractor**

Introduced in 1928, the Kay-Gee 25-50 tractor remained in production into the early 1930s. This 9,800 pound tractor retailed for $2,850. Originally sold as a 22-45 tractor, it carried a LeRoi four-cylinder engine having a 5-1/4 x 7 inch bore and stroke.

**30-60 tractor**

Rounding out the 1928 Keck-Gonnerman line was the big 30-60 tractor. Originally billed as a 27-55, this model used a four-cylinder LeRoi engine having a 5-1/2 x 7 inch bore and stroke. Active production of the 30-60 continued until the late 1930s, and it is possible that a few were built after that time.

**K-G 18-36 tractor**

In 1946 the Keck-Gonnerman tractors were listed for the last time. Back in 1935 the 18-35 was revamped to include a four-cylinder Waukesha engine having a 5-1/8 x 6-1/4 inch bore and stroke. It also had four forward speeds of 2, 4, 7, and 10 mph. Full production of the K-G tractor line was suspended during World War Two, and after the war ended, many companies went into other industries or sold their factory buildings to the government.

# Kenison Mfg. Company
*Solomon, Kansas*

**Kenison 12-24 tractor**

Kenison advertised their 12-24 tractor for a brief period in 1919. Aside from this, no other information has surfaced on the company or the tractor. It is shown here at a plowing demonstration, but even the location of this event is unknown.

## Kenney-Colwell Tractor Company
*Norfolk, Nebraska*

In 1913 A. J. Colwell patented a tractor and joined with Albert Kenney to build it. Efforts continued until 1916 when Albaugh-Dover Company, Chicago, Illinois bought the firm. The company then continued at Norfolk as the *Square Turn Tractor Company*. See this heading for further information.

## Keystone Iron & Steel Works
*Los Angeles, California*

**Keystone crawler tractor**

Keystone offered their crawler tractor in the 1920-1925 era. The unique track design used two idlers with a large drive sprocket in the center; the latter also served as a track carrier. A Waukesha four-cylinder engine was used for power; it was built with a 5 x 6-1/2 inch bore and stroke.

**Keystone Model 30**

By 1923 the Keystone Model 30 had gained a 20-35 horsepower rating, although the engine remained essentially the same. In addition, the fenders and

hood saw a slight redesign. After 1924 the Keystone slips from view, although it may have remained on the local market for a time.

## Killen-Strait Mfg. Company
## Killen-Walsh Mfg. Company
*Appleton, Wisconsin*

**"Strait's Tractor"**

In 1913 Killen-Walsh Mfg. Company was organized to built "Strait's Tractor." Initially it had a rating of 40 brake horsepower, but soon became the 30-50 model. The company name was changed to Killen-Strait in 1914. "Strait's Tractor" was equipped with a four-cylinder Doman engine having a 6 x 7 inch bore and stroke.

**Model 3, 15-30 tractor**

Shortly after the 1914 name change to Killen-Strait Company, the Model 3, 15-30 tractor appeared. This model was nearly identical in appearance to the larger size, but used a four-cylinder, 30 horse-power engine with a 4-1/2 x 5-3/4 inch bore and stroke. It appears that the company survived until 1917, or perhaps a short time longer.

## Kimble & Dentler Company
*Vicksburg, Michigan*

**Kimble & Dentler tractor**

In 1913 Kimble & Dentler attempted to enter the tractor business with a 40 horsepower model. It had several unique features, including a specially designed front axle that permitted short turns. The tractor venture appears to have gone no farther than the prototype stage. Kimble & Dentler was a scion of Dentler Bagger Company. The latter had a long career manufacturing tally boxes and other thresher accessories.

## King-Wyse Inc.
*Archbold, Ohio*

In 1950 and 1951 the King-Wyse garden tractor was advertised. It used either a Clinton or a Wis-

**King-Wyse garden tractor**

consin air-cooled single-cylinder engine of about 4-1/2 horsepower. Little other information has been found.

## Kinkead Tractor Company
*Minneapolis, Minnesota*

**Kinkead tractor**

Production of the Kinkead tractor began in April 1915. However, production seems to have ended when R. S. Kinkead, the moving force in the company, was drafted into the military during World War One. The Kinkead was of three-wheel design, using a single drivewheel in the rear. It was equipped with a four-cylinder crossmounted engine with a 4-1/4 x 5-3/4 inch bore and stroke. It was rated at 12 drawbar and 25 belt horse-power. Operating weight was 5,000 pounds.

## Kinnard-Haines Company
*Minneapolis, Minnesota*

The first Flour City Gasoline Traction Engine was built in 1900; Kinnard Press Company had built

**Flour-City Gasoline Traction Engine**

its first gasoline engine in 1896. Through 1907 the Flour City tractors were of this general design, adapting the company's own stationary engines to the tractor chassis.

**Flour City tractor**

A platform view shows the first design of the Flour City tractors. They were built in 8, 12, and 16 horsepower sizes having a single-cylinder engine. They were also available in 20 and 25 horsepower models using a two-cylinder engine. The 8 horsepower model weighed 5,500 pounds, while the 25 horsepower size weighed 15,000 pounds.

In 1908 an entirely new tractor design was unveiled. Rated at 30 drawbar horsepower, it used the company's own four-cylinder engine; it

**Kinnard-Haines tractor**

had a 6-1/4 x 7 inch bore and stroke. Ground speed was 2-1/2 mph. Production of this model continued until about 1910.

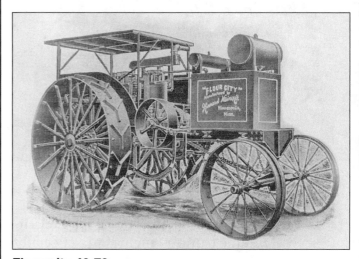

**Flour-city 40-70**

The Flour City 40-70 emerged in 1910, and remained available until 1927. Weighing about 21,000 pounds, the 40-70 used a four-cylinder engine having a 7-1/2 x 9 inch bore and stroke. In Nebraska Test No. 52 of 1920 the 40-70 delivered almost 73 belt horsepower and on the drawbar this model delivered nearly 53 horsepower.

Kinnard-Haines announced their 40-70 Flour City in 1911. Along with it came the Flour City Junior. This model used a two-cylinder engine that was apparently of the same dimensions as

**Kinnard-Haines 40-70 Flour City**

**Flour City 30-50 tractor**

Three sizes of Flour City tractors were introduced in 1911 and continued to be available until 1927. They were the 40-70, the 20-35, and the 30-50 shown here. This model was equipped with a four-cylinder engine with a 6-1/4 x 7 inch bore and stroke. Rated speed was 800 rpm. All three models used engines built by Kinnard-Haines Company, later known as Kinnard & Sons Mfg. Company.

the larger four-cylinder size. The Flour City Junior remained in the line until 1919 when it was replaced with an improved version.

**Flour City 20-35 tractor**

A four-cylinder engine with a 5-1/4 x 6 inch bore and stroke powered the Flour City 20-35 tractor. Introduced in 1911, it remained in the line until 1927. In Nebraska Test No. 50 of 1920 it delivered 19-1/2 drawbar horsepower. Total weight of this tractor was about 10,000 pounds.

**Flour City Junior**

The Flour City Junior was a two-cylinder tractor built until 1919. At that point it was replaced with the Flour City Junior 14-24 tractor. The latter was built with a four-cylinder engine having a 5-inch bore and stroke. This tractor weighed 6,700 pounds. It remained in the Flour City line until 1927.

**Kinnard Four-Plow Tractor**

In 1915 the Kinnard Four-Plow Tractor was introduced. This tractor was offered through 1917. It used two drivewheels with a narrow space between, and was essentially a three-wheel tractor although it had four on the ground. In 1918 the company name was changed to Kinnard & Sons Mfg. Company. The company had a long history going back to 1882 as the Kinnard Press Company. At that time the primary product was a hay press.

**Kinnard 15-25 tractor**

Apparently the Kinnard 15-25 tractor was built for only a short time. This tractor used a four-cylinder 5 x 5 inch engine as did the Flour City Junior of 1919. Kinnard four-cylinder engines used a two-piece crankshaft that was coupled in the center. Thus the obvious space between the two sets of engine cylinders.

# Klumb Engine & Machine Company
*Sheboygan, Wisconsin*

**Klumb 10-20 Model C tractor**

In 1918 Klumb offered their 10-20 Model C tractor. It used a two-cylinder opposed engine with a 6 x 6-1/2 inch bore and stroke. Total weight of this tractor was 4,000 pounds. The firm was organized in 1913, and was incorporated in 1916. By June 1919 the company had moved to Dubuque, Iowa and reorganized as Liberty Tractor Company. In a short time the firm again reorganized as Dubuque Truck & Tractor Company. The latter firm remained in the tractor business for only a short time.

# W. Chandler Knapp
*Rochester, New York*

**Knapp's Farm Locomotive**

By the time this 1912 model of Knapp's Farm Locomotive appeared, Knapp had been building tractors for several years. This one, with a single drivewheel to the rear typified the Knapp design. By 1917 the Gray Tractor Company was organized at Minneapolis, Minnesota to build a tractor that closely followed the design shown here; the Gray Tractor Company continued for several years.

# Knickerbocker Motors Inc.
*Poughkeepsie, New York*

**Kingwood Model 5-10 tractor**

Knickerbocker Motors began building a tractor conversion outfit already in 1909. In 1917 the company started building their Kingwood Model 5-10 tractor. It used a LeRoi four-cylinder engine with a 3-1/8 x 4-1/2 inch bore and stroke. Numerous attachments were available so that the tractor could be driven from various implements. The Kingwood Jr. disappeared from the market after 1920.

# Wm. Knudsen
*Fremont, Nebraska*

**Knudsen 25-40 tractor**

The Knudsen tractor of 1920 carried a 25-40 horsepower rating and used a four-cylinder engine having a 5 x 9 inch bore and stroke. The engine was of Knudsen's design and manufacture. For reasons unknown, this tractor was advertised for only a short time, and does not appear to have gone past a few copies.

# Kohl Tractor Company
*Cleveland, Ohio*

The *Power Wagon Reference Book* of 1919 lists this firm as the manufacturer of the 17-35 Kohl tractor. No other information has been found.

# Kreider Machine Company
*Lancaster, Pennsylvania*

**Lancaster Traction Engine**

Kreider Machine Co. advertised their Lancaster Traction Engine in 1907 for $150. It consisted of a small engine mounted on a suitable chassis, and made to pass through a door or gate only 31 inches wide. It is listed in various directories as late as 1911. No other information has been found.

# Kroyer Motors Company
*San Pedro, California*

**Wizard 4-Pull tractor**

The Wizard 4-Pull tractor made its debut in 1919. Of four-wheel-drive design, it was steered by clutches on each side of the machine, much like today's modern skid-steer loaders. Wizard Tractor Corporation, Los Angeles, California acquired the 4-Pull in 1924.

## Kruger Mfg. Company

*Marshalltown, Iowa*

In the 1946-1953 period, the Superior garden tractors from Kruger were listed in various directories, but no other information has been found.

## L. C. Kuhnert & Company
## Kuhnert & Ryde Company

*Chicago, Illinois*

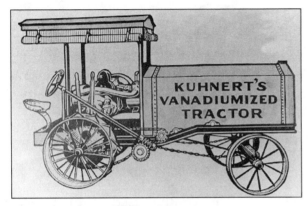

**Kuhnert's Vanadiumized Tractor**

L. C. Kuhnert & Company was organized in 1913 to build Kuhnert's Vanadiumized Tractor. The fancy title was a reference to the fairly recent discovery of vanadiumized steel which was a new high-strength alloy. The company advertised this small tractor as the "Lightest Weight [and] lowest price per horse power in the world." It was also sold on a free trial basis direct from the manufacturer.

**Kuhnert & Ryde Utility tractor**

In 1915 a name change resulted in Kuhnert & Ryde Company. Their 1916 catalog shows the

Utility tractor. It used a four-cylinder engine having a 4-1/2 x 6-3/4 inch bore and stroke. Total weight of the tractor was 5,500 pounds; the tractor was not rated in the conventional manner but was said to have a pull "equal to 8 to 10 horses." The Kuhnert Utility tractor disappears from view before 1920.

## Kultor King Mfg. Company

*Portland, Oregon*

This company is listed in the 1946-1948 period as building the Kultor King garden tractor, but no illustrations or specifications have been located.

| 1 | 2 | 3 | 4 |
|---|---|---|---|
| $750 | $600 | $400 | $200 |

## Kut-Kwick Tool Corporation

*Brunswick, Georgia*

**Kut-Kwick J-5 garden tractor**

In 1951 the Kut-Kwick J-5 garden tractor appeared. It was powered by a Wisconsin AKN single-cylinder, air-cooled engine capable of about 5-1/2 horsepower. Numerous attachments were available, ranging from various kinds of plows and cultivators to a hay rake and a sprayer. Little other information has been found.

# L

## L.A. Auto Tractor Company
*Los Angeles, California*

**Little Bear**

About 1919 the Little Bear tractor appeared. It was largely built from Ford Model T parts, even including the steering wheel. Weighing only 1,600 pounds, it apparently was designed as a low-priced outfit, and given the ample supply of Model T parts then available, servicing should never have presented a problem. Production continued until about 1921.

## La Crosse Boiler Company
*La Crosse, Wisconsin*

See: Fairbanks-Morse and Townsend

La Crosse Boiler Company acquired the Townsend Tractor Company in 1931. La Crosse continued building this 12-25 model until about

**Model 12-25**

1939. It was a two-cylinder model using a 6 x 8 inch bore and stroke. By 1935 electric starting and lighting equipment was an extra-cost option.

**Townsend 20-40 tractor**

The Townsend 20-40 tractor of an earlier time became the Lfsa Crosse 20-40 after 1931. This model carried a two-cylinder engine with a 7-1/2 x 9 inch bore and stroke. Engine speed ranged from 400 to 480 rpm.

A two-cylinder engine with a 9-1/2 x 12 inch bore and stroke was used in the La Crosse 30-60 tractor. This model had a speed range of 375 to 450 rpm, for a ground speed of 2 to 2-1/4 mph.

**La Crosse 30-60 tractor**

La Crosse continued building these tractors until 1939 or 1940. In any event, production was halted by World War Two, if indeed it did not end sooner.

## La Crosse Tractor Company
*La Crosse, Wisconsin*

**8-16 Model A**

Late in 1916 the La Crosse Tractor Co. was organized. It was a consolidation of the Happy Farmer Tractor Company of Minneapolis and the Sta-Rite Engine Co. of La Crosse. Between 1916 and 1918 the company offered the 8-16 Model A and the 12-24 Model B. Both were designed with a two-cylinder engine; the 8-16 had a 5 x 6-1/2 inch bore and stroke.

Model F La Crosse-Happy Farmer tractors were built in the 1918-1920 period. The Model F used a single front wheel as formerly, and carried a two-cylinder engine having a 5-3/4 x 7 inch

**Model F La Crosse-Happy Farmer tractors**

bore and stroke. Weighing 3,800 pounds, it was priced at $975. It offered only a single speed forward and reverse of 2-1/2 mph.

|  | 1 | 2 | 3 | 4 |
|---|---|---|---|---|
| Model F | $17,000 | $12,000 | — | — |

**Model G 12-24 tractor**

The Model G 12-24 tractor was built in the same time frame as the Model F. In fact, the only difference between them was that the Model G used a conventional four-wheel chassis, while the Model F was of three-wheel design. Both could be equipped in the field with a line drive system to permit operation of the tractor from a wagon, a grain binder, or other attached implement.

|  | 1 | 2 | 3 | 4 |
|---|---|---|---|---|
| Model G | $16,000 | $11,000 | — | — |

In 1921 La Crosse brought out their Model M, 7-12 line drive tractor. In 1921 it sold for $900, but a year later the price had dropped to $650. Concurrently the company produced the Model

**La Crosse Model M, 7-12 line drive tractor**

H, 12-24 tractor. It was an upgraded version of the earlier Model G. Oshkosh Tractor Co. purchased the assets of the tractor division in 1921, with plans of moving the factory to Oshkosh, Wisconsin. The plan fell through in 1922 and La Crosse announced they would continue building the tractor, but these plans never materialized.

|  | **1** | **2** | **3** |
|---|---|---|---|
| Model M 7-12 |  |  |  |
| $20,000 | — | — | — |

## Lambert Gas Engine Company
*Anderson, Indiana*

**Lambert tractor**

Lambert was an early gasoline engine builder with a career going back to 1890. Apparently the company built a tractor already in 1894, but it was not a commercial success. About 1904 the firm began mounting their engines on the Morton traction trucks and sold these tractors on a regular basis for a number of years.

**Lambert Steel Hoof tractor**

The Lambert Steel Hoof tractor emerged in 1912. It had a unique drivewheel design with retractable pads that functioned much like a horse's hoof. No specifications have been found for this tractor. It was produced until about 1916 when the company was taken over by Buckeye Mfg. Company.

## Lambert Mfg. Company
*Los Angeles, California*

This company is listed as a tractor manufacturer in 1914, and probably before. No other information has been found.

## Lamson Truck & Tractor Company
*Wausau, Wisconsin*

From various sources it is learned that this company was organized in 1917 to manufacture tractors, but no other information has been located.

## Lang Tractor Company
*Minneapolis, Minnesota*

The Lang tractor made its appearance in 1917. This design used a four-cylinder Waukesha engine with a 4-1/4 x 5-3/4 inch bore and stroke.

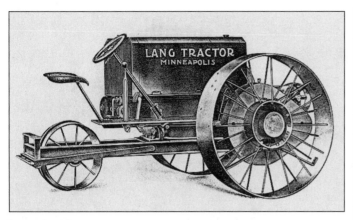

**Lang tractor**

It featured two forward speeds of 2-1/2 and 5 mph. While the company made a serious effort to become a force in the tractor business, it appears that they left the market by 1920.

## Lapeer Tractor Company
*Lapeer, Michigan*

Lapeer Tractor Co. was organized in 1917, with plans to begin tractor production by July 1918. After the initial announcement, nothing further is heard of the company.

## Homer Laughlin Engineers Corporation
*Los Angeles, California*

**Laughlin Little Husky tractor**

In 1919 the Laughlin Little Husky tractor appeared. It was also sold as the Laughlin Farm & Orchard Tractor. Originally it carried an 8-16 horsepower rating, but by 1920 it was being sold as a 10-20 model. The company used their own

four-cylinder engine having a 4-3/8 x 5-1/2 inch bore and stroke. Total weight was 6,000 pounds. The Laughlin disappears from the directories in the early 1920s.

## Laughlin Tractor Company
*Marshall, Texas*

**Laughlin Row Crop**

The Laughlin Row Crop appears in the 1948 tractor directories. This was apparently the only model. It used a Continental four-cylinder, 162ci engine with a 3-7/16 x 4-3/8 inch bore and stroke. Four forward speeds were available, ranging from 2-1/2 to 9-3/4 mph.

## Laurel Mfg. Company
*Denver, Colorado*

By 1955 the Laurel Series L tractor was on the market. This $700 outfit featured a Briggs & Stratton 23R6 engine and was available with numerous attachments, including a dozer blade

**Laurel Series L tractor**

**Lauson 15-25 or 20-35**

and sickle bar mower. The Series L weighed 960 pounds. After 1955 it disappears from the industry listings.

| | 1 | 2 | 3 | 4 |
|---|---|---|---|---|
| Series L | $2,000 | $1,500 | $1,000 | $800 |

## Stephen Laurenchick & Company
*Toledo, Ohio*

In 1953 this firm is listed as the manufacturer of the C-E garden tractor, but no specifications have been found.

See: C-E Tractor Company; Cleveland Engineering Company

## C. P. & J. Lauson
*Milwaukee, Wisconsin*

This famous gasoline engine manufacturer apparently sold gasoline tractors for a time, probably using their own modified engine as the power unit. The company is listed as a tractor manufacturer in trade directories of the 1905-1908 period, but in 1908 the company was purchased by Christensen Engineering Company of Milwaukee.

## John Lauson Mfg. Company
*New Holstein, Wisconsin*

Lauson entered the tractor business in late 1915 with a 15-25 and a 20-35. Both tractors had the

same external appearance, and in fact, the chassis was similar for both. However, the 15-25 used an Erd four-cylinder engine with a 4 x 6 inch bore and stroke, while the 20-35 carried an Erd engine with a 4-3/4 x 6 inch engine.

**Lauson 15-25 model**

By 1918 the Lauson tractors had lost the operator's cab of the original design. In addition, a Beaver engine replaced the Erd motor formerly used in the 15-25 model. It was of four-cylinder design and carried a 4-1/2 x 6 inch bore and stroke. By this time the "24 Jeweled" tradename had been associated with the Lauson tractors.

In 1919 Lauson upgraded the 15-25 tractor and gave it a new 15-30 rating. This resulted from replacing the earlier 4-1/2 x 6 Beaver engine with a 4-3/4 x 6 motor. A 15-30 was sent

**Lauson 15-30 model**

to Nebraska's Tractor Test Laboratory, and in September 1920 it demonstrated almost 18 horsepower on the drawbar. This model weighed 6,500 pounds.

**Lauson High-Powered 12-25 tractor**

at 1,200 rpm. During Nebraska Test No. 75 the 12-25 delivered over 37 maximum brake horsepower. This tractor carried a list price of $1,295.

**Lauson Road Model**

The 15-30 Lauson was available in several configurations, including a Lauson Road Model shown here. It was essentially the same tractor, but was equipped with heavy cast rear wheels to provide additional weight for soil compaction. The 15-30 was also built in a special Ricefield design.

In late 1920 or early 1921 the Lauson High-Powered 12-25 tractor appeared. It was designed around a Midwest four-cylinder engine having a 4-1/8 x 5-1/4 inch bore and stroke, and was rated

**Lauson 20-40 model**

Lauson came out with a new series of tractors in 1926. Included was the 20-40 model. It was equipped with a Beaver four-cylinder engine having a 4-3/4 x 6 inch bore and stroke. Rated at 1,040 rpm, the 20-40 was easily capable of its load rating. This model disappeared by 1930.

Along with the 20-40 farm tractor, Lauson also built the 20-40 Thresherman's and Roadbuilders Special. This model developed over 50 belt horsepower, and used extra heavy wheels.

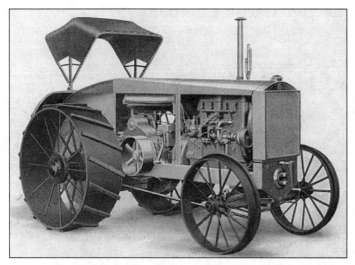

**Lauson 20-40 Thresherman's and Roadbuilder's Special**

For instance, the drive wheels on this model used 1-inch spokes, and could be furnished with 16 or 20-inch rims, as desired. With 20-inch road wheels, this model weighed 8,650 pounds.

|  | 1 | 2 | 3 | 4 |
|---|---|---|---|---|
| 20-40 Special | $8,000 | $6,000 | $4,500 | $2,000 |

**Lauson 20-35 tractor**

Lauson 20-35 tractors first appeared in 1927. Weighing 7,580 pounds, this model was furnished with Bosch lighting equipment as a standard feature. A Beaver four-cylinder engine was featured, and the sun canopy was standard equipment.

Emerging in 1926, the Lauson 16-32 was tested at Nebraska the following year. Test No. 131 revealed a maximum of nearly 37 belt horsepower for this model. It was built with a Beaver four-cylinder engine having a 4-1/2 x 6 inch bore and stroke; rated speed was 1,100 rpm.

*Lauson 16-32 tractor*

**Lauson 25-45 tractor**

The Lauson 25-45 emerged in 1929. This was a six-cylinder tractor with a LeRoi 4-1/2 x 6 inch engine. It was available with Bosch electric starting and lighting equipment by the mid-1930s. Total weight of this tractor was 9,060 pounds. Production ended about 1937.

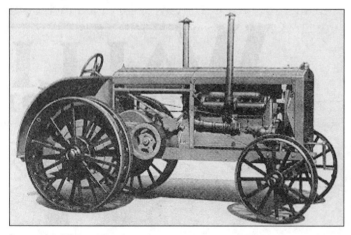

**Lauson 65 tractor**

Lauson 65 tractors carried a 22-35 horsepower rating. The six-cylinder engine was a Wisconsin, and it used a 3-7/8 x 5 inch bore and stroke. Like the 25-45, it came onto the market in 1929. During the 1930s the company continued offering the 20-35 and the 25-45 models in addition to the Lauson 65 shown here. However, the Lauson tractors disappear from the tractor directories after 1937.

# Lawter Tractor Company
*St. Marys, Ohio*

**1914 Model**

In 1913 Lawter Tractor Company was incorporated at Newcastle, Indiana. Later that year the company purchased the Universal Tractor Mfg. Co., also at Newcastle. The following year the company moved to St. Marys, Ohio. The 1914 model was rated at 20 drawbar and 40 belt horsepower. However, by 1916 the tractor was given an 18-38 rating. Production of the Lawter continued for several years, apparently ending about 1918. Weighing 6,500 pounds, it retailed at $1,750.

# Leader Engine Company
*Detroit, Michigan*

**Leader tractor**

Leader Engine Company is shown operating at Detroit, Michigan as well as at Grand Rapids, Michigan. In 1913 the Sintz-Wallin Co. of Grand Rapids merged with Midland Tractor Co. at

Detroit to form Leader Engine Co. Rated at 12 drawbar and 18 belt horsepower, the Leader used a two-cylinder opposed engine of the company's own design and manufacture. Production appears to have ended by 1915.

## Leader Tractor Mfg. Company
*Cleveland, Ohio*

**Leader Model B tractor**

By 1946 the Leader tractor was on the market. The 1947 Model B shown here was furnished with a Hercules four-cylinder engine having a 3-1/4 x 4 inch bore and stroke. Total weight of the tractor was 2,500 pounds. A belt pulley and a pto shaft both came as standard equipment. Production of the Leader tractors continued into the early 1950s.

|         | 1       | 2       | 3       | 4     |
|---------|---------|---------|---------|-------|
| Model B | $2,900  | $1,800  | $1,100  | $400  |

## Leader Tractor Mfg. Company
*Des Moines, Iowa*

Leader emerged in 1918 with their 12-25 Rex tractor. Weighing 5,600 pounds, the Rex sold for $1,800. The company was apparently a successor

**12-25 Rex tractor**

to the defunct Ohio Tractor Mfg. Company of Marion, Ohio. The latter had gone broke in 1916 and was acquired by others to build motor trucks. Perhaps the new owners sold off the tractor business to Leader. In any case, the Rex tractor did not remain on the market for any length of time, likely being out of business by 1920. The Rex 12-25 was powered by a Waukesha four-cylinder engine having a 4-1/4 x 5-3/4 inch bore and stroke.

## Harry W. Leavitt
*Waterloo, Iowa*

Harry Leavitt appears to have been in the tractor business for a time. Without a doubt, he was involved with Waterloo Gasoline Engine Co. for several years in the design of various tractors. Once the company was sold to Deere & Co., Leavitt appears to have continued with them for a time as well. At any rate, any tractor production from Leavitt was very limited indeed.

## LeClaire Mfg. Company
*LeClaire, Iowa*

In the 1950-1952 period, the Handy Dandy "K" garden cultivator appeared from LeClaire Mfg. Company. Weighing only 107 pounds, it was powered by various makes of small air-cooled

**Handy Dandy "K" garden cultivator**

engines. Very few specific details have been found regarding this small garden tractor.

## Legner Engineering Works
*Littleton, California*

No information has been found regarding this company or its activities in the tractor business.

## Leland Detroit Mfg. Company
*Detroit, Michigan*

**Terra-Tiller No. 47**

Beginning about 1950 and continuing until about 1953, the Terra-Tiller No. 47 was offered by Leland Detroit. This 256 pound garden tractor was available with numerous attachments,

and was powered by a Briggs & Stratton 2 horsepower engine with a 2 x 2-1/4 inch bore and stroke.

| <u>1</u> | <u>2</u> | <u>3</u> | <u>4</u> |
|------|------|------|------|
| $500 | $350 | $200 | $100 |

## Lenox Motor Car Company
*Hyde Park, Massachusetts*

**Lenox American Model 20, 22-30 tractor**

The Lenox American Model 20, 22-30 tractor came out in 1916. Priced at $2,500 this four-wheel-drive tractor was powered with a Wisconsin four-cylinder engine. It used a 4-3/4 x 5-1/2 inch bore and stroke. Specific information has been difficult to locate on this company, but it appears that production ended about 1920.

## Leonard Tractor Company
*Gary, Indiana*

**Leonard four-wheel-drive**

Built in the 1918-1922 period, the Leonard was a four-wheel-drive design. Initially it was built with a 12-35 horsepower rating, but about 1920 this was raised to 20 drawbar horsepower, while the belt rating remained constant. The company appears to have operated at Joliet, Illinois and Jackson, Michigan as well as at the Indiana address.

## Levene Motor Company

*Philadelphia, Pennsylvania*

This company is often referred to as a tractor manufacturer. However, it appears that Levene often bought out failing or bankrupt tractor manufacturers and then continued to supply repair parts. The tractors they built and/or sold appear to have been left-over stocks from the companies they purchased.

## Liberty Tractor Company

*Dubuque, Iowa*

**Liberty tractor**

Liberty began business in 1919. The company began in 1913 as Klumb Engine & Machinery Co. in Sheboygan, Wisconsin. Within months after beginning operations at Dubuque, the company name was again changed to Dubuque Truck & Tractor Company. It appears that few tractors were built before the company went out of business.

## Liberty Tractor Company

*Hammond, Indiana*

Although it was organized and incorporated in 1918, no further information has been located relative to this company's activities in the tractor business.

## Liberty Tractor Company

*Minneapolis, Minnesota*

**Liberty tractor**

Organized in 1917, Liberty did not begin making any large number of tractors until the following year. A large distributing house, P. J. Downes & Co., sold the tractor, and when Downes went broke, Liberty lost its sales organization. Downes reorganized, Liberty came to life again, but the second attempt was not successful. Initially, the tractor was built as a 15-30, but late in production it was sold as an 18-32 model. Power came from a Climax Model K four-cylinder engine with a 5 x 6-1/2 inch bore and stroke.

## Lincoln Steel Works

*Lincoln, Nebraska*

In the mid-1950s Lincoln offered their Kitty Krawler. This was a small tracklaying tractor that weighed only 1,500 pounds. It was powered

**Lincoln Kitty Krawler**

by a Wisconsin air-cooled single-cylinder engine with a 3 x 3 inch bore and stroke, and capable of about 8 horsepower. Three forward speeds were available. Little other information has been found on the Kitty Krawler.

## Lincoln Tractor & Farm Implement Company
*Sandusky, Ohio*

After Dauch Mfg. Company went broke, Lincoln was organized to build a new tractor design. Organized in November 1921 the company announced plans to begin tractor production by February of the following year. By October 1922 the company announced plans to begin production in February of 1923. None of the plans materialized, and only a few tractors were made. Unfortunately, the only image in the Author's collection was too poor to reproduce.

## Lincoln Tractor Company
*Los Angeles, California*

The Lincoln garden tractor was on the market by 1947. This model used a Salsbury single-cylinder engine of 6-1/2 horsepower. Weighing 750 pounds, it was available with various options

**Lincoln garden tractor**

including several different cultivators. It was also equipped with a pto shaft, both to the front and to the rear of the tractor. Nothing is known of the Lincoln after 1948.

## Line Drive Tractor Company
*Milwaukee, Wisconsin*

**Line Drive Tractor**

The Line Drive Tractor first appeared about 1915. As shown here, it was designed for operation with a pair of leather lines, just like driving a team of horses. The company persisted in business until 1917 when it was taken over by Automotive Corporation, Fort Wayne, Indiana. Curiously, a trademark application from The Line Drive Tractor Company, Chicago, Illinois appeared that year, claiming first use of this mark on March 3. Whether the two companies are connected in any way is unknown.

## Linn Mfg. Company
*Morris, New York*

Linn Mfg. Company came out with their tractor-truck in 1916. For a time the firm attempted to enter the tractor market with their machine, but it was better suited to construction and other rough terrain uses than to farming. Initially the Linn Tractor-Truck was powered by a Continental four-cylinder engine, but as it evolved, larger engines were used. The company remained in operation until about 1950.

## Lion Tractor Company
*Minneapolis, Minnesota*

Billed as "King of the Farm" the Lion tractor made its first appearance in 1914. It was designed by D. M. Hartsough who had also designed the popular Bull tractor made in Minneapolis. Rated at 8 drawbar and 16 belt horse-

**"King of the Farm" Lion tractor**

power, the Lion used a two-cylinder engine having a 5 x 6-1/2 inch bore and stroke. The company sold a substantial number of tractors for a time, but vanished from the market in 1918.

**Linn tractor**

## Litchfield Mfg. Company

*Waterloo, Iowa*

In 1912 and 1913 this firm is listed as a farm tractor manufacturer. The company actively built numerous farm machines, and for a time, also built gasoline engines. No information on their farm tractor has been found.

## Little Dilly Tractor Works

*Wichita Falls, Texas*

The Little Dilly Jr. and Little Dilly Sr. garden tractors are listed in 1947 and 1948, but no illustrations have been found. The Jr. was equipped with a Lauson 2-1/4 horsepower engine, and the Sr. used a Briggs & Stratton or Wisconsin engine of 3 horsepower. Both models had an optional belt pulley drive.

## Little Giant Company

*Mankato, Minnesota*

**Model B, 16-22 tractor**

Mayer Bros. Company began building tractors in 1913, and in June 1918 changed the company name to Little Giant Company. By this time two tractor models were available, the smallest of which was the Model B, 16-22. This 5,200 pound tractor retailed at $1,650 in 1918. The engine was a four-cylinder design built by Little Giant; it used a 4-1/2 x 5 inch bore and stroke. Toward the end of production in 1927 the engine bore was raised to 4-1/2 inches.

**Little Giant Model A, 26-35 tractor**

Little Giant tractors maintained the same general design throughout their production run ranging from 1913 to 1927. The Model A, 26-35 tractor carried the company's own four-cylinder engine; it used a 5-1/4 x 6 inch bore and stroke. Probably for the sake of convenience, the cylinders were cast in pairs. The Model A weighed 8,700 pounds and sold for $2,500 in 1918.

## Little Oak

See: Humber-Anderson; and Willmar Tractor Co.

## C.M. Livingston & Son

*Tulsa, Oklahoma*

**Livy "5HP" garden tractor**

Beginning about 1950 and continuing for about 5 years, the Livy "5HP" garden tractor was available. It is shown here with a rotary brush cutter that could also be used for felling small trees.

Power came from a Briggs & Stratton Model 14 engine with a 2-5/8 inch bore and stroke. It was capable of about 5 horsepower. Various attachments were available.

# Lobb Bros.
*Fairmont, Minnesota*

This company is listed in a 1918 tractor directory as a tractor manufacturer, but no other information has been found.

# Lodge & Shipley Company
*Cincinnati, Ohio*

**Choremaster garden tractor**

Beginning about 1947 the Special Products Division of Lodge & Shipley started producing their Choremaster garden tractor. The simple design was equipped with a Clinton 700 engine having a 2 x 1-7/8 inch bore and stroke. A perusal of the tractor directories leads to the conclusion that the Choremaster was built for only a short time.

# Lombard Auto-Tractor-Truck Corporation
*New York, New York*

**Lombard tractor-truck**

Alvin O. Lombard organized this company in 1901 to build a steam log hauler. In 1917 the company was incorporated and began building a tractor-truck. Power came from a six-cylinder engine with a 5-1/2 x 6-3/4 inch bore and stroke for 140 horsepower. Two forward speeds were available of 4 and 6 mph. Under suitable conditions this machine had a drawbar pull of 15,000 pounds. The company endured until 1920.

# London Motor Plow Company
*Springfield, Ohio*

**London motor plow**

Little history has been found on this company, but as late as 1923 the firm was offering its motor plow. Rated at 12 drawbar and 25 belt horsepower, it used a Midwest four-cylinder engine with a 4-1/8 x 5-1/4 inch bore and stroke. The tractor weighed 4,600 pounds, with the detachable plows adding considerably to that figure.

# Long Mfg. Company

*Tarboro, North Carolina*

**Long Model A tractor**

By 1948 the Long Model A tractor was on the market. Weighing 3,225 pounds, it was tested at Nebraska under No. 410 of 1949. A Continental four-cylinder, F-162 engine was featured. It had a 3-7/16 x 4-3/8 inch bore and stroke. In Nebraska Test No. 410 this tractor delivered almost 29 drawbar horsepower, along with nearly 32 horsepower at the belt pulley.

# A. H. Loomis

*Belleville, Kansas*

A.H. Loomis appears in the annals of tractor history as a manufacturer, but no information has been found.

# Los Angeles Motor Car Company

*Los Angeles, California*

No information on this firm has been found, either regarding tractors it may have built, nor even in the automotive directories we checked; the company title certainly suggests that automobiles were part of the scene.

# Louisville Motor Plow Company

*Louisville, Kentucky*

No specific information has been located regarding this firm. It seems plausible that it was somehow connected with B. F. Avery Company of the same city; the latter built and sold a motor plow for a short time.

# Love Tractor Company

*Eau Claire, Michigan*

**Love J51 tractor**

Beginning about 1950 and continuing through the decade, Love offered several tractor models. Included was the J51, a small two-plow tractor. This one was built with a Willys CJ2A engine. Much of the tractor was built up of OEM parts. A belt pulley was standard equipment. Total weight of the tractor was 2,650 pounds.

**Love C51 or CP51 tractor**

While production of the J51 appears to have ended in the early 1950s, the C51 and CF51 tractors were apparently available through the decade. Three distinct "51" models were built. The C51 used a Chrysler 217ci engine; the CF51 used a Chrysler 230.5ci engine and had a slightly longer wheel base. The F51 tractor was virtually the same, but used a Ford 7HNN5H engine with a 226ci displacement.

| | 1 | 2 | 3 | 4 |
|---|---|---|---|---|
| C51, CP51 | $5,000 | $3,500 | $1,500 | $750 |

# Harry A. Lowther Company

*Shelbyville, Indiana*

**Custom Model C tractor**

The Custom Model C emerged from Custom Mfg. Co. at Shelbyville in 1948. By 1950 what appears to be the same tractor was being built by Lowther. By 1953 the Custom reappears at Hustisford, Wisconsin. For 1950 the Custom was built in two sizes. The ER and EW designators were for tricycle or adjustable wide-front axles. This model used a Chrysler Industrial 8 engine with a displacement of 250.6ci. The HR and HW models used a Chrysler Industrial 6 engine with a 230.2ci displacement. Both models offered five forward speeds and both were equipped with Fluid Drive drive couplings.

# Lyons Atlas Company

*Indianapolis, Indiana*

In 1917 Lyons Atlas bought out Hume Mfg. Company at Hume, Illinois. The latter had developed the Hume tractor, and Lyons Atlas continued to build it under their own name for a short time. The Lyons Atlas had a 16-26 horsepower rating, and through its special design had a turning radius of only 9 feet. The four-cylinder engine used a 4-1/4 x 5-3/4 inch bore and stroke and was rated at 1,000 rpm. Weighing 5,100 pounds, it was priced at $1,465. When Lyons Atlas went broke the Midwest Engine Company was formed.

**Lyons Atlas 16-26 tractor**

# M

## McCadden Machine Works

*St. Cloud, Minnesota*

McCadden was building gasoline engines by 1904. In March 1916 the company incorporated and announced plans to build a tractor. Whether it got past the prototype stage is unknown, since no other information has been found.

## S. McChesney

*Pipestone, Minnesota*

For a brief time in 1911 S. McChesney offered his E-Z Built Tractor. It was essentially a set of traction trucks, and less than that, appears to have been little more than the essential gearing and accessories. The buyer then furnished wheels, frame, and his own stationary engine. Little else is known of this machine.

## McCormick Harvesting Machine Company

*Chicago, Illinois*

See: International Harvester Company

## McCormick Tractor Company

*Denver, Colorado*

In 1918 the McCormick Tractor Company was induced to change its name, admitting they had adopted the name partly because of the advertising value that had been established by International Harvester Company. The company announced that they would choose a new name, but no further information has been found regarding the venture, nor is it known whether any tractors were built.

## Tyler McDonald

*La Mesa, California*

About 1956 this firm offered their Jiffy-Cart 4-Wheel-Drive garden tractor. It was powered by a Kohler K-90 engine of about 3-1/2 horsepower. It used a 2-3/8 x 2-1/4 inch bore and stroke. Little else is known of the Jiffy Cart, and no illustrations have been found.

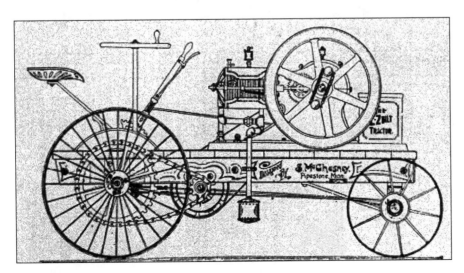

**McChesney E-Z Built Tractor**

# McDougall-Duluth Company
*Duluth, Minnesota*

This company has been identified as a tractor manufacturer but no other information has been found.

# McFarland & Westmont Tractor Company
*Sauk City, Wisconsin*

See: Wisconsin Farm Tractor Company

# McIntyre Mfg. Company
*Columbus, Ohio*

**Farmer Boy tractor**

The Farmer Boy tractor was developed in 1915 and appeared on the market the following year. From various advertising, it appears that two models were built, including a small 10-20 size and the larger 18-30 model. Both models used four-cylinder engines. Few details of the Farmer Boy tractors have been found. In 1918 the company was reorganized as Columbus Tractor Company.

# McKinney Traction Cultivator Company
*St. Louis, Missouri*

Organized at Gainesville, Georgia in 1910, the McKinney Traction Cultivator Company moved to St. Louis, Missouri the following year. Their

**McKinney Traction Cultivator**

initial design used an 8 horsepower gasoline engine for power. The 1910 model was equipped with a single lever to control all functions of forward, reverse and steering.

**McKinney motor cultivator**

After the move to St. Louis in 1911, McKinney offered two different motor cultivators of 18 and 25 brake horsepower, with the largest model being shown here. Power came from a two-cylinder, two-cycle engine, and steering was achieved through friction wheels working on the countershafts. Nothing more is known of the firm after its 1911 announcements.

# D. M. McLaughlin Company
*Emeryville, California*

Although this company is listed as a tractor manufacturer, no information has been found regarding what was built, or when it was built.

# McVicker Engineering Company

*Minneapolis, Minnesota*

**McVicker Engineering Company tractor**

McVicker Engineering Company began offering a tractor through Joy-Wilson Sales Company in 1909. By the following year the firm was building three sizes of 40, 70 and 140 brake horsepower. The latter had a four-cylinder engine with a 10 x 10-1/2 inch bore and stroke for a displacement of some 3,300 ci. Walter J. McVicker was a prominent mechanical engineer and designed several different tractors, most notably the early Twin City models of Minneapolis Steel & Machinery Company. The company's career in tractor manufacturing appears to have ended after 1910.

# M&M Tractor Company

*Minneapolis, Minnesota*

In 1914 this company announced that they would be starting production of a new tractor, and claimed great things for their prototype model. After the initial announcements, nothing more was heard of the company.

# Macultivator Company

*Sandusky, Ohio*

This example of the Motor Cultivator was gleaned from an unknown magazine, the date of which is also unknown. Given the design of this garden tractor and the style of engine, it would

**Macultivator Motor Cultivator**

certainly seem to be of pre-1920 vintage. Perhaps additional information might be found for a later edition of this book.

| 1 | 2 | 3 | 4 |
|---|---|---|---|
| $800 | $600 | $400 | $200 |

# Magnet Tractor Company

*Minneapolis, Minnesota*

**Magnet Tractor Co. 14-28 model**

Incorporated in 1919, Magnet Tractor Co. offered their 14-28 model in 1920 and 1921. Priced at $1,875, this tractor weighed 4,400 pounds. Power came from a Waukesha Model DU four-cylinder engine with a 4-1/2 x 6-1/4 inch bore and stroke. The 14-28 used a worm gear final drive.

# Manitoba Universal Farm Tractor Company Ltd.

*Winnipeg, Manitoba*

This company was incorporated in 1915 to build farm tractors, but no other information has been found.

## Manley Engineering & Machine Works
*Copley, Ohio*

Various references are found regarding the Blue Ox Garden Tractor built by Manley in the 1948-1953 period. However, no illustrations or specifications have been found.

## Marine Iron Works
*Tacoma, Washington*

**Mighty Man Garden Tractor**

By 1947 the Farm Equipment Division of Marine Iron Works had developed the Mighty Man Garden Tractor. In 1950 the line included three models, including the Mighty Man "5" shown here. This model used a Clinton Model 700 air-cooled engine capable of about 1-1/2 horsepower.

**Mighty Man "7" model**

The 1950 line of Mighty Man garden tractors included the Mighty Man "7" model shown here, along with the Mighty Man "10" garden tractor. These two were essentially the same, but used

different wheels and on the "10" a four-speed belt reduction was available; this was not used on the Mighty Man "7" tractor. Both styles used a Wisconsin ABN engine capable of over 4 horsepower. It carried a 2-1/2 x 2-3/4 inch bore and stroke. Numerous attachments were available. The Mighty Man line continued at least into the mid-1950s.

## Market Garden Tractor Company
*Minneapolis, Minnesota*

**Market Garden Tractor**

Organized and incorporated in 1918, this firm continued until mid-1921. At that point the company name was changed to Aro Tractor Company. Priced at $295, the Market Garden Tractor was set up especially for garden and orchard cultivating and spraying. Power came from a single-cylinder, two-cycle engine with a 4-inch bore and stroke, and capable of about 4-1/2 belt horsepower.

## Maroa Motor Plow Company
*Maroa, Illinois*

Although the company was organized in 1911 to build the Maroa Motor Plow, little other information has been located.

# Marschke Motor Plow Company
*Valley City, North Dakota*

**Marschke Motor Plow**

By 1908 R. B. Marschke had developed the Marschke Motor Plow. That year a company was organized to manufacture the machine. The company lasted at least into 1909 when they tried to promote it. After that time, further references to the company have not been found.

# Martin Tractor Company
*Indianapolis, Indiana*

During 1912 this firm was organized and incorporated to manufacture tractors, but no further information has been found.

# Martin Tractor Company
*Springfield, Massachusetts*

This firm was incorporated in 1913 to build farm tractors. It is unknown whether there was a connection to the company of the same name, organized a year earlier at Indianapolis, Indiana.

# Marvel Tractor Company
*Columbus, Ohio*

In 1921 Marvel applied for this trademark, noting that it had been first used August 20, 1920. While

**Marvel trademark**

it is known that Marvel built at least a few tractors, production did not come up to expectations and lasted for only a short time.

# Massey-Harris Company
*Toronto, Ontario and Racine, Wisconsin*

# Massey-Ferguson Inc.
*Detroit, Michigan*

Massey-Harris was organized at Toronto in 1891, and was a merger of Massey Mfg. Company and A. Harris & Son. Until about 1910 the company was primarily a Canadian firm and catered mainly to the Canadian trade. With the purchase of Deyo-Macey Co. of Binghamton, New York in 1910 the company began a serious attempt to enter the U.S. market as well.

By 1917 the company had entered the tractor business, first selling the Bull tractor made in Minneapolis. The following year Massey-Harris contracted with Parret Tractor Company of Chicago, Illinois to design and build the Massey-Harris No. 1. Three different models were produced, and production was entirely suspended in 1923.

During 1927 Massey-Harris began selling the Wallis tractor of J. I. Case Plow Works, and the following year M-H bought out this company for

$1.3 million in cash, plus guaranteeing another $1.1 million in bonds.  Massey-Harris Company was organized and incorporated at Racine, Wisconsin, and the company now was able to successfully penetrate the U. S. tractor market.

In 1953 Massey-Harris acquired Harry Ferguson Inc. to form Massey-Harris-Ferguson.  In March 1958 the name was abbreviated to Massey-Ferguson.  Massey-Harris-Ferguson and Massey-Ferguson tractors may be found under the Massey-Ferguson heading.

**Bull tractor**

In 1917 Massey-Harris entered the tractor market as a sales wing for the Bull Tractor Company of Minneapolis.  The Bull had phenomenal sales when it first came on the market, but by 1917 it had already reached its zenith.  Thus, the company's first entry into farm tractors was a failure.

**Parrett Tractor**

During 1918 Massey-Harris made an agreement with Parrett Tractors of Chicago, Illinois.  Under this plan, Parrett was to design and build the tractor for M-H.  Before production ended in

1923, three different models were built, and it appears that at least some of them were built at the company's Weston (Ontario) plant.

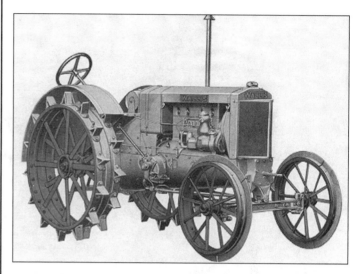

**Wallis 20-30**

From 1923 to 1927 Massey-Harris abstained from the tractor business, but in the latter year they contracted with J. I. Case Plow Works to sell their Wallis tractor.  The following year Massey-Harris bought out the Racine, Wisconsin factory of J. I. Case Plow Works, and set up their own Massey-Harris Company plant at Racine.  The 20-30 Wallis was their first model.  The 20-30 was tested at Nebraska (No. 134) in 1927 and displayed well over its rated power.

**20-30 Orchard tractor**

J. I. Case Plow Works had developed the 20-30 Orchard tractor in the late 1920s, and after the 1928 Massey-Harris takeover, the latter contin-

**20-30 Industrial tractor**

ued to offer this specialized model. Aside from the special fenders and other accessories, it was essentially the same as the ordinary 20-30.

Several of the larger tractor manufacturers developed industrial models during the 1920s. This brought tractor power to factories and assembly plants. The 20-30 Industrial was equipped with solid rubber tires and with different transmission gearing, but was otherwise a conversion of the farm model.

Massey-Harris introduced the Model 25 tractor in 1931. It replaced the earlier 20-30 model. The Model 25 was also known as the Massey-Harris 26-41. Its four-cylinder engine carried a 4-3/8 x 5-3/4 inch bore and stroke, and was rated at 1,200 rpm. The pto shaft shown on this model was an extra equipment item. The Model 25 continued the unit frame design using a boiler plate frame; it went back to the Wallis Cub of 1913.

**Massey-Harris Model 25 tractor**

**Massey-harris 12-20 tractor**

In late 1928 or early 1929, Massey-Harris introduced its 12-20 tractor. This companion to the 20-30 and later, the Model 25 tractor, was tested at Nebraska under No. 164 of June 1929. This model used a four-cylinder engine having a 3-7/8 x 5-1/4 inch bore and stroke. The 12-20 was capable of well over 24 belt horsepower.

**Massey-Harris 12-20**

Besides the regular farm version, the Massey-Harris 12-20 was also available in orchard and industrial models. No major changes were made to the tractor chassis or the engine, but special fenders and relocated air stack and exhaust were all necessary. Production of the 12-20 continued until about 1936.

Nebraska Test No. 177 was run on the Massey-Harris General Purpose tractor in May 1930. Rated as a 15-22, it was equipped with a four-cylinder Hercules engine having a 4 x 4-1/2 inch

**Massey-Harris General Purpose tractor**

bore and stroke. Production of this model continued for several years, but no specific production data has been located.

**Massey-Harris Challenger**

The Massey-Harris Challenger first appeared in February 1936. It marked the company's entry into row-crop tractors, and continued to use the boiler plate unit frame design that had been pioneered on the Wallis Cub of 1913. The engine was built by Massey-Harris; its four-cylinder design carried a 3-7/8 x 5-1/4 inch bore and stroke. In Nebraska Test No. 265 of August 1936 the Challenger was capable of 20 drawbar horsepower. Production of this model ended in 1938.

**Twin Power Challenger**

Late model Challenger tractors sported a stream-lined hood and grille. Emerging in 1937, the Twin Power Challenger was rated at 1,200 and 1,400 rpm. At the higher speed, this model delivered over 36 belt horsepower. Essentially, this tractor was the same as the original Challenger design which it replaced. The Twin Power Challenger performance data may be found in Nebraska Test No. 293. The Challenger remained in production until about 1942.

**Massey-Harris Pacemaker**

The Massey-Harris Pacemaker first appeared in 1936. It used the same four-cylinder engine as the Challenger, namely, with a 3-7/8 x 5-1/4 inch bore and stroke. Total weight was about 4,000 pounds. This model was built into 1937 when it was replaced with the Twin Power Pacemaker. In Nebraska Test No. 266 the Pacemaker demonstrated approximately 27 belt horsepower.

**Massey-Harris PA Orchard tractor**

In addition to the regular standard-tread Pacemaker, Massey-Harris also offered a special Model PA Orchard tractor. It was identical to the regular model but had a 40-inch tread width, special hood and fenders, and no belt pulley. Production of the Pacemaker ended in 1937 when it was replaced with the Twin Power Pacemaker models.

**Twin Power Pacemaker**

Production of the Twin Power Pacemaker began in 1937. This model had a streamlined hood and grille. The engine was virtually identical to that of the original 1936 Pacemaker, but had a dual rating of 1,200 and 1,400 rpm, thus the Twin-Power tradename. In Nebraska Test No. 294 of November 1937 the Twin Power Pacemaker exhibited nearly 42 belt horsepower. Production apparently continued until about 1942.

Production of the Massey-Harris Model 81 and Model 82 Standard-Tread tractors began in 1941 and ended in 1946. This two-plow tractor was capable of about 27 belt horsepower and

**Massey-Harris Model 81 Standard**

used a Continental four-cylinder engine with a 3 x 4-3/8 inch bore and stroke.  Production of this model was seriously limited by the requirements of World War Two.

|  | 1 | 2 | 3 | 4 |
|---|---|---|---|---|
| 81 Standard | $2,500 | $1,750 | $1,200 | $650 |
| 82 Standard | $2,500 | $1,750 | $1,200 | $650 |

In Nebraska Test No. 376 of 1941 the Massey-Harris Model 81 Row-Crop tractor delivered nearly 21 drawbar horsepower.  Like others of this series, it had a dual speed rating.  For belt work and for road gear, it could be operated at 1,800 rpm, while for drawbar work it was rated at 1,500 rpm.  The Model 81 Row-Crop used the same four-cylinder engine as the 81 Standard.  Production of the Model 81 and 82 tractors ended in 1946.

**Massey-Harris Model 81 Row-Crop tractor**

|  | 1 | 2 | 3 | 4 |
|---|---|---|---|---|
| 81/82 Row-Crop | $2,100 | $1,550 | $1,000 | $400 |

**Twin Power 101 Standard**

No Nebraska test was run on the 101 Jr. or 102 Jr. standard-tread tractors. Initially, the Twin Power 101 Standard was equipped with a 3-1/4 x 4-3/8 inch, four-cylinder engine, but this was later changed to a 3-5/16 inch bore. The 102GS Junior was a 2-3 plow tractor that used a four-cylinder Continental engine having a 3-7/16 x 4-3/8 inch bore and stroke. Production of the 101 Jr. and 102 Jr. tractors began in 1939.

**Massey-Harris 101 Junior tractor**

In October 1940, Nebraska Test No. 359 was run on the Massey-Harris 101 Junior tractor. This test demonstrated over 30 belt horsepower from the 162 ci, four-cylinder, Continental engine. It used a 3-7/16 x 4-3/8 inch bore and stroke. The 102 Junior was of similar design. Production of these models ended in 1946.

Primiary differences between the 81/82 models and the 101/102 models are the 82 and 102 models were Canadian built and usually had larger displacement engines as the Canadian output was meant for the use of kerosene and distillate fuels which require larger displacement engines in order to keep the horsepower ratings commensurate with the gas engine models

| | 1 | 2 | 3 | 4 |
|---|---|---|---|---|
| 101/102 Junior Standard | $2,300 | $1,350 | $800 | $400 |
| 101/102 Junior Row-Crop | $2,200 | $1,200 | $600 | $300 |

**101 Senior Row-Crop**

Production of the 101 Senior tractors began in 1938. The row-crop model was equipped with a Continental six-cylinder engine having a 3-5/16 x 4-3/8 inch bore and stroke. This tractor had a dual speed rating of 1,500 rpm for drawbar work and 1,800 rpm for road and belt work. The pto shaft and power lift system both came as extra equipment. Production of the 101 Sr. tractors continued into 1945.

| | 1 | 2 | 3 | 4 |
|---|---|---|---|---|
| 101 Senior Standard | $2,600 | $1,875 | $1,300 | $700 |
| 101 Senior Row-Crop | $2,500 | $1,700 | $1,200 | $600 |
| 101 Super with Crysler engine | $4,500 | $3,000 | $2,000 | $1,200 |

**101 Senior standard-tread tractor**

The standard-tread version of the 101 Senior tractors was virtually identical in design, except of course for the chassis itself. Both tractors used a six-cylinder 226 ci Continental engine. While the 101 Senior tractors were rated in the three-plow class, they were not tested at Nebraska, and no specific horsepower data was generally published. Production of the 101 Senior Standard and Row-Crop models ran from 1938 to 1946. The 102 Senior Standard and Row-Crop tractors were built from 1941 to 1946.

|  | 1 | 2 | 3 | 4 |
|---|---|---|---|---|
| 102 Senior Standard | $2,550 | $1,700 | $1,200 | $800 |
| 102 Senior Row-Crop | $2,500 | $1,700 | $1,250 | $850 |

The Massey-Harris 201 was built in 1942-43 and used a Chrysler T-100 6 cylinder engine.

|  | 1 | 2 | 3 | 4 |
|---|---|---|---|---|
| 201 | $3,800 | $2,500 | $1,500 | $1,200 |

The Massey-Harris 202 (223 units were built) used a Continental M-290 6 cylinder engine.

|  | 1 | 2 | 3 | 4 |
|---|---|---|---|---|
| 202 | $6,200 | $4,400 | $3,200 | $1,500 |

**Massey-Harris 203 Distillate tractor**

Production of the Massey-Harris 203 Distillate tractor began in 1940, followed the next year by the 203 Gasoline model. Both remained in production until 1947. The 203 used a six-cylinder Continental engine having a 4 x 4-3/8 inch bore and stroke. It was rated at 1,700 rpm for drawbar work and 2,000 rpm for belt and road work.

|  | 1 | 2 | 3 | 4 |
|---|---|---|---|---|
| 203 Distillate | $3,700 | $2,700 | $2,000 | $900 |
| 203 Gasoline | $6,000 | $4,000 | $3,500 | $2,000 |

**Massey-Harris 20**

The Massey-Harris 20 saw first light in 1946, and remained in production until 1948. A Continental F124 engine was used in the M-H 20. It was designed with a 3 x 4-3/8 inch bore and stroke, like its predecessor, the Massey-Harris 81 tractor.

Although M-H advertising notes that the row-crop 20 and the standard-tread 20 differed "only in the front axle design," at least one 1947 industry listing shows the 20-K standard-tread model with a Continental F140 engine; it used a 3-3/16 x 4-3/8 inch bore and stroke. Since the 20-K was designed for use with kerosene fuel, perhaps the larger engine bore was needed to

**Massey-Harris 20-K**

deliver the same horsepower as the gasoline engine. In any circumstance, the 20-K was built only in 1947 and 1948; a 20 Gas Standard was offered only in 1948.

| | 1 | 2 | 3 | 4 |
|---|---|---|---|---|
| 20 Gas Row-Crop | $2,100 | $1,550 | $1,000 | $400 |
| 20 Gas Standard | $2,500 | $1,750 | $1,200 | $650 |
| 20-K Row-Crop | $2,100 | $1,550 | $1,000 | $400 |
| 20-K Standard | $2,500 | $1,750 | $1,200 | $650 |

**Massey-Harris "30" tractor**

In 1946 Massey-Harris introduced the "30" tractor. It was built in standard-tread and row-crop designs, with several versions of the latter being

available. Included was this single-front wheel design, along with the standard tricycle and the high-arch, adjustable-width front axle. The Model 30 used a Continental F-162 four-cylinder engine having a 3-7/16 x 4-3/8 inch bore and stroke. In Nebraska Test No. of May 1949 the Model 30 yielded in excess of 33 belt horsepower. This popular design was built into 1952 when it was replaced with the M-H "33" tractor.

| | 1 | 2 | 3 | 4 |
|---|---|---|---|---|
| 30 Gas Row-Crop | $2,500 | $1,800 | $1,300 | $700 |
| 30 Gas Standard | $2,600 | $1,900 | $1,350 | $750 |
| 30-K Row-Crop | $2,500 | $1,800 | $1,300 | $700 |
| 30-K Standard | $2,600 | $1,900 | $1,350 | $750 |

**Model 11 Pony tractor**

The Model 11 Pony tractor first appeared in 1948 and was built until 1957. Smallest in the Massey-Harris line, it was powered by a Continental four-cylinder engine with a 2-3/8 x 3-1/2 inch bore and stroke. In Nebraska Test No. 401 of September 1948 it delivered nearly 11 belt horsepower.

| | 1 | 2 | 3 | 4 |
|---|---|---|---|---|
| Model 11 Pony | $3,000 | $2,300 | $1,250 | $500 |

**Massey-Harris Model 22**

**Massey-Harris "33" Row-Crop**

Production of the Massey-Harris Model 22 row-crop and standard-tread tractors began in 1948 and continued until 1952. It used the Continental F-140 four-cylinder engine having a 3-3/16 x 4-3/8 inch bore and stroke. The row-crop model was tested at Nebraska in 1948 under Test No. 403. It demonstrated nearly 24 maximum drawbar horsepower.

| | **1** | **2** | **3** | **4** |
|---|---|---|---|---|
| Model 22 Row-Crop | | | | |
| | $3,300 | $2,450 | $1,400 | $900 |
| Model 22 Standard | | | | |
| | $3,500 | $2,500 | $1,500 | $1,000 |

Massey-Harris "33" tractors used the company's own Model E-201 four-cylinder engine. It had a 3-5/8 x 4-7/8 inch bore and stroke for a 201 cid. Live hydraulics and a live pto system came as standard equipment. The row-crop model was available in several configurations, such as tricycle front, single front, and adjustable wide-front axles.

| | **1** | **2** | **3** | **4** |
|---|---|---|---|---|
| Model 33 Row-Crop | | | | |
| | $3,500 | $2,500 | $1,100 | $600 |

All models of the Massey-Harris "33" tractors were built in the 1952-1955 period. All used a 201 cubic inch, four-cylinder engine, capable of over 36 belt horsepower. The "33" row-crop was

**Massey-Harris "33" Standard**

tested at Nebraska under No. 509 of October 1953. The standard-tread model was not tested, but was capable of similar performance.

| | 1 | 2 | 3 | 4 |
|---|---|---|---|---|
| Model 33 Standard | $3,800 | $2,800 | $1,400 | $1,000 |

**Massey-Harris "44" tractor**

Production of the Massey-Harris "44" tractor began in 1947 and continued until 1955. This four-cylinder tractor used the company's own engine; it carried a 3-7/8 x 5-1/2 inch bore and stroke. It was tested under No. 389 at Nebraska in October 1947 and demonstrated 44 maximum belt horsepower.

**Massey-Harris "44" standard-tread model**

In addition to several row-crop styles, the Massey-Harris "44" was also built in a standard-tread model. It was essentially the same as the row-crop, except of course, for the modified chassis. Standard-tread models were popular in certain areas, although the row-crop was sold in far greater numbers.

| | 1 | 2 | 3 | 4 |
|---|---|---|---|---|
| Model 44 Row-Crop | $2,500 | $1,500 | $800 | $400 |
| Model 44 Standard | $2,300 | $1,300 | $700 | $400 |

**Massey-Harris "44" tractor LP gas version**

For a time during its 1946-1955 production run, the "44" was available in an LP gas version with an 8.7 to 1 compression ratio. During the 1950s LP gas for tractor fuel gained considerable popularity, and many companies responded with specially equipped LP gas tractor models.

| | 1 | 2 | 3 | 4 |
|---|---|---|---|---|
| Model 44 LP Row-Crop | $3,500 | $2,500 | $2,000 | $1,500 |

Orchard and Vineyard models of the Massey-Harris "44" were available during its entire production run. These tractors were built over the "44" standard-tread model, and included the special hood and fenders required for this duty. In addition, the air stack and exhaust were

**Massey-Harris "44" Orchard (Vineyard) model**

placed low, and a special shield helped protect the operator. The Vineyard was built on a narrower chassis than the Orchard and used 44 Standard sheet metal.

| 1 | 2 | 3 | 4 |
|---|---|---|---|
| Model 44 Orchard/Vineyard | | | |
| $8,000 | — | — | — |

**44 Special Cane tractor**

The 44 Special Cane tractor was yet another version adapted to specific crop needs. This high-clearance model was also used for other growing crops. Production of these models only came to a small fraction of all "44" models that were built.

| 1 | 2 | 3 | 4 |
|---|---|---|---|
| Model 44 Special Cane | | | |
| $8,000 | — | — | — |

**"44" Diesel standard-tread tractor**

Production of the "44" Diesel standard-tread tractor began in 1948 and continued until 1955. The following year the "44" Diesel row-crop tractor emerged; it also remained in production until 1955. This model used a four-cylinder engine with a 3-7/8 x 5-1/2 inch bore and stroke. It featured a Bosch fuel injection system. In Nebraska Test No. 426 of 1949 the "44" Diesel delivered nearly 42 belt horsepower.

| 1 | 2 | 3 | 4 |
|---|---|---|---|
| Model 44 Diesel | | | |
| $3,500 | $2,500 | $1,300 | $900 |

**Massey-Harris "44-6" tractor**

In 1947 Massey-Harris introduced their "44-6" tractor as a companion to the four-cylinder Model 44. The "44-6" was intended for those who preferred six-cylinder smoothness, and aside from this, had no distinct advantage over the four-cylinder model. A Continental F-226 engine was used; it had a 3-5/16 x 4-3/8 inch bore and stroke. Production of the "44-6" standard tread model ended in 1948; the row-crop style survived until 1951.

| | 1 | 2 | 3 | 4 |
|---|---|---|---|---|
| Model 44-6 | $3,500 | $2,750 | $1,500 | $800 |

**"44" Special**

Built in the 1953-1955 period, the "44" Special used a four-cylinder engine with a 4 x 5-1/2 inch bore and stroke for a displacement of 277 ci. In Nebraska Test No. 510 of 1953, this tractor came up with over 45 belt horsepower. A standard-tread model was the only one tested at Nebraska. A "44" Special Diesel model was also built.

| | 1 | 2 | 3 | 4 |
|---|---|---|---|---|
| 44 Special Standard | $3,300 | $2,500 | $1,900 | $1,200 |
| 44 Special Row-Crop | $3,000 | $2,200 | $1,600 | $1,000 |

When the Massey-Harris "55" was introduced in 1946, it was the largest wheel-type farm tractor on the market. This model used a four-cylinder engine with a 4-1/2 x 6 inch bore and stroke. In Nebraska Test No. 394 of 1948, the "55"delivered nearly 56 belt horsepower. However, the "55" gasoline model was again tested at

**Massey-Harris "55"**

Nebraska in 1951 under No. 455. In this test it delivered 63-1/2 belt horsepower. Production of the 55 ran until 1955. It was only built as a standard tractor.

**"55" Diesel tractor**

Production of the "55" Diesel began in 1949 and continued until 1955. This model used a 382 ci four-cylinder engine with a 4-1/2 x 6 inch bore and stroke, and during Nebraska Test No. 452 of 1950 it delivered almost 60 belt horsepower. The "55" was built only in a standard-tread design, but variations included a "55" Rice tractor and a "55" Wheatland tractor.

**Massey-Harris Colt standard-tread**

Built only during 1952 and 1953, the Massey-Harris Colt was a two-plow tractor. Shown here is the standard-tread design. The Colt was equipped with a Continental F-124 four-cylinder engine with a 3 x 4-3/8 inch bore and stroke. The engine was rated at 1,500 rpm for drawbar work and 1,800 rpm on the belt.

|          | **1**   | **2**   | **3**   | **4**   |
|----------|---------|---------|---------|---------|
| 21 Colt  | $4,850  | $3,600  | $2,550  | $1,980  |

**Massey-Harris Colt Row-Crop**

Colt and Mustang tractors were both available in a row-crop design in lieu of the standard-tread model. The row-crop models could be purchased with standard tricycle front end, single wheel front, or an adjustable-width, high-arch front axle. All tractors of this series included live hydraulics as standard equipment.

**Massey-Harris Model 23 Mustang**

Massey-Harris built the Model 23 Mustang tractor between 1952 and 1955. This model followed the M-H 22 tractor, and used the same Continental F-140 four-cylinder engine. The Mustang was available in row-crop design, with the choice of dual-front wheels, single-front wheel, or a high-arch adjustable wide-front axle. This tractor was also built in a standard-tread design.

|            | **1**   | **2**   | **3**   | **4**   |
|------------|---------|---------|---------|---------|
| 23 Mustang | $4,500  | $3,400  | $2,200  | $1,700  |

**Massey-Ferguson "333" tractor**

Massey-Harris and Ferguson joined in October 1953 to form Massey-Harris-Ferguson Inc. The "Harris" name was dropped in 1958, thus, Massey-Ferguson. In 1956 production of the "333" tractors began. They were an updated version of the Model 33. The "333" was built in gasoline, distillate, LP gas and diesel models, with the latter being shown here. In Nebraska Test No. 577 of June 1956 the "333" diesel delivered over 37 belt horsepower. This model used a 3-11/16 x 4-7/8 inch bore and stroke in its four-cylinder engine. The "333" gasoline model appears in Nebraska Test No. 603. It had a similar horsepower rating. Production of the "333" series ended in 1957.

| | 1 | 2 | 3 | 4 |
|---|---|---|---|---|
| 333 - Row Crop Gas | | | | |
| | $6,000 | $4,500 | $3,000 | $1,800 |
| Standard Gas | | | | |
| | $6,000 | $4,500 | $3,000 | $1,800 |
| Row Crop Diesel | | | | |
| | $6,300 | $4,800 | $3,300 | $2,000 |
| Standard Diesel | | | | |
| | $6,500 | $5,000 | $3,500 | $2,200 |
| Row Crop LP | | | | |
| | $6,500 | $5,000 | $4,000 | $2,500 |
| Standard LP | | | | |
| | $7,000 | $5,500 | $4,300 | $2,500 |

**Massey-Harris "444" tractor**

Massey-Harris "444" tractors were built in gasoline, LP gas distillate, and diesel versions. In addition, there were several different chassis and axle styles available. Live hydraulics and a live pto were standard equipment. These tractors used an engine designed by M-H-F and built by Continental. The four-cylinder design carried a 4 x 5-1/2 inch bore and stroke. This model delivered a maximum of 47 belt horsepower. Produc-

tion of the "444" tractors ran from 1956 to 1958. Until the latter date, the company was known as Massey-Harris-Ferguson Inc., with headquarters at Racine, Wisconsin.

| | 1 | 2 | 3 | 4 |
|---|---|---|---|---|
| 444 - Row Crop Gas | | | | |
| | $4,500 | $3,500 | $2,500 | $1,600 |
| Standard Gas | | | | |
| | $4,300 | $3,300 | $2,300 | $1,400 |
| Row Crop Diesel | | | | |
| | $4,800 | $3,800 | $2,800 | $1,500 |
| Standard Diesel | | | | |
| | $4,500 | $3,500 | $2,700 | $1,400 |
| Row Crop LP | | | | |
| | $5,000 | $4,000 | $3,000 | $2,000 |
| Standard LP | | | | |
| | $5,000 | $4,000 | $3,000 | $2,000 |

**Massey-Harris "555" tractor**

Production of the Massey-Harris "555" tractor began in 1955 and continued into 1958. These tractors were built in gasoline, LP gas, distillate and diesel-powered versions. All were essentially the same except for the power plant. The big four-cylinder engine had a displacement of 382 cubic inches, and used a 4-1/2 x 6 inch bore and stroke. These tractors were rated at about 58 belt or pto horsepower.

| | 1 | 2 | 3 | 4 |
|---|---|---|---|---|
| 555 - Gas | $5,000 | $4,000 | $2,500 | $1,500 |
| Diesel | $4,500 | $3,800 | $2,300 | $1,700 |
| LP | $5,000 | $4,200 | $2,700 | $2,000 |

**MH-50 tractor**

When the "Harris" part of the corporate name was dropped in 1958, the end likewise came for Massey-Harris tractors. From this point on, the Massey-Ferguson name would predominate. The stage was set for a new line of tractors with the 1956 introduction of the MH-50. This was an entirely new design, and was followed in 1958 with the MF-50 tractor. The MH-50 appears in Nebraska Test No. 595 of September 1956. Its four-cylinder engine used a 3-5/16 x 3-7/8 inch bore and stroke, and delivered nearly 30 belt horsepower.

# Master Tractor Company

*Minneapolis, Minnesota*

**Master Jr. 6-12 garden tractor**

Master Tractor Co. was incorporated at Minneapolis in 1918. By 1920 the company appeared as Master Truck & Tractor Co., but by 1922 the original title was once again assumed. F. A. Valentine who was associated with tractor manufacturing in previous years was a business partner. The company built an 18-35 tractor, but no illustrations have been found of this model. During 1921 the company offered the Master Jr. 6-12 garden tractor. This unique design used a four-cylinder LeRoi engine with a 3-1/8 x 4-1/2 inch bore and stroke.

# Masterbilt Truck & Tractor Company

*Decatur, Illinois*

Although this firm was incorporated in 1918, no other information has been located.

# Matthews Tractor Company

*Brockport, New York*

See: Wheat Tiller & Tractor Company

**Matthews tractor**

Hession Tractor & Tiller Company began building the Wheat tractor in 1917. By 1920 or 1921 the company was reorganized as Wheat Tractor & Tiller Corporation. In the 1922-1924 period the Wheat tractor was built by Matthews Tractor Company. The 12-24 Wheat tractor was equipped with an Erd four-cylinder engine having a 4 x 6 inch bore and stroke. The Wheat tractor disappears from trade listings after 1924.

## Maxfer Truck & Tractor Company

*Harvey, Illinois*

This firm was offering the Maxfer Tractor-Truck in 1918. It was apparently more of a truck than a tractor, and the latter term seems to have applied more to an industrial tractor than to one built for farm use. No other information has been found.

## Maxim Munitions Corporation

*New York, New York*

**Maxim Model A, 12-24 tractor**

Apparently, the Maxim Model A, 12-24 tractor was offered only in 1919. Industry listings make no other mention of this model. Maxim used their own four-cylinder engine in the 12-24. It carried a 4-1/4 x 5-1/2 inch bore and stroke. The Model A was priced at $1,685.

## Maxwell Motor Sales Corporation

*Detroit, Michigan*

In 1918 Maxwell started with a tractor known previously as the 'Chief' but which was then renamed as 'Flanders.' The Flanders automobile was under control of Studebaker. At this point it is not known with certainty whether Maxwell Motor Sales was connected with the famous Maxwell automobile, or whether the choice of corporate name was a mere coincidence.

## Mayer Brothers Company

*Mankato, Minnesota*

**Mayer Brothers Model A 26-35 tractor**

This firm went back to 1876 when Louis and Lorenz Mayer opened a machine shop at Mankato, Minnesota. About 1911 the company began experimenting with tractors, and by 1914 the company was building tractors exclusively. Included was the Model A 26-35 tractor; it sold for $2,000 in 1916.

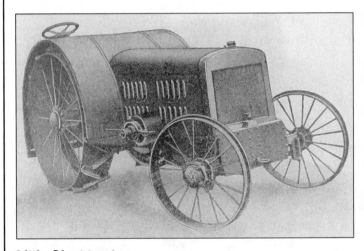

**Little Giant tractor**

The Little Giant tractors were built in two sizes, the Model A 26-35 and the Model B 16-22 shown here. Both used engines built in the Mayer Bros. shops. These tractors had a rather advanced design, notably that ball and roller bearings were used exclusively in an age when plain bearings were still used to a great extent. In 1918 the corporate name was changed to Little Giant Company. Further information may be found under that heading.

# Mayrath Incorporated
*Dodge City, Kansas*

**Mayrath Mobile tractor**

Two sizes of the Mayrath Mobile Tractor were offered, namely, the "5 HP" and the "8-1/4 HP." Few specifics have been found, but apparently these tractors were built in the 1950-1952 period. Trade directory information leads to the conclusion that both used the same chassis, varying only as to the engine.

# Maytag Company
*Newton, Iowa*

**Maytag 12-25 tractor**

This famous manufacturer of home appliances made a brief entry into the tractor business during 1916. Rated as a 12-25, the Maytag tractor was a 5,000 pound machine powered by a four-

cylinder Waukesha engine. Very few specifics have been found for this tractor, probably because it was only marketed for a few months.

# M. B. M. Mfg. Company
*Milwaukee, Wisconsin*

**Red-E garden tractor**

The Red-E garden tractor first appeared under that title in September 1923. Through 1927 it was built by M.B.M. Mfg. Company, but late in 1927 the Red-E appears from Modern Machine Works, also of Milwaukee. By 1928 the Red-E, still keeping to its original design, appears under Pioneer Mfg. Company of nearby West Allis. Priced at $275, the Red-E used a single-cylinder engine of 3-3/4 x 4 inch bore and stroke; it was built by M.B.M. It was named the Red-E because "it was always READY to go to work" according to the company.

|       | **1**    | **2**    | **3**  | **4**  |
|-------|----------|----------|--------|--------|
| Red-E | $1,500   | $1,000   | $750   | $350   |

# Mead-Morrison Mfg. Company
*Boston, Massachusetts*

Beginning about 1924 and continuing until about 1930, the Mead-Morrison Bear "55" was offered. Obvious in this view is the unique front suspension system. Weighing 8,700 pounds the Bear

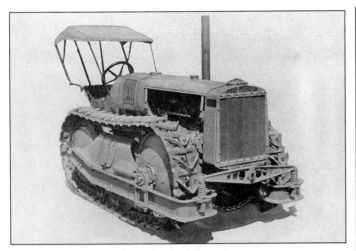

**Mead-Morrison Bear "55" tractor**

"55" used a Stearns four-cylinder engine with a 4-3/4 x 6-1/2 inch bore and stroke. Also of interest, the Bear "55" used a conventional steering wheel to handle the machine.

|  | **1** | **2** | **3** | **4** |
|---|---|---|---|---|
| Bear "55" | $10,000 | $7,5000 | $5,000 | $2,250 |

## Mead Specialties Company Inc.
*Chicago, Illinois*

**Mead Mighty Mouse Model M-6 crawler tractor**

Beginning about 1951 and continuing for several years Mead offered their Mighty Mouse Model M-6 crawler tractor. Weighing 1,250 pounds, the Mighty Mouse sold for $1,180. It was equipped with either a Briggs & Stratton 14FB or a Wisconsin AKN engine, either of which was capable of 5 to 6 horsepower.

|  | **1** | **2** | **3** | **4** |
|---|---|---|---|---|
| M-6 | $3,200 | $1,800 | $1,500 | — |

## Megow Tractor Company
*St. Paul, Minnesota*

Megow was organized in 1916, ostensibly to manufacture farm tractors, but no other information has been found.

## Melin Industries
*Cleveland, Ohio*

**Garden-Craft "15" garden tractor**

By 1950 Melin Industries was offering their Garden-Craft "15" and their Soil-Craft "30" garden tractors. The "15" and "30" were of similar design, with the smaller model using a Kohler K7 2 horsepower engine, while the "30" was equipped with a Kohler K12 3 horsepower motor. Kohler advertising noted the "over 22 different attachments" were available.

**Farmcraft "45" garden tractor**

The Melin line included the Farmcraft "45", Farmcraft "60", and Farmcraft "75" models. All were of similar design and utilized the "Unitool" carriage system for use with various implements. All three sizes used Wisconsin engines. For the

"45" it was the ABN 4 horsepower model. The "60" used the AKN 6 horsepower motor and the "75" used the AEN 7-1/2 horsepower engine. Production of these tractors continued at least into the mid-1950s.

## Mellinger Mfg. Company
*Willow Street, Pennsylvania*

The Garden Spot garden tractor was listed from Mellinger in 1953, but no other information has been located.

## Mercer-Robinson Company Inc.
*New York, New York*

By 1952 the Mercer "30" tractor was on the market. Two models were offered; the BD was a diesel version, and the CK was powered with a gasoline engine. These tractors originated about 1948 as the Farmaster FD-33 and the Farmaster FG-33, both from Farmaster Corporation at Clifton, New Jersey. These models appear in Nebraska Test Numbers 419 and 421 respectively. Both were equipped with 153 ci Buda four-cylinder engines. Production of the Mercer models continued at least into the late 1950s.

## Mercury Mfg. Company
*Chicago, Illinois*

No information has been found on this company.

## Merry Mfg. Company
*Edmonds, Washington*

By 1950 the Merry "Tiller" was on the market. Power came from a Briggs & Stratton Model N engine capable of 2 horsepower. Numerous

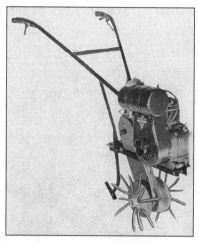

**Merry "Tiller"**

attachments were available for this unit, including a sickle bar and a reel mower. Little other information has been found after 1951.

## Messinger Mfg. Company
*Tatamy, Pennsylvania*

Various sources indicate that Messinger Mfg. Co. built garden tractors for a time, but the meager information we have is conflicting, so perhaps we will be able to offer further information in a subsequent edition of this book.

## Metal Products Corporation
*Racine, Wisconsin*

See: Haas Foundry Company

## W.E. Metzler Company
*Azusa, California*

This firm is listed as manufacturing garden tractors in the 1948-1953 period, but no other information has been found.

## J.J. Meyer
*Shepard, Michigan*

J.J. Meyer is listed for 1920 as the builder of the Chippewa Chief tractors. No other information has been found.

# M. F. M. Combination Saw & Machinery Company
*Denton, Texas*

**M.F.M. Combination Saw**

By 1950 the M.F.M. Combination Saw had been put on the market. Shown here with its mounted saw, this outfit was also available with several other attachments to further extend its usefulness. Weight of this unit was 680 pounds. Relatively little is known of the machine.

# Michigan Tractor Company
*Detroit, Michigan*

**All-wheel-drive machine**

Organized in 1915, Michigan Tractor Co. developed a unique all-wheel-drive machine. As shown in this illustration, the tractor had a very short turning radius because the powered front steering wheel could be turned virtually upon itself. By late 1915 the company was taken over by the A. T. Harrow Tractor Company, but very little is known of the latter venture.

# Middletown Machine Company
*Middletown, Ohio*

This firm was well known as the manufacturer of the Woodpecker gasoline engines, and is listed as a tractor manufacturer in trade directories for 1911, 1912 and 1913. However, no information regarding these tractors has been located. Thus, it is assumed that if Middletown built any tractors at all, production was quite limited.

# Midget Tractor Company
*Minneapolis, Minnesota*

**Midget small cultivating tractor**

Organized in 1918, Midget produced a small cultivating tractor designed for one-row cultivation. From this firm, Shaw-Enochs Tractor Company was organized in November 1919. Few specifics have been found regarding the Midget tractor.

# Midland Company
*Milwaukee, Wisconsin*

**Dandy Boy "Town & Country" model**

Beginning about 1950, and continuing for several years, Midland offered several sizes of garden tractors. Typical of the line was the Dandy Boy "Town & Country" model. This one used a Briggs & Stratton 3 horsepower engine. Other models included the Dandy Boy Clipper, a 2 horsepower size, and the Dandy Boy "Super." The latter was equipped with a 5 horsepower Briggs & Stratton motor.

# Midland Tractor Company
*Detroit, Michigan*

**Midland Tractor**

Midland Tractor Co. was organized in 1912 to build a medium-size tractor weighing about 4,800 pounds, and retailing for $1,250. The following year, 1913, the company was bought out by Leader Engine Company, Grand Rapids, Michigan.

# Midwest Company
*Minneapolis, Minnesota*

In 1948 this firm is listed as a manufacturer of garden tractors, but no other information has been found.

# Midwest Engine Company
*Indianapolis, Indiana*

**Midwest Utilitor garden tractor**

Midwest first adopted the Utilitor tradename in June 1919. For some years to follow, the company offered the Midwest Utilitor garden tractor. This was a 750 pound machine equipped with a single-cylinder engine having a 3-1/2 x 4-1/2 inch bore and stroke. Numerous attachments were available including plows, cultivators and a planter. The basic tractor unit was priced at $295.

# Milwaukee Equipment Company
*Milwaukee, Wisconsin*

Beginning about 1946 the Milwaukee rotary tillers appeared in several models. Shown here is the JR16, a new model which first appeared about 1950. It used a Wisconsin 4-1/2 horsepower engine. The JR12 was the smallest of the line and was powered by a Clinton 3 horsepower motor. Other models included the G18 with a

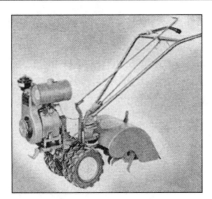

**JR16 tiller**

Wisconsin 7-1/2 horsepower engine. The big G26 machine was available with a Wisconsin 7-1/2 horsepower engine or an Onan 10 horsepower motor.

|  | 1 | 2 | 3 | 4 |
|---|---|---|---|---|
| All models | $600 | $500 | $200 | $100 |

## Minneapolis-Moline Company
*Minneapolis, Minnesota*

In 1929 three companies merged to form Minneapolis-Moline. Included were the Moline Plow Company, Moline, Illinois; Minneapolis Threshing Machine Company, Hopkins, Minnesota; and Minneapolis Steel & Machinery Company, Minneapolis, Minnesota.

Moline Plow Company went back to 1870 and over its career developed an extensive line of tillage tools.

Minneapolis Threshing Machine Company began operations in 1887 as a manufacturer of steam engines and threshers. Subsequently the company developed a substantial tractor line.

Minneapolis Steel & Machinery Company was organized in 1902, and subsequently developed the Twin City tractor line.

Minneapolis-Moline was taken over by White Farm Equipment Company in 1963.

The Minneapolis-Moline tractor line had unusual production patterns that sometimes overlapped one another. Model designators are sometimes difficult to decipher, and conflicts appear even within the company's own serial number listings. Thus, it is entirely possible that certain

M-M models are inadvertently omitted from the following series of illustrations. With help from readers of this book, these difficulties can be corrected in future editions of this volume.

**M-M Twin City 17-28**

The M-M Twin City 17-28 had previously been developed and marketed by Minneapolis Steel & Machinery Company. It was carried into the 1929 merger, and M-M continued to produce it until 1935. The 17-28 was first built in 1926 and was a re-rated version of the Twin City 12-20 model introduced about 1919. This model used a four-cylinder, 4-1/4 x 6 inch engine. This 5,900 pound tractor was capable of over 22 drawbar horsepower.

|  | 1 | 2 | 3 | 4 |
|---|---|---|---|---|
| 17-28 | $7,250 | $6,000 | $4,000 | $1,000 |

**17-30 Type A tractor**

Minneapolis Threshing Machine Co. introduced its 17-30 Type A tractor about 1920. This model carried on into the 1929 merger and remained in production until 1934. Nebraska Test No. 70 of 1921 notes that this model was equipped with a four-cylinder, 4-3/4 x 7 inch engine and was capable of nearly 32 belt horsepower.

**17-30 Type B tractor**

About 1925 Minneapolis Threshing Machine Co. released the 17-30 Type B tractor. It was quite similar to the 17-30 Type A, but had a longer chassis, and a slightly larger engine of 4-7/8 x 7 inch bore and stroke. In Nebraska Test No. 118 the Type B delivered almost 35 belt horsepower. Production of the 17-30 Type B ended in 1934.

**M-M Twin City KT tractor**

The M-M-Twin City KT tractor was developed in 1929 and was marketed until 1934. The KT stood for Kombination Tractor. This model had a rating of 11 drawbar and 20 belt horsepower. In

Nebraska Test No. 175 of 1930 it delivered almost 26 belt horsepower. Subsequent to Test No. 175 the KT was sometimes billed as a 14-23 model.

**KT Orchard tractor**

By 1932 Minneapolis-Moline was marketing the KT Orchard tractor, a specially designed model built over the regular KT chassis. The major difference was the special hood and fender design. M-M also built the KT Industrial tractor in the 1932-1935 period.

**Model KT-A tractor**

During 1934 the improved Model KT-A tractor was introduced, replacing the earlier KT model. The KT-A continued to use the four-cylinder, 4-1/4 x 5 inch engine that was featured in the earlier KT tractor. Various improvements and modifications prompted the change to a new model designation.

| | 1 | 2 | 3 | 4 |
|---|---|---|---|---|
| KTA Tractor | $4,750 | $3,000 | $1,800 | $900 |

**Type FT 21-32 tractor**

During 1926 Minneapolis Steel & Machinery Co. introduced their Type FT 21-32 tractor. In Nebraska Test No. 127 of 1926 this model developed nearly 36 belt horsepower. The 21-32 was rated at 1,000 rpm and used a four-cylinder engine having a 4-1/2 x 6 inch bore and stroke. Minneapolis-Moline continued building the 21-32 tractor until 1934. About this time the FT designation was used, minor changes were made, and the tractor continued in production until 1937.

**Twin City 20-35**

Nebraska Test No. 67 was run on the Twin City 20-35 in 1920. In 1926 the same basic tractor was again tested under No. 122 as the 27-44. The 27-44 used a four-cylinder engine having a 5-1/2 x

6-3/4 inch bore and stroke. In Test No. 122 this tractor delivered nearly 50 belt horsepower. Production of the 27-44 continued until 1935.

|  | **1** | **2** | **3** | **4** |
|---|---|---|---|---|
| 20-35 | — | $7,000 | $4,500 | $2,000 |

**M-M 27-42 tractor**

Production of the M-M 27-42 tractor ended in 1934. This model originated with Minneapolis Threshing Machine Co. about 1928. The 27-42 used a four-cylinder crossmounted engine having a 4-7/8 x 7 inch bore and stroke. In Nebraska Test No. 162 of 1929 the 27-42 delivered nearly 35 drawbar horsepower.

**M-M row-crop model 13-25**

The first M-M row-crop model was the Universal 13-25. Introduced in 1931, it remained in production until 1934. Nebraska Test No. 197 indicates that the Universal was capable of nearly 27 belt horsepower. The 13-25 was equipped with a four-cylinder engine having a 4-1/4 x 5 inch bore and stroke.

**M-M Universal "J" tractor**

Production of the M-M Universal "J" tractor began in 1934 and continued until 1938. In addition to the row-crop model, a standard-tread tractor was also produced. This small tractor weighed only 3,450 pounds, and was equipped with a four-cylinder engine having a 3-5/8 x 4-3/4 inch bore and stroke. It was available on steel wheels or rubber tires.

|    | <u>1</u> | <u>2</u> | <u>3</u> | <u>4</u> |
|----|----|----|----|----|
| JT | $3,000 | $2,500 | $1,800 | $800 |

Production of the Universal "M" tractor began in 1934, following the introduction of the Universal "MT" model in 1931. The latter model was tested at Nebraska under No. 197 of October 1931. It demonstrated nearly 27 belt horsepower, using a four-cylinder engine with a 4-1/4 x 5 inch

**Universal "M" tractor**

bore and stroke. Production of the Universal M continued until 1939.

|    | <u>1</u> | <u>2</u> | <u>3</u> | <u>4</u> |
|----|----|----|----|----|
| MT | $2,200 | $1,500 | $800 | $600 |

**FT 21-32 tractor**

An improved version of the FT 21-32 tractor came along in 1935. The new FT-A was essentially the same, and continued to carry the same 21-32 horsepower rating. Slight changes in styling and accessory items were the main differences over the earlier model. Production of the FT-A continued until 1938.

|  | **1** | **2** | **3** | **4** |
|---|---|---|---|---|
| FT | $6,250 | $5,000 | $3,000 | $1,000 |

**Type R streamlined tractor**

Production of the Type R streamlined tractors began in 1939 and continued until 1947. The R-Series tractors used a M-M Model EE engine with

four-cylinders and having a 3-5/8 x 4 inch bore and stroke. The "N" suffix apparently denotes a single-front wheel design.

|  | **1** | **2** | **3** | **4** |
|---|---|---|---|---|
| RTN | $1,950 | $1,500 | $1,000 | $350 |

**Minneapolis-Moline RTU tractor**

The Minneapolis-Moline RTU tractor was tested at Nebraska in May 1940. This small tractor was capable of 20 drawbar horsepower and over 23 horsepower in the belt. The engine design was unique with its unusual side-valve arrangement.

|  | **1** | **2** | **3** | **4** |
|---|---|---|---|---|
| RTU | $1,800 | $1,400 | $900 | $350 |

**Minneapolis-Moline RTS standard-tread tractor**

Minneapolis-Moline RTS standard-tread tractors were yet another version of the basic Model R series. Production of the R-Series tractors began in 1939 and continued until 1947, although production was seriously hampered during World War Two.

|     | **1** | **2** | **3** | **4** |
|-----|-------|-------|-------|-------|
| RTS | $2,250 | $1,800 | $1,200 | $650 |

**Minneapolis-Moline ZTU Row-Crop**

Minneapolis-Moline tractors were sold under the M-M Twin City tradename into the early 1940s. The M-M ZTU row-crop model was introduced in 1936 and continued in production until 1948. In Nebraska Test No. 352 of 1940, the ZTU demonstrated nearly 28 belt horsepower under its rated load. Power came from a four-cylinder engine having a 3-5/8 x 4-1/2 inch bore and stroke. Subsequently, in 1949, M-M revamped the Z-Series tractors with the ZA series.

|     | **1** | **2** | **3** | **4** |
|-----|-------|-------|-------|-------|
| ZAE | $2,800 | $2,350 | $1,650 | $1,000 |
| ZAN | $2,600 | $2,000 | $1,600 | $800 |
| ZAS | $3,000 | $2,600 | $1,800 | $900 |
| ZBE | $2,150 | $1,800 | $1,000 | $600 |
| ZBN | $2,150 | $1,800 | $1,200 | $600 |
| ZBU | $2,100 | $1,800 | $1,200 | $600 |
| ZTU | $2,500 | $1,650 | $1,350 | $650 |

Built in the same 1936-1948 period as the ZTU row-crop tractor was this ZTN with a single-front wheel design. In all other respects the trac-

**Minneapolis-Moline ZTN tractor**

tor was the same, but the single-front design was essential for certain crops.

|     | **1** | **2** | **3** | **4** |
|-----|-------|-------|-------|-------|
| ZTN | $2,500 | $1,650 | $1,350 | $650 |

**Minneapolis-Moline Model ZTS tractor**

Between 1937 and 1947 Minneapolis-Moline produced their Model ZTS tractor. It was the standard-tread version of the Z-Series. In the 1936-39 period, M-M also built the ZTI, an industrial tractor especially set up for factory and warehouse work. All models used the same engine and the same basic chassis design.

**M-M GT Standard-Tread tractor**

Topping the M-M line in the 1938-1941 period was the GT Standard-Tread tractor. It was equipped with the company's own Model LE engine, a four-cylinder design having a 4-5/8 x 6 inch bore and stroke. With some changes in sheet metal work and other minor differences, the GT-A tractor appeared in 1942 and continued in production until 1947.

|  | 1 | 2 | 3 | 4 |
|---|---|---|---|---|
| GT Tractor | $3,500 | $2,800 | $2,100 | $1,400 |
| GTA Tractor | $3,500 | $2,800 | $2,100 | $1,400 |

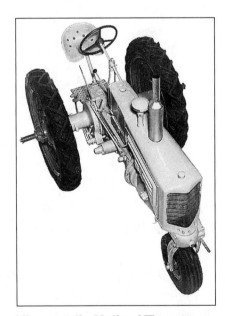

**Minneapolis-Moline YT tractor**

During 1937 Minneapolis-Moline built a few copies of their YT tractor. This was a two-cylinder design, and was essentially one half of the Model R tractor. For reasons unknown the YT was never put into production, with assembly ending after a couple dozen were sent into the field. Fourteen specimens exist today.

|  | 1 | 2 | 3 | 4 |
|---|---|---|---|---|
| YT Tractor | $28,500 | — | — | — |

**UTU row-crop tractor**

Production of the U-Series tractors began in 1938 and extended into 1948. The UTU shown here was the ordinary row-crop style. Weighing about 6,700 pounds, it used the company's own Model KEF four-cylinder engine; it had a 4-1/4 x 5 inch bore and stroke. In Nebraska Test No. 319 it yielded nearly 43 belt horsepower.

|  | 1 | 2 | 3 | 4 |
|---|---|---|---|---|
| UB Special | $3,250 | $3,000 | $1,850 | $1,000 |
| All other U-Series models | $2,400 | $1,800 | $1,950 | $1,00 |

**UTS tractor**

In Nebraska Test No. 310 the UTS tractor had a maximum drawbar pull of nearly 5,000 pounds.

This model was equipped with the same KEF engine as the UTU tractor, and could deliver 39 drawbar horsepower. Production of the U-Series tractors continued into 1948.

|     | 1 | 2 | 3 | 4 |
|-----|------|------|------|------|
| UTS | $2,650 | $2,000 | $1,400 | $900 |

**Minneapolis-Moline UDLX (U-Deluxe) tractor**

In 1938 Minneapolis-Moline introduced their UDLX (U-Deluxe) tractor. It was essentially the same as the remainder of the U-Series tractors, but was equipped with a special cab, headlights, radio and other accessories. Unfortunately, the concept was ahead of its time; farmers were not yet ready to accept an enclosed tractor cab. Thus, production of this model ended in 1939.

|     | 1 | 2 | 3 | 4 |
|-----|------|------|------|------|
| UDLX Tractor | $65,000 | $45,000 | $30,000 | $20,000 |

**Minneapolis-Molie RTU row-crop model**

Minneapolis-Moline revamped their R-Series tractors in 1948. The RTU row-crop model continued in production until 1954, while the RTN

single-front wheel style was built in the 1948-51 period. Other styles included the RTE, built from 1948 to 1953, and the RTI Industrial style shown here. It was offered only in 1953. It was equipped with the M-M Model EE four-cylinder engine having a 3-5/8 x 4 inch bore and stroke.

**GTE standard-tread model**

Introduced in 1947, the GTB standard-tread model was built until 1954. In Nebraska Test No. 437 of 1950, the GTB delivered almost 56 belt horsepower. The engine was an M-M 403A-4 with a 4-5/8 x 6 inch bore and stroke. This big tractor weighed 6,400 pounds. During 1953 and 1954 Minneapolis-Moline also offered their GTB Diesel model.

**UTS standard-tread tractor**

Beginning in 1948, Minneapolis-Moline introduced new and improved models of the U-Series tractors. The UTS standard-tread came along in 1948 and continued until 1957. Weighing 5,500 pounds, it was equipped with a four-cylinder 283 ci engine. In Nebraska Test No. 310 it delivered 39 drawbar horsepower. This tractor was also tested at Nebraska using propane fuel under No. 411. M-M pioneered the use of propane fuel for tractors during the 1940s and remained active in this field for at least twenty years.

**Minneapolis-Moline UTU row-crop**

The Minneapolis-Moline UTU row-crop of the 1948-1955 period was greatly updated from the original UTU model. It was capable of 38 drawbar and 45 belt horsepower. Details are found in Nebraska Test No. 319. In addition, M-M also offered the UTC model in the 1954-55 period, the UTE from 1951-1954 and the UTN between 1950 and 1952.

An improved series of M-M "Z" tractors appeared in 1949 and continued until 1952. Typical of the line was the ZAU row-crop style. It was a 206 ci four-cylinder engine. Along with

**M-M ZAU row-crop tractor**

the row-crop model, the Z-Series tractors were offered in numerous other chassis configurations.

|  | 1 | 2 | 3 | 4 |
|---|---|---|---|---|
| GB Tractor | $3,200 | $2,000 | $1,6850 | $1,000 |
| GB LP | $3,500 | $2,500 | $2,000 | $1,000 |

**Avery BF tractor**

B. F. Avery Company at Louisville, Kentucky brought out their Avery BF tractor in 1945. Minneapolis-Moline bought out Avery in 1951 and continued to market the BF until 1955. This small tractor was capable of about 26 belt horsepower.

It was equipped with a four-cylinder Hercules engine with a 3-1/4 x 4 inch bore and stroke for a displacement of 133 ci.

|  | 1 | 2 | 3 | 4 |
|---|---|---|---|---|
| Avery BF | $3,000 | $2,400 | $1,500 | $800 |
| Avery BG | $3,800 | $2,750 | $2,500 | $1,200 |
| Avery BH | $3,600 | $2,700 | $1,600 | $1,200 |

**MM-Avery Model V tractor**

Production of the MM-Avery Model V tractor paralleled that of the Model BF. The Model V was half the size of the BF, using a Hercules ZXB-3 four-cylinder engine with a 2-5/8 x 3 inch bore and stroke for a displacement of 65 ci. Production of this model was rather limited.

|  | 1 | 2 | 3 | 4 |
|---|---|---|---|---|
| Avery V | $3,000 | $2,500 | $2,050 | $1,000 |

# Minneapolis Steel & Machinery Company

*Minneapolis, Minnesota*

Organized in 1902, Minneapolis Steel & Machinery Co. entered the tractor business in 1910. The design caught on, and the following year the company registered their "Twin City" trademark. Numerous models were built in the following years. In 1929 Minneapolis Steel merged with Moline Plow Co. and the Minneapolis Threshing Machine Co. to form Minneapolis-Moline Power Implement Co.

**Twin City "40" tractor**

In January 1910 Minneapolis Steel & Machinery Co. began developing a four-cylinder tractor, with the Twin City "40" emerging late in 1911. Initially the tractor used a four-cylinder engine having a 7 x 10 inch bore and stroke, but by late 1911 the engine bore was increased to 7-1/4 inches.

**Twin City "40" 40-65 tractor**

By 1913 the Twin City "40" had achieved its final form. This model was rated as a 40-65, meaning it was capable of 40 drawbar and 65 belt horsepower. It was, in fact, underrated. In Nebraska Test No. 48 this tractor delivered nearly 66 belt horsepower and almost 50 horsepower on the drawbar. Production of the 40-65 continued until 1924.

The Twin City "40" was available in several variations, including this special road roller model. Designed especially for road work, it had

**Twin City "40" road roller model**

a heavy front steering drum, along with special heavy rear wheels. Production of this model was probably measured in rather small numbers.

**Twin City "40" crawler model**

It is unknown whether the Twin City "40" crawler model ever went into production, or whether it was strictly a special order tractor. Obviously, at least one was built, and a few catalogs illustrate or mention this special model.

**Minneapolis Steel & Machinery Co. 60-90 tractor**

During the 1913-1920 period Minneapolis Steel & Machinery Co. built their 60-90 tractor. Weigh-

ing 28,000 pounds, this was one of the largest tractors built; in 1917 it sold for $6,000. The 60-90 had the same 7-1/4 x 9 inch bore and stroke as the 40-65, but had a huge six-cylinder engine.

**Twin City "25" tractor**

Production of the Twin City "25" tractor ran from 1913 to 1920. This model used a four-cylinder engine with a 6-1/4 x 8 inch bore and stroke. Weighing 16,000 pounds, the "25" sold for $3,850. Aside from physical size, the design was virtually identical to the Twin City "40" tractor.

**Twin City "25" special road roller tractor**

Little is known of the Twin City "25" special road roller tractor. Presumably, production was rather limited, and few, if any of these special tractors still exist. The road roller model was the same as the regular Twin City "25" except for the modifications needed for this special duty.

Between 1913 and 1917 there were three different models of the Twin City "15" tractor.

**Twin City "15" tractor**

Shown here is the earliest version with a complete hood over the engine. This model has all the appearances of the larger Twin City tractors except for the physical size.

**Twin City "15"**

Perhaps the most popular of the Twin City "15"models was this one, a virtual clone of the larger sizes. These tractors were equipped with a four-cylinder engine having a 4-3/4 x 7 inch bore and stroke. As with all other Twin City models, the engine was built by Minneapolis Steel & Machinery Co.

Toward the end of production in 1917, Minneapolis Steel modified the Twin City "15" to include a cellular radiator. This was a much more efficient method of cooling and greatly

**Twin City "15" with cellular radiator**

reduced the weight of the tractor and the required amount of water. Another obvious change was the use of a sun canopy instead of the heavy canopy of previous years.

**Twin City 16-30 tractor**

In 1918 the Twin City 16-30 tractor appeared, probably as a replacement for the Twin City "15" model. The 16-30 used a four-cylinder engine having a 5 x 7-1/2 inch bore and stroke. Early models included a canopy over the operator's platform. Production of this model ended in 1920.

During 1919 Minneapolis Steel & Machinery Co. announced their little 12-20 Twin City tractor. It utilized the unit frame design and had all the gearing enclosed. The four-cylinder engine

**Twin City 12-20 tractor**

**Twin City 17-28 Model TY tractor**

was unique with four valves per cylinder for better performance and increased power. This was the first farm tractor to use this design. In 1927 the 12-20 was re-rated as the 17-28 tractor.

horsepower. Production of this model continued into the 1929 merger that formed Minneapolis-Moline.

| | 1 | 2 | 3 | 4 |
|---|---|---|---|---|
| Twin City 17-28 | $6,000 | $4,000 | $2,000 | $1,000 |

**Twin City 20-35 tractor**

**Twin City 27-44 tractor**

Weighing 8,100 pounds, the Twin City 20-35 made its debut in 1919. This model used a four-cylinder engine having a 5-1/2 x 6-3/4 inch bore and stroke. In Nebraska Test No. 67 of 1920 the 20-35 delivered over 34 drawbar horsepower. This model was built until 1927 when it was re-rated and sold as a 27-44 tractor.

| | 1 | 2 | 3 | 4 |
|---|---|---|---|---|
| Twin City 20-35 | $8,000 | $6,000 | $4,000 | — |

In 1926 the 12-20 tractor was again submitted for testing at Nebraska. In Test No. 121 the new 17-28 Model TY tractor delivered 22-1/2 drawbar

Nebraska Test No. 122 was run on the Twin City 27-44 tractor in May 1926. This tractor was simply an updated version of the 20-35 that saw first light in 1919. Production of the 27-44 continued into the 1929 Minneapolis-Moline merger.

| | 1 | 2 | 3 | 4 |
|---|---|---|---|---|
| Twin City 27-44 | $8,000 | $6,000 | $4,000 | — |

**Twin City FT 21-32 tractor**

During 1926 Minneapolis Steel & Machinery Co. introduced their Twin City FT 21-32 tractor. This model used a four-cylinder engine with a 4-1/4 x 6 inch bore and stroke. In Nebraska Test No. 127 of October 1926 this model produced almost 36 belt horsepower. The 21-32 weighed about 6,200 pounds. Production continued into the 1929 Minneapolis-Moline merger.

|  | **1** | **2** | **3** | **4** |
|---|---|---|---|---|
| Twin City 21-32 | $3,400 | $2,800 | $2,000 | $1,200 |

## Minneapolis Threshing Machine Company

*Hopkins, Minnesota*

Minneapolis Threshing Machine Co. had an ancestry going back to 1874. That year, Fond du Lac Threshing Machine Co. was organized at Fond du Lac, Wisconsin. In 1887 John S. McDonald left Fond du Lac and organized Minneapolis Threshing Machine Co.

Traction engines became a part of the Minneapolis line in 1891, and by 1897 the company was investigating the gasoline engine as tractor power. MTM became interested in gasoline tractors in 1910, and built a few in 1911, with full production coming the following year.

MTM built several tractor models in the following years, but never marketed a row-crop design. The company was a part of the Minneapolis-Moline merger of 1929.

**MTM 20 horsepower Universal tractor**

Minneapolis Threshing Machine Co. (MTM) entered the tractor business in 1911 by marketing the 20 horsepower Universal tractor. Built by Universal Tractor Co., Stillwater, Minnesota this model was offered under several different brand names such as Universal, Skibo, and the Rumely GasPull. MTM continued to offer this model as late as 1913.

|  | **1** | **2** | **3** | **4** |
|---|---|---|---|---|
| Universal | $26,000 | $20,000 | $16,000 | $10,000 |

**Minneapolis Farm Motor**

The first Minneapolis Farm Motor was designed by McVicker Engineering Company in 1910 and

1911. During 1911 MTM contracted with Northwest Thresher Company at Stillwater, Minnesota to build 25 of these tractors.

**Minneapolis 25-50 tractor**

Built in the 1912-1914 period, the Minneapolis 25-50 was apparently the immediate successor to the Minneapolis Farm Motor of 1911. The 1912 production of 48 tractors was built by Northwest Thresher Company, but by 1913 MTM was building their own tractors.

**MTM 40-80 tractor**

During 1912 MTM perfected its 40-80 tractor. This huge four-cylinder model carried a 7-1/4 x 9 inch bore and stroke. The impressive operator's cab could be furnished with windows for cold weather operation. Production of this model continued until 1920 when it was re-rated as a 35-70 tractor.

| | 1 | 2 | 3 | 4 |
|---|---|---|---|---|
| 35-70 and 40-80 | | | | |
| | $40,000 | $35,000 | $20,000 | $8,000 |

**MTM 20-40 tractor**

In late 1913 or early 1914 MTM introduced its 20-40 tractor. This one used a four-cylinder engine having a 5-3/4 x 7 inch bore and stroke. This model used an L-head engine, while the 40-80 and many other MTM tractors carried a valve-in-head engine. Production of this model continued until about 1919 when it was replaced with the slightly larger 22-44 tractor.

| | 1 | 2 | 3 | 4 |
|---|---|---|---|---|
| 20-40 and 22-44 | | | | |
| | $20,000 | $15,000 | $10,000 | $4,000 |

**MTM "15" tractor**

Minneapolis Threshing Machine made their entry into the small tractor market in late 1915. The "15" used a 4-1/2 x 7 inch four-cylinder engine, and built until 1920 when it was re-rated downward to a 12-25 model.

**Minneapolis 40-80 tractor**

In Nebraska Test No. 15 of 1920 the Minneapolis 40-80 tractor developed slightly over 74 belt horsepower. Subsequently the company re-rated it as a 35-70, even though it was capable of nearly 50 drawbar horsepower. This tractor used a four-cylinder, 7-1/4 x 9 inch engine and was rated at 550 rpm. Production ended with the 1929 Minneapolis-Moline merger.

**Minneapolis 22-44 model**

About 1919 the Minneapolis 22-44 appeared as a replacement for the earlier 20-40 model. The 22-44 used a 6 x 7 inch four-cylinder engine. In Nebraska Test No. 14 of 1920 this model delivered over 46 belt horsepower. Production of the 22-44 ended in 1927.

Had it not been for snow and cold weather, the Minneapolis 12-25 tractor would have been the first tractor tested at Nebraska. It was initially presented as a 15-30 model but failed to

**Minneapolis 12-25 tractor**

come up to MTM expectations, and was then re-rated as the 12-25. This model was built until 1926.

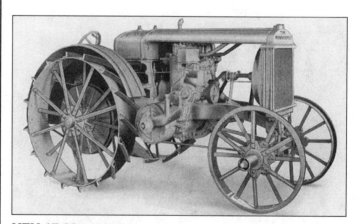

**MTM 17-30 tractor**

MTM announced their 17-30 tractor in 1920. It was an entirely new lightweight design, and was the first tractor tested at Nebraska in 1921. (Test No. 70). The 17-30 used a four-cylinder engine having a 4-3/4 x 7 inch bore and stroke. In testing, the 17-30 was capable of nearly 20 drawbar horsepower. About 1926 this model became known as the 17-30 A tractor. This designation was primarily to prevent confusion with the newly released 17-30 B model.

**17-30 A tractor**

Specifications for the 17-30 A tractor were essentially the same as for the original 17-30. However, minor changes were made during production, and the 17-30 A continued in the Minneapolis-Moline lineup until 1934. The 17-30 A used the same 4-3/4 x 7 inch bore and stroke that had been used on the original 17-30 tractor.

|         | 1      | 2      | 3      | 4      |
|---------|--------|--------|--------|--------|
| 17-30 A | $7,200 | $5,500 | $3,900 | $1,000 |

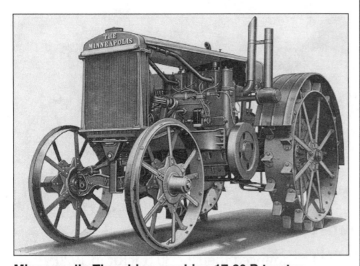

**Minneapolis Threshing machine 17-30 B tractor**

About 1925 Minneapolis Threshing Machine Company introduced their 17-30 B tractor. This model had a slightly longer chassis, and the engine bore was increased to 4-7/8 inches. Aside from this, the two tractors were virtually identical. Production of the 17-30 B continued into 1934, several years after the Minneapolis-Moline merger.

|        | 1      | 2      | 3      | 4    |
|--------|--------|--------|--------|------|
| 7-30 B | $6,750 | $5,000 | $3,500 | $800 |

**MTM 27-42 tractor**

Shortly before the Minneapolis-Moline merger of 1929, MTM announced their 27-42 tractor. It used an engine with the same 4-7/8 x 7 inch bore and stroke as the 17-30 B tractor. However, the 17-30 B was rated at 825 rpm, and the 27-42 had a rated speed of 925 rpm. This model was capable of nearly 34 drawbar horsepower. Production ended in 1934.

**MTM 39-57 tractor**

During 1928 MTM developed their 39-57 tractor. However the Minneapolis-Moline merger occurred in 1929, and when the tractor was tested at Nebraska in June of that year, it was under the auspices of Minneapolis-Moline Power Implement Company. The 39-57 carried a huge four-cylinder engine having a 5-1/2 x 6-1/2 inch bore and stroke. Rated at 1,000 rpm, this tractor was capable of nearly 48 drawbar horsepower. Production of this model apparently ended shortly after the Minneapolis-Moline merger.

## Minnesota-Nilson Corporation
*Minneapolis, Minnesota*

See: Nilson Tractor Company

## Minnesota Farm Tractor Company
*St. Cloud, Minnesota*

In August 1915 it was announced that Minnesota Farm Tractor Co. had been organized and incorporated at St. Cloud to build a three-plow tractor. Aside from this information, nothing else is known of the company.

## Minnesota Tractor Company
*Minneapolis, Minnesota*

**Minnesota 18-36 tractor**

During 1919 the Minnesota 18-36 tractor appeared. It was advertised for only a short time and then disappeared. It used a two-cylinder engine with a 7-1/2 x 8 inch bore and stroke.

## Mitchell Motor Plow Company
*Pueblo, Colorado*

Mitchell Motor Plow Co. was organized and incorporated in 1918, ostensibly to manufacture motor plows. No other information on this company has been found.

## Mobile Tractor Company
*Mobile, Alabama*

**Mobile tractor**

A very poor photograph is the only one found thus far for this company. Organized in 1919, Mobile launched a major stock sale campaign early the following year. The Mobile tractor was a one-man outfit driven by leather lines, much like driving a team. After a few brief notices in 1920, nothing more can be found.

## Model Gas Engine Works
*Peru, Indiana*

**Model Gasoline tractor**

Model had an ancestry in the gasoline engine business going back to the 1890s. By 1906 the company was making engines in single-cylinder models from 2 to 125 horsepower. Two and four-cylinder stationary and marine engines were built in sizes from 15 to 500 horsepower. The Model Gasoline and Kerosene Traction Engine was available in sizes from 16 to 60 horsepower. Aside from a few advertisements, no specific information has been found.

# Modern Machine Works

*Milwaukee, Wisconsin*

**Red-E garden tractor**

The Red-E garden tractor appears only in the 1927 directories from Modern Machine Works. In the 1923-1927 period it was built by M.B.M. Mfg. Company of Milwaukee, and subsequently, from 1928 onward, it was built by Pioneer Mfg. Company. The Red-E used the company's own single-cylinder engine having a 3-3/4 x 4 inch bore and stroke.

|  | **1** | **2** | **3** | **4** |
|---|---|---|---|---|
| Red-E | $1,500 | $1,000 | $750 | $350 |

# Donald K. Moe Company

*Portland, Oregon*

This company is listed in 1948 as the manufacturer of the Garden Pal garden tractors, but no other information has been located.

|  | **1** | **2** | **3** | **4** |
|---|---|---|---|---|
| Garden Pal | $500 | $400 | $250 | $100 |

# Moline Plow Company

*Moline, Illinois*

This famous plow and implement manufacturer has roots going back to 1852 as the firm of Candee, Swan & Company. After steady growth the company reorganized as Moline Plow Company in 1870. Subsequently the firm acquired numerous other companies, and by 1900 had become a formidable competitor in the farm equipment business.

In 1915 the company bought out the Universal Tractor Company at Columbus, Ohio, and continued to develop their design. Into 1918 Moline Plow Company built a two-cylinder "universal" tractor with a two-cylinder engine, but then changed over to a larger four-cylinder style.

Production of the Moline Universal tractor continued until 1923. In 1929 Moline Plow Co. merged with Minneapolis Steel & Machinery Co., and Minneapolis-Threshing Machine Co. to form Minneapolis-Moline.

**Moline two-cylinder motor cultivator**

When Moline Plow Company bought out Universal Tractor Co. in 1915, the latter had already developed a small cultivating tractor. This two-cylinder design was built into 1917. The Moline Universal tractor could be equipped with a variety of implements, all of which became an integral part of the tractor.

|  | **1** | **2** | **3** | **4** |
|---|---|---|---|---|
| B and C, 2-cylinder opposed engine | $12,000 | $10,000 | $6,000 | $3,000 |

During the 1918-1923 period, Moline Plow Company built the Model D Moline Universal tractor. The four-cylinder design was rated at 9 drawbar and 18 belt horsepower. This engine carried a 3-1/2 x 5 inch bore and stroke and operated at 1,800 rpm. It included many unique fea-

**Model D Moline Universal tractor**

tures, including electric starter and lights, and an electric governor. Moline Plow Co. offered numerous implements and hitches for the Model D Universal tractor.

|   | **1** | **2** | **3** | **4** |
|---|---|---|---|---|
| D | $9,000 | $6,000 | $4,000 | $2,000 |

## Moline Pump Company
*Moline, Illinois*

In 1910 it was announced that Moline Pump Co. would be bringing out a new line of farm tractors. The plan apparently did not materialize, since no other information has been found.

## Monarch Iron Works
*San Francisco, California*

No information has been found regarding this company.

## Monarch Machinery Company
*New York, New York*

Aside from a single advertisement, virtually nothing is known of the Monarch Gasoline Traction Engine of 1904. This particular design con-

**Monarch Gasoline Traction Engine**

sists of an unknown make of engine mounted on a set of Morton traction trucks. The latter was rather popular at this time, since it permitted virtually any engine manufacturer to instantly enter the tractor business.

## Monarch Tractor Company
*Springfield, Illinois*

**Monarch Lightfoot 6-10**

Monarch Tractor Co. was organized at Watertown, Wisconsin in 1913. Little is known of the company until 1916 when their Lightfoot 6-10 appeared. This small tractor was ostensibly intended for farm and light construction work. It was powered by a Kermath four-cylinder engine having a 4-inch bore and stroke. Production apparently ended about 1918.

**Monarch 12-20 Neverslip tractor**

The Monarch 12-20 Neverslip tractor made its debut about 1916, and continued in production for several years. This model weighed 6,200 pounds and was powered by an Erd four-cylinder engine with a 4 x 6 inch bore and stroke. It sold for $1,650.

**Monarch 18-30 tractor**

By 1919 the Monarch 18-30 had appeared; by 1920 it had a new rating of 20 drawbar and 30 belt horsepower. In 1924 this model was revamped, speeded up, and became the Model C, 25-35 crawler. In Nebraska Test No. 56 of 1920 the 18-30 delivered over 21 drawbar horsepower. It was equipped with a Beaver four-cylinder engine having a 4-3/4 x 6 inch bore and stroke.

|        | 1        | 2        | 3       | 4       |
|--------|----------|----------|---------|---------|
| 18-30  | $15,000  | $13,000  | $5,000  | $2,000  |

Production of the Monarch 20-30 continued until about 1924 or early 1925 when it was superseded by the Monarch Model C, 25-35 tractor. The increased power level came from raising the

**Monarch 20-30 tractor**

rated speed to 1,200 rpm, compared to 950 rpm for the 20-30. The Model C was capable of about 38 belt horsepower.

|        | 1        | 2        | 3       | 4       |
|--------|----------|----------|---------|---------|
| 20-30  | $15,000  | $10,000  | $6,000  | $2,000  |

**Monarch 6-60 tractor**

In 1924 Monarch introduced their 6-60 tractor. It was powered by a Beaver six-cylinder engine having a 4-3/4 x 6 inch bore and stroke. Weighing over 8-1/2 tons, the 6-60 was capable of over 70 belt horsepower and in excess of 51 horsepower at the drawbar. This tractor became part of the AC-Monarch line when Allis-Chalmers bought out Monarch in 1927.

The Model F, 10-Ton Monarch came onto the market in 1926, with production ending in February 1928. At this time it was replaced with the Model F, "75" tractor; Allis-Chalmers continued building this model until 1931. The Model F

**Montana tractor**

Virtually nothing is known of the company, nor is it known whether this company was connected with a firm of the same name at Oconto, Wisconsin, or yet another at Tinley Park, Illinois

**Model F, 10-Ton Monarch**

pulled over 20,000 pounds in low gear. Power came from a LeRoi four-cylinder engine with a 6-3/4 x 7 inch bore and stroke. Following the history of the Monarch tractor line is extremely difficult. Monarch literature is difficult to find, and many Monarch models were not listed in the farm tractor directories since they were intended primarily for heavy construction work.

|  | **1** | **2** | **3** | **4** |
|---|---|---|---|---|
| Model F, 10-Ton | | | | |
|  | $15,000 | $12,000 | $6,000 | $3,000 |

## Monroe Motors
*Pontiac, Michigan*

Monroe Motors was in the automobile business in the 1914-1923 period, operating at Pontiac from 1916 to 1918. Apparently the company had plans of entering the tractor business, but no information on this venture has been found.

## Montana Tractor Company
*Minneapolis, Minnesota*

Developed in 1916, the Montana tractor was marketed in 1917. After that time it drops out of sight.

## Montana Tractor Company
*Oconto, Wisconsin*

**Montana 15-20 tractor**

Only during 1921 was the Montana 15-20 tractor listed in some of the tractor directories. Rated at 15 drawbar and 20 belt horsepower, it was equipped with a two-cylinder Reliable engine. Power was applied to all three wheels of this machine. The Montana 15-20 weighed 5,200 pounds.

## Montana Tractor Company
*Tinley Park, Illinois*

During 1920 Montana Tractor Co. offered their 15-20 model. The horsepower rating leads to the assumption that this tractor may have been the

**Montana 15-20 model**

predecessor of the one built the following year at Oconto, Wisconsin. Unfortunately, no specific information has been found.

## Moon Tractor Company
*San Francisco, California*

**Moon Pathmaker 12-25 crawler**

About 1920 the Moon Pathmaker 12-25 crawler made its way into some of the tractor listings. However, nothing is known of the company before or after that time. The 12-25 weighed 7,500 pounds and retailed for $2,875. It was powered by a Buda XTU four-cylinder engine having a 4-1/4 x 6 inch bore and stroke.

## Tom Moore Tractor Inc.
*Mantua, Ohio*

**Moore Farm-Ette garden tractor**

Beginning about 1950, Moore offered their Farm-Ette garden tractors in four different models, all having the same general design. The Farm-Ette "B" used a single drive wheel; all others were of two-wheel design. This model was equipped with a Kohler 2 horsepower motor. The Farmette "A" used a 3-1/2 horsepower Ultimotor, as did the Farmette "D" with a 3-1/2 horsepower Ultimotor. Farmette "C" garden tractors were furnished with a 2 horsepower Kohler engine. The firm was active into the mid-1950s but no other information has been found.

## Morgan Engine Works
*Alliance, Ohio*

No information has been found regarding this company.

## Geo. W. Morris
*Racine, Wisconsin*

Few details can be found regarding this 60 horsepower, four-cylinder tractor developed in 1910 by Geo. W. Morris. The latter had begun with tractor development a year earlier, and was building a four-cylinder model with an 8 x 10

**Morris 60 horsepower tractor**

inch bore and stroke. Also in the works was a six-cylinder model having a 7-1/2 x 9 inch bore and stroke. It does not appear that any of these models ever went into production.

**Morris tractor**

Another Geo. W. Morris tractor of the 1909-1910 period was this huge four-cylinder model with a crossmounted engine. No details have been found regarding the size of the tractor, but as with other Morris tractors, it does not appear that any number were built. Prior to his work at Racine, Morris had founded the Morris Threshing Machine Company at Brantford, Ontario.

## Otho A. Morris
*Wichita Falls, Texas*

Aside from a single listing, no other information has been found for this individual or his efforts at tractor building.

## S. S. Morton
*York, Pennsylvania*

In 1904 Morton Traction Company was listed as a tractor manufacturer. To be more precise, Morton built a special tractor chassis. A variety of "stationary" engines could be fitted to this chassis for power. Numerous companies did so, with the best known example being the early International Harvester designs. The company thrived for a few years, but as the tractor evolved, there was little need to use a huge single-cylinder engine with an unfavorable weight-to-horse-power ratio.

## Morton-Heer Company
*Portsmouth, Ohio*

Organized in 1910, this firm was incorporated the following year. It was an alliance of Chris Heer and the Morton interests at Ohio Mfg. Company. When the tractor finally came onto the market in 1912, it was under the auspices of Heer Engine Company. The latter operated until 1916 when it was reorganized as Reliable Tractor & Engine Co. The tractor is illustrated under the *Heer Engine Company* heading.

## Morton Motor Plow Company
*Columbus, Ohio*

**Morton Motor Plow**

Little is known of the Morton Motor Plow. Introduced in 1914, it remained on the market for only a short time. Its salient feature was the two-bottom plow mounted to the rear of the tractor. Briefly, the company appears at Galion, Ohio.

## Morton Tractor Company

*Fremont, Ohio*

**Morton Tractor Co. four-wheel-drive tractor**

During 1911 Morton Tractor Co. announced its four-wheel-drive tractor. This was the same tractor offered by Heer Engine Company and by Morton-Heer Company. All were connected, and by 1912 it appears that Heer Engine Company won out as the sole manufacturer of the Heer tractor.

## Morton Truck & Tractor Company

*Harrisburg, Pennsylvania*

**Morton "60 h.p. four-wheel double worm drive tractor"**

Morton billed this model as their "60 h.p. four wheel double worm drive tractor." Weighing 12,000 pounds, it was equipped with a four-cylinder engine having a 5-3/4 x 7 inch bore and stroke. This 1912 model had three forward speeds ranging from 2-1/2 to 8-1/4 mph. This firm was of the same Morton family involved in other tractor building ventures going back to 1899.

## Motor Driven Implement Company

*Galion, Ohio*

Although it was incorporated in 1916 to build tractors and implements, no other information has been found.

## Motor Macultivator Company

*Toledo, Ohio*

**Motor Macultivator**

Our research has not determined the origins of Motor Macultivator Company. However, it appears that the firm was taken over by American Swiss Magneto Co. about 1925. This 1924 model was equipped with a Briggs & Stratton engine having a 2-1/2 inch bore and stroke. It was priced at $162.50.

See: Macultivator Company

## Motor Truck & Tractor Company

*Knoxville, Tennessee*

Although it was organized and incorporated in 1918 to build tractors, nothing further can be found regarding this firm.

# B. H. Mott Company
*Huntington, West Virginia*

**Utilitor Model 25**

The Utilitor Company was apparently taken over by B. H. Mott Co. about 1945. The latter continued advertising the Utilitor until about 1950. A Wisconsin single-cylinder engine was used on the Utilitor Model 25 shown here. It carried a 3 x 3-1/4 inch bore and stroke.

|  | **1** | **2** | **3** | **4** |
|---|---|---|---|---|
| Utilitor Model 25 |  |  |  |  |
|  | $450 | $600 | $400 | $250 |

# Mountain State Fabricating Company
*Clarksburg, West Virginia*

See: Fate-Root-Heath; Plymouth; Silver King

**Silver King Model 370**

Fate-Root-Heath Company at Plymouth, Ohio closed out its tractor line in 1954, sending all parts and tooling to Mountain State Fabricating Company. The following year, the Silver King Model 370 appears from Mountain State Fabricating Company. This model weighed 3,550 pounds and was equipped with a Continental F-162 four-cylinder engine. This tractor was capable of road speeds up to 19 mph.

**Silver King tractor Model 371**

The Silver King Model 371 was a standard-tread version of the Model 370, and used the same Continental F-162 engine. Mountain State built fewer than 75 tractor before closing their doors, apparently in 1956.

# M-R-S Mfg. Company
*Flora, Mississippi*

The first origins of M-R-S Mfg. Co. are unknown, but it appears that the company began building four-wheel-drive tractors in the late 1950s, continuing for several years. It also appears that the tractors were sold primarily into specialty markets; there is no indication that the M-R-S was widely sold into the grain country of the western

**M-R-S A-100**

and midwestern states. Several sizes were built, including the A-100 shown here. It was capable of 265 maximum brake horsepower, and was powered by a GM 6V-7IN diesel engine.

## Mulsifier Corporation

*Detroit, Michigan*

No illustrations have been found for the Mulsifier garden tractor. It was a 225 pound unit equipped with a Wisconsin Model ABS engine having a 2-1/2 x 2-3/4 inch bore and stroke. This

machine is listed in the trade directories about 1947, but no information regarding the history of the firm has been located.

| 1 | 2 | 3 | 4 |
|---|---|---|---|
| $350 | $250 | $150 | $75 |

## Multi-Tractor Company

*Lincoln, Nebraska*

In 1914 this tractor was displayed at the Fremont Tractor Demonstration. It was essentially a motor plow and was powered by a two-cylinder Cushman engine; the latter was also located at

**1914 Motor plow**

Lincoln, Nebraska.  Very little information is available on this tractor, and there is every likelihood that only a few were built.

## Multonomah Mfg. Company
*Portland, Oregon*

In 1909 it was announced that this firm would be building a 35 horsepower tractor equipped with a six-cylinder engine.  Since no other references have been found, it is assumed that if the tractor ever went into production, it was only for a short time.

## Muncie Wheel Company
*Muncie, Indiana*

No information has been found on this company.

## Muscatine Motor Company
*Muscatine, Iowa*

**Golden West tractor**

The Golden West tractor was advertised in a 1910 issue of *Canadian Thresherman Magazine*.  Aside from this, no other references have been found to this tractor.  It is shown here with an automatic plow guide and a canopy, so it must have been intended as a plowing tractor.

## Mustang Motorcycle Corporation
*Glendale, California*

A trademark application of 1953 indicates that the "Mustang" trademark was first applied to "Tractors" on February 9, 1952.  No other references to this 'tractor' have been found.

# N

## Napco Industries
*Minneapolis, Minnesota*

**Napco "Crab" tractor**

In early 1958 the Napco "Crab" tractor was announced. It featured front wheel steer, front and rear steer, or oblique steering. This tractor was also equipped with four-wheel power steering, hydraulic brakes, and a mechanical pto shaft. No other information has been found.

## National Brake & Electric Company
*Milwaukee, Wisconsin*

No information available on this firm.

## National Engine Company
*Waterloo, Iowa*

This firm was organized in 1913 to "take over the business of the Handt Tractor Company." No other information has been found on either company.

## National Equipment Co. of Texas
*Marshall, Texas*

Information is sketchy, but it appears that this tractor is actually the Nateco Laughlin C-24 tractor of 1946. This model apparently then became the Intercontinental tractor referred to previously in this book. No specifications for the Nateco have been found.

**1946 Nateco Laughlin C-24 tractor**

# National Farm Equipment Company
*New York, New York*

In 1947 this firm advertised their National Garden King garden tractor. It was a 500 pound outfit, and was powered by a Wisconsin AB single-cylinder engine. The engine was rated at 3 horsepower and used a 2-1/2 x 2-3/4 inch bore and stroke. Apparently this machine was built as late as 1953, perhaps later. No illustrations have been found.

# National Farm Machinery Cooperative
*Bellevue, Ohio*

About 1945 National Cooperatives began selling the Cockshutt tractors in the United States. This continued into the late 1950s. The Cockshutt "20" was sold as the Co-op E-2, the Cockshutt "30" was sold as the Co-op E-3, and the Cockshutt "40" was sold as the Co-op E-4. These tractors are illustrated under the *Cockshutt* heading in this book. In 1947 National Cooperatives was selling the Blackhawk Model C garden tractor through its Ohio Cultivator Division at Bellevue. This model was equipped with a Briggs & Stratton Model B engine rated at 2 - 3/4 horsepower. No illustrations of this model have been found.

# National Pulley & Mfg. Company
*Chicago, Illinois*

**National Pulley 10-20 Paramount tractor**

The 10-20 Paramount tractor from National Pulley made its debut in 1916. Production of this tractor was probably very limited, since it does not appear in the tractor directories in subsequent years. No information has been found indicating the type of engine used, or other specifications. Operating weight was 4,000 pounds.

# National Steel & Shipbuilding Corporation
*San Diego, California*

**Lincoln tractor**

In the early 1950s the Lincoln tractor was offered; it is listed during 1953 and 1954, but may have been built for a longer period. This tractor was equipped with a Wisconsin AEH single-cylinder engine rated at 6-1/2 horsepower. Shipping weight was 800 pounds.

# National Track-Tractor Company
*Milwaukee, Wisconsin*

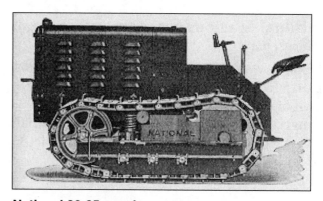

**National 20-25 crawler**

In 1931 the *Tractor Field Book* illustrates the National 20-25 crawler tractor. Weighing some 5,400 pounds, it was powered by a Continental S12, four-cylinder engine that used a 4-1/4 x 5 inch bore and stroke.

Apparently the National crawler tractors were built only in the 1930-1931 period. No other references to these tractors have been found. The National 25-35 shown here in a line drawing was

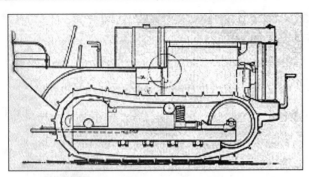

**National 25-35 crawler**

powered by a Continental four-cylinder engine having a 4-3/4 x 6 inch bore and stroke. Both National crawler models were equipped with a rear pto shaft.

## National Tractor Company
*Wichita, Kansas*

Although this company was organized and incorporated in December 1916, no other information has been found on National Tractor Co. or its activities.

## National Tractor & Machinery Company
*Chicago, Illinois*

This firm was organized and incorporated early in 1918 to build the Uncle Sam farm tractors. In April of that year the company name was changed to U. S. Tractor & Machinery Company at Menasha, Wisconsin. The Uncle Sam tractor is illustrated under the latter heading.

## National Tractor Company
*Cedar Rapids, Iowa*

National Tractor Company was the reorganized version of the former Denning Tractor Company. National was a subsidiary of General Ordnance Co with offices in New York City. Denning took bankruptcy in late 1919, with National tractors being built under this title until 1920 when the G-O tractor appeared from General Ordnance

**National tractor**

Co. The tractors were all essentially the same as the former Denning models. The Model E was rated as a 9-16 model, and the Model F was rated at 12 drawbar and 22 belt horsepower.

## Natvik & Company
*Columbus, Wisconsin*

**Natvik Little Giant garden tractor**

Beginning about 1946 Natvik produced their Little Giant garden tractor. It remained in the tractor directories until at least 1953, but any specific history of the firm has not been found. The Little Giant was available with numerous attachments, but few details have been found on this model.

|  | **1** | **2** | **3** | **4** |
|---|---|---|---|---|
| Little Giant | $500 | $400 | $250 | $100 |

**Nevada Auto Plow**

## Nelson Blower & Furnace Company
*Boston, Massachusetts*

**Nelson four-wheel-drive tractor**

Apparently the Nelson four-wheel-drive tractor was introduced in 1919 and remained on the market for a couple of years. It was built in three sizes; 15-24, 20-28, and 35-50. All models were of the same general design. All models used four-cylinder Wisconsin engines. The 15-24 had a 4 x 5 inch bore and stroke; the 20-28 used a 4-3/4 x 5-1/2 inch bore and stroke, and the 35-50 had a 5-3/4 x 7 inch bore and stroke. Operating weight was 5,000, 7,000, and 10,000 pounds respectively.

## Nelson Machine Works
*Seattle, Washington*

In 1948 this company was listed as the manufacturer of the Mity Midget garden tractor. No details, photographs or specifications have been found.

## Nevada Auto Plow Company
## Nevada Truck & Tractor Company
*Nevada, Iowa*

The Nevada Auto Plow first appeared in 1912. This machine was rated at 12 drawbar and 25 belt horsepower. Shortly after it was organized, the firm changed the name to Nevada Truck & Tractor Co. The machine shown here was equipped with a three-bottom plow. Within a couple of years the Nevada quietly disappeared from the market.

## New Age Tractor Company
*Minneapolis, Minnesota*

**New Age 10-18 tractor**

First built in 1915, the New Age tractor was designed by Alex W. Sutherland. It appears that early in development the company was known as Sutherland Manufacturing Co. In 1917 New Age Tractor Co. was incorporated, and continued building the 10-18 model shown here. It carried a two-cylinder engine having a 5 x 6-1/2 inch bore and stroke. During 1919 the New Age tractor was remodeled and began using a Beaver four-cylinder engine with a 4-1/2 x 6 inch bore and stroke. That same year the company was renamed as Sutherland Machinery Company. By 1921 the New Age tractor disappeared.

## New Beeman Tractor Company
*Minneapolis, Minnesota*

**Beeman garden tractor**

This firm was incorporated in 1916 as the Beeman Garden Tractor Company. Three years later, in 1919, the name was changed to *Beeman Tractor Company*. In 1925 the name was again changed to New Beeman Tractor Company. The firm continued at least into the late 1940s.

## New Britain Machine Company
*New Britain, Connecticut*

**New Britain tractor-cultivator**

About 1919 New Britain began building two sizes of their tractor-cultivator. Both used a water-cooled two-cylinder engine having a 2-3/4 x 4 inch bore and stroke. The NB No. 1 retailed at $400, while the NB No. 2 sold for $450. This machine was rated at 6 horsepower. NB No. 2

has an adjustable left wheel for varying row width. Both models used many Fordson and Model T engine parts. The New Britain disappears from the trade directories after 1925. Only one is known to exist today.

|  | **1** | **2** | **3** | **4** |
|---|---|---|---|---|
| NB No. 1 | $4,000 | — | — | — |

## New Deal Tractor Company
*Wyoming, Minnesota*

During the 1930s this company built a limited number of tractors, but little information has been found regarding the company.

## New Way Machinery Company
*Eau Claire, Wisconsin*

This company is listed as a tractor manufacturer in 1918, but no other information has been found.

## New Way Motor Company
*Lansing, Michigan*

New Way was a well known engine builder. Various references also point to this firm as a tractor manufacturer. In a 1911 trademark application, New Way claimed first use of their trademark on traction engines as February 1, 1905. The firm is also listed in various trade directories as a tractor manufacturer as late as 1911. No illustrations of the New Way tractors have been found.

## Nichols & Shepard Company
*Battle Creek, Michigan*

Nichols & Shepard Company had its beginnings in 1848, and in the early 1850s the partnership of John Nichols and David Shepard began building grain threshers.

The partnership was incorporated in 1886 as Nichols & Shepard Company. By this time the company was a major manufacturer of threshing machines and steam traction engines. The Red River Special line appeared about 1900 and continued through the remaining years of the company.

Tractor development began about 1911, and at least one model was built as late as 1927. In 1929 Nichols & Shepard became a part of the merger that formed Oliver Farm Equipment Company.

**Nichols & Shepard prototype**

By December 1911 Nichols & Shepard had developed a large tractor; the prototype is shown here pulling ten plows. A limited number of these tractors were built in 1912. The Nichols & Shepard design was extremely heavy, and from the beginning the largest model was rated at 35 drawbar and 70 belt horsepower.

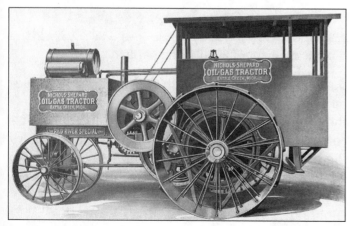

**35-70 tractor**

The big 35-70 tractor came into full production in 1913. This huge tractor had a two-cylinder engine with a 10-1/2 x 14 inch bore and stroke. The crank-

shaft had a diameter of 4-3/4 inches! Various tests run at the time indicated over 90 belt horsepower at rated engine speed of 375 rpm. Production of the 35-70 was fairly small. Active production appears to have continued until 1920, although it also is apparent that this model was available on special order into the late 1920s.

| | 1 | 2 | 3 | 4 |
|---|---|---|---|---|
| 35-70 | $100,000 | $85,000 | — | — |

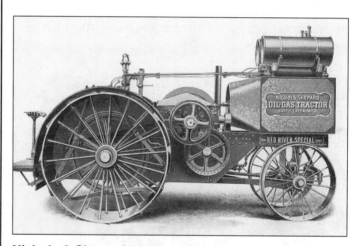

**Nichols & Shepard 25-50 model**

With the 1913 introduction of the 35-70 tractor, Nichols & Shepard also announced their 25-50 model. Although modified somewhat over the years, it remained in production until 1927. The 25-50 was probably underrated to some degree since it appears that it was capable of well over 60 belt horsepower. This model used a two-cylinder engine having a 9 x 12 inch bore and stroke. Among other things, Nichols & Shepard claimed their tractors to have the heaviest gearing of anything on the market.

| | 1 | 2 | 3 | 4 |
|---|---|---|---|---|
| 20-40 or 25-50 | | | | |
| | $30,000 | $20,000 | $15,000 | $7,500 |

About 1920 the 25-50 tractor was modified to some degree. The basic specifications remained the same, but the radiator was changed, the fuel

**25-50 tractor**

**Nichols & Shepard 20-42 tractor**

tanks were relocated, and the canopy was modified. Production of this model continued until 1927.

**Nichols & Shepard 18-36 tractor**

About 1918 Nichols & Shepard developed their 18-36 tractor. Within a year it was re-rated as the 20-42 tractor. The latter continued on the market until about 1925. The same general design was used in the 18-36 as in the larger models. N & S tractor designs were mastered by R. P. Hawthorne who had formerly been associated with Fairbanks, Morse & Company.

The Nichols & Shepard 20-42 tractor was built from 1919 until about 1925. Like the earlier 18-36 it used a two-cylinder engine having an 8 x 10 inch bore and stroke. The company advertised their tractors very little outside of their annual

catalogs, thus accounting in part for the low production of the various models. None of the Nichols & Shepard tractors were tested at Nebraska.

**Nichols & Shepard 20-40 Thresherman's Special**

Beginning about 1927 Nichols & Shepard supplemented their tractor line with three models from the John Lauson Company at New Holstein, Wisconsin. The 20-40 Thresherman's Special typified the line, although this model had heavier drive wheels and other features not found on regular farm tractors. Also included in the series was the 20-40 farm tractor, along with a smaller 20-35 model. The Nichols & Shepard line was amalgamated into Oliver Farm Equipment Company in a 1929 merger.

# Nichols Tractor & Equipment Company
*El Cajon, California*

**Nichols "410" garden tractor**

During the 1946-1948 period the Nichols "410" garden tractor was listed in various directories. No listings have been found after that time, although this does not presume that the "410" went out of production at that time. Weighing 500 pounds, this garden tractor was powered by a Wisconsin AK single-cylinder engine with a 2-7/8 x 2-3/4 inch bore and stroke. Various tools and implements were also available.

# Nilson Tractor Company
*Minneapolis, Minnesota*

**Nilson Farm Machine Co. tractor**

Nilson Agricultural Machine Co. was incorporated in March 1913. A few months later the name was changed to Nilson Farm Machine Co. During 1915 the company introduced their first tractor. It had two steering wheels in the front and a single drive wheel in the rear.

**Nilson 20-40 tractor**

By 1916 the Nilson tractor had been streamlined somewhat, and was given a 20-40 horsepower rating. Retailing at $1,485, this tractor weighed 5,250 pounds. Late in 1915 the company announced plans to move to Waukesha, Wisconsin, but eventually the company moved into a factory area of the former Bull Tractor Company in Minneapolis.

**Nilson 20-40 tractor**

Late in 1916 the Nilson 20-40 took on a new look. The single driver of earlier models gained two smaller drivers outside the chassis. This provided better stability and increased traction. In December of that year the company was reorganized as Nilson Tractor Company.

Production of the Nilson Junior 16-25 tractor began in 1917. However it had an initial rating of 15 drawbar and 30 belt horsepower…the new rating did not come until 1918. Nilson Tractor

**Nilson Junior 16-25 tractor**

Company went into receivership in late 1918 and the assets were sold the following year. In February 1920 the Minnesota-Nilson Company was organized, and again built the Nilson tractors.

**Nilson Senior 24-36 tractor**

During 1918 the Nilson Senior 24-36 tractor appeared as a replacement for the original 20-40 models. However, the 24-36 took on a 20-40 horsepower rating in 1920. This model used a Waukesha four-cylinder engine having a 4-3/4 x 6-3/4 inch bore and stroke. Production of this model continued until about 1925.

**Nilson tractor**

In the late 1920s, Shotwell-Johnson Company attempted to sell stock in the Nilson Company. The newest tractor design was illustrated in their literature, although no details or specifications were included. Apparently this venture did not have great success. The company went into dissolution in 1929. Repair parts were available for the Nilson tractors as late as 1936.

# Noble Automatic Company
*Kansas City, Missouri*

No information can be found regarding this company or any tractors it may have built.

# Northwest Thresher Company
*Stillwater, Minnesota*

During 1911 Northwest Thresher Co. and Universal Tractor Co., both of Stillwater, consolidated their interests. The following year M. Rumely Company of LaPorte, Indiana bought out Northwest, and with it, their Universal tractor. The latter was then marketed as the Rumely GasPull for a short time.

**Northwest Universal tractor**

# O

## Ogburn Tractor Company
*Indianapolis, Indiana*

This firm was organized in 1917 by A. R. and H. R. Ogburn and others. No other information has been found.

## Ohio Cultivator Company
*Bellevue, Ohio*

In the late 1940s this firm is listed as the manufacturer of the Blackhawk garden tractor, but little other information has been found.

## Ohio General Tractor Company
*Cleveland, Ohio*

**Ohio General crawler**

About 1919 the Ohio General crawler came onto the market. It was rated at 25 drawbar and 30 belt horsepower. It was on the market for only a

short time, perhaps as little as a year. No specifications are details regarding this tractor have been located.

## Ohio Mfg. Company
*Upper Sandusky, Ohio*

**Morton Traction Truck**

In the late 1890s the Morton Traction Truck first appeared. As shown here from a 1906 advertisement, it was simply the chassis and gearing. Any engine from 6 to 50 horsepower could be fitted to the Morton trucks. Numerous engine manufacturers offered tractors using their own engines and the Morton traction trucks. They were available as late as 1913.

**Whitney 9-18 tractor**

In 1916 the Whitney 9-18 tractor appeared. Retailing at $1,175 it was equipped with a Gile two-cylinder engine having a 5-1/2 x 6-1/2 inch

**Marion 45 hp tractor**

bore and stroke. Ohio Manufacturing Co. continued building the 9-18 until about 1921. At this time the company name was changed to Whitney Tractor Company. The latter continued for only a short time.

## Ohio Steel Wagon Company
*Wapokoneta, Ohio*

In 1911 this firm bought out the Smith Tractor Mfg. Company at Harvey, Illinois. The company was moved to Ohio, and late in 1911 the firm name was changed to Thompson-Breese Company. The tractor is illustrated under that heading.

## Ohio Tractor Mfg. Company
*Marion, Ohio*

This firm began building tractors in 1908, and in 1910 bought out the Marion Mfg. Company, builders of Leader steam traction engines. The Ohio tractors were built in four sizes of 20, 30, 45, and 70 horsepower. The 45 horsepower model is shown here, although all were of the same general design. Production continued until 1915 when the company took bankruptcy. No specific details have been found for the Ohio tractors.

## Ohio Tractor Company
*Columbus, Ohio*

About 1920 the Ohio 15-30 tractor appeared. This model was powered by a Wisconsin four-

**Ohio 15-30 tractor**

cylinder engine having a 4-1/2 x 6 inch bore and stroke. Weighing 4,500 pounds, it had a list price of $2,800. This tractor was of modern design for its time; a 12-volt electrical system was available as a factory option. Production of the Ohio 15-30 continued until about 1922.

## Oklahoma Auto Mfg. Company
*Muskogee, Oklahoma*

This firm is listed as a tractor manufacturer in 1919, but no other information has been found.

## Olds Gas Engine Works
*Lansing, Michigan*

**Olds tractor**

Already in 1905 Olds is listed as a tractor manufacturer, and a catalog of 1908 illustrates their design. It was powered by a single-cylinder Olds stationary engine. It was available in several sizes, but few specific details have been found.

## Oldsmar Tractor Company
*Oldsmar, Florida*

**Oldsmar garden tractor**

Organized in 1917, Oldsmar Tractor Company was a brainchild of R. E. Olds of automobile fame. Olds bought out the Kardell Truck & Tractor Company, St. Louis, Missouri as a start to the project. The Oldsmar garden tractor was rated at 2-1/2 drawbar and 4-1/2 belt horsepower. Its single-cylinder engine had a 5 x 5-1/2 inch bore and stroke. Production continued until about 1920.

## Olin Gas Engine Company
*Buffalo, New York*

Olin was a well known manufacturer of gasoline engines. About 1915 the company developed the Olin –7 garden tractor. This rather heavy design was built somewhat like a "universal" tractor with its hinged frame. Rated at 7 belt horsepower, the Olin appears to have left the market by 1920 or before.

## Oliver Farm Equipment Company
*Chicago, Illinois*

On April 1, 1929, four companies merged to form Oliver Farm Equipment Company. Oliver Chilled Plow Works at South Bend, Indiana had roots going back to 1855. Nichols & Shepard Company at Battle Creek, Michigan originated in 1848, as did the American Seeding Machine Company. The Hart-Parr Company at Charles City, Iowa began in 1897, and was the first company devoted exclusively to manufacturing tractors.

**Oliver 18-28 tractor**

Various acquisitions followed, but in 1969 Oliver Corporation, Minneapolis-Moline, and Cockshutt merged their interests into White Farm Equipment.

Specific details on these companies and their products can be found in the author's title, *Oliver Hart-Parr*, Motorbooks: 1993.

| | 1 | 2 | 3 | 4 |
|---|---|---|---|---|
| 900 Industrial | $5,000 | $3,500 | $2,000 | $1,500 |
| 18 Industrial | — | — | $12,000 | — |
| 35 Industrial | $4,000 | $3,000 | $2,500 | $1,500 |
| 44 Industraial | $4,250 | $3,500 | $3,000 | $2,000 |
| 50 Industrial | $4,500 | $3,000 | $2,000 | $1,000 |

In 1930, only a few months after the merger, Oliver came out with their new 18-28 tractor. It marked a new epoch in Oliver tractor design with its unit frame, and lightweight design. The 18-28 was available in Standard, Western, Ricefield, and Orchard versions. Production continued until 1937. This model used a four-cylinder engine having a 4-1/8 x 5-1/4 inch bore and stroke.

| | 1 | 2 | 3 | 4 |
|---|---|---|---|---|
| 18-28 Tractor | $3,750 | $2,200 | $1,500 | $800 |
| 18-28 Orchard | — | — | — | $1,000 |

**Oliver big 28-44 tractor**

Like the 18-28 tractor, the big 28-44 was built in the 1930-1937 period. This model used a four-cylinder engine having a 4-3/4 x 6-1/4 inch bore and stroke. Rated speed was 1,125 rpm. The 28-44 weighed in at 5,600 pounds.

|  | 1 | 2 | 3 | 4 |
|---|---|---|---|---|
| 28-44 Tractor | $4,000 | $2,500 | $1,500 | $800 |

**18-27 row-crop model**

Another new tractor design for 1930 was the 18-27 row-crop model. A unique feature was the single front wheel of this style. Oliver used their own four-cylinder engine; it had a 4-1/8 x 5-1/4 inch bore and stroke. Rated at 1,150 rpm, the engine in the 18-27 was essentially the same as in the 18-28 standard-tread model. Production of the 18-27 single-wheel model ended in 1931.

|  | 1 | 2 | 3 | 4 |
|---|---|---|---|---|
| 18-27 single | $4,500 | $3,000 | $1,500 | $1,000 |

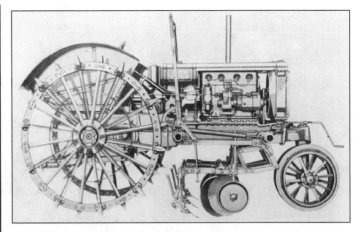

**18-27 dual front wheel design**

Replacing the 18-27 single-front wheel design was the 18-27 dual front wheel design in 1931. This model continued until 1937. This tractor used the same engine as the 18-28 model. In Nebraska Test No. 176 of April 1930 the 18-27 demonstrated nearly 30 belt horsepower, using kerosene fuel.

|  | 1 | 2 | 3 | 4 |
|---|---|---|---|---|
| 18-27 Dual | $3,500 | $1,700 | $1,000 | $500 |

**Oliver "28" tractor**

The Oliver "28" Industrial tractor was the first to use pneumatic tires. It was simply a rubber-tired version of the 28-44 on steel wheels. For industrial purposes though, this model had regular features that included an upholstered seat, headlights and many more optional features. Production of this model ran from 1931 to 1937. A similar model was the Oliver Hart-Parr 80 Industrial. It too had its beginnings with the original 18-28 tractor.

**Oliver Hart-Parr 99 Industrial**

Oliver Hart-Parr 99 Industrial tractors were essentially the same as the 28-44 Industrial model. Built in the 1932-1947 period, this tractor underwent some cosmetic changes along the way, but the engine and chassis were changed but little. Originally this tractor was sold as the Oliver Special High-Compression 28-44.

**Oliver 70 Row-Crop tractor**

During 1935 Oliver introduced its Oliver Hart-Parr 70 Row-Crop tractor. It was the first Oliver tractor to use a six-cylinder engine. Rated at 1,500 rpm, the engine was designed with a 3-1/8 x 4-3/8 inch bore and stroke. In Nebraska Test No. 252 of 1936 this model demonstrated nearly 17 drawbar horse-

power, and approximately 27 belt horsepower. Production of this model continued until 1937. At that point it was dressed up with a streamlined hood and other niceties. Production of the stream-lined model continued until 1948.

|  | 1 | 2 | 3 | 4 |
|---|---|---|---|---|
| 70 Hart-Parr | $3,600 | $2,500 | $750 | $300 |
| 70 Hart-Parr Orchard | $7,500 | — | — | — |

**Oliver 70 Row-Crop**

Few basic changes were made to the Oliver 70 Row-Crop from the time it was introduced in 1935 until production finally ended in 1948. In 1940 an entirely new hood and grille were introduced, but these changes were mainly cosmetic in nature. The unusual skeleton wheels were called "Power on Tiptoe" and were a salient feature until pneumatic tires took over.

**Oliver 70 Standard model**

Numerous variations of the Oliver Row-Crop 70 tractor were built. An example is the Oliver

Hart-Parr 70 Standard model, built in the 1935-1937 period. The chassis and engine were virtually the same as in the row-crop tractor, but special features included expanding differential disk brakes. A live pto was an optional feature.

| | **1** | **2** | **3** | **4** |
|---|---|---|---|---|
| 70 Industrial | $4,250 | $2,500 | $1,800 | $800 |
| 70 Row-Crop | $2,900 | $1,500 | $750 | $500 |
| 70 Standard | $4,500 | $2,750 | $1,200 | $750 |
| 70 Row-Crop wide front | $3,500 | $2,000 | $1,250 | $1,000 |

In 1937 the Oliver 80 Row-Crop tractor appeared, with production continuing until 1948. In 1940 the 80 Diesel Row-Crop was introduced. Initially it used a Buda-Lanova engine, but later on an Oliver diesel engine was installed. The 80

**Oliver 80 Row-Crop tractor**

Diesel Row-Crop is shown here; the 80 Gasoline model was virtually identical except for the engine itself.

Another style in the 80-Series tractors was the 80 Standard. This model was built in the same 1937-1948 time period as the Row-Crop model

**Oliver 80 Standard**

and was essentially the same tractor except for the chassis configuration. A very few of these tractors were also offered with a diesel engine.

| | 1 | 2 | 3 | 4 |
|---|---|---|---|---|
| 80 Industrial | $3,400 | $2,000 | $1,600 | $800 |
| 80 Row-Crop | $3,000 | $1,700 | $1,000 | $600 |
| 80 Standard | $3,200 | $2,200 | $1,500 | $700 |
| 80 Row-Crop Diesel | $10,000 | — | — | — |

**Oliver 99 tractor**

Nebraska Test No. 451 the Oliver 99 delivered over 62 belt horsepower. Production of this model ended in 1957.

| | 1 | 2 | 3 | 4 |
|---|---|---|---|---|
| 90 & 99 | $4,100 | $2,500 | $1,800 | $800 |
| 99 Super Gas or Diesel | $6,000 | $3,000 | $2,200 | $100 |

**Oliver 90 tractor**

Oliver 90 tractors were a continuation of the original 28-44 series. The four-cylinder engine used a 4-3/4 x 6-1/4 inch bore and stroke. The same Nebraska Test No. 183 was used for the 28-44 as well as for the Oliver 90. Electric starting was an important feature for these tractors. Production ran from 1937 to 1953.

The Oliver 99 tractors were essentially a continuation of the earlier 90-Series tractors. However, the 99 used a high compression four-cylinder engine designed for 70-octane fuel. In

**Oliver 60 Row-Crop2,000**

Oliver 60 Row-Crop tractors were built between 1940 and 1948. This model used a four-cylinder engine having a 3-5/16 x 3-1/2 inch bore and stroke. Rated speed was 1500 rpm. It was capable of about 18 belt horsepower. It was tested at Nebraska in 1941 under No. 375.

**Oliver 60 Standard-tread model**

A standard-tread model of the Oliver 60 was also built in the 1940-1948 period. It was virtually identical to the Row-Crop tractor except for the chassis configuration. The Oliver 60 was also available in an Industrial style.

| | 1 | 2 | 3 | 4 |
|---|---|---|---|---|
| 60 Industrial | $3,800 | $2,000 | $1,200 | $600 |
| 60 Row Crop | $3,500 | $2,000 | $1,200 | $400 |
| 60 Standard or adjustable | $4,200 | $2,500 | $1,400 | $500 |

**Oliver 88 tractor (high clearance version)**

Oliver 88 tractors made their debut in 1948, with production continuing until 1954. The Oliver 88 Diesel was introduced in 1949. A six-cylinder engine powered the Oliver 88. It used a 3-1/2 x 4 inch bore and stroke. In Nebraska Test No. 388 of October 1947 the Oliver 88 delivered a maximum of 41 belt horsepower.

**Oliver Super 88**

The Oliver Super 88 was the last of this series. It was built between 1954 and 1958. The gasoline model was tested at Nebraska under No. 525, and displayed almost 37 drawbar horsepower. It used a six-cylinder engine having a 3-3/4 x 4 inch bore and stroke. Test No. 527 for the Super 88 Diesel revealed nearly 38 drawbar horsepower. Both of these tests were run in October 1954.

| | 1 | 2 | 3 | 4 |
|---|---|---|---|---|
| 88 Standard | $3,800 | $2,200 | $1,500 | $900 |
| 88 Row Crop | $3,500 | $1,800 | $900 | $500 |
| 88 Super Standard | $6,000 | $4,000 | $2,000 | $1,500 |
| 88 Super | $3,800 | $2,200 | $1,500 | $900 |

In 1948 the Oliver 77 tractor appeared; it remained in production until 1954. Late in 1948 this tractor was tested (Nebraska No. 404) and indicated a maximum of over 37 belt horsepower. This tractor was available in many differ-

**Oliver 77 tractor**

ent configurations, including an LP-gas model. The Oliver 77 Standard was a popular model. Oliver 77 tractors were also available in diesel-powered models.

Oliver Super 77 tractors were built between 1954 and 1958. Shown here is the high clearance design, but the Super 77 was available in many different configurations, depending on customer needs. The six-cylinder, 216 ci engine used a 3-1/2 x 3-3/4 inch bore and stroke.

|  | 1 | 2 | 3 | 4 |
|---|---|---|---|---|
| 77 Row Crop | $3,100 | $1,700 | $1,000 | $500 |
| 77 Standard | $3,800 | $2,200 | $1,500 | $900 |
| 77 Super | $3,800 | $2,200 | $1,500 | $900 |

Production of the Oliver 66 tractor ran from 1949 to 1954. In the 1951-1954 period it was available with a diesel engine, in addition to the gasoline and LP-gas models. In Nebraska Test No. 412 the Oliver 66 delivered nearly 25 belt horsepower.

**Oliver Super 77 tractor (high clearance version)**

**Oliver 66 tractor**

Test No. 467 was run on the diesel version. Shown here is the standard-tread model, just one of many different available styles.

**Oliver Super 66 Diesel tractor**

Nebraska Test No. 544 was run on the Oliver Super 66 Diesel tractor and demonstrated nearly 30 drawbar horsepower for this model. A 12-volt electrical system came as standard equipment on this model. The four-cylinder engine used a 3-5/16 x 3-3/4 inch bore and stroke. Production of the Super 66 ran from 1954 to 1958.

|  | 1 | 2 | 3 | 4 |
|---|---|---|---|---|
| 66 Row Crop | | | | |
|  | $5,500 | $3,000 | $1,000 | $400 |
| 66 Row Crop adjustable wide front | | | | |
|  | $6,300 | $3,800 | $1,800 | $1,000 |

| 66 Standard or Diesel | | | | |
|---|---|---|---|---|
|  | $5,750 | $3,300 | $1,300 | $500 |
| 66 Super | $5,500 | $3,000 | $1,000 | $400 |

**Oliver Super 55 tractor**

Introduced in 1954, the Oliver Super 55 was the company's first utility tractor. It remained on the market until 1958. In Nebraska Test No. 524 of 1954 the Super 55 gasoline model demonstrated almost 31 maximum drawbar horsepower, using a four-cylinder engine with a 3-1/2 x 3-3/4 inch bore and stroke. The Super 55 was also available with a diesel engine.

|  | 1 | 2 | 3 | 4 |
|---|---|---|---|---|
| 55 Super | $4,500 | $2,700 | $1,800 | $800 |
| 44 Super | $8,000 | $5,000 | $3,500 | $1,500 |

**Oliver Super 99 tractor**

Production of the Oliver Super 99 began in 1954, and was a continuation of the Oliver 99, going back to 1937. These tractors were available with gasoline or diesel engines, the latter being the most popular. One variation was the Super 99 – GM. This model was equipped with a General Motors diesel, although the 99 was also available with Oliver's own diesel model.

|  | **1** | **2** | **3** | **4** |
|---|---|---|---|---|
| 99-GM | $10,000 | $6,000 | $4,000 | $2,200 |

**Oliver Cletrac HG**

Oliver Corporation bought out the Cletrac line in 1944. Cletrac had already introduced several small farm crawlers, including the HG. The latter was available in several track widths to accommodate various farming practices. Numerous implements were tailored especially for the HG tractors, and special cab equipment could be furnished for cold weather operations.

|  | **1** | **2** | **3** | **4** |
|---|---|---|---|---|
| 1916-1936 | $4,500 | $2,500 | $1,500 | $500 |
| Model 20-C | $5,000 | $4,000 | $2,500 | $1,000 |
| Model 25 | $3,500 | $2,500 | $1,500 | $500 |
| Model 30 Diesel | $3,500 | $2,500 | $1,500 | $500 |
| Model 30 Gas | $3,500 | $2,500 | $1,500 | $500 |
| Model 35 | $5,000 | $4,000 | $2,500 | $1,000 |
| Model 35 Diesel | $3,500 | $2,500 | $1,500 | $500 |
| Model 40 | $3,500 | $2,500 | $1,500 | $500 |
| Model 40/30 | $3,500 | $2,500 | $1,500 | $500 |
| Model 80/60 | $5,000 | $4,000 | $1,500 | $300 |
| Model 80 Diesel | $5,000 | $4,000 | $1,500 | $300 |
| Model AD | $2,500 | $2,000 | $1,500 | $300 |
| Model AD-2 | $2,500 | $2,000 | $1,500 | $500 |
| Model AG | $4,000 | $3,000 | $2,000 | $500 |
| Model AG-6 | $3,000 | $2,000 | $1,500 | $500 |
| Model B-30 | $3,500 | $2,500 | $1,500 | $300 |
| Model BD | $3,500 | $2,500 | $1,500 | $300 |
| Model BD-2 | $3,500 | $2,500 | $1,500 | $300 |
| Model BG | $4,500 | $3,000 | $2,000 | $500 |
| Model BGS | $3,500 | $2,500 | $1,500 | $300 |
| Model CG | $3,500 | $2,500 | $1,500 | $300 |
| Model DD | $3,000 | $2,500 | $1,500 | $300 |
| Model DG | $3,000 | $2,500 | $1,500 | $500 |
| Model E | $3,000 | $2,000 | $1,500 | $500 |
| Model E-38 | $3,000 | $2,000 | $1,500 | $500 |
| Model E-42 | $3,000 | $2,000 | $1,500 | $500 |
| Model ED-2 | $3,000 | $2,000 | $1,500 | $500 |
| Model ED-38 | $3,000 | $2,000 | $1,500 | $500 |
| Model ED2-38 | $3,000 | $2,000 | $1,500 | $500 |
| Model ED-42 | $3,000 | $2,000 | $1,500 | $500 |
| Model ED2-42 | $3,000 | $2,000 | $1,500 | $500 |
| Model EHD-2 | $3,000 | $2,000 | $1,500 | $500 |
| Model EHG | $3,500 | $2,500 | $1,500 | $500 |
| Model EN | $3,500 | $2,500 | $1,500 | $500 |
| Model FD | $8,000 | $6,000 | $3,000 | $1,500 |
| Model FDE | $8,000 | $3,500 | $2,500 | $500 |
| Model FDLC | $8,000 | $3,500 | $2,500 | $500 |
| Model FG | $8,000 | $3,500 | $2,500 | $500 |

Model GG (wheel tractor)

|  | 1 | 2 | 3 | 4 |
|---|---|---|---|---|
| Model GG (wheel tractor) | $2,000 | $1,500 | $1,000 | $400 |
| Model HG | $4,500 | $3,000 | $2,500 | $500 |
| Model HGR | $10,000 | $7,500 | $5,000 | $500 |
| MG-1 | $8,000 | $6,000 | $3,000 | $1,500 |

**HG crawler on rubber tracks**

During the 1940s the HG crawler could be furnished with special rubber tracks. The idea was far ahead of its time. Unfortunately, the rubber tracks were unable to stand the stress of heavy work and inevitably they stretched beyond usefulness. These and other problems prompted the company to retrofit these machines with ordinary steel tracks. Only a very few of these machines still exist.

Oliver OC-6 crawler tractors used the same engine as the Oliver 66 row-crop model. In Nebraska Test No. 516 the gasoline-powered OC-6 delivered almost 33 horsepower at the drawbar. Test No. 517 indicated over 34 horsepower for the diesel model. Oliver built many different crawler tractors, and for additional reference, the reader is referred to the author's title, *Oliver Hart-Parr*, Motorbooks: 1993. Oliver abruptly ended production of crawler tractors in 1965.

|  | 1 | 2 | 3 | 4 |
|---|---|---|---|---|
| Oliver OC-3 | $7,000 | $4,500 | $2,500 | $1,000 |
| Oliver OC-4 | $7,000 | $4,500 | $2,500 | $1,000 |

**Oliver OC-6 crawler**

| | 1 | 2 | 3 | 4 |
|---|---|---|---|---|
| Oliver OC-4-3G | $7,000 | $4,500 | $2,500 | $1,000 |
| Oliver OC-6G | $6,000 | $9,000 | $2,500 | $1,000 |
| Oliver OC-9 | $6,000 | $4,000 | $2,500 | $1,000 |
| Oliver OC-12D | $8,000 | $6,000 | $3,000 | $1,500 |
| Oliver OC-12G | $8,000 | $6,000 | $3,000 | $1,500 |
| Oliver OC-15 | $10,000 | $6,000 | $3,500 | $1,500 |
| Oliver OC-18 | $12,000 | $7,500 | $3,500 | $1,500 |

## Oliver Tractor Company
*Knoxville, Tennessee*

During 1919 Oliver offered two crawler tractor models. The Model B 12-20 used a Buda four-cylinder engine with a 4-1/2 x 5-1/2 inch bore and stroke. A 15-30 horsepower rating was given the Model A crawler. The latter carried a Chief four-cylinder engine with a 4-1/2 x 6 inch bore

**Oliver Model B 12-20 crawler**

and stroke. Little is known of the company, and it does not appear that they were in the tractor business for more than a short time.

## Olmstead Gas Traction Company
*Great Falls, Montana*

**Olmstead four-wheel-drive tractor**

During 1912 Olmstead developed their four-wheel-drive tractor. Although plans were made to market the machine, less than forty were actually built. In 1914 the company announced plans to move to Decatur, Illinois, but apparently this did not materialize and the firm faded into obscurity. Few details have been found regarding this tractor.

|     | **1**    | **2** | **3** | **4** |
|-----|----------|-------|-------|-------|
| 4WD | $95,000  | —     | —     | —     |

## Omaha-Park Tractor Company
*Omaha, Nebraska*

No information concerning this company or its tractors has been found.

## Omaha Tractor & Engine Company
*Omaha, Nebraska*

Omaha Tractor was incorporated in 1913, ostensibly to manufacture engines and tractors. No other information has been found.

## Once Over Tiller Corporation
*New York, New York*

**Once Over Tiller tractor**

About 1920 the 15-25 Once Over Tiller tractor appeared. This 4,000 pound machine was powered by a Buda four-cylinder engine. The plows were equipped with special rotary units that pulverized the soil as it came from the moldboards. Apparently the Once Over was marketed for only a short time.

## One Wheel Truck Company
*St. Louis, Missouri*

In 1917 this firm developed the Autohorse; it was apparently a self-powered conversion unit for pulling various vehicles or wagons. No other information has been found.

## Oneman Tractor Company
*Ann Arbor, Michigan*

This firm was organized in 1917 to build the Oneman Tractor Plow. No other information has been found.

## Opsata Motor Plow Company

*Eau Claire, Wisconsin*

This firm was organized in 1913 by Martin S. Opsata to build a motor plow he had developed. In 1916 the company was taken over by Eau Claire Machine Company. No illustrations of the Opsata Motor Plow have been located.

## Orchard Machinery Mfg. Company

*Gasport, New York*

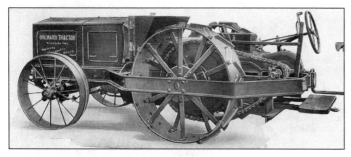

**Orchard 20 horsepower tractor**

A 1913 catalog illustrates the 20 horsepower tractor. Its low profile design was especially suited for orchard work, although the tractor was equally capable of general farm work. A two-cylinder vertical engine was used in this model. It had a top rated speed of 600 rpm and used a 6-1/4 x 8 inch bore and stroke. The tractor weighed 6,000 pounds.

## Osco Motors Corporation

*Philadelphia, Pennsylvania*

**Osco "65" garden tractor**

About 1947 the Osco "65" garden tractor appeared, remaining on the market into the early 1950s. It was equipped with a Wisconsin AEN 7-1/2 horsepower engine. A pto shaft was standard equipment, as was a belt pulley. Numerous tools were available.

## Oshkosh Tractor Company

*Oshkosh, Wisconsin*

In September 1921 this firm was to have bought the La Crosse Tractor Company, La Crosse, Wisconsin. The announced intention was to move the factory to Oshkosh and continue manufacturing tractors there. From all appearances, little or nothing came of this venture.

## Ostenburg Mfg. Company

*Salina, Kansas*

In 1953 this company is listed as the manufacturer of the OMC garden tractors. No other information has been found.

## Otto Gas Engine Works

*Philadelphia, Pennsylvania*

**Otto Gas Engine Works 42 hp model**

Otto Gas Engine Works was the American equivalent to the German company founded by N. A. Otto. The latter was the inventor of today's four-cycle engine. The first Otto traction engine was this big 42 horsepower model. Weighing 15,000 pounds, it was powered by a single-cylinder Otto engine having a 12 x 18 inch bore and stroke. This engine was built in 1896-1897.

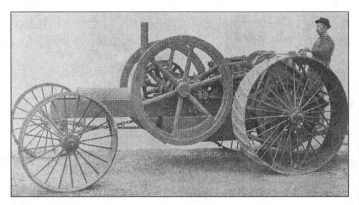

**Otto 1897 tractor**

By 1897 the Otto tractor had been redesigned, and the tractor was showing commercial promise. Thus, this tractor was scheduled for shipment to Hope, North Dakota for field trials. No other information has been found regarding this tractor.

**Otto 1904 tractor**

The Otto gas tractor of 1904 was a rather attractive looking machine, complete with a canopy. Of course these tractors were powered with an Otto stationary engine. At this time they were available in sizes from 6 to 25 horsepower.

**Otto 1912 tractor**

For 1912 the Otto gasoline tractor was built in sizes of 8, 10, 12, 15, and 21 horsepower. This tractor varied but little from the 1904 model, although the engine itself was somewhat improved of course. Otto Gas Engine Works is not listed as a tractor manufacturer after 1913.

## Owatonna Tractor Company
*Owatonna, Minnesota*

During 1912 this company was organized and incorporated to build tractors, but no other information has been found.

# P

## Pacific Coast Tractor Company

*Los Angeles, California*

This firm was organized and incorporated in 1918 to manufacture tractors, but no other information has been found.

## Pacific Iron & Machine Company

*San Diego, California*

**Pacific H6 garden tractor**

The Pacific H6 garden tractor appeared about 1950. It used an articulated chassis and steering brakes for steering of the machine. Power came from a Wisconsin AEH engine capable of about 5 horsepower. Few other details have been found for this unit.

## Pacific Power Implement Company

*Oakland, California*

Only in 1921 does the All-in-One 12-25 tractor appear in the trade directories. This interesting design was an all-wheel-drive tractor. Weighing 4,800 pounds it was powered by a Weidely four-cylinder engine having a 3-3/4 x 5-1/2 inch bore and stroke. Few other details have been found on this tractor.

## Page Dairy & Farm Equipment Company

*Milwaukee, Wisconsin*

This firm appears in 1948 as the manufacturer of the Page garden tractors, but no other details have been located.

| 1 | 2 | 3 | 4 |
|---|---|---|---|
| $550 | $400 | $250 | $125 |

## Pan Motor Company

*St. Cloud, Minnesota*

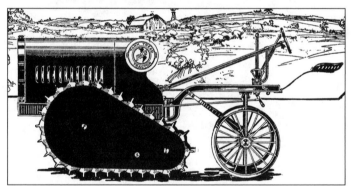

**Pan 12-24 tractor**

Pan Motor Company was established at St. Cloud in 1916, and by May 1918 about 40 cars had been built. In December 1917 the Pan tractor was announced, and a non-working prototype was displayed at several fairs in 1918. Late in 1919 the prototype operated under its own power. Never-ending legal difficulties plagued the Pan Motor Company, and as a result, the much-heralded Pan 12-24 tractor never went into production.

# Panther Tractor Corporation

*Garland, Texas*

**Panther tractor**

In 1948 the Panther tractor appeared. Presumably it had been developed during 1947. The Panther was built with a four-cylinder Waukesha engine having a 2-1/2 x 3-1/8 inch bore and stroke. It was rated at 16 horsepower. By special order the engine could be secured with the manifold, carburetor, and auxiliary fuel tank required for burning kerosene fuel. Numerous attachments were available for the Panther tractors.

# Park Tractor Company

*Chicago, Illinois*

James D. Park apparently organized this firm in 1918. The following year he filed a trademark application noting that he had first used the "Park" tradename on tractors in May 1918. No other information has been found.

# Parker Motor Plow Company

*Bedford City, Virginia*

By 1913 Parker Bros. had developed a heavy duty motor plow. It was powered by a two-cylinder engine of 9 horsepower. Various implements were available. It appears that the company was incorporated in 1915, but no other information has been found regarding the Parker Motor Plow.

# Parrett Motors Corporation

*Chicago, Illinois*

**Parrett Motor Cultivator**

About 1919 this firm was organized as a totally separate entity from Parrett Tractor Company. Its purpose was to build the Parrett Motor Cultivator. Rated at 6 drawbar and 12 belt horsepower, this machine was powered by the well known LeRoi four-cylinder engine with a 31/8 x 4-1/2 inch bore and stroke. A great many small tractors were equipped with this engine. The Parrett Cultivator is listed only during 1920 and 1921.

# Parrett Tractor Company

*Chicago, Illinois*

**Parrett tractor**

In 1913 Dent and Henry Parrett completed their first tractor. Initially they set up a small plant at Ottawa, Illinois, and the first 25 tractors were built at the Plano, Illinois factory of Independent Harvester Company. The Parrett was compact and lightweight for its time, and soon became very popular.

**10-20 Parrett tractor**

**Parrett Model K 15-30 tractor**

Early in 1915 Parrett Tractor Co. moved to Chicago and began building the 10-20 Parrett tractor. Within a short time the Parrett became a very popular design, with thousands of them being sold. The 10-20 was sold between 1915 and 1917.

Between 1918 and 1920 Parrett sold the 12-25 Model H tractor. Among its features was a three-speed transmission. Power came from a Buda four-cylinder engine having a 4-1/4 x 5-1/2 inch bore and stroke. In 1918 this tractor retailed at $1,450.

During 1919 Parrett developed their Model K 15-30 tractor. Its design was virtually the same as its predecessors except for the increased power

level. However, the company was experiencing financial problems by this time, and it does not appear that the Model K experienced the sales of its ancestors. Parrett Tractor Company is not found in the trade listings after 1922.

**Hicks-Parrett 18-30 crawler**

Hicks-Parrett Tractor Co. offered their 18-30 crawler model in 1921. The firm was a brief attempt at a new life, since Parrett Tractor Co. was experiencing financial difficulties. In fact,

**Parrett 12-25 Model H tractor**

the company had previously been reorganized in 1918, even though at the time they were building 50 tractors per day. Little is known of the Hicks-Parrett 18-30.

## Parrett Tractors Inc.
*Benton Harbor, Michigan*

**Parrett tractor**

During 1935 Dent Parrett introduced a new light-weight tractor design. This design weighed only 2,600 pounds, and came with electric starter and lights as standard equipment. Power came from a four-cylinder Hercules IXB engine. This tractor was capable of road speeds up to 20 mph. Within a short time this tractor design was taken over by *Co-operative Mfg. Company*.

## Bert B. Parrott
*Jackson, Michigan*

This individual is listed as a tractor manufacturer in 1917, and apparently was the moving force behind the Highway Tractor Company incorporated at that time. No other information has been found.

## Patch Bros. Tractor Company
*Sand Springs, Oklahoma*

Patch Bros. was organized in 1915, and the following year changed the company name to Farm Engineering Company. The latter built tractors during 1916 and 1917.

## Peco Mfg. Company
*Philadelphia, Pennsylvania*

In 1948 the Peco Model TR47 garden tractor is listed in the directories, but no illustrations of this machine have been found. Few details of this machine have been located.

|  | **1** | **2** | **3** | **4** |
|---|---|---|---|---|
| Model TR47 | $850 | $650 | $400 | $250 |

## Peerless Motor Tractor Works
*Freeport, Illinois*

**Peerless tractor**

In 1911 the Peerless tractor was developed. The front-wheel-drive system could be engaged with a separate clutch, and was intended mainly to facilitate short turns and as a power boost in poor conditions. A two-cylinder horizontal opposed engine was used; it was capable of 20 belt horse-power. Little else is known of the Peerless; nothing has been found subsequent to the 1911 announcements.

## Pennsylvania Tractor Company
*Philadelphia, Pennsylvania*

For 1920 Pennsylvania Tractor Co. offered the Morton Four-Wheel-Drive 40 tractor. Priced at $3,000 the "40" used a 40 horsepower Buda four-

**Morton Four-Wheel-Drive 40 tractor**

cylinder engine. This tractor followed the designs of the Morton Truck & Tractor Company, Harrisburg, Pennsylvania

**Morton Four-Wheel-Drive model**

In addition to the Four-Wheel-Drive 40, Pennsylvania Tractor Company also offered the Morton Four-Wheel-Drive model in 1920. This huge four-drive outfit was equipped with a six-cylinder engine having a 5-1/2 x 7 inch bore and stroke. It was priced at $5,000. Pennsylvania Tractor Company was in operation for only a short time, and does not appear in the 1921 directories.

## Peoria Tractor Company
*Peoria, Illinois*

In 1914 Peoria introduced their three-wheeled 8-20 tractor. By 1916 it had been re-rated as a 10-20, although the tractor was essentially

**Peoria three-wheeled 8-20 tractor**

unchanged. The Peoria used a Beaver four-cylinder engine having a 3-3/4 x 5 inch bore and stroke. Total weight of the tractor was 3,950 pounds; in 1916 it sold for $685.

**Peoria 12-25 tractor**

By 1917 the Peoria 12-25 replaced the original 10-20 model. The 12-25 used a Climax four-cylinder engine having a 5 x 6-1/2 inch bore and stroke. An important feature was full pressure lubrication through a drilled crankshaft. Weighing 4,750 pounds, the 12-25 was priced at $1,585.

**Peoria Model J 12-25 tractor**

About 1919 the Peoria Model J 12-25 tractor replaced the original 12-25. This tractor was nearly identical to its immediate ancestor but used a fully hooded design. Also, a conventional two-wheel standard-tread front axle was used instead of the original one-wheel design.

**Peoria Model L 12-25 tractor**

The Peoria Model L 12-25 tractor first appeared about 1920, and was apparently the last Peoria tractor model, since the firm is not listed after 1921. The Peoria L tractor was again quite similar to the earlier style, although the main frame was changed, and heavier wheels were used. Through its relatively short lifespan, Peoria Tractor Company was reorganized several times.

## Perkins Tractor Company
*Boston, Massachusetts*

This firm was incorporated in 1915 to manufacture tractors, but no other information has been found.

## Ray Perrin Tractor Company
*Portland, Oregon*

In 1948 this company was listed as the manufacturer of the Perrin tractor, apparently a machine in the garden tractor class. No other information has been found.

## Petro-Haul Mfg. Company
*Chicago, Illinois*

**Petro-Haul tractor**

Petro-Haul tractors first appeared in 1913 and remained on the market a couple of years. The Petro-Haul used a unique drive wheel design with retractable lugs. Weighing 5,400 pounds, it was equipped with a Waukesha four-cylinder engine capable of 24 horsepower.

## Phillips-Palmer Tractor Company
*Kansas City, Missouri*

Incorporated in 1916, Phillips-Palmer apparently intended to build farm tractors, but no other information has been found.

## Phoenix Tractor Company
*Winona, Minnesota*

**Phoenix tractor**

The Phoenix tractor appeared in 1912. Rated at 20 drawbar and 30 belt horsepower, it weighed some 7,000 pounds. Within a year of its appearance, the Phoenix tractor was bought out by American Gas Engine Company at Kansas City, Missouri. The latter marketed this design as the Weber tractor.

## Piasa Tractor Company

*Jayton, Texas*

This company was incorporated in 1913 to build tractors, but no other information has been found.

## Piedmont Motor Car Company

*Lynchburg, Virginia*

This company is listed as a tractor manufacturer in 1919 but no other information is available.

## Pioneer Mfg. Company

*Milwaukee, Wisconsin*

See: Red-E; Page; MBM

**Pioneer Red-E 12 garden tractor**

In 1946 Pioneer appears as the manufacturer of the Red-E garden tractors, with the Red-E 12 being shown here. This model used the company's own single-cylinder vertical engine; it was designed with a 3-3/4 x 4 inch bore and stroke. Rated speed was from 500 to 1,500 rpm. The company was also listed as the manufacturer of the Page Model Z garden tractor.

## Pioneer Tractor Mfg. Company

*Winona, Minnesota*

Pioneer was incorporated in April 1909 as Pioneer Tractor Company. A year later Pioneer Tractor Mfg. Co. was organized at Winona, and by the summer of 1910 the Pioneer 30 tractor was on the market. The company persevered in the tractor business until 1925 when it was reorganized as Pioneer Tractors Inc., but the reorganized venture only lasted for a short time.

**Pioneer 30 tractor**

The Pioneer 30 used a four-cylinder horizontal opposed engine with a 7 x 8 inch bore and stroke. The drive wheels were 96 inches high. An enclosed cab featured removable windows and a back curtain. The Pioneer 30 was listed in the directories as late as 1927, apparently the last year the company was in the tractor business.

|          | 1 | 2 | 3 | 4 |
|----------|---|---|---|---|
| 30 (1910) | — | — | $40,000 | $30,000 |

**Pioneer 45-90 tractor**

In 1912 the Pioneer 45 appeared. This huge 45-90 tractor carried a six-cylinder engine having a 7 x

8 inch bore and stroke. Three forward speeds were available on the 30 and 45 models, ranging from 2 to 6 mph. Production of this model continued into 1914; it is likely that it was also available on special order after that time. The company also built a four-cylinder Pioneer Jr. tractor but no illustrations of this model have been located.

**Pioneer Pony tractor**

About 1916 the Pioneer Pony tractor appeared, and was advertised for a short time. This model had a 15-30 horsepower rating, but few specific details of this tractor have been found. In 1916 it listed at $765.

**Pioneer Special 15-30 tractor**

During 1917 the Pioneer Special appeared. Rated as a 15-30, it used a four-cylinder engine with a 5-1/2 x 6 inch bore and stroke. In Canada this tractor was sold as the Winona Special, even though it was the same tractor. Production of this model continued into 1919.

**Pioneer 18-36 model**

Sometime in 1919 Pioneer replaced their "Special" with a new 18-36 model. This tractor was equipped with a four-cylinder horizontal opposed engine having a 5-1/2 x 6 inch bore and stroke. The 18-36 weighed 6,000 pounds. This model remained active until the company left the tractor business in 1927.

## Plano Tractor Company
*Plano, Illinois*

**12-24 Motox tractor**

The 12-24 Motox tractor first appeared in 1917. Initially it had a list price of $1,850. Power came from a Buda four-cylinder engine having a 4-1/4 x 5-1/2 inch bore and stroke. There was only one forward speed and reverse. Sometime in 1919 the Motox was taken over by Wabash Tractor Company.

## Plantation Equipment Company
*Valley Park, Missouri*

For 1916 this company is listed as the manufacturers of the Ultimate tractor line. Included was the Ultimate 8-16, the Ultimate 12-25, and the Ultimate 16-32. No illustrations of these tractors have been found.

## Plowboy Tractor Company

*Phoenix, Arizona*

This company was organized in 1913 to manufacture the Plowboy tractors, but no other information has been found.

## Plowman Tractor Company

*Waterloo, Iowa*

**Plowman 15-30 tractor**

The Plowman 15-30 tractor appeared in 1920. It was actually the same tractor that had been offered previously by Interstate Tractor Company, also of Waterloo. The Plowman 15-30 was equipped with a Buda YTU four-cylinder engine having a 4-1/2 x 6 inch bore and stroke. The Plowman 15-30 was marketed for only a short time.

## Pocahontas Mfg. Company

*Charles City, Iowa*

This firm was organized at Minneapolis in 1917, and shortly afterwards, bought out the Charles City Engine Company, Charles City, Iowa. The latter had been building the Armstrong gasoline engines, formerly of Waterloo, Iowa. At this same time the company announced its Poco tractor, but no illustrations or other information on it has been found. The Poco is listed as late as 1919.

## Geo. D. Pohl Mfg. Company

*Vernon, New York*

This famous gasoline engine manufacturer is also listed as a tractor manufacturer as late as 1913. No illustrations of the Pohl tractor have been found.

## Pond Garden Tractor Company

*Ravenna, Ohio*

Harold Pond first began using the Speedex garden tractor name in 1935, but no illustrations of the earliest machines have been located. The Speedex Model B garden tractor was fitted with a Briggs & Stratton Model ZZ engine having a 3 x 3-1/4 inch bore and stroke.

| | **1** | **2** | **3** | **4** |
|---|---|---|---|---|
| Speedex Model B | $450 | $350 | $250 | $100 |

## Pontiac Tractor Company

*Pontiac, Michigan*

**Pontiac 15-30 tractor**

Apparently the Pontiac 15-30 tractor was developed during 1918, and marketed into 1919. This tractor used a single-cylinder engine having a 9 x 12 inch bore and stroke. Unfortunately, very little else is known of the company or its tractors.

## Pony Tractor Company

*LaPorte, Indiana*

A 1919 trade note indicates that Pony Tractor Co. was incorporated that year, ostensibly to manufacture tractors. No other information has been found.

# Pope Mfg. Company
*Watertown, South Dakota*

**Dakota 15-27 tractor**

The Dakota 15-27 tractor was offered in 1920 by Pope Mfg. Co. It was apparently a takeoff from the earlier Dakota tractors built by G. W. Elliott & Son at DeSmet, South Dakota. Power for this tractor came from a Doman four-cylinder engine having a 4-3/4 x 6 inch bore and stroke.

# Port Huron Engine & Thresher Company
*Port Huron, Michigan*

**Port Huron 12-25 tractor**

Port Huron had an ancestry going back to the 1850s as a small grain thresher manufacturer. The company continued to grow, and in 1890 the name was changed from Upton Mfg. Co. to Port Huron. The company offered its gas tractor

between 1918 and 1922. Rated as a 12-25, the Port Huron used a four-cylinder Chief engine with a 4-3/4 x 6 inch bore and stroke. The tractor weighed 6,200 pounds and was priced at $1,700. This tractor used an infinitely variable drive system much like the Heider tractors.

# Porter Tractor Company
*Des Moines, Iowa*

**Porter 20-40 tractor**

In 1919 the Porter Tractor Co. began operations at Colfax, Iowa. Within a few months the firm moved to nearby Des Moines. Rated as a 20-40, the Porter tractor featured a Waukesha engine with a 4-3/4 x 6-3/4 inch bore and stroke. A unique feature was the special extension attachment whereby many different implements could be operated from the seat of the connected machine, such as a grain binder. The Porter disappeared after 1920.

# Post Tractor Company
*Cleveland, Ohio*

Post Tractor Company was organized and incorporated in 1918. By the following year the Post 12-20 tractor was on the market. This unique design used two centrally placed drive wheels, with an outrigger support wheel on each side. Power came from a four-cylinder Waukesha

**Post 12-20 tractor**

engine having a 4-1/4 x 5-3/4 inch bore and stroke. Weighing 3,300 pounds, the Post 12-20 sold for $1,250. Production apparently ended during 1920.

## Powell Tractor Company
*Elwood, Indiana*

**Powell 16-30 tractor**

During 1919 the Powell 16-30 appeared. Few details are available for this model except that it offered two forward speeds of 2-1/2 and 5 mph. This tractor has great similarities to the Elgin tractor, built earlier at Elgin, Illinois.

## Power Garden Cultivator Company
*Minneapolis, Minnesota*

In 1918 this company appeared, and their advertising brochure leads to the conclusion that the company was in full operation. Apparently

**Midget tractor**

though, the company was operating on a shoe-string, and whether the Midget tractor ever became more than a figment of the artist's imagination is unknown.

## Power King Tractor Company
*Milwaukee, Wisconsin*

**Power King tractor**

The Power King appears in the 1953 directories, but no information has been found to determine the career of the company or its tractors. The 1953 model was capable of about 8 horsepower and used either a Briggs & Stratton or a Wisconsin engine. Numerous attachments were available.

| 1 | 2 | 3 | 4 |
|---|---|---|---|
| $1,200 | $900 | $750 | $500 |

# Power Truck & Tractor Company
*Detroit, Michigan*

**Power Truck & Tractor Company 15-32 tractor**

During 1919 Power Truck & Tractor Co. offered this 15-32 tractor. Power came from a single-cylinder engine having a 9 x 12 inch bore and stroke. This tractor is quite similar to the Pontiac 15-30, a tractor of virtually identical design, and offered a year earlier by Pontiac Tractor Co.

# Powerall Farm Tools Company
*Chula Vista, California*

The Powerall garden tractor was listed in 1948, but no illustrations or specifications have been found.

# Pow-R-Trak Company
*Wichita, Kansas*

During 1948 the Pow-R-Trak garden tractor was on the market, but no photographs or specifications on this unit have been located.

# Prairie Queen Tractor Mfg. Company
*Temple, Texas*

In the early 1920s the Prairie Queen 8-16 tractor appeared. This small tractor was priced at only $765. For reasons unknown it left the market

**Prairie Queen 8-16 tractor**

during 1922. No details of the company have been found, nor have detailed specifications been located.

# Progressive Machinery Company
*Minneapolis, Minnesota*

**Peters garden tractor**

In 1931 the Peters garden tractor was being built by Progressive Machinery Co. This model was powered by a Briggs & Stratton Model PB engine having a 2-1/2 inch bore and stroke. Alternatively, a Toro Model ME engine was used; it was slightly larger with its 2-5/8 x 3-1/4 inch bore and stroke.

|  | **1** | **2** | **3** | **4** |
|---|---|---|---|---|
| Peters Garden Tractor | $2,500 | $2,000 | $1,000 | $650 |

# Providence Engineering Works

*Providence, Rhode Island*

**Providence tractor**

In early 1914 the Providence tractor was announced, leading to the assumption that it had been developed the previous year. An interesting feature was that the body of the tractor was of a single iron casting. Power came from a three-cylinder engine of 20 horsepower. After the initial announcements, nothing more is known of the Providence tractor.

# Pull-Away Garden Tractor Company

*Stockton, California*

During 1948 this firm was listed as the builder of the Pull-Away Garden Tractor, but no other information has been found.

# Pullet Tractor Company

*Minneapolis, Minnesota*

A trademark application of 1918 notes that the Pullet trademark had first been applied to tractors in October 1917. In 1919 the Pullet tractor with a 40 horsepower belt rating was displayed at several demonstrations, and the company is listed as a tractor manufacturer as late as 1921. No illustrations or specifications regarding this tractor have been found.

# Pullford Company

*Quincy, Illinois*

**Pullford conversion attachment**

Hundreds of companies built conversion units to make a tractor out of a car. One of the most successful of these was the Pullford attachment. By 1917 it was available for the Model T Ford at only $135. It continued on the market into the 1930s, and during that decade was also available for the Model A Ford.

# Puritan Machine Company

*Detroit, Michigan*

**New Elgin 12-25 tractor**

During 1920 Puritan offered the New Elgin 12-25 tractor. It was apparently the immediate successor to the Waite and Elgin tractors found elsewhere in this volume. The New Elgin 12-25 used a four-cylinder Erd engine with a 4 x 6 inch bore and stroke.

# Q

## Quick Mfg. Company
*Springfield, Ohio*

**Springfield garden tractor**

During 1953 Quick Mfg. offered their Springfield 2001, 2002 and 2003 garden tractors. The 2001 was furnished with a Briggs & Stratton NPR-6 engine capable of 2 horsepower. Model 2002 and 2003 tractors were equipped with a Briggs & Stratton 8R6 engine or a Clinton D1162 engine, both capable of 2-1/2 horsepower.

|  | <u>1</u> | <u>2</u> | <u>3</u> | <u>4</u> |
|---|---|---|---|---|
| All models | $850 | $600 | $300 | $100 |

## Quincy Engine Company
*Quincy, Pennsylvania*

By 1912 Quincy Engine Company had entered the tractor business. This small tractor appears to have been capable of about 6 or 8 belt horsepower. The engine was simply a Quincy portable mounted to the company's own chassis.

**Quincy 10-20 tractor**

The Quincy 10-20 tractor shown here was powered by a Quincy 20 horsepower single-cylinder engine. This model came onto the market in 1912 and remained as late as 1916. At that time it sold for $1,200. This tractor weighed 10,000 pounds.

**1912 Quincy tractor**

# R

## R & P Tractor Company
*Alma, Michigan*

**R & P 12-20 tractor**

Between 1918 and 1920 the R & P 12-20 appeared. A unique feature was the unique track-pad wheels. They were originally developed in Italy for their military tractors. The R & P was designed with a Waukesha four-cylinder engine having a 3-3/4 x 5-1/2 inch bore and stroke. At least one R & P tractor remains in existence; it is in Australia.

## Ranger Tractor Company
*Houston, Texas*

No information available.

## S. W. Raymond Tractor Company
*Adrian, Michigan*

About 1922 the Raymond tractor appeared. It had a unique chassis design and was powered by a Ford Model T engine. The Raymond used individual rear brakes and also featured a unique mechanical lift system for the plow. A cultivator

**Raymond tractor**

could be mounted directly to the tractor frame. After using the engine, transmission, radiator and fuel tank for the tractor, the remaining parts could be used for making a four-wheel trailer.

## Redden Truck & Tractor Company
*Harvey, Illinois*

**Redden Farmer-Tractor-Truck**

By 1919 the Redden Farmer-Tractor-Truck appeared. This combination machine was intended as a tractor and a two-ton truck. A Buda four-cylinder engine powered this machine; it used a 4-1/4 x 5-1/2 inch bore and stroke. Standard features included a belt pulley. This machine had a list price of $2,600.

## Red-E-Tractor Company
*Richfield, Wisconsin*
See: M.B.M. Mfg. Co.

In 1953 this firm is listed as the manufacturer of the M.B.M. garden tractor. No other information is available.

# Reed Foundry & Machine Company
*Kalamazoo, Michigan*

**Reed 12-25 tractor**

About 1916 the Reed 12-25 tractor appeared. Initially the 12-25 used a Waukesha four-cylinder engine having a 3-1/2 x 5-3/4 inch bore and stroke, but within a year the engine bore was increased to 4 inches. This model sold at about $1,650. Production of the 12-25 ended in 1920.

**Reed 12-25 tractor**

A redesigned Reed 12-25 appeared in 1921. The new tractor featured a Doman four-cylinder engine of the same size as the Waukesha used in the original model. Shortly after it appeared on the market this new tractor was known as the Model A 15-30 tractor. The company also developed a tractor using a Doman 5 x 6 inch, four-cylinder motor, but mounted in the same chassis. By the following year the Reed tractor disappeared.

# Reeves & Company
*Columbus, Indiana*

Reeves began building grain threshers in 1874 and began building steam traction engines about

**Reeves "40" tractor**

ten years later. The Reeves tractor was developed in 1910 and came out the following year. In 1912 Emerson-Brantingham Company bought out Reeves and continued building the tractor for several years. The Reeves "40" was rated at 40 drawbar and 65 belt horsepower, and was the same engine used in the Twin City 40-65 model. It was of four-cylinder design and used a 7-1/4 x 9 inch bore and stroke.

# Reierson Machinery Company
*Portland, Oregon*

No information available.

# Rein Drive Tractor Company Ltd.
*Toronto, Ontario*

**Rein Drive tractor**

During April 1917 the Rein Drive tractor was developed. As the name implies it was intended to be driven by reins, just like driving a team of horses. For reasons unknown the company succeeded for only a short time. The Rein Drive was advertised into 1918, but after that it disappeared from the scene. No specific details have been found.

## Reliable Tractor & Engine Company

*Portsmouth, Ohio*

See: Morton Tractor Company; Morton-Heer; Heer Engine Co.

**10-20 Reliable tractor**

In 1915 Reliable Tractor & Engine Co. was organized to take over the assets of Heer Engine Company, also of Portsmouth. The 10-20 Reliable was equipped with a two-cylinder engine having a 6 x 7 inch bore and stroke. It weighed 3,800 pounds and sold for $985. This tractor was also sold by Fairbanks, Morse & Company as their Fair-Mor tractor for several years. Production of this model ended about 1921.

## Remy Bros. Tractor Company

*Kokomo, Indiana*

In 1917 this firm was incorporated by Remy Brothers of magneto fame, and Elwood Haynes of automotive fame to build a tractor. The Remy 15-30 tractor was announced in 1918, but no other information about the company or its tractors has been located.

## Renno-Leslie Motor Company

*Philadelphia, Pennsylvania*

This firm was organized and incorporated in 1917 to build tractors, but no other information has been located.

## Rexroth Industries

*Riverside, California*

**Rexroth Bobbette Model L garden tractor**

In the late 1950s the Rexroth Bobbette Model L garden tractor appeared. It was powered with a Wisconsin Model AKN engine having a 2-7/8 x 2-3/4 inch bore and stroke. This produced over 6 horsepower. Numerous attachments were available, and features included three forward speeds. Total weight was 520 pounds.

## Ripley Cultivator & Motor Tractor Mfg. Company

*Aurora, Illinois*

This firm was organized in 1920 to manufacture tractors, but no other information has been found.

# Rock Island Plow Company

*Rock Island, Illinois*

See: Heider Mfg. Company

Rock Island Plow Co. had its beginnings in the plow business in 1855. The company prospered and took the Rock Island name in 1882. By 1912 the firm offered one of the largest lines of tillage implements in the entire industry.

During 1914 and 1915 Rock Island Plow Co. expanded their line with the addition of the Heider tractor built at Carroll, Iowa. In January 1916 Rock Island bought out the Heider tractor line and launched themselves permanently into the tractor business. This continued until Rock Island Plow Co. was taken over by J. I. Case Company in 1937.

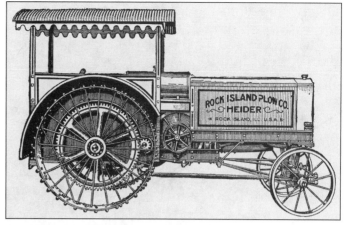

**12-20 Model C Heider tractor**

bore and stroke. Total weight was 6,000 pounds. The salient feature of the Heider tractor was the use of a friction drive system that permitted seven different speeds, forward or reverse.

**10-20 Model C Heider**

Rock Island Plow Co. entered the tractor business in 1914 by contracting to sell the output of the Heider Tractor Co., Carroll, Iowa. The Heider proved to be very popular, and in 1916 Rock Island bought out the Heider tractor line. The original 10-20 Model C Heider gave way to a 12-20 Model C in 1916.

During 1916 the 12-20 Model C Heider tractor appeared. It remained on the market until 1924 when it was replaced with the improved 15-27 Model C. A Waukesha four-cylinder engine was used in the 12-20; it carried a 4-1-2 x 6-3/4 inch

**Hieder Model C, 15-27 tractor**

The Heider Model C, 15-27 tractor was built in the 1924-1927 period. This model used a Waukesha four-cylinder engine having a 4-3/4 x 6-3/4 inch bore and stroke. In Nebraska Test No. 114 of 1925 the 15-27 proved itself with over 17 drawbar horsepower and 30 horsepower on the belt pulley.

Introduced in 1916, the Heider Model D 9-16 tractor remained on the market until 1929. Weighing 4,000 pounds, the 9-16 featured a Waukesha four-cylinder engine having a 4-1/4 x 5-3/4 inch bore and stroke. In Nebraska Test No.

**Heider Model D 9-16 tractor**

17 of 1920 the 9-16 delivered nearly 12 drawbar horsepower. When the 9-16 was taken out of production in 1929 the Heider tradename was dropped.

**Heider 6-10 cultivator**

Rock Island Plow Co. introduced its Heider 6-10 cultivator in 1920; actually, it was sold as the M-1 (one-row) or the M-2 (two-row) cultivator. Power came from a four-cylinder LeRoi engine with a 3-1/8 x 4-1/2 inch bore and stroke. This unit was available through 1926.

Production of the Rock Island Model F 18-35 tractor began in 1927. This tractor was furnished with a Buda four-cylinder engine having a 4-1/2 x 6 inch bore and stroke. In Nebraska Test No. 144 of 1927 the 18-35 demonstrated over 30 drawbar horsepower. Production of this model con-

**Rock Island Model F 18-35 tractor**

tinued until the firm was bought out by J. I. Case Co. in 1937. A Model FA was also available. The only difference was that the transmission was geared more slowly than the Model F.

| | 1 | 2 | 3 | 4 |
|---|---|---|---|---|
| Model F 18-35 | $6,500 | $4,500 | $2,500 | — |

**Rock Island G-2, 15-25 tractor**

In 1929 the Rock Island G-2, 15-25 tractor appeared. This tractor was of a design similar to the Model F. Weighing 4,200 pounds, the G-2 was furnished with a Waukesha four-cylinder engine having a 4-1/4 x 5-3/4 inch bore and stroke. Starting and lighting equipment were available for the Model F and Model G-2 tractors as an extra-cost option. When J. I. Case bought out Rock Island Plow Co. in 1937 all production of Rock Island tractors ceased.

| | 1 | 2 | 3 | 4 |
|---|---|---|---|---|
| Model G-2 | $5,500 | $4,000 | $2,500 | — |

# Rockford Engine Works
*Rockford, Illinois*

This firm is listed as a tractor manufacturer between 1906 and 1908. Rockford certainly was an active engine builder at the time, and most likely produced a few "gasoline traction engines" using their stationary designs. No illustrations of the Rockford tractors have been found.

# Rogers Tractor & Trailer Company
*Albion, Pennsylvania*

**Rogers four-wheel-drive tractor**

Rogers offered this four-wheel-drive tractor in 1923. Little information can be found on the company, so it may have been on the market for a few years during the early 1920s. The Rogers had two speeds forward and reverse. It was powered by a Buffalo four-cylinder engine.

# Ross Motors Ltd.
*Chicago, Illinois*

This firm is listed as a tractor manufacturer but no other information has been found.

# Roths Industries
*Alma, Michigan*

By 1947 Roths was offering several styles of garden tractors, and by 1950 this included the Model R Bes-Ro tractor shown here. It was equipped with a 7-1/2 horsepower engine and an automotive-type differential. Also included was the Model W Gar-

**Model R Bee-Ro tractor**

den King, a two-wheeler with a 5 horsepower engine, and the Model G, a two-wheeler with the choice of a 2 or 3 horsepower engine. Roths was active at least into the late 1950s.

# Roto-Hoe & Sprayer Company
*Newbury, Ohio*

**Roto-Hoe 148H rotary tiller**

In the early 1950s the Roto-Hoe 148H rotary tiller was available. It was equipped with a Lauson Model RSH engine that used a 2 x 1-7/8 inch bore and stroke. It was capable of 2 horsepower.

|      | **1**  | **2**  | **3** | **4** |
|------|--------|--------|-------|-------|
| 148H | $150   | $100   | $75   | $35   |

## Rototiller Incorporated
*Troy, New York*

**Rototiller**

Rototiller first used its tradename for soil cultivators on February 9, 1929. The company built various models of Rototillers during the years. Initially the firm operated at Wilmington, Delaware, but by the late 1940s was located at Troy, New York. Shown here is the Model T Rotoette from Rototiller. This 1950 model was equipped with a Briggs & Stratton Model N engine having a 2-inch bore and stroke. No detailed history of Rototiller has been found.

|            | **1**  | **2**  | **3**  | **4**  |
|------------|--------|--------|--------|--------|
| All models | $750   | $600   | $450   | $175   |

## Royal Motors Company
*Napoleon, Ohio*

In 1917 Royal Motors announced their new line-drive tractor. Rated at 35 belt horsepower, it also featured electric starting and lights. The Royal

**Royal Line-Drive tractor**

Line-Drive apparently remained on the market for only a short time. Virtually nothing is known of the machine aside from introductory announcements.

## Royer Tractor Company
*Wichita, Kansas*

**12-25 Royer tractor**

Royer Ensilage Harvester Co. was organized and incorporated at Wichita in 1914. By 1919 the company was building their 12-25 Royer tractor. It was equipped with a four-cylinder Erd engine having a 4 x 6 inch bore and stroke. The company was incorporated in 1920, but little is known of the Royer enterprise after that time.

# Ruby Tractor Company
*Minneapolis, Minnesota*

This firm is listed as a tractor manufacturer in 1916, and remains listed as late as 1920. The company exhibited their tractor at various shows during this period. However the company operated from the same address as the Pullet Tractor Company, so apparently they were actually one and the same. No specific information has been found on the Ruby tractor.

# Leo Rumely Tractor Company
*LaPorte, Indiana*

**Hoosier tractor**

The Hoosier tractor was announced in January 1916. It was a revised version of the Wolf tractor, previously built in LaPorte by Wolf Tractor Company. The Hoosier had a rating of 8 drawbar and 18 belt horsepower. Power came from a Waukesha four-cylinder engine having a 3-3/4 x 5-1/4 inch bore and stroke. The Hoosier remained on the market for only a short time.

# Rumely Products Company
*LaPorte, Indiana*

See: Advance-Rumely Thresher Company

# Russell & Company
*Marion, Ohio*

Russell & Company had its roots all the way back to 1842 when the Russell brothers formed a company to build threshing machines. In 1878 the company was incorporated, and a couple of years later they began building steam traction engines.

Russell & Co. entered the gasoline traction engine business in 1909 and subsequently offered several sizes of tractors. The company was sold at auction in March 1927 and Russell Service Co. provided repair parts until 1942.

**American Gas Traction Engine**

The three-cylinder American Gas Traction Engine made its debut in 1909. It used a three-cylinder engine having an 8 x 10 inch bore and stroke for 22 drawbar horsepower. The American weighed 17,000 pounds and sold for $2,400. This tractor was available as late as 1914.

**Russell 30-60 tractor**

Between 1911 and 1913 Russell offered this 30-60 tractor with a single front wheel. A four-cylinder engine powered this model, but no specifications or detailed information has been found.

**Russell 30-60 tractor**

During 1913 the Russell 30-60 tractor was redesigned to include a conventional front axle instead of the single front wheel as before. Another change was the use of a large tubular radiator. From this design came the Russell Giant of 1914.

From 1914 until 1921 the Russell Giant was rated as a 40-80 tractor. The big four-cylinder engine used an 8 x 10 inch bore and stroke, but in

Nebraska Test No. 78 it only developed 66 belt horsepower. From that time on, until production ended in 1927, it was sold as a 30-60 tractor. The Russell Giant weighed 24,000 pounds.

**Russell Jr. 12-24 tractor**

Production of the Russell Jr. 12-24 tractor began in late 1915. This model used a Waukesha engine with a 4-1/2 x 5-3/4 inch bore and stroke. This tractor was available into the mid-1920s.

**Russell Giant 40-80 tractor**

**Russell Little Boss 15-30 tractor**

The Russell Little Boss 15-30 tractor first appeared in 1917. It used a four-cylinder Climax engine having a 5 x 6-1/4 inch bore and stroke. Test No. 93 was run at Nebraska in 1923, and the 15-30 delivered over 24 drawbar horsepower.

**Russell 20-40 Big Boss tractor**

Nebraska Test No. 94 was run on the Russell 20-40 Big Boss tractor in 1923, although production of this model had begun already in 1917. This model used a Climax four-cylinder engine having a 5-1/2 x 7 inch bore and stroke. In Test No. 94 this tractor was capable of almost 31 drawbar horsepower, considerably more than its manufacturer's rating. Production of the Russell tractors ended in 1927 when the company was sold at auction.

| | 1 | 2 | 3 | 4 |
|---|---|---|---|---|
| 20-40 Big Boss | $25,000 | $15,000 | $10,000 | $5,000 |

## Russell Tractor Company
*Chicago, Illinois*

This firm was organized in 1914 to manufacture tractors, but no other information has been located.

# S

## Sageng Threshing Machine Company
*St. Paul, Minnesota*

**Sageng Combination Gasoline Thresher**

Halvor O. and Ole O. Sageng organized the Sageng Threshing Machine Company in 1908. The Sageng Combination Gasoline Thresher was their primary interest, and was one of the first such machines to be built. A large four-cylinder engine was situated beneath the driver's platform. The machines were built by Minneapolis Steel & Machinery Company.

During 1911 the Sageng Farmer's Tractor appeared. Rated at 16 drawbar and 30 belt horsepower, it used a two-cylinder opposed engine having a 7 x 8 inch bore and stroke. Unfortunately, the Farmer's Tractor lasted only a short time, since Sageng Threshing Machine Co. went broke in April 1912.

## Samson Iron Works
*Kansas City, Missouri*

No information available.

**Sageng Farmer's Tractor**

# Samson Iron Works
*Stockton, California*

See: General Motors

**Samson tractor**

As early as 1914 the Samson tractor was on the market. The smallest model used a single-cylinder engine having a 7 x 9 inch bore and stroke. It was rated at 10 belt horsepower. Weighing 4,200 pounds, it was priced at $675. This model was built until about 1917. Only three specimens are known to exist.

**Samson Sieve Grip tractor**

By 1916 the Samson Sieve Grip tractor line included a four-cylinder model with a rating of 20 belt horsepower. It was furnished with an engine having a 4-1/4 x 6-3/4 inch bore and stroke. Weighing 5,500 pounds, it sold for $1,150. General Motors Corporation bought out the Samson tractor line in 1918 and moved the manufacturing operation to Janesville, Wisconsin. Samson Iron Works had its start in the gasoline engine business as early as 1904.

| | **1** | **2** | **3** | **4** |
|---|---|---|---|---|
| Sieve Grip | $30,000 | $26,000 | — | — |

# Savage Harvester Company
*Denver, Colorado*

**Savage 20-35 tractor**

A full cab came as standard equipment on the Savage 20-35 tractor. Listed only in 1921, this model weighed 7,500 pounds and was priced at $3,500. Power came from a Climax four-cylinder engine having a 5-1/2 x 7 inch bore and stroke. Little else is known of the Savage 20-35.

# Savidge Tractor Mfg. Company
*Alton, Illinois*

Although this firm was organized and incorporated in 1917, no other information has been located.

# Savoie-Guay Company Ltd.
*Plessisville, Quebec*

In 1914 Savoie-Guay developed a one-man motor plow and advertised it the following year. This machine used a three-cylinder engine capable of 35 belt horsepower. Very little information can

**Savoie-Guay one-man motor plow**

be found on this unit, and it seems unlikely that any substantial number were built.

## Sawyer-Massey Company
*Hamilton, Ontario*

**Sawyer-Massey 22-45 tractor**

During 1910 Sawyer-Massey introduced its new tractor, demonstrating it at various fairs and expositions. Its performance was sufficiently good to warrant continued tractor development, and from this prototype came the Sawyer-Massey 22-45 of the following year. The 22-45 was typical of the Sawyer-Massey line until production ended in the early 1920s. In the 1912-1917 period Sawyer-Massey offered the 10-20, 16-32 and 25-50 models; the latter was nothing more than the original 22-45 production model of 1911.

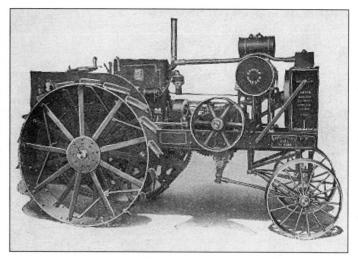

**Sawyer-Massey 11-22 tractor**

By 1918 the Sawyer-Massey line included the 11-22 tractor. This model was designed with a four-cylinder Erd motor having a 4 x 6 inch bore and stroke. Weighing 5,400 pounds, it was priced at $1,750.

**Sawyer-Massey 17-34 tractor**

A Twin City four-cylinder engine was used in the Sawyer-Massey 17-34 tractor. It used a 5-1/2 x 7-1/2 inch bore and stroke. The 17-34 weighed 11,500 pounds and was priced at $2,900. Production continued into the early 1920s.

**Sawyer-Massey 20-40 tractor**

Sawyer-Massey used their own four-cylinder engine in the 20-40 tractor. It was designed with a 5-5/8 x 7 inch bore and stroke. Apparently this tractor was built over the same chassis as the 17-34 tractor. The 20-40 was priced at $3,750.

**Sawyer-Massey 27-50 tractor**

Priced at $4,000 the Sawyer-Massey 27-50 weighed 17,500 pounds. This model was equipped with the company's own four-cylinder engine having a 6-1/4 x 8 inch bore and stroke. Production of the Sawyer-Massey tractors ended in the early 1920s when the company moved into the construction of road building machinery.

|  | 1 | 2 | 3 | 4 |
|---|---|---|---|---|
| 10-20 | $20,000 | $18,000 | $10,000 | $6,500 |
| 11-22 | $20,000 | $18,000 | $10,000 | $6,500 |
| 16-32 | $25,000 | $20,000 | $18,000 | $15,000 |
| 17-36 | $25,000 | $20,000 | $18,000 | $15,000 |
| 20-40 | $35,000 | $30,000 | $20,000 | $15,000 |
| 25-50, 25-45 or 30-60 |  |  |  |  |
|  | $50,000 | $40,000 | $20,000 | $15,000 |

# Schofield Auto Tractor Company
*Kansas City, Missouri*

**Schofield Auto Tractor Attachment**

The Schofield Auto Tractor Attachment was offered in 1919, and perhaps for a few seasons on either side of that year. Nearly fifty different companies were building automobile-tractor conversion kits at the time, and this one simply drove the entire automobile onto a chassis, connected the drive chains and the steering linkage for an instant tractor.

# Scientific Farming Machinery Company
*Minneapolis, Minnesota*

**Princess Pat VI 10-20 model**

Incorporated in 1916, this firm offered their machines to the U. S. Government the following year in a "Win the War" effort. During 1920 the company gave a manufacturing franchise to Once-Over Tiller Corporation to build a similar machine. The latter was also known as U. S. Farming Machinery Co. The Princess Pat VI 10-20 model is shown here. Its two plow bottoms were equipped with powered revolving blades that pulverized the soil as it left the moldboards.

**Mark 4 tractor**

By 1922 the "Once-Over" design was available as the Mark 4, a one-plow horsedrawn unit, the Mark 5, one-plow "Baby" tractor, the Mark 6 two-plow tractor shown here, and the Mark 10 four-plow crawler unit. The plowing units could be removed so that other implements could be used, and a belt pulley was also provided.

**Mark 10 tractor also known as the Tank-Tread X tractor**

For 1922 the equipment line included the Mark 10 shown here. It was also known as the Tank-Tread X tractor. This unit had a 25-50 horsepower rating; the higher horsepower was required to operate the whirling tines which pulverized the soil as it left the plows. This machine sold for $3,750, compared to $1,750 for the Princess Pat model of 1919. The company does not appear in the trade directories after 1924.

# Seager Engine Works
*Lansing, Michigan*

**Seager tractor**

In 1910 Seager Engine Works, manufacturers of the Olds gasoline engines, came out with the Seager tractor. It was rated at 20 drawbar horsepower and used a four-cylinder engine. The tractor weighed 6,000 pounds and had two forward and two reverse speeds. Few specific details of this tractor have been found.

# Sears, Roebuck & Company
*Chicago, Illinois*

**Handiman garden tractor**

About 1930 Sears & Roebuck introduced their Handiman garden tractor. It was equipped with a 2-1/2 horsepower gasoline engine having a 2-1/2 inch bore and stroke. Ordinarily it was furnished with battery ignition and priced at $149.50, but in 1932 it was also available with magneto ignition at a price of $165. This unit weighed 400 pounds.

**Sears Bradley General Purpose tractor**

Few details have been found on the Sears Bradley General Purpose tractor. It is listed briefly in the 1932 catalog, but reference is given to a special tractor catalog detailing this machine. It was available with a single-row or a two-row cultivator. The rear wheel tread width was adjustable to accommodate various row spacings.

**Sears & Roebuck conversion attachment**

During the 1930s Sears & Roebuck offered a conversion attachment whereby any Ford Model T or Model A could be converted into a small utility tractor. Priced at $100 this conversion was capable of ground speeds up to 2-1/2 mph. Various tillage equipment was also available for this unit.

For 1938 Sears & Roebuck offered the Sears New Economy tractor. Priced at $495, it was powered by a rebuilt Ford Model A engine. This tractor could be furnished on steel wheels, with

**Sears New Economy tractor**

rubber tires being an extra-cost option. Various cultivators and implements were available for use with this tractor.

**Sears Handiman garden tractor**

By 1942 the Sears Handiman garden tractor was available in an entirely new design that featured rubber tires and weighed only 220 pounds. It was powered by a 1-horsepower Briggs & Stratton engine, and was available with numerous implements and attachments.

**David Bradley Super Power garden tractor**

The David Bradley Super Power garden tractor was tested at Nebraska in 1953. Test No. 515 indicates a maximum of 6.7 belt horsepower for this unit. It was powered by a Continental Red Seal engine having a single cylinder with a 2-1/4 x 2 inch bore and stroke.

**David Bradley Tri-Trac tractor**

In 1954 Sears & Roebuck offered their David Bradley Tri-Trac tractor. It used a 6 horsepower Wisconsin engine having a 2-7/8 x 2-3/4 inch bore and stroke. The Tri-Trac weighed 894 pounds and had a cultivating clearance of nearly 20

inches. Sears & Roebuck offered an extensive number of garden tractors in the 1940s and 1950s but we have not had access to their special tractor catalogs during our research.

## Self-Contained Power Plow Company
*Chapman, Kansas*

Trade reports indicate that this firm was in operation in 1913 but no details or illustrations of this machine have been found.

## Sexton Tractor Company
*Albert Lea, Minnesota*

No information has been found regarding this company, but it appears that a company of similar name at Asbury Park, New Jersey was led by the same George L. Sexton; the latter was the moving force behind this company.

**Sexton 12-25 tractor**

In 1918 the Sexton 12-25 tractor appeared. This tractor was designed around an Erd four-cylinder engine having a 4 x 6 inch bore and stroke. Westinghouse electric starting and lighting equipment came as an extra-cost option. After a very short time the Sexton tractor disappeared from the scene.

# S.G. Stevens Company
*Duluth, Minnesota*

**Stevens Auto Cultivator**

Early in 1913 the Stevens Auto Cultivator was announced; it was the invention of S.G. Stevens. The cultivating units revolved about an axis, and were powered by a 5 horsepower motorcycle engine. Little else is known of this machine; it is assumed that production lasted for only a short time.

# Sharpe Mfg. Company
*Joliet, Illinois*

**Sharpe tractor**

In 1917 Sharpe offered this design, noting their heavy use of ball and roller bearings in their tractor. Few details can be found regarding the Sharpe tractor; apparently it was in production for only a short time.

# Shaw-Enochs Tractor Company
*Minneapolis, Minnesota*

In 1918 the Midget Tractor Co. was organized at Minneapolis. By November of the following year

**Shawnee 6-12 tractor**

the company was renamed as Shaw-Enochs Tractor Co. The Shawnee 6-12 shown here was a 2,600 pound machine that was powered by a four-cylinder LeRoi engine having a 3-1/8 x 4-1/2 inch bore and stroke. In this instance it is connected to a cultivator, but the Shawnee could be used with a variety of implements.

**Shawnee 9-18 model tractor**

During 1919 the Shaw-Enochs tractor line included the Shawnee 9-18 model. This one was powered by a four-cylinder Gray engine having a 3-1/2 x 5 inch bore and stroke. This 9-18 is shown with a road grader, and from this design came the Shawnee Township Road Boss road grader. Its success prompted the firm to discontinue farm tractors in 1921 and concentrate solely on road building machinery.

# Shaw Mfg. Company
*Galesburg, Kansas*

By 1930 the Shaw Du-All garden tractor was being actively promoted and sold. This early model used a Briggs & Stratton one-cylinder engine, but

**Shaw Du-All garden tractor**

few specifics have been found on this early model. Shaw Mfg. Company apparently started in the manufacturing business already in 1903.

**Shaw tractor conversion unit**

During the 1930s Shaw promoted their tractor conversion units, using the Ford Model A or Model T engine and parts of the chassis. These units were offered for a number of years, and were fairly successful. Of course, much of the success laid with the condition of the engine that was used and the skill of the mechanic assembling this unit.

In 1934 the Shaw Du-All T45D tractor appeared. It was built in 2, 3 and 4 horsepower sizes. All models were equipped with Briggs & Stratton engines. These tractors were available with steel wheels or rubber tires; in 1934 the 4 horsepower unit on steel wheels was priced at

**Shaw Du-all T45D tractor**

$221.50. By 1936 these tractors became known as the Du-All Model D tractors; they remained on the market until about 1940.

**Shaw HY-8 tractor**

The Shaw HY-8 tractor first appeared about 1940. This small tractor used a Wisconsin single-cylinder engine having a 3-5/8 x 4 inch bore and stroke. A belt pulley was standard equipment. The plow shown here was one of many optional implements.

**Model H2 Peppy Pal garden tractor**

Several models of Peppy Pal garden tractors appeared about 1945. One was the 1-1/2 horsepower model; it was available with several different attachments. The Model H2 Peppy Pal offered many features, including an adjustable tread width ranging from 18 to 28 inches.

**Shaw T24 riding tractor**

About 1954 the Shaw T24 riding tractor appeared. This model was offered with the choice of 2-1/2, 2-3/4, 3 and 3-1/2 horsepower engines. A mower attachment was a $45 extra, and various other implements were available, such as a cultivator, a plow, and a snowplow. At this time Shaw also offered a Model D24 riding mower, and a Model D32 riding mower; it was equipped with a 6 horsepower engine.

## Shaw Tractor Company
*Minneapolis, Minnesota*
No information available.

## John Shelburne
*New London, Missouri*
A trade note of 1912 indicates that this individual or firm was beginning to build a new tractor design. No other information has been found.

## Shelby Truck & Tractor Company
*Shelby, Ohio*

**Shelby 9-18 tractor**

In 1919 the Shelby 9-18 tractor appeared. It was powered by a four-cylinder Waukesha engine having a 3-3/4 x 5-1/4 inch bore and stroke. In 1921 this model was given a 10-20 horsepower rating, but production ended shortly thereafter.

**Shelby 15-30 tractor**

Between 1919 and 1921 Shelby produced their 15-30 tractor. Weighing 5,000 pounds, it was equipped with a four-cylinder Erd engine having a 4-3/4 x 6 inch bore and stroke. Little is known of the company, despite the fact that they operated for at least three years.

# Sheldon Engine & Sales Company

*Waterloo, Iowa*

**Sheldon Three Purpose Tractor Attachment**

During World War One the Sheldon Three Purpose Tractor Attachment appeared. This device was intended primarily for use with the Ford Model T, but could also be adapted to other automobiles. The complete conversion kit was priced at $175. The company rated this machine to have a drawbar pull of 900 pounds, assuming that the Model T engine was in good condition.

# R. H. Sheppard Company

*Hanover, Pennsylvania*

**Sheppard SD-1 tractor**

Sheppard began building their own diesel engines in 1940. During World War Two the firm developed several sizes and styles of diesel engines using the unique Sheppard design. The Sheppard SD-1 tractor first appeared about 1948. Weighing 1,100 pounds, it was equipped with a Sheppard single-cylinder diesel engine having a 3 x 4 inch bore and stroke. This tractor was apparently out of production by 1950.

**Sheppard SD-2 Diesel tractor**

The Sheppard SD-2 Diesel tractor first emerged about 1948, with production continuing for about ten years. This model used a two-cylinder diesel engine of Sheppard's own design. Rated at 1,650 rpm, it used a 4-1/4 x 5 inch bore and stroke for a displacement of 141.9 ci.

**Sheppard SD-3 Diesel tractor**

A three-cylinder Model 6B Sheppard engine was used in the SD-3 Diesel tractor. The design was built around a 4 x 5 inch bore and stroke for a displacement of 188.5 ci. Production of the Sheppard tractors continued into the late 1950s.

**Sheppard SDO-3 model**

In addition to standard row-crop farm tractors, Sheppard also provided various Industrial and Orchard models, including this SDO-3 model. It was essentially built over the SD-3 chassis but included the necessary fenders, hood and other accessories for orchard and vineyard work.

**Sheppard SD-4 Diesel tractor**

Production of the SD-4 Sheppard Diesel began about 1948 and continued into the late 1950s. This model used the company's own Model 16, four-cylinder diesel engine; it had a 319 cid. Rated speed was 1,650 rpm. A Sheppard-built transmission was used in the Sheppard tractors; the SD-4 had ten forward speeds. Another important feature was the independent hydraulic system, introduced at a time when few farm tractors were thus equipped. The engine in this tractor used a 4-1/2 x 5 inch bore and stroke. Sheppard also built a conversion unit whereby the Farmall M and selected other models could be converted to Sheppard Diesel power.

# P. E. Shirk
*Blue Ball, Pennsylvania*

**Shirk tractor**

By 1911 the Shirk tractor was on the market. It consisted of a traction chassis which P. E. Shirk had designed. In this instance, a Woodpecker engine from Middletown Machine Co., Middle-

town, Ohio serves as the power plant. It was capable of 8 belt horsepower. Probably the chassis could be fitted with other engines as well.

**Shirk gasoline tractor**

The Shirk gasoline tractor was capable of plowing and various other farm duties. Although the 8 horsepower model is shown here, the company was prepared to furnish this machine in 4, 6, 10, 12 and 15 horsepower sizes. Little is heard of the Shirk tractor after its 1911 announcement.

# Short Turn Tractor Company
*Bemidji, Minnesota*

**Short Turn 20-30 tractor**

Short Turn Tractor Co. was organized in 1916, and by 1918 a factory was established at Bemidji. The Short Turn 20-30 of that year was built with a four-cylinder engine having a 4 x 6 inch bore and stroke. Production continued into 1920, and during the last year of production the Short Turn got a larger engine with a 4-3/4 inch bore. At that time it sold for $1,500.

## Siemon Tractor Corporation
*Buffalo, New York*

**Siemon's Iron Horse Tractor**

During 1919 Siemon's Iron Horse Tractor was demonstrated at various points, and company advertising noted that "The Siemon-McCloskey Tractor has already created a sensation in many parts of the world." Aside from some advertisements, little is known of this tractor; it is not believed that production lasted more than a short time.

## Silver King
*Plymouth, Ohio*

See: Fate-Root-Heath; Mountain State Engineering

## Simplex Tractor Company
*Minneapolis, Minnesota*

## Simplex Tractor Company
*Wichita, Kansas*

**Simplex 15-30 tractor**

The Simplex tractor first appeared in 1914. Rated as a 15-30, it weighed 5,500 pounds and sold for $950. The Simplex was displayed at various fairs and expositions into 1917. Late that year the company folded up at Minneapolis and reorganized itself at Wichita, Kansas. Little came of the Wichita venture.

## Simplicity Mfg. Company
*Port Washington, Wisconsin*

**Turner Simplicity tractor**

Simplicity Mfg. Co. began as Turner Mfg. Company in 1911. This firm built Simplicity gasoline engines in many sizes, and began building the Turner Simplicity tractor in 1915. The company was liquidated in 1920 and the following year Simplicity Mfg. Co. was organized. Simplicity began in the garden tractor business by building a garden tractor for Montgomery, Ward & Co. in 1937. From this came the extensive Simplicity garden tractor line. Shown here is the Model L 2 horsepower tractor of about 1950.

**Model M 3 hp garden tractor**

During the 1950s the Simplicity garden tractor line expanded considerably, and included the

Model M 3 horsepower size shown here. In 1961 Simplicity began building garden tractors for Allis-Chalmers, and in 1965 Allis-Chalmers bought out the Simplicity factories.

|         | **1**  | **2**  | **3**  | **4**  |
|---------|--------|--------|--------|--------|
| Model M | $600   | $500   | $250   | $125   |

# Sioux City Foundry & Mfg. Company
*Sioux City, Iowa*

**Sioux City Foundry & Mfg. Company tractor**

In 1911 this lightweight tractor appeared. The company noted that it was an experimental model, and that full production had not yet begun. Apparently it never got into production, since nothing further is heard of the machine. The engine was a two-cycle model built by Ottumwa-Moline Pump Co. at Ottumwa, Iowa.

# S. K. & S. Company
*El Paso, Illinois*

This firm developed the Jim Dandy Motor Cultivator about 1916, and subsequently General Motors bought it out. The latter then redesigned the Jim Dandy and produced the Samson Iron Horse cultivator.

# Smathers Mfg. Company
*Brevard, North Carolina*

In 1948 Smathers was building the Inexco garden tractor, also known as the Acme. Inexco Tractor

**Inexco garden tractor**

Co. was the exclusive foreign distributor, and it appears that the majority of production was for export. The Inexco used a Clinton Model 1100 engine, capable of about 3 horsepower. Total weight of this machine was 500 pounds.

# Smith Form-A-Truck Company
*Chicago, Illinois*

**Smith Form-A-Tractor**

About 1920 the Smith Form-A-Tractor appeared. It was a sister device to the Smith Form-A-Truck; the latter was intended to convert an automobile into a light truck. Numerous tractor attachments were available in the 1915-1930 period, but only a few continued into the 1930s.

# Smith Tractor Mfg. Company
*Harvey, Illinois*

In 1911 this company was bought out by Ohio Steel Wagon Company at Wapokoneta, Ohio. Little else is known of either firm.

## H. J. Smith Tractor Company
*Minneapolis, Minnesota*

In 1915 it was announced that this firm would begin building tractors at Minneapolis. No other information has been located.

## Smith & Sons
*Kansas City, Missouri*

No information available.

## Sollberger Engineering Company
*Marshall, Texas*

**Sollberger C-24 tractor**

In 1948 Sollberger listed their C-24 tractor. It was also known as the Laughlin C-24 tractor, and was sold by Laughlin Engineering under that title until the early 1950s. The C-24 used a Continental F162, four-cylinder engine. It was designed with a 3-7/16 x 4-3/8 inch bore and stroke.

## South Texas Tractor Company
*Houston, Texas*

This firm was incorporated in 1917 but no other information is available.

## Southern Corn Belt Tractor Company
*Sioux Falls, South Dakota*

Organized in 1916, this company displayed their tractor at the 1917 Tractor Demonstration at Atchison, Kansas. The company was building the Corn Belt 7-18 tractor. Priced at $750, it weighed 3,700 pounds. It was powered by a Gile two-cylinder engine having a 5 x 6-1/2 inch bore and stroke. No illustrations of the Corn Belt 7-18 have been found.

## Southern Motor Mfg. Company Ltd.
*Houston, Texas*

**Ranger Motor Cultivator**

The Ranger Motor Cultivator was developed in 1918. Initially it was given a 6-12 horsepower rating, but this was soon raised to an 8-16 rating. Southern apparently remained in business until 1923 or 1924, and then disappeared from the scene. The Ranger 8-16 sold for $1,100.

## Southern Tractor Mfg. Corporation
*Camden, South Carolina*

This firm is listed as the manufacturer of the Southern garden tractor in 1953, but no other information has been found.

## Speedex Tractor Company
*Ravenna, Ohio*

See: Pond Garden Tractor Company.

# Springfield Boiler Mfg. Company
*Springfield, Illinois*

No information available for this company.

# Springfield Gas Engine Company
*Springfield, Ohio*

This company was listed as a tractor manufacturer in the 1906-1910 period, but no illustrations of the Springfield tractors have been found. The company was a well known manufacturer of gasoline engines.

# Square Deal Mfg. Company
*Delaware, Ohio*

This firm is listed as a tractor manufacturer in 1909 but no other information has been located.

# Square Turn Tractor Company
*Norfolk, Nebraska*

**Square Turn 18-35 tractor**

In December 1917 Square Turn Tractor Co. was organized from the Kenney-Colwell Co., also of Norfolk. The Square Turn 18-35 was powered by a four-cylinder Climax engine having a 5 x 6-1/2 inch bore and stroke. A 3-bottom Oliver plow came as standard equipment, and the friction drive transmission eliminated clutch, transmission gears and differential. Total weight of the tractor was 7,800 pounds, and in 1920 it sold for $1,875. The company was sold at a sheriff's sale in 1925.

| | 1 | 2 | 3 | 4 |
|---|---|---|---|---|
| Square Turn — | — | — | — | $10,000 |

# Standard-Detroit Tractor Company
*Detroit, Michigan*

**Standard-Detroit tractor**

In 1916 the Standard-Detroit tractor appeared. Rated at 10 drawbar and 20 belt horsepower, the Standard-Detroit was equipped with a four-cylinder engine having a 3-1/4 x 5 inch bore and stroke. Production of this tractor only continued for a couple of years.

**Tracford Tractor conversion attachment**

The Tracford tractor conversion attachment first appeared about 1916 and remained on the market for several years. It was one of many tractor conversion kits available at the time, and was built especially for the Ford Model T automobile chassis.

## Standard Engine Company
*Minneapolis, Minnesota*

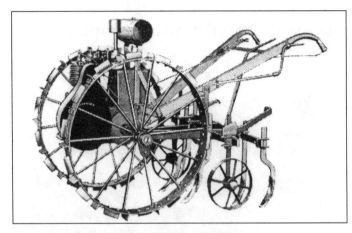

**Standard 3-1/2 model garden tractor**

Standard began building garden tractors in the early 1930s. For 1933 the Standard 3-1/2 model used the company's own engine having a 3-inch bore and stroke. This unit weighed 300 pounds and retailed at $219. Ignition was by battery and timer, but a magneto could be supplied at extra cost.

**Walsh tractor**

At an undetermined point, Standard took over the Walsh Garden Tractor Co. and continued building and selling the Walsh tractor. It was quite similar in design to the Standard 3-1/2

model. A confusing picture of makes and models emerged from Standard into the 1950s. These also included the Standard Twin and the Viking garden tractors.

| | 1 | 2 | 3 | 4 |
|---|---|---|---|---|
| Walsh | $750 | $500 | $350 | $250 |
| Viking Twin | $1,200 | $950 | $600 | $350 |
| Standard Twin | $1,200 | $950 | $600 | $350 |
| Viking Single | $1,500 | $1,000 | $800 | $450 |

## Standard Mfg. & Sales Company
*Lebanon, Indiana*

This firm is listed in 1953 as the builder of the Standard-Bantam tractor, but no photographs or specifications have been located.

## Standard Tractor Company
*St. Paul, Minnesota*

**Standard 22-45 tractor**

Originally, this firm was organized in 1913 as Humber-Anderson Co. In 1915 the company moved to Willmar, Minnesota and operated as Willmar Tractor Co. Standard Tractor Co. emerged in 1917, and continued building the Standard 22-45 into 1920. Originally this model was built as the 20-40. It weighed 8,000 pounds and was designed around a Waukesha four-cylinder engine having a 4-3/4 x 6-3/4 inch bore and stroke.

## Standard Tractor Company

*New York, New York*

This firm was organized in 1914 to manufacture tractors, but no other information has been found.

## Star Tractor Company

*Findlay, Ohio*

**Star 5-10 tractor**

Developed in 1917, the Star 5-10 tractor made its appearance in 1918. This small tractor used a LeRoi four-cylinder engine having a 3-1/8 x 4-1/2 inch bore and stroke. In 1919 Indiana Tractor Company took over Star Tractor Company.

## E. G. Staude Mfg. Company

*St. Paul, Minnesota*

**Staude Mak-a-Tractor**

The Staude Mak-a-Tractor first appeared in 1918 and remained on the market for several years. Priced at $225, this conversion unit was designed especially for the Ford Model T automobile.

## Steam Tractor & Auto Mfg. Company

*Sioux City, Iowa*

About 1912 this firm attempted to get into the tractor business with a special steam tractor design, but apparently it never got past the experimental stage. No other information has been found.

## Stearns Motor Mfg. Company

*Ludington, Michigan*

**Stearns Model Q 15-35 tractor**

Stearns bought out Gile Engine & Tractor Co. in 1919 and began producing the Stearns Model Q 15-35 tractor. It was essentially the same as the Gile Model Q 15-35 of the previous year. The four-cylinder Stearns engine used a 4-3/4 x 6-1/2 inch bore and stroke. The 15-35 weighed 6,800 pounds. Production continued for only a short time.

## Steel King Motor Plow Company

*Detroit, Michigan*

**Steel King Motor Plow**

During 1914 the Steel King Motor Plow appeared. The rear-mounted plows were detachable so that the tractor could be used for other drawbar work. Rated as a 9-18 tractor, the Steel King was priced at $950. Production continued for only a short time.

## Chas. H. Stehling Company

*Milwaukee, Wisconsin*

In 1948 this company was listed as supplying 'repairs only' for the Dependable garden tractors. No other information has been located.

## Steiger Tractor Company

*Fargo, North Dakota*

This volume carries the history of the farm tractor into the 1950s. However, Steiger Tractor Company began operations in 1957-1958 when Douglass and Maurice Steiger built their first prototype model. Their original four-wheel-drive design was powered with a 238 horsepower Detroit Diesel engine. Subsequently this machine logged over 10,000 hours of farm duty. From this model came an extensive line of Steiger tractor models, beginning in the mid-1960s.

## Sterling Engine Works Ltd.

*Winnipeg, Manitoba*

**Sterling 12-24 tractor**

During 1916 the Sterling 12-24 tractor was offered to the market. This $1,170 tractor weighed 5,400 pounds, and was sold direct to the farmer. Sterling offered to pay the travel expenses for anyone wishing to come to Win-

nipeg and inspect the new tractor; this was a novel approach to selling tractors. Aside from their 1916 advertising, little else has been found on this tractor.

## Sterling Machine & Stamping Company

*Wellington, Ohio*

**Wellington tractor**

In 1920 Sterling offered their Wellington tractor in two sizes. The Wellington F 12-22 tractor shown here sold for $1,600. It was equipped with an Erd four-cylinder engine having a 4 x 6 inch bore and stroke. The Wellington B 16-30 tractor used a Chief four-cylinder engine with a 4-3/4 x 6 inch bore and stroke. It weighed 5,000 pounds. No other information on the company has been found.

## Stewart Tractor Company

*Waupaca, Wisconsin*

See: Topp-Stewart

## Stinson Tractor Company

*Minneapolis, Minnesota*

The Stinson 15-30 tractor made its first appearance in 1917. This model used an Erd four-cylinder engine with a 4-1/2 x 5 inch bore and stroke,

**Stinson 15-30 tractor**

but it could also be equipped with a Herschell-Spillman V-8 engine.

**Stinson 18-36 tractor**

For 1918 the Stinson tractor gained an 18-36 horsepower rating. In 1917 the Stinson was manufactured by Gile Engine Co. at Ludington, Michigan. The 1918 model was built by Imperial Machinery Company at Minneapolis. This model used a four-cylinder Beaver engine having a 4-3/4 x 6 inch bore and stroke.

**Stinson Heavy Duty 18-36 tractor**

In 1920 the Stinson Heavy Duty 18-36 tractor appeared. From then until production ended in 1922, this was the only model in the Stinson tractor line. Numerous changes were made in the company organization, including a move to Superior, Wisconsin about 1922, just at the end of production.

## St. Marys Machinery Company
*St. Marys, Ohio*

This company is listed as a tractor manufacturer about 1910, and actually may have mounted some of their stationary engines to a traction chassis, but no illustrations have been found.

## Stockton Tractor Company
*Stockton, California*

**Stockton Model A 8-16 tractor**

In 1920 the Stockton Model A 8-16 tractor appeared. Very little is known of this model, probably because it was on the market for only a short time.

**Stockton Model B Sure-Grip tractor**

The Stockton Model B Sure-Grip tractor made its debut in 1920. Apparently the Model A and Model B tractors both used a four-cylinder Herschell-Spillman engine with a 3-1/2 x 5 inch bore and stroke. The company does not appear in the 1921 directories.

## Stone Tractor Company
*Texarkana, Texas*

**Stone 20-40 tractor**

In 1917 Stone Tractor Co. was organized, and began building the Stone 20-40 tractor. Weighing 5,450 pounds, it was built with a Beaver four-cylinder engine having a 4-1/2 x 6 inch bore and stroke. The 20-40 sold for $1,850. Production continued until about 1920.

## Stone Tractor Mfg. Company
*Quincy, Illinois*

This firm was incorporated in 1917, presumably to manufacture a new tractor design, but no other information has been found.

## Stover Engine Works
*Freeport, Illinois*

**Stover tractor**

In 1906 Stover shipped three of these 40 horsepower tractors to Argentina. This model used a single-cylinder Stover engine having a 12-1/2 x 18 inch bore and stroke. Between 1906 and 1911 Stover built a handful of these tractors. The last one was a 30 horsepower model, built in 1911.

**Stover prototype**

Stover built this prototype in 1915. Aside from the photograph, nothing is known of the tractor, even from the extensive Stover records still in the author's possession. Compared to numerous other tractors of the day, this one was fairly attractive, and given the size of the company, could have probably been sold in quantity. However, an internal company photograph is the only evidence that this tractor ever existed.

## St. Paul Machinery & Mfg. Company
*St. Paul, Minnesota*

**St. Paul 24-40 tractor**

Organized in 1910, St. Paul Machinery & Mfg. began building tractors shortly after that time. By 1912 the St. Paul had taken the form shown here, and was equipped with a four-cylinder engine capable of about 35 belt horsepower. The mounted plows came as standard equipment, and were detachable for other drawbar work. Production of this tractor continued as late as 1917. By that time the tractor had a 24-40 horsepower rating.

## Strite Tractor Company
*Minneapolis, Minnesota*

Already in 1913 the Strite 3-Point tractor was on the market. It was thus named because of its three-wheel chassis configuration. By 1917 this model had an 18-36 horsepower rating and used

**Strite 3-Point tractor**

a Waukesha four-cylinder engine with a 4-1/2 x 6-3/4 inch bore and stroke. It was priced at $1,485.

**Strite 12-25 tractor**

In 1919 the Strite 12-25 tractor appeared. At this point, Strite Tractor Co. had its offices in New York City, but the connection between the Minneapolis and the New York offices has not been established. The 12-25 used a four-cylinder engine with a 3-1/2 x 5-1/4 inch bore and stroke. Production of this model apparently ended by 1921.

## Stroud Motor Mfg. Association
*San Antonio, Texas*

During 1919 Stroud developed their 16-30 tractor. It was powered by a Climax four-cylinder engine having a 5 x 6-1/2 inch bore and stroke. Curiously, the Stroud 16-30 embodied most of the features that would be essential for the soon-

**Stroud 16-30 tractor**

to-come Farmall row-crop tractor. For reasons unknown, they did not put these into practice, or perhaps did not remain in the tractor business long enough to implement them.

## Stuts-Mar Tractor Company
*San Jose, California*

This firm is listed as a tractor manufacturer in 1918 and 1919, but no other information has been found.

## Sullivan Tractor Company
*Oakland, California*

**Sullivan 8-28 tractor**

An industry listing of 1915 lists the Sullivan 8-28 tractor. It used a four-cylinder Beaver engine and weighed 4,000 pounds. The engine carried a 4-3/4 x 5-1/2 inch bore and stroke. In 1916 this tractor listed at $1,250. Production apparently ended after 1916.

## Sumner Iron Works
*Everett, Washington*

This company is listed as a tractor manufacturer in 1921 but no other information has been found.

## Sun Tractor Company
*Columbus, Ohio*

**Sun 8-16 tractor**

About 1916 the Sun 8-16 tractor appeared. It was of the universal design, meaning that it hinged in the middle and the driver was seated on the towed implement. This model remained on the market for only a short time.

## Super-Diesel Tractor Company
*Manhattan, New York*

In 1917 Edward A. Rumely and others incorporated the Super-Diesel Tractor Co. Rumely had formerly been the moving force at M. Rumely Company, builders of the Rumely OilPull tractors. Rumely had been a close friend of Rudolph Diesel and others. As a result, Rumely was convinced that diesel power was ultimately the way to go in the tractor business. Unfortunately, Rumely's ideas were ahead of his time and technology, so the Super-Diesel never made it into production.

## Super-Trac Incorporated
*Chicago, Illinois*

This company is listed as the manufacturer of the Super-Trac tractor in 1948, but no other information has been found.

## Superior Traction Company
*Duluth, Minnesota*

This firm announced in 1910 that they would be building a new tractor, but no other information has been found.

# Superior Tractor Company
*Cleveland, Ohio*

**Superior 15-30 tractor**

The Superior 15-30 was developed in 1919 and remained on the market until about 1922. This model was powered by a four-cylinder Beaver engine having a 4-3/4 x 6 inch bore and stroke. Weighing 4,500 pounds, it had two forward speeds.

# Sweeney Tractor Company
*Kansas City, Missouri*

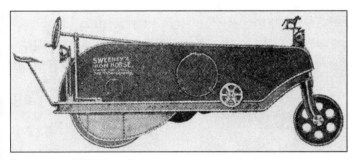

**Sweeney 15-25 tractor**

During 1916 the Sweeney tractor appeared. Sweeney was also operating a tractor school so that interested parties could learn how to operate and repair tractors. Rated as a 15-25, the Sweeney was built for only a short time.

# SWH Engineering Company
*Cleveland, Ohio*

Little information is available on the SWH 15-30 tractor. Introduced in 1919, it apparently left the market the same year. The 15-30 was equipped

**SWH 15-30 tractor**

with a four-cylinder engine having a 4-3/4 x 6 inch bore and stroke. It weighed 4,800 pounds and had two forward speeds.

# Sylvester Mfg. Company Ltd.
*Lindsay, Ontario*

**Sylvester auto thresher**

In 1907 Sylvester Mfg. Co. developed their first auto thresher, or in other words, a self-propelled threshing machine. This machine differed from most other auto threshers because it was capable of heavy drawbar work, while the rest were content to just move themselves from place to place.

Sylvester began building farm implements at Lindsay, Ontario in 1876 and began building gasoline engines in 1902. With the 1907 introduction of the auto thresher came the announcement of

**Sylvester gasoline traction engine**

the Sylvester gasoline traction engines. These were powered by a two-cylinder opposed engine, but few details have been found.

**Sylvester tractor**

By 1910 the Sylvester tractors had been modified somewhat, although the basic design remained the same. These tractors were offered until 1914 when the company reverted back to its farm equipment line. In 1920 the firm quit the farm equipment business to concentrate on railway equipment and track cars. The firm remained in operation until 1956.

## Synmotor Company
*Magnolia, New Jersey*

No information has been found on this company.

# T

## Taylor-Jenkins Tractor Company
*Jonesboro, Arkansas*

In 1918 this company was listed as the manufacturer of the 30-40 TJ tractor. No other information has been found.

## Temple Pump Company
*Chicago, Illinois*

**Temple Pump tractor**

This firm went back to the 1850s in the pump business, and began building gasoline engines by 1903. In 1908 the company offered a tractor, noting in their advertising that they had been building their 'traction engine' for some time. It was built in 5, 7, 10, 15, 20, 30, and 45 horsepower sizes, the largest two being of four-cylinder design, and the others being of two-cylinder design.

## Termaat & Monahan Company
*Oshkosh, Wisconsin*

In 1913 Termaat & Monahan offered small tractor with a 7 horsepower engine of their own manufacture. Weighing 4,200 pounds, it had two forward speeds. The company also indicated that larger engines could be mounted on the same chassis if desired. Termaat & Monahan was a sizable gasoline engine builder. The company went into receivership in 1917 but recovered and subsequently built the Wiscona Pep engines.

## Texas Motor Car Association
*Fort Worth, Texas*

A trade note of 1918 indicates that this firm was organized to "build a tractor." The company was formed in December 1917 to build the Texan automobile, but the latter never made it to the market until 1920, and was out of the market by 1922. It is assumed that if in fact, the tractor was ever built, it met the same fate.

## Texas Tractor & Farm Machinery Company
*Amarillo, Texas*

In 1917 this firm was organized to build a farm tractor, but no further information has been found.

## Texas Truck & Tractor Company
*Dallas, Texas*

This firm is said to have built an assembled automobile in 1920. The Wharton Pull 12-22 tractor was listed from this company in 1920. It used a four-cylinder engine with a 4 x 6 inch bore and stroke. The Wharton Pull weighed 3,700 pounds. No illustrations have been found.

# Thieman Harvester Company
*Albert City, Iowa*

**Thieman tractor**

In 1936 the first Thieman tractor appeared. This was actually a $185 tractor chassis to which the customer fitted a Ford Model A engine, driveshaft, and rear axle. The Thieman chassis could also be supplied for the 1928 Chevrolet or the Dodge Four. The Thieman chassis was sold until World War Two, when production was halted because of the war effort.

|         | 1 | 2      | 3 | 4 |
|---------|---|--------|---|---|
| Thieman | — | $2,100 | — | — |

# Thompson-Breese Company
*Wapokoneta, Ohio*

**Thompson-Breese tractor**

During 1911 Thompson-Breese was formed from the Ohio Steel Wagon Company. Their tractor was also announced that year, but few details have been found. It was powered by a two-cylinder opposed engine and was equipped with a rear-mounted plow.

# Thomson Machinery Company
*Thibodaux, Louisiana*

**Thomson UCD tractor**

The Thomson UCD tractor was originally built as the Allis-Chalmers Model U Cane Tractor. When production of this tractor ended in 1941, Allis-Chalmers apparently continued building the UC rear end for Thomson, and they in turn modified it suitably for a cane tractor. By the mid-1950s the UCD appeared with a GM 2-71 diesel engine.

**Thomson XTD four-wheel-drive tractor**

By the late 1950s Thomson Machinery Co. was offering their XTD four-wheel-drive tractor. Like the UCD, it was equipped with a General Motors 2-71 diesel engine. This 12,600 pound tractor included features such as four hydraulic brakes and an optional hydraulic system.

## Thorobred Tractor & Mfg. Company
*Mobridge, Ohio*

This company is listed as a tractor manufacturer in 1918, but no further information has been found.

## Three-P Auto Tractor Company
*Davenport, Iowa*

Three-P was incorporated in 1917 to manufacture tractors, but no other information has been found.

## Three Wheel Drive Tractor Company
*Indianapolis, Indiana*

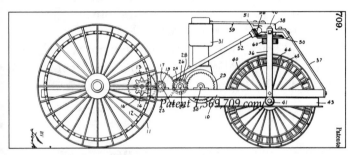

**Patent 1,369,709 copy**

In 1919 J. B. Schuman applied for a patent covering a three-wheel-drive tractor design. It was issued in February 1921, and assigned to the above company. Aside from the patent, nothing more has been found regarding this tractor or the company organized for its manufacture.

## Tiger Tractor Corporation
*Keyser, West Virginia*

**Tiger tractor**

In the late 1940s the Tiger tractor was being built by Inexco Tractor Company. However, by 1953

the Tiger was being produced by Tiger Tractor Corporation. The Tiger PTD6 shown here was built with a Briggs & Stratton Model 14 engine, capable of over 5 horsepower. Priced at $520, it was available with numerous attachments.

| | 1 | 2 | 3 | 4 |
|---|---|---|---|---|
| PTD 6 | $750 | $650 | $350 | $150 |

## Tillavator Company
*New York, New York*

**Tillavator DP55 rotary tiller**

By the late 1930s the Tillavator DP55 rotary tiller was on the market. It was designed with single-cylinder, two-cycle engine capable of 5 horsepower. The company was listed as a garden tractor manufacturer at least into the early 1950s.

| | 1 | 2 | 3 | 4 |
|---|---|---|---|---|
| Late models | — | — | $100 | — |

## Tillermobile Company
*Minneapolis, Minnesota*

**Tillermobile 2-6 garden tractor**

Tillermobile Company was organized in 1920, and offered the Tillermobile 2-6 garden tractor that same year. It used the company's own single-cylinder horizontal engine having a 4-inch bore and stroke. Weighing 625 pounds, it sold for $350. Production apparently ended soon after it began.

## Tioga Mfg. Company

*Philadelphia, Pennsylvania*

**Tioga 15-27 tractor**

Tioga Tractor Company apparently began operations at Philadelphia, Pennsylvania about 1920. Initially the Tioga 15-27 was equipped with a Wisconsin four-cylinder engine having a 4-1/2 x 6 inch bore and stroke. By 1923 the company had moved to Baltimore, Maryland, and by 1925 had begun building the Tioga 3, 18-32 tractor. It was of the same essential design, and even continued to use the same Wisconsin engine as the 15-27 model. Production ended in the late 1920s.

## Titan Truck & Tractor Company

*Milwaukee, Wisconsin*

This firm was organized in 1917 to build trucks and tractors. Before the year ended, the firm had dropped "Tractor" from the corporate name, probably indicating a hasty end to the tractor business. The company continued building trucks into the late 1920s.

## Tom Thumb Tractor Company

*Minneapolis, Minnesota*

**Thom Thumb 12-20 tractor**

Developed during 1915, the Tom Thumb 12-20 tractor featured a Waukesha four-cylinder engine with a 4-1/4 x 5-3/4 inch bore and stroke. This 4,500 pound tractor was propelled by a single rear-mounted track, and the two large front wheels gave a three-point chassis design. The firm was taken over by Federal Tractor Company in 1917.

## Topeka Farming & Machinery Company

*Topeka, Kansas*

No information has been found on this company.

## Topp-Stewart Tractor Company

*Clintonville, Wisconsin*

**Topp-Stewart tractor**

G.F. Stewart, a native of Antigo, Wisconsin, developed the principle of a four-wheel-drive tractor using conventional straight drive axles mounted on wagon-type (bolster) drive axles driven by conventional universal joint drive shafts front and rear. The bolster-type axles were used because this tractor featured four-wheel steer. That is, the front and rear axles were connected with cross chains that caused both axles to turn in opposite directions for a shorter turning radius. A Waukesha engine of 4-3/4 inch bore by 6-3/4 stroke, mounted conventionally, was used. Beceause of the axle arrangement the engine could not be cranked from the front and a disengageable bevel-gear system was devised to crank the engine from the left side and cranking counter-clockwise.

Lacking the financial resources to proceed with production in Antigo, Stewart moved to Waupaca, Wisconsin. Still in need of funding, the company received the investment it needed from Dr. Charles Topp of Clintonville, Wisconsin. At that point the company moved to Clintonville and was renamed the Topp-Stewart Tractor Company, and there it thrived until it was sold to the Atlas Tractor Company. Later the company ceased making tractors and became known as the Atlas Conveyor Company. It was later sold to the Rex-Nord Company of Milwaukee, Wisconsin, and continues to operate under that name today.

At no time was the Topp-Stewart Tractor Company associated with the FWD Auto Company of Clintonville.

**Topp-Stewart 30-45**

By 1918 the Topp-Stewart tractor was furnished with an upholstered seat and a styled hood. This tractor continued to use the same engine as before, giving it 30 drawbar and 45 belt horsepower. The 30-45 weighed 7,500 pounds and sold for $3,250.

# Toro Motor Company
*Minneapolis, Minnesota*

**Toro two-row power cultivator**

Toro Motor Co. announced its two-row power cultivator in 1918. It was powered by a LeRoi four-cylinder engine having a 3-1/8 x 4-1/2 inch bore and stroke. The "Toro" name reflected an earlier connection with the Bull Tractor Company; "toro" is the Spanish word for "bull."

**Toro cultivator**

An interesting play on words is noted on the radiator shell of this Toro cultivator of the 1920s. Splitting the word To-Ro also could be pronounced as "two-row" and that described the Toro cultivator exactly. During the 1920s this outfit sold for about $500. In September 1927 the Toro Motor Cultivator was sold to Advance-Rumely Thresher Company. The latter then revamped it as the Rumely DoAll Tractor.

During the 1920s Toro introduced their small Toro tractor, but unfortunately, no specifications for this unit have been found. The company also built engines for power lawn mowers, beginning in 1914. Self-propelled tractors for pulling mow-

**Toro tractor**

ers were added in 1919, and self-contained lawn mowers were added in 1925. Over the years the company continued with an extensive line of garden tractors and mowers.

# E. F. Townsend Tractor Company
*Los Angeles, California*

**EFT 6-12 crawler**

The EFT 6-12 crawler appeared in 1921 and remained on the market at least into 1922. This small tractor was powered by a Light four-cylinder engine having a 3-1/4 x 4-1/2 inch bore and stroke. Towed implements were attached to the trailing trucks.

# Townsend Mfg. Company
*Janesville, Wisconsin*

See: Fairbanks-Morse; La Crosse Boiler

Townsend began the tractor business by offering a 10-20 two-cylinder model in 1915. Known as the Bower City 10-20, it was sold until 1918 when it

**Bower City 10-20 tractor**

was replaced with the 12-25 tractor shown here. The 10-20 used a 6 x 8 inch bore and stroke; the two-cylinder 12-25 carried a 7 x 8 inch bore and stroke. In 1919 the 12-25 was re-rated as the 15-30 tractor. In Nebraska Test No. 63 of 1920 the 15-30 delivered nearly 18 drawbar horsepower.

|  | 1 | 2 | 3 | 4 |
|---|---|---|---|---|
| 12-25, 15-30 | — | $22,000 | — | — |

**Townsend 25-50 tractor**

By 1924 the Townsend line included the 25-50 and 30-60 tractors. Both were of two-cylinder design, and like previous Townsend models, used a boiler shell that served as the tractor frame as well as the engine radiator. The 25-50 carried an 8-1/2 x 10 inch bore and stroke, while the 30-60 was designed with a 9-1/2 x 12 inch bore and stroke.

|  | 1 | 2 | 3 | 4 |
|---|---|---|---|---|
| 25-50 | — | $35,000 | — | — |

**Townsend 20-40**

Production of the Townsend 20-40 began about 1923 and continued for several years after the company sold out in 1931. At that time, LaCrosse Boiler Co. at LaCrosse, Wisconsin bought out the firm and continued building several models until the onset of World War Two.

**Townsend 12-20**

During 1924 the Townsend 12-20 tractor appeared. This model used a two-cylinder engine having a 6 x 8 inch bore and stroke, as did the original 10-20 tractor of 1915. The 12-20 weighed 4,000 pounds. After the 1931 takeover by La Crosse Boiler Co., the 12-20 was re-rated upwards to a 12-25 tractor.

## Traction Engine Company
*Boyne City, Michigan*

In 1918 this company was incorporated to build the Heinze four-wheel-drive tractor. This design remained on the market into 1919. The company

**Heinze four-wheel-drive tractor**

used their own four-cylinder engine having a 4-1/4 x 6 inch bore and stroke. Weighing 4,000 pounds, this tractor retailed at $2,000.

## Traction Motor Corporation
*Kalamazoo, Michigan*

**Traction tractor**

In 1920 the Traction Motor tractor appeared. It was quite a modern tractor for the time, with electric starting and lights, a three-speed transmission, and full pressure lubrication to all engine bearings. The engine was a 65 horsepower V-8 from Herschell-Spillman. Nothing is known of this tractor after its 1920 appearance.

## Tractor Mfg. Company
*South Gate, California*

In 1947 and 1948 the Garden Master Model B garden tractor was listed in the trade directories. It was powered by a Briggs & Stratton Model B engine. Ratchet hubs were used for steering. This tractor weighed 525 pounds. No illustrations of the Garden Master have been found.

## Tractor Motor Corporation

*Kalamazoo, Michigan*

This company was incorporated in 1918 to build the "Hans" tractor, but no other information has been found.

## Tractor Producing Corporation

*New York, New York*

A 1918 trademark application from this firm indicates that they were building the Liberty tractor and first used this tradename on February 1, 1917. No other information has been found.

## Transit Thresher Company

*Minneapolis, Minnesota*

**Transit 35 tractor**

Transit Thresher Co. was organized in 1907 to build the Transit 35 (drawbar) horsepower tractor. The four-cylinder engine had a 6 x 8 inch bore and stroke. This was one of the first four-cylinder tractors to be built. In 1908 the firm was reorganized as Gas Traction Company. In 1912 the latter was bought out by Emerson-Brantingham Co., Rockford, Illinois.

## Traylor Engineering Company

*Cornwells, Pennsylvania*

**Traylor 6-12 tractor**

About 1920 the Traylor 6-12 tractor appeared. It remained on the market, virtually unchanged, until the late 1920s. A four-cylinder engine was used, in this instance it was the LeRoi with a 3-1/8 x 4-1/2 inch bore and stroke. A cultivator could be attached and removed at will.

## Trenam Tractor Company

*Stevens Point, Wisconsin*

Built in the 1917-1920 period, the Trenam 12-24 was fairly popular. This 4,500 pound tractor used various engines, including the Erd four-cylinder style with a 4 x 6 inch bore and stroke.

## Triple Tractor Truck Company

*Minneapolis, Minnesota*

**Triple tactor Truck**

During 1915 the Triple Tractor Truck appeared. It was an all-wheel-drive affair powered by a four cylinder engine. The latter used a 4-1/4 x 5-1/4 inch bore and stroke. It was also designed with a pulley for belt work. Nothing is heard of this design after its 1915 announcement.

## Triumph Truck & Tractor Company
*Kansas City, Missouri*

**Triumph 18-36 tractor**

During 1920 the Triumph 18-36 tractor was offered to the market. This model was built with a Climax four-cylinder engine having a 5 x 6-1/2 inch bore and stroke. Weighing 5,200 pounds, it sold for $2,250. Nothing is known of the Triumph after the 1920 listings.

## Trojan Unit Tractor Company
*Waterloo, Iowa*

In 1917 the Trojan Unit Tractor appeared. This design had a manufacturer's rating of 32 drawbar and 40 belt horsepower. Power came from a Waukesha Type L, four-cylinder engine having a

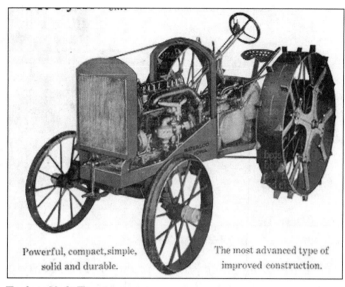

Powerful, compact, simple, solid and durable. The most advanced type of improved construction.

**Trojan Unit Tractor**

4-3/4 x 6-3/4 inch bore and stroke. The combination planetary transmission provided three forward speeds. Production of this tractor continued for only a short time.

## Turner Mfg. Company
*Port Washington, Wisconsin*

**Turner Simplicity 12-20 tractor**

Turner Mfg. Co. had a career as gas engine builders going back to 1902. In 1915 the Turner Simplicity 12-20 tractor appeared. Weighing 4,200 pounds, it sold for $1,350. Power came from a Waukesha four-cylinder engine having a 3-3/4 x 5-1/4 inch bore and stroke. Production of this model continued until about 1919.

**Turner Simplicity 14-25 tractor**

The Turner Simplicity 14-25 tractor first appeared about 1918. This model was of the same general design as the 12-20 but used a larger Buda four-cylinder engine; it was designed with a 4-1/4 x 5-1/2 inch bore and stroke. Turner went into receivership in 1920, and the following year it was reorganized as Simplicity Mfg. Company.

|  | **1** | **2** | **3** | **4** |
|---|---|---|---|---|
| 12-20 or 14-25 | | | | |
| | $8,500 | $6,000 | $4,000 | $2,000 |

## Twin Ports Steel & Machinery Company
*Superior, Wisconsin*

No information available on this company or its tractors.

## Two-Way Tractor Plow Company
*Denver, Colorado*

In 1921 this company was listed as a tractor manufacturer, but no other information is available.

# U

## Uncle Sam Tractor & Machinery Company
*Menasha, Wisconsin*

See: U. S. Tractor & Machinery Company

## Union Iron Works
*Minneapolis, Minnesota*

**New Gearless tractor**

In 1913 the New Gearless tractor appeared from Union Iron Works. This unique design transmitted power to the rear wheels without the use of gears, chains, and sprockets. It soon proved itself impractical, although it stayed on the market until about 1915. The New Gearless was rated at 12 belt horsepower.

## Union Tool Corporation
*Torrance, California*

The Union 12-25 crawler was listed in the tractor directories for 1921 and 1922. Quite possibly it was built for a time before and after those years. Power came from the company's own four-cylinder engine; it was designed with a 4-3/4 x 6 inch bore and stroke. Already in 1914 the com-

**Union 12-25 crawler**

pany came out with their Velvettread crawler, but no information has been found on this unit.

## Union Tractor Company
*San Francisco, California*

The Union Bulldog 18-30 crawler appeared for a short time in 1917 and then disappeared from the scene. Little is known of this tractor. In many instances, new tractors barely got past a few prototypes; sometimes they never got past the drawing board.

## Unit Power Wheel Company
*Cleveland, Ohio*

No information is available on this company.

## United States Tractor Corporation
*Dover, Delaware*

No information has been found on this company or its tractors except that it was organized and incorporated in 1917.

## United Tractor & Equipment Company
*Chicago, Illinois*

First appearing in 1929, the United was actually a Model U Allis-Chalmers except for the "United" logo appearing on the radiator. Over 30 independent implement makers and distributors

**United tractor**

banded together to form this company, but it marketed the United only into 1930.

## United Tractor Company
*Des Moines, Iowa*

This firm was incorporated in 1917 to build tractors, but no other information has been found.

## United Tractors Corporation
*New York, New York*

**7-12 Cultitractor**

About 1918 the 7-12 Cultitractor appeared. This small tractor used a Light Model H, four-cylinder engine having a 3-1/4 x 4-1/2 inch bore and stroke. Weighing 2,350 pounds, the Cultitractor retailed at $785. By 1920, essentially the same tractor was known as the Mohawk 8-16.

**Mohawk 8-16 tractor**

For 1921 the Mohawk 8-16 was slightly redesigned, but continued to use the same engine, chassis, and drivetrain as before. The company guaranteed that this tractor would pull at least 1,000 pounds on the drawbar, and deliver at least 16 horsepower in the belt. Production ended in the early 1920s.

## Unitractor Company
*Indianapolis, Indiana*

**Unitractor Model 47**

The Unitractor first appeared in June 1939. By 1947 it had taken the form shown here, with this being the Model 47. It was equipped with a Briggs & Stratton Model N engine having a 2-inch bore and stroke. Various equipment was available for the Unitractor.

## Unity Steel Tractor Company
*Antigo, Wisconsin*

This company was organized in 1914 by D. S. Stewart and others. Stewart was involved with the Topp-Stewart Tractor Company, as well as the Antigo Tractor Company of 1919.

## Universal Machinery Company
*Portland, Oregon*

**Universal garden tractor**

By 1948 the Universal garden tractor line was on the market. A typical model of 1950 was the Universal pattern shown here. This tractor was powered by a Lauson single-cylinder engine having a 2-1/4 inch bore and stroke. The Universal was available at least into the mid-1950s.

## Universal Mfg. Company
*Indianapolis, Indiana*

In 1953 this company is listed as the manufacturer of the McLean garden tractor. No other information is available.

| | 1 | 2 | 3 | 4 |
|---|---|---|---|---|
| McLean garden tractor | $1,500 | $1,200 | $850 | $500 |

## Universal Motor Company
*Newcastle, Indiana*

In 1910 the concept of a combination truck and tractor was not at all uncommon. The Universal was a unique combination outfit in several ways. First of all, a large six-cylinder engine was direct-coupled to a generator. Electric motors were con-

**Universal**

nected to each wheel, and operated from the generator. Production of this unit continued for only a short time.

## Universal Motor Truck & Traction Engine Company
*St. Louis, Missouri*

Although it was organized and incorporated in 1912, no other information has been found on this company.

## Universal Motor Company
*Oshkosh, Wisconsin*

**Universal motor cultivator**

Aside from a single illustration, almost nothing is known of the Universal motor cultivator of 1920. It used a single rear drive wheel, and the operator was seated to the very front of the machine.

## Universal Products Company
*Madison, Wisconsin*

Although organized and incorporated in 1919, no other information has been found for this company.

## Universal Tractor Company
*Brooklyn, New York*

No information available.

## Universal Tractor Company
*Indianapolis, Indiana*

Universal was organized and incorporated in 1913, but no other information has been found.

## Universal Tractor Company
*Stillwater, Minnesota*

**Universal tractor**

Production of the Universal tractor began at Crookston, Minnesota in July 1909. The following year the company was taken over by Northwest Thresher Company at Stillwater, and in 1912 the latter was bought out by M. Rumely Company, LaPorte, Indiana. At that point the Universal became the Rumely GasPull tractor. The Universal used a two-cylinder opposed engine having a 7-1/2 x 8 inch bore and stroke, and capable of 18 horsepower.

## Universal Tractor Mfg. Company
*Columbus, Ohio*

Beginning in 1914, Universal came out with a 10 horsepower motor cultivator outfit. It used a two-cylinder engine and was priced at $385. Moline Plow Company bought out the company in November 1915 for $150,000. Initially, Moline

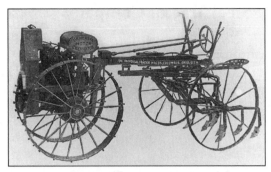

**Universal 10hp motor cultivator**

continued to build the two-cylinder design pioneered by Universal, but eventually converted to a larger four-cylinder model.

|                | __1__   | __2__   | __3__   | __4__   |
|----------------|---------|---------|---------|---------|
| 10hp cultivator | $8,000  | $7,000  | $5,000  | $2,000  |

## Universal Tractor Mfg. Company
*Newcastle, Indiana*

The beginnings of this company are unknown, but in 1913 Universal went into receivership, and late that year, merged with Lawter Tractor Company, also of Newcastle.

## Universal Tractors Ltd.
*Bartonville, Ontario*

**Universal garden tractor**

In 1947 the Universal garden tractor was listed; however, it is unknown if the company built other models. The Universal was equipped with a Briggs & Stratton NPR-6 engine having a 2-inch bore and stroke. Total weight was 200 pounds.

## U. S. Farming & Machinery Company
*Minneapolis, Minnesota*

No information available on this company.

## U. S. Tractor & Machinery Company
*Menasha, Wisconsin*

**Uncle Sam 20-30 tractor**

Organized at Chicago, Illinois in 1918, this company had moved to Menasha by the following year. Two sizes of the Uncle Sam tractor were built. Initially, it was a 12-20 model, followed by the 20-30 shown here. The 20-30 was equipped with a Beaver four-cylinder engine having a 4-3/4 x 6 inch bore and stroke. Production of this tractor continued into the early 1920s.

## U. S. Tractor Company
*Minneapolis, Minnesota*

**U.S. 12-24 tractor**

In 1917 the Challenge Tractor Co. was organized at Minneapolis. Challenge Co. of Batavia, Illinois also had a major branch house at Minneapolis, and the latter also was building a tractor so lots of confusion ensued. Finally, Challenge Tractor Co. changed its name to U. S. Tractor Co. in 1918. The U.S. 12-24 tractor only remained on the market a short time.

## U. S. Tractor Corporation
*Warren, Ohio*

## U. S. Tractor Sales Inc.
*Peoria, Illinois*

**USTRAC Model 10 crawler**

In 1948 U. S. Tractor Sales Division and U. S. Tractor Corp. are both listed as manufacturers of the USTRAC Model 10 crawler. Then within a year or so, production was taken over by Federal Machine & Welder Company. The Model 10 was capable of about 27 belt horsepower. It used a Continental F-124 engine and had four forward and four reverse speeds.

## Utilitor Company
*Dayton, Ohio*

**Utilitor Model 7 garden tractor**

About 1925 the Utilitor Model 502 garden tractor appeared. It used the company's own single-cylinder engine having a 3-1/2 x 4-1/2 inch bore and stroke. About 1927 it was replaced with the Utilitor Model 7 shown here. This model was nearly identical except that the engine size was increased to 3-5/8 x 5 inches. The exact origins of Utilitor are unknown.

| | 1 | 2 | 3 | 4 |
|---|---|---|---|---|
| Early Utilitors (no model numbers) | | | | |
| | $2,500 | $2,000 | $1,500 | $850 |

**Model 8 Utilitor**

In the early 1930s the Model 8 Utilitor appeared. It remained in production until about 1940. During later years it could be purchased with steel wheels or rubber tires. The Model 8 used a Novo engine having a 3-3/8 x 4 inch bore and stroke. Total weight of this tractor was 840 pounds.

| | 1 | 2 | 3 | 4 |
|---|---|---|---|---|
| Model 7/Model 8 | | | | |
| | $1,200 | $1,000 | $850 | $600 |

**Utilitor Model 25**

Late in the 1930s the Utilitor Model 25 appeared, and it remained in production until the company faded from view in the early 1950s. The Model 25 weighed 640 pounds, and was equipped with a Wisconsin engine having a 3 x 3-1/4 inch bore and stroke. The Model 25 had three forward speeds ranging from 1/2 to 5 mph.

| | 1 | 2 | 3 | 4 |
|---|---|---|---|---|
| Model 25 | $800 | $500 | $300 | $150 |

In addition to above models, Utilitor Company also manufactured a riding tractor called the "Red Label". Produced in the 1930's it had rubber tires all around, a PTO and was powered by a two-cylinder water cooled Wisconsin engine. At this writing, it appears that only one exists and is owned by a collector in Wisconsin.

| | 1 | 2 | 3 | 4 |
|---|---|---|---|---|
| Red Label | $5,000 | $4,000 | $3,000 | $2,500 |

## Utility Products Company
*Auburn, Indiana*

In 1948, Utility Products Co. was listed as the manufacturer of the Tractorette garden tractor. No other information has been found.

## Utility Steel Tractor Company
*Antigo, Wisconsin*

**Utility Steel Tractor**

Announced in 1915, the Utility Steel Tractor was one of the first successful four-wheel-drive designs, and ultimately led to the FWD designs of Atlas Engineering Company, Clintonville, Wisconsin. The model shown here weighed about 5,000 pounds and was equipped with a four-cylinder engine capable of about 40 belt horsepower. All parts of the tractor were cast steel wherever it was possible to use it.

# V

## Vail-Rentschler Tractor Company
*Hamilton, Ohio*

**Vail Oil Tractor**

Incorporated in 1916, Vail-Rentschler began producing their Vail Oil Tractor that same year. Initially it was rated as a 9-18, but by 1918 it was rated as a 10-20 model. The Vail used a two-cylinder engine with a 6 x 7 inch bore and stroke. Total weight was 3,700 pounds. Production apparently ended about 1920.

## Valentine Bros. Mfg. Company
*Minneapolis, Minnesota*

**Imperial tractor**

During 1908 Valentine Bros. announced their Imperial tractor. Priced at $3,400 it was equipped with a horizontal opposed engine of four cylinders with a 7-1/2 x 9 inch bore and stroke. In 1910 Valentine Bros. and the Shock & Hay Loader Company merged to form Imperial Mfg. Company.

## Van Duzen Gas & Gasolene Engine Company
*Cincinnati, Ohio*

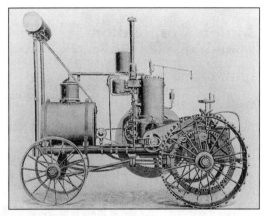

**Van Duzen gasoline traction engine**

Benjamin C. Van Duzen was a prolific inventor of gasoline engines and their accessory parts. Shown here is the Van Duzen gasoline traction engine of 1898, for which he received Patent No. 609,253. Huber Mfg. Company at Marion, Ohio bought out Van Duzen in 1898, and built a prototype or two, then left the 'gasoline traction engine' business for a decade before returning with an entirely different design.

## Van Nostrand Plow Company
*Omaha, Nebraska*

This company announced a rotary motor plow design about 1912 but no more is known after this time.

## Vaughan Motor Company
*Portland, Oregon*

**Flex-tread garden tractor**

In the late 1930s Vaughan developed their Flex-tread garden tractors. The Model W shown here is of 1939 vintage, and was powered by the company's own single cylinder engine. It used a 3-3/4 x 4 inch bore and stroke. Vaughan still listed their Flextread tractors into the 1950s.

## Velie Motors Corporation
*Moline, Illinois*

**Velie Biltwell tractor**

Velie began building tractors in 1916. The company went back to 1901 as the Velie Carriage Company, and in 1908 the Velie Motor Vehicle Company was organized to build automobiles. Another firm, Velie Engineering Co. was organized in 1911 to build trucks. The Velie Biltwell had a rating of 12 drawbar and 24 belt horsepower.

**Velie 12-24 tractor**

About 1917 Velie modified the 12-24 tractor by giving it a different hood and removing the canopy. Velie built their own engine for the 12-24. It was of four-cylinder design and used a 4-1/8 x 5-1/2 inch bore and stroke. Production of the 12-24 continued until 1920.

## Versatile Mfg. Company
*Winnipeg, Manitoba*

Versatile Mfg. Co. began building farm equipment in 1945, and began making self-propelled swathers in 1954. The company did not begin building tractors until 1966, a decade after the scope of this volume. Hopefully, another edition will cover tractors from the 1960s onward, as well as picking up on a great many for which we could find little or no information.

## Victor Tractor Company
*Minneapolis, Minnesota*

**Victor tractor**

The Victor tractor was first built in 1918 and remained on the market for only a short time. It was powered by a Climax four-cylinder engine having a 5 x 6-1/2 inch bore and stroke. Weighing 4,500 pounds, the Victor sold for $1,685.

## Victor Traction Gear Company
*Loudonville, Ohio*

**Victor conversion attachment**

At least into the early 1920s, Victor offered a variety of "Traction Equipment for Converting Portable Engines into Tractors." Shown here are the components of a two-speed system, complete with all gears, clutches, and other items. The concept was popular enough at the time to provide room for several manufacturers of these conversions.

## Victory Tractor Company
*Greensburg, Indiana*

**Victory 9-18 tractor**

This company was organized in 1918 and built the Victory tractor until 1921. The best known model is the 9-18 built during the entire existence of the company. It was equipped with a Gray four-cylinder engine having a 3-1/2 x 5 inch bore and stroke. In the 1919-1921 period the company also built a 15-30 model. It was of the same design as the 9-18 but used a Waukesha four-cylinder engine having a 4-1/4 x 5-3/4 inch bore and stroke.

## Victory Tractor Company
*Minneapolis, Minnesota*

No information is available on this company or its tractors.

## Vim Tractor Company
*Schleisingerville. Wisconsin*

**10-20 Vim tractor**

Vim took over the factories of Standard Machinery Company in 1919 and began building the 10-20 Vim tractor. Shortly after the firm added the Vim 15-30; it is shown here. The 10-20 was of similar appearance; it used a Waukesha four-cylinder engine having a 3-3/4 x 5-1/2 inch bore

and stroke. No specifications have been found for the 15-30 model. Production ended by 1920 or shortly thereafter.

## Vincennes Tractor Company
*Vincennes, Indiana*

**Vincennes tractor**

During 1911 this company was organized to manufacture tractors, and in 1913 the first Vincennes tractor appeared. It was powered by a four-cylinder engine having a 6 x 7-1/2 inch bore and stroke, for something like 50 belt horsepower. Little is known of the company, and it is entirely possible that the prototype shown here was the only copy built.

## James Vis
*Grand Rapids, Michigan*

**Peters garden tractor**

Into the early 1930s the Peters garden tractor was built by Progressive Mfg. Company of Minneapolis, Minnesota. Subsequently, the Peters was offered by James Vis, at least until the beginning of World War Two. The 1939 model used a Briggs & Stratton Model PB engine having a 2-1/2 inch bore and stroke. Alternatively, the Peters could be supplied with a Briggs & Stratton Type T engine with a 2-5/8 x 3-1/4 inch bore and stroke.

# Wabash Tractor Company
*Wabash, Indiana*

**Motox 18-20 tractor**

The Motox 18-30 was advertised by Wabash in 1919; at the same time, the Motox was being promoted by Plano Tractor Company at Plano, Illinois. The connection between the two firms has not been established. A Buda four-cylinder engine having a 4-1/4 x 6 inch bore and stroke was used in the Motox. This 5,000 pound tractor retailed for $2,000.

# R. M. Wade & Company
*Portland, Oregon*

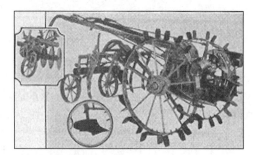

**Wade garden tractor**

By the late 1930s the Wade garden tractor was on the market; this one is of 1937 vintage. It was powered by a 4 horsepower Briggs & Stratton

engine and permitted power turns through ratchet hubs. The Wade garden tractor appears as late as 1953.

# Wagner Tractor Inc.
*Portland, Oregon*

**Wagner TR-14 tractor**

In the early 1950s the Wagner four-wheel-drive tractors appeared. For 1955 three models were available. The TR-6 was equipped with a 302ci diesel engine, and the TR-9 was built with a 495 cubic inch diesel. Shown here is the TR-14 tractor. This model weighed about 16,000 pounds and was designed around a 672 cubic inch diesel. Wagner tractors were built at least into the 1960s, possibly even later.

# Waite Tractor Sales Corporation
*Chicago, Illinois*

**Waite tractor**

H. C. Waite was the designer of this tractor, going back to 1913 and a factory at Elgin, Illinois.

The company continued building this model, and attempted to raise the capitalization of the firm in 1916. However, in July of that year the company was forced into reorganization. Waite tractors used a friction-drive system.

## Wallis Tractor Company
*Racine, Wisconsin*

See: J. I. Case Plow Works

## Walsh Tractor Company
*Minneapolis, Minnesota*

See: Standard Engine Co.

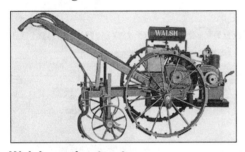

**Walsh garden tractor**

The Walsh garden tractor of 1931 used the company's own single-cylinder engine; it had a 2-1/2 inch bore and stroke, and was rated at 2-1/2 horsepower. With an engine speed of 800 to 2,000 rpm, it could travel from 1/2 to 2 mph. This machine weighed 231 pounds and could be furnished with a variety of implements. The tractor shown here is equipped with a double engine. This option effectively doubled the horsepower.

|  | **1** | **2** | **3** | **4** |
|---|---|---|---|---|
| Walsh | $750 | $500 | $350 | $250 |
| Viking Single | $1,500 | $1,000 | $850 | $450 |
| Viking Twin | $1,200 | $950 | $600 | $350 |
| Standard Twin | $1,200 | $950 | $600 | $350 |

## Ward Tractor Company
*Lincoln, Nebraska*

**Ward tractor**

During 1912 the Ward tractor was announced. This unique design was powered by a Cushman 20 horsepower, two-cylinder engine. (The Cushman was also built at Lincoln, Nebraska.) Despite many favorable comments on this tractor, it does not appear that it was built beyond 1914.

## Warehouse Point Company
*Warehouse Point, Connecticut*

**Terra Farma garden tractor**

In 1946 this firm offered their Terra Farma garden tractor. It was powered by a 1-1/2 horsepower engine. This machine retailed for $350. According to advertising, it was offered to "distributors and exporters." Nothing further is known of this machine.

## Warren Motor & Mfg. Company
*Minneapolis, Minnesota*

In 1919 this company is listed as the manufacturer of the Dakota King tractor. No other information has been found.

## Waterbury Tool Division
*Waterbury, Connecticut*

**Waterbury Model R riding tractor**

In the early 1950s Waterbury offered several different models of garden tractors. Shown here is the Waterbury Model R riding tractor. Weighing 545 pounds, it sold for $395. Power came from a Briggs & Stratton engine capable of over 5 horsepower. This firm was a subsidiary of Vickers Incorporated.

## Waterloo Boy Kerosene Tractor Company
*Chicago, Illinois*

Little is known of this company except that it was organized and incorporated in 1916. It had no connection with Waterloo Gasoline Engine Company, the builders of the Waterloo Boy tractors.

## Waterloo Foundry Company
*Waterloo, Iowa*

In 1911 the 8-15 Big Chief tractor was announced. Little is known of this tractor, although it bears

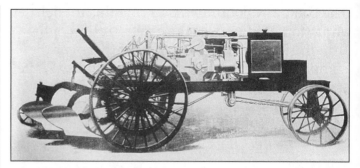

**8-15 Big Chief tractor**

unmistakable signs of being a forerunner to the Waterloo Boy tractor. The latter was built by Waterloo Gasoline Engine Company. No specific details of the Big Chief tractor have been found.

## Waterloo Gasoline Engine Company
*Waterloo, Iowa*

**Froehlich gasoline traction engine**

As early as 1886 John Froehlich conceived the idea of building a replacement for the steam traction engine. In 1892 he built his first engine at Froehlich in Clayton County, Iowa. That year his gasoline traction engine was shipped to South Dakota where it threshed over 62,000 bushels of grain without a single breakdown. Subsequently, Froehlich was an organizer of the Waterloo Gasoline Traction Engine Company, but due to the limited market at the time, the company organizers preferred to build gasoline engines. Froehlich disagreed, and the resulting Waterloo Gasoline Engine Co. became a major gas engine builder until they themselves entered the tractor business in 1912.

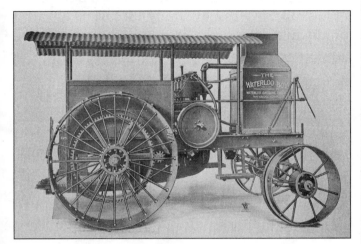

**Waterloo Boy One-Man tractor**

After the Froehlich tractor of the 1890s, Waterloo Gasoline Engine Co. stayed out of the tractor business until announcing the Waterloo Boy One-Man tractor in 1912. This model used a four-cylinder engine with a 5-1/2 x 6 inch bore and stroke. It was available with rear-mounted plows if so desired. Production of this model ended in 1913.

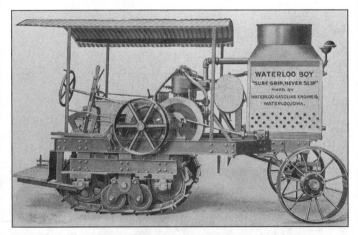

**Waterloo Boy Sure-Grip (Waterloo Catapillar)**

The Waterloo Boy Sure-Grip, also known as the Waterloo Catapillar, used the same engine as the One-Man tractor of 1912. This tractor, like the One-Man, owed its existence to the design work of Harry Leavitt.

**Waterloo One-Man tractor**

By 1913 the Waterloo One-Man tractor was discontinued, and in its place came a new Waterloo One-Man tractor of an entirely different design. This 15 horsepower model used a two-cylinder opposed engine with a 5-1/2 x 7 inch bore and stroke. Production continued into 1914.

**Waterloo Boy Small Farm tractor**

Sometime in 1914 the Waterloo Boy Small Farm tractor appeared. This model continued to use the same engine as the 15 horsepower One-Man, but used a cellular radiator, along with other changes.

**Waterloo Boy Style R tractor**

During 1914 the first Waterloo Boy Style R tractor appeared. It used a two-cylinder engine with a 5-1/2 x 7 inch bore and stroke. First known as the Type A, this tractor underwent numerous changes in the coming months. By 1915 it was the Model R, Style D, but all used the same 5-1/2 x 7 engine.

In 1916 the engine of the Style R Waterloo Boy was changed to a 6 x 7 inch bore and stroke. It remained thus until 1917 when it was again changed to include a 6-1/2 x 7 inch bore and stroke. Production of the Style R ended in 1918.

**Waterloo Boy Style N tractor**

Production of the famous Waterloo Boy Style N tractor began in 1917 and continued until 1924. When the Nebraska Tractor Tests began in 1920, the Model N, 12-25 was the first tractor tested. It yielded almost 16 maximum drawbar horsepower during Test No. 1. This tractor carried a two-cylinder engine having a 6-1/2 x 7 inch bore and stroke. (See Deere & Co. for price information)

## Waterloo Mfg. Company Ltd.
*Waterloo, Ontario*

**Waterloo Bronco Model 100 tractor**

In 1953 the Waterloo Bronco Model 100 was listed in a few of the tractor directories. This small trac-

tor was equipped with a Wisconsin two-cylinder Model TE engine having a 3 x 3-1/4 inch bore and stroke. It was rated at slightly over 11 horsepower. Options included a pto shaft and a belt pulley. Also available was a hydraulic lift system. Exact production dates of the Bronco 100 are not known.

|  | **1** | **2** | **3** | **4** |
|---|---|---|---|---|
| Bronco Model 100 | $3,500 | $3,000 | $2,500 | $1,000 |

## Waterloo Motor Works
*Waterloo, Iowa*

This firm was organized in 1902 after a buyout of the Davis Gasoline Engine Works of Waterloo, Iowa. The latter had also organized the Davis Gasoline Traction Engine Works, and possibly built a few tractors. In any event, the activities of Waterloo Motor Works in the tractor business probably followed the pioneering work of Davis. No illustrations of the Waterloo Motor Works tractors have been found.

## Waterous Engine Company
*St. Paul, Minnesota*

**Waterous tractor**

By 1904 the Waterous tractor was on the market, and remained so until 1911. Few details of this tractor have been found, although it appears to be of 30 or more horsepower. Waterous began building steam fire engines in the 1880s, and began building gasoline engines in the late 1890s. After leaving the tractor business, Waterous Fire Engine Co. specialized in building firefighting equipment.

## Wayne Tractor Company
*Detroit, Michigan*

Although it was organized and incorporated in 1916, nothing further is known of this company or its tractors.

## Welborn Corporation
*Kansas City, Kansas*

This firm succeeded Coleman Tractor Company in 1920. It appears that a few tractors may have been built by Coleman-Welborn Corporation, and even a few by Welborn Corporation, but the Coleman was essentially gone after 1920.

## Wellman-Seaver-Morgan Company
*Akron, Ohio*

**Akron 15-30 tractor**

During the 1920-1922 period Wellman-Seaver-Morgan offered their Akron 15-30 tractor. The

company used their own four-cylinder engine; it was designed with a 4-3/4 x 6 inch bore and stroke. Four forward speeds were provided, ranging from 1-1/2 to 6 mph.

## Western American Industries
*Longmont, Colorado*

See: Gibson

**Gibson Super D tractor**

In the late 1950s Western American appeared as the manufacturer of the Gibson tractors, apparently succeeding Gibson Mfg. Corporation of Longmont, Colorado. Shown here is the Gibson Super D tractor. This model was equipped with a Wisconsin single-cylinder engine having a 3 x 3-1/4 inch bore and stroke. It was rated at nearly 8-1/2 horsepower.

## Western Farm Machinery Company
*Denver, Colorado*

No information available for this company or its tractors.

## Western Implement & Motor Company
*Davenport, Iowa*

In 1912 Western Implement & Motor Company was organized. This was a new name for what had formerly been the National Co-operative Farm Machinery Company. To launch itself into the tractor business, Western bought out the Colby Motor Works at Mason City, Iowa. Shown

**Creeping Grip 40-30 tractor**

here is the Creeping Grip 40-30 tractor, rated to have 40 drawbar horsepower.

**Creeping Grip 75-55 model**

Aside from an occasional illustration, few specifications have been found on the Creeping Grip tractors. Even some occasional advertising literature provides little in-depth data. Obviously the 75-55 model shown here was built with a four-cylinder engine. Western went out of business late in 1913.

## Western Mfg. Company
*Watertown, South Dakota*

In 1914 this company offered a 20-35 tractor weighing 8,200 pounds and using a two-cylinder opposed engine. No other information has been found, nor have any photographs been located.

## Western Tool & Mfg. Company
*Kansas City, Missouri*

No information has been located for this company or its tractors.

## Western Tractor Company
*El Monte, California*

In 1947 this company offered the Western "400" garden tractor. It was powered by a Briggs & Stratton engine having a 2-1/4 inch bore and stroke. Shipping weight was 400 pounds. Little else is known of this garden tractor, and no illustrations have been found.

## Western Tractor Company
*Minneapolis, Minnesota*

This company announced in early 1917 that they would soon be building tractors, but no other information has been found.

## Western Tractor Company
*Regina, Saskatchewan*

No information has been located on this company except that it went out of business in 1919.

## Western Tractor Company
*Tulsa, Oklahoma*

Organized in 1916, this firm offered the Western 8-15 tractor at least into 1917. It used a Toro two-cylinder vertical engine with a 5-1/4 x 6-1/2 inch bore and stroke. Weighing 4,200 pounds, it sold for $735. No illustrations of this tractor have been found.

# Western Tractor Company
*Wichita, Kansas*

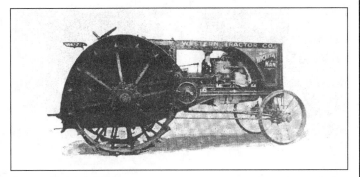

**Western 16-32 tractor**

Developed about 1919, the Western 16-32 tractor remained on the market for only a short time. This 5,900 pound tractor had a 1920 retail price of $2,100. It featured a Climax four-cylinder engine having a 5 x 6-1/2 inch bore and stroke.

# Wetmore Tractor Company
*Sioux City, Iowa*

**Wetmore 12-25 tractor**

During 1919 the Wetmore 12-25 tractor appeared. This lightweight design weighed only 3,000 pounds and had a list price of $1,385. Power came from a Rutenbur four-cylinder engine having a 4-1/8 x 5-1/2 inch bore and stroke. Originally the tractor was built by H. A. Wetmore, but the company name was changed to Wetmore Tractor Co. in the early 1920s. Production of the 12-25 continued into the early 1930s.

# Wharton Motors Company
*Dallas, Texas*

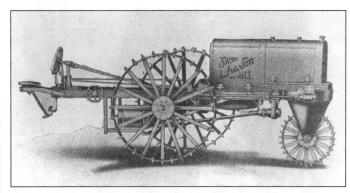

**Wharton 3WD, 12-22 tractor**

By 1920 the Wharton 3WD, 12-22 tractor was on the market. It was of a unique three-wheel-drive design, and was powered by an Erd four-cylinder engine with a 4 x 6 inch bore and stroke. By 1921 the Wharton tractors were being built by Texas Truck & Tractor Company.

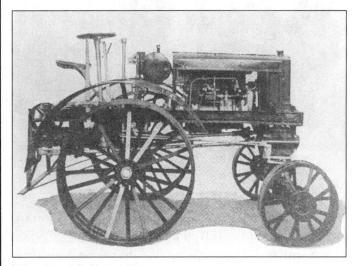

**Wharton 20-40 tractor**

The Wharton 20-40 was a four-wheel-drive design, but few details have been found for this tractor. Probably, as with the 12-22, production was rather limited, since the company was under the auspices of Texas Truck & Tractor Company by 1921; it is not thought that the latter built any large number of Wharton tractors.

# Wheat Tiller & Tractor Company
*Buffalo, New York*

See: Hession

**Wheat 12-24 tractor**

The Wheat 12-24 tractor appeared in 1921; it had formerly been built by Hession Tiller & Tractor Corporation. This unique design was a combination farm and road tractor. As shown in the top illustration, the tractor was ready for the road, but in the bottom illustration it is ready for the field. In the 1922-1924 period the Wheat tractor was built by Matthews Tractor Company at Brockport, New York.

# Whitney Tractor Company
*Cleveland, Ohio*

About 1918 the Whitney 9-18 tractor appeared, but remained on the market for only a short time.

**Whitney 9-18 tractor**

Whitney was the successor to the Ohio Mfg. Company, and the latter had roots going back to the late 1890s. The 9-18 was powered by a Gile two-cylinder engine. It sold for $1,175; weight of the 9-18 was 3,000 pounds.

# Wichita Falls Motor Company
*Wichita Falls, Texas*

**Wichita 20-30 tractor**

By 1920 the Wichita 20-30 was on the market. Weighing 5,500 pounds, this tractor listed at $2,500. Power came from a Beaver four-cylinder engine having a 4-1/2 x 6 inch bore and stroke. The Wichita does not appear in the 1921 listings.

# Wichita Tractor Company
*Wichita, Kansas*

The Wichita 8-16 tractor was announced in 1917 and was built until 1920. At that time it was taken over by Agrimotor Mfg. Company, also of Wichita.

**Wichita 8-16 tractor**

This tractor was also known as the Midwest 8-16. Power came from a Gile two-cylinder opposed engine having a 5 x 6-1/2 inch bore and stroke. For 1920, this 3,300 pound tractor sold for $1,085.

## Will-Burt Company
*Orrville, Ohio*

**Little Farmer garden tractor**

In the early 1950s the Little Farmer garden tractor appeared from Will-Burt. Weighing only 180 pounds, it sold for $100. Power came from a Briggs & Stratton Model 5S engine capable of 1 horsepower. Very little information has been found on this company.

|  | **1** | **2** | **3** | **4** |
|---|---|---|---|---|
| Little Farmer | | | | |
|  | $700 | $500 | $250 | $100 |

## H. C. Williams Mfg. Company
*Rootstown, Ohio*

In 1950 Williams offered their Norm Garden Tractor in two different sizes. The 14R6 weighed 435 pounds and was powered by a 4 horsepower

**Norm U-2R6 garden tractor**

Briggs & Stratton engine. Shown here is the Norm U—2R6 garden tractor. This model was equipped with a 3-1/2 horsepower Ultimotor engine. Little more is known of the Norm garden tractors aside from a 1950 listing.

## Willmar Tractor Company
*Willmar, Minnesota*
See: Humber-Anderson Mfg. Co.

**Little Oak tractor**

Humber-Anderson Mfg. Co. was organized at St. Paul, Minnesota in 1913 to build the Little Oak tractor. Shortly afterward, Willmar Tractor Mfg. Company took over the Little Oak, and the latter continued until December 1916. At that time the company was reorganized as Standard Tractor Co. As built by Willmar, the Little Oak carried a 22-44 horsepower rating. It was equipped with a four-cylinder engine having each cylinder cast separately. It used a 5-5/8 x 7-1/2 inch bore and stroke.

## Willys-Overland Motors
*Toledo, Ohio*

**Willys CJ-2A**

In the late 1940s and early 1950s, Willys offered their famous Jeep, specifically the CJ-2A for farm use. A wide number of options were available, including a three-point hitch system, pto shaft, and belt pulley. The CJ-2A had a curb weight of 2137 pounds. It was equipped with the Jeep CJ-2A engine; this motor was of four-cylinder design and used a 3-1/8 x 4-3/8 inch bore and stroke.

## Wilson Tractor Company
*Peoria, Illinois*

**Two-row cultivator**

Developed by 1918 this two-row cultivator made its appearance in 1919. It was powered by a four-cylinder LeRoi engine having a 3-1/8 x 4-1/2 inch bore and stroke. Apparently, Parrett Motors Corporation at Chicago, Illinois took over the Wilson cultivator in 1919, and marketed their own machine in 1920 and 1921.

## Wilson Tractor Mfg. Company
*Ottumwa, Iowa*

**Wilson 12-20 four-wheel-drive tractor**

Rated as a 12-20, the Wilson four-wheel-drive tractor appeared in 1920. Weighing only 3,700 pounds, it was powered by a Weidely four-cylinder engine having a 4 x 5-1/2 inch bore and stroke. This company was bought out by Austin Mfg. Company, Chicago, Illinois in 1922, and from this design the latter built their own four-wheel-drive tractor for a time.

## Winchell Mfg. Company
*Fort Scott, Kansas*

The Clean Row Garden Tractor was offered by this firm in the late 1940s and at least into the early 1950s. No illustrations or specifications of the Clean Row have been found.

|  | **1** | **2** | **3** | **4** |
|---|---|---|---|---|
| Clean Row | $300 | $200 | $150 | $75 |

# Windolph Tractor Company
*Portland, Oregon*

**Windolph Garden Maker "M"**

In the early 1950s and extending through the decade, Windolph offered several models of its garden tractors. Shown here is the Windolph Garden Maker "M" which was essentially a rotary tiller. This small machine was powered by a Clinton Model 700 engine of 1-1/2 horsepower.

**Windolph Chain-Tred Deluxe garden tractor**

Weighing 480 pounds, the Windolph Chain-Tred Deluxe garden tractor was a crawler machine that sold for $549. Power came from a 6 horsepower Wisconsin Model AK engine. The Windolph tractors appear to have been built during the 1950s, but no specific information on the company has been found.

Topping the Windolph line was the Riding "C" tractor, a crawler design that weighed 1,500 pounds. This model was powered by a 13 horsepower Wisconsin Model TF engine. Numerous attachments were available for the Windolph,

**Windolph Riding "C" tractor**

including a moldboard plow, various harrows, cultivators, mowers, and other accessories.

|  | **1** | **2** | **3** | **4** |
|---|---|---|---|---|
| All models | $4,000 | $3,000 | $1,200 | $800 |

# Winkley Company
*Minneapolis, Minnesota*

This firm is listed as the manufacturer of the Winkley garden tractor in 1953, but no other information has been found.

# Winnebago Tractor Company
*Rockford, Illinois*

**Winnebago Chief tractor**

About 1920 the Winnebago Chief tractor made a very brief appearance. Little is known of this model except that it used the company's own four-cylinder engine.

## Winona Mfg. Company
*Winona, Minnesota*

In 1896 this company gained manufacturing rights for the Otto Gasoline Traction Engines with a territory covering much of the northwest. The manufacturing arrangement lasted for only a year or two. No illustrations of the Winona-built Otto gasoline traction engines have been found.

## Winslow Mfg. Company
*Kansas City, Missouri*

This company appears in 1917 as the manufacturer of the Coleman 10-20 tractor. The Coleman operation went through numerous title changes and reorganizations; the role of Winslow is unknown.

## Winter Mfg. Company
*Tacoma, Washington*

The Mighty Man garden tractors first appeared in April 1946. Beyond this, no information had been found, nor have any photographs appeared.

| | **1** | **2** | **3** | **4** |
|---|---|---|---|---|
| Mighty Man | $750 | $500 | $250 | $100 |

## Wisconsin Farm Tractor Company
*Sauk City, Wisconsin*

**Wisconsin "Thirty" tractor**

In 1917 McFarland & Westmont Tractor Co. began building tractors. Within a short time the name was changed to Wisconsin Farm Tractor Company. Initially the tractor was known as the Wisconsin "Thirty" with a 15-30 horsepower rating. The rating was soon changed to 16-32. In Nebraska Test No. 21 of 1920, this model was officially given a 16-30 horsepower rating. Power came from a Climax four-cylinder engine having a 5 x 6-1/2 inch bore and stroke. Toward the end of production in 1923 this model took on a 20-35 horsepower rating.

**Wisconsin 22-40 tractor**

By 1918 the Wisconsin 22-40 tractor was on the market. It was built over the same chassis as the 16-30. This model used a Climax four-cylinder engine having a 5-1/2 x 7 inch bore and stroke. At its rated speed of 800 rpm, this engine was capable of 50 belt horsepower.

**Wisconsin 25-45 tractor**

The 22-40 and the 25-45 Wisconsin tractors used the same Climax engine. However, the 25-45 was claimed to have a maximum of 60 belt horsepower, even though the rated engine speed was the same 800 rpm for both models. Production of the Wisconsin tractors ceased in 1923.

## Wisconsin Truck & Tractor Company
*Madison, Wisconsin*

Although it was organized and incorporated in 1917 to manufacture tractors, nothing further is known of this company or its activities.

# Wizard Tractor Corporation
*Los Angeles, California*

**Wizard 4-Pull tractor**

During the 1920s the Wizard 4-Pull tractor was marketed. Rated as a 20-35 tractor, this machine was of the four-wheel-drive design. Power came from a four-cylinder engine having a 5-1/4 x 6-1/2 inch bore and stroke. Few specific details have been found on the Wizard 4-Pull.

# Wolf Tractor Company
*LaPorte, Indiana*

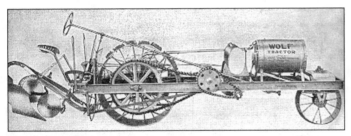

**Wolf tractor**

In 1913 or 1914 the Wolf Tractor Company was organized. John Wolf was the inventor; he had formerly been the manager of the Rumely Hotel in LaPorte. During 1915 the Leo Rumely Tractor Co. was organized to take over the Wolf operation. No details of the Wolf tractor have been found.

# Wolverine Tractor Company
*Detroit, Michigan*

# Wolverine Tractor Company
*Saginaw, Michigan*

In 1917 Wolverine purchased a factory at Dearborn to build the Wolverine 15-30 tractor. This model was designed with an Erd four-cylinder

**Wolverine 15-30 tractor**

engine having a 4 x 6 inch bore and stroke. The tractor weighed 5,500 pounds. In 1918 the company moved to a different factory at Saginaw, Michigan. Little is known of the Wolverine activities after that time.

# Wood, Knight, Hawk Plow Company
*Oklahoma City, Oklahoma*

**Wood, Knight, Hawk motor plow**

This company was incorporated in 1911 to build a motor plow. The prototype machine shown here was equipped with a three-cylinder engine. A descriptive article notes that this was merely an experimental engine and that the production model would use an engine ranging from 60 to 75 belt horsepower. However, no further information has been found. This machine was built under the tradename of Alivator.

# S. A. Woods Machine Company
*Boston, Massachusetts*

During 1953 this firm was listed as the manufacturer of the GHN and Sprywheel garden tractors. No other information has been located.

|  | 1 | 2 | 3 | 4 |
|---|---|---|---|---|
| All models | $3,500 | $3,000 | $2,000 | $800 |

**World Harvester Corp. Auto-Tiller**

## World Harvester Corporation
*New York, New York*

In 1919 the Auto-Tiller was available from World Harvester Corp. This machine was rather large, and used a single-cylinder engine with a 5 x 7 inch bore and stroke. It weighed 800 pounds. Few other details have been found on this machine, and none are known to exist.

## Worthington Pump & Machinery Corporation
*Cudahy, Wisconsin*

Worthington bought out International Gas Engine Company of Cudahy in 1916. The latter had earlier

**Ingeco 10-20 tractor**

brought out their 10-20 Ingeco tractor. Worthington revamped the Ingeco 10-20 and sold it as late as 1919. At that time it was priced at $1,175. Power came from the company's own two-cylinder engine; it used a 6 x 7 inch bore and stroke.

# Y

## Yankee Boy Tractor Corporation
*Chicago, Illinois*

**Yankee Boy 16-32 tractor**

Developed in 1918, the Yankee Boy 16-32 remained on the market for a couple of years. Power came from a Buda engine, but no details of the engine or other tractor components have been found. In 1919 though, the Yankee Boy sold for $2,295.

## Ypsilanti Hay Press Company
*Ypsilanti, Michigan*

**Wolverine tractor**

In 1912 the Wolverine tractor was offered in 18, 25, and 35 horsepower sizes. Little is known of

these tractors, and it is not believed that they were marketed for any length of time. About the only evidence that they existed comes from a few magazine advertisements.

## Yuba Mfg. Company
*Maryville, California*

**Yuba Model 12 and Model 18**

The Yuba Ball Tread tractor began with the Ball Tread Tractor Co., Detroit, Michigan. In 1912 they built their first 12-25 tractor. Yuba Construction bought the company in 1914 and continued with the 12-25 and 18-35 models developed by Ball Tread Co. Shown here is the early design of the Yuba Model 12 and Model 18 tractors.

**Yuba Ball Tread 12-20 tractor**

Production of the Yuba Ball Tread 12-20 tractor ran from about 1916 to 1921. This model then became the 15-25 tractor; it was built from 1921 to 1925. Initially a Continental four-cylinder engine powered the 12-20, but the 15-25 used a Waukesha engine.

**Yuba Ball Tread 20-35 tractor**

The Yuba Ball Tread 20-35 was apparently a take-off from the Yuba Model 18 that had been developed by Ball Tread Company. Production of this model ran from 1916 to 1921. Various engines were used during the production run. Toward the latter part of production a Wisconsin four-cylinder engine was used. It had a 5-3/4 x 7 inch bore and stroke.

**Yuba Ball Tread 40-70 tractor**

The Yuba Ball Tread 40-70 tractor was only listed in 1919, so it was probably developed in 1918 and remained on the market into 1920. This big crawler weighed 21,000 pounds and used a four-cylinder engine having a 6-1/2 x 8-1/2 inch bore and stroke. It had three forward speeds.

**Yuba Rodebilder 25-40**

In the early 1920s the Yuba Rodebilder appeared. The 25-40 model was likely a takeoff from the earlier 20-35 model. This tractor used a four-cylinder Yuba-built engine with a 5-1-4 x 7 inch bore and stroke. Production of this model continued until the company ceased building tractors about 1931.

**Model 15-25 Yuba tractor**

The Model 15-25 Yuba tractor was equipped with a Wisconsin four-cylinder engine having a 4-1/4 x 6 inch bore and stroke. This model appears to have been an improved version of the earlier 12-20 tractor. Perhaps because of the onset of the Great Depression, Yuba tractors were not listed in the trade directories after 1931.

# Z

## Geo. Zalesky & Company
*Cedar Rapids, Iowa*

This firm was organized to build the G-O tractors after General Ordnance Company closed its doors in the early 1920s. The venture lasted only a short time.

## Zelle Tractor Company
*St. Louis, Missouri*

**Zelle 12-25 tractor**

Zelle Tractor Company was organized and incorporated in 1916, having taken over the Plantation Equipment Co., previously referred to in this volume. Zelle offered their 12-25 tractor in the 1916-1921 period. It was rated at 12 drawbar and 25 belt horsepower, using a four-cylinder engine with a 4-1/4 x 5-1/2 inch bore and stroke. Weighing 4,000 pounds, it sold for $1,500.

## Zimmerman Auto Tractor Company
*Chicago, Illinois*

This company built a tractor conversion unit and may also have built farm tractors, but no other information has been found.

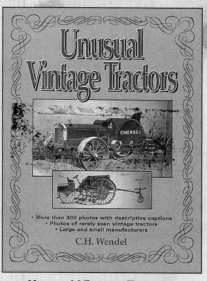
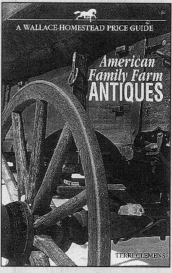
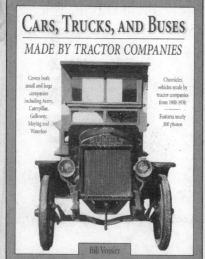
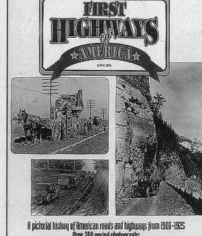